MW01283150

A History of Canadian Horror Cinema

THEY CAME FROM WITHIN

Caelum Vatnsdal

ARBEITER RING PUBLISHING

Copyright © 2004 Caelum Vatnsdal

Arbeiter Ring Publishing
201E-121 Osborne St.
Winnipeg, MB
Canada R3L 1Y4
www.arbeiterring.com

Printed in Canada by the workers at Kromar Printing Ltd.
Book design by Steph Whitehouse/Public Image Co.
National Library of Canada Cataloguing in Publication

Vatnsdal, Caelum
        They came from within : a history of Canadian horror
cinema/Caelum Vatnsdal.

Includes bibliographical references and index.
ISBN 1-894037-21-9

        1. Horror films—Canada—History and criticism. I. Title.

PN1995.9.H6V38 2004   791.43'6164'0971   C2004-902203-2

Canada Council   Conseil des Arts
for the Arts   du Canada

The publishers have made every effort to contact the copyright holders of all text and
images in this publication and believe they have met all conditions of copyright. If anyone
knows of these conditions not being met, they are urged to contact the publishers.

A History of Canadian Horror Cinema

THEY CAME FROM WITHIN

Caelum Vatnsdal

Table of Contents

FORWARD *by David DeCoteau*　　　　　　　　　　　　　*page 6*

INTRODUCTION　　　　　　　　　　　　　　　　　　*page 11*
TERROR ON THE TUNDRA

I.　PUT THE MASK ON!　　　　　　　　　　　　　　*page 21*
　　(*The Beginning to 1967*)

II.　I'M DREAMING OF A BLACK CHRISTMAS　　　　*page 55*
　　(*1968 – 1971*)

III.　"YOU SHOULD KNOW HOW BAD THIS MOVIE IS;　*page 95*
　　AFTER ALL, YOU PAID FOR IT."
　　(*1975 – 1977*)

IV.　SLASH FOR CASH　　　　　　　　　　　　　　*page 121*
　　(*1978 – 1982*)

V.　MONSTER CHILLER　　　　　　　　　　　　　*page 169*
　　(*1983 – 1999*)

VI.　IT TAKES A NATION OF HOSERS TO HOLD US BACK　*page 221*
　　(*2000 and onward*)

FOOTNOTES   *page* 232

BIBLIOGRAPHY AND REFERENCES   *page* 234

APPENDIX: FILMS   *page* 236

CREDITS   *page* 248

INDEX   *page* 249

ACKNOWLEDGEMENTS   *page* 256

FORWARD

David DeCoteau

I'D WANTED TO BE IN THE MOVIE BUSINESS since I was a kid, and in Portland, Oregon, working in a movie theatre was the closest thing to it—and I got free passes as well. I worked in the Broadway Theatre—one of those Grand Old Movie Palaces that typically populate the downtown centres of most major North American cities—but I could use my passes at any cinema in the Luxury Theatre chain.

I grew up in the multiplex theatres that dotted Portland. The Mall 205 played double bills on the order of *Screams of a Winter Night* and *Beyond Atlantis;* or *Zombie* back-to-back with *Up From the Depths;* or even *Tourist Trap* paired up appropriately enough with Wes Craven's classic *The Hills Have Eyes.* My favourite multiplex was the Rose Moyer Sixplex in the Portland suburb of Gresham. It was brand new, and they played genre pictures like Charles Band's *Crash, Death Race 2000, The Young Cycle Girls,* the black-and-white British import *The Fiendish Ghouls, And Now The Screaming Stops, The Day After Halloween,* and my personal favourite, *Infra-Man.* For this one, the theatre had to be equipped with a special stereo sound system called INFRA-STEREO or something like that. Since I saw these movies on the Saturday and Sunday matinee screenings, and the Rose Moyer was so new and rather remote, they usually had very few customers. Most of the time I sat alone in these auditoriums, as my friends, who had no idea why I might want to sit and watch *Eat My Dust* back-to-back with *Crazy Mama,* refused to join me. It was like a private screening. I saw everything that came out—but I usually seemed to dig the B horror flicks the most. They were weird, creative and unpredictable.

The Broadway, my theatre, was, naturally, situated on Broadway. It had lost its lustre and was eventually renovated to become a four-plex. I was a projectionist there for a few years, and since it was a non-union job I also worked the candy counter. We had the bigger Hollywood movies in the main auditorium, and the remaining screens usually played curious double-bills like *Attack of the Killer Tomatoes* and *Winter Kills.* The fourth auditorium played the most obscure of the B movies—*Grave of the Vampire,* for example, or *Garden of the Dead.*

One week at the Broadway we played *Mad Max.* I liked the nifty poster art right away, but then, as I was building the print, I realized it was in 'Scope. I knew that if a movie was in 'scope—that is, in a nice widescreen format—it was going to at least look good even if the movie itself was mediocre. I threaded the projector and started the film, and what I saw was one of the most original B movies I'd ever run across. Beautifully photographed, dazzling action scenes, kick ass music and a very handsome leading man. One thing weirded me out, though: the film was clearly dubbed, even though the actors seemed to be speaking English. I figured maybe the film was German, so I watched the end credits and notice that the film had been produced in association with the Australian Film Development Corporation. Australian? I thought Australia was nothing but red rocks and desert!

I started to check out the credits more often, trying to find out the origins of these wild movies. The Broadway got *The Brood* and a co-feature called *The Evil.* Both of these, I noticed, came from a company called New World Pictures. Studying the end credits of *The Brood,* I saw that this film had been made in association with the Canadian Film Development Corporation. Wait a minute—Canadian? I thought Canada was nothing but blinding white snow and Eskimos on the frozen tundra. It was then that I realized how many other countries outside my own were either in or just getting into the exploitation movie business. The USA made its fair share, of course, but since we played just about everything in Portland, I saw South Africa's *Kill or Be Killed* and *Kill and Kill Again,* Italy's gorefest *The Last Survivor* and *The Tempter,* Japan's *Shogun Assassin,* and the Mexican animal-lovers' trilogy *Barracuda, Killer Fish* and *The Bees.* I was beginning to see that the United States didn't have the monopoly on weird flicks.

Christmas of 1980 was a big time for me. I was 18 years old, and I moved down to Los Angeles to give the movie business—the real movie business—a shot. I started as a production assistant for New World Pictures, and on the weekends I worked as a projectionist. I was a kind of an alternate with the local projectionist's union, so I might get a last-minute call to show up at the Sundown, a Spanish-language drive-in in Whittier; or maybe at one of the many Pussycat (which is to say, hardcore) theatres. On my nights off I wandered the Hollywood Boulevard streets watching the sidewalk freak shows, often popping in to catch a triple bill at my favourite L.A. theatre, the World. Here my education in worldwide exploitation cinema continued.

Like everyone in film production, I read the industry tome *Variety*, which reviewed everything that came out, from gay porn on down. Sometimes they would pick on one of the little Canadian flicks, labelling it a "shoddy tax shelter movie from Canada." Tax shelter movie? What did that mean? I guessed—correctly, as it turns out—that there was some kind of tax scheme in Canada that was designed to help jump-start the country's flagging film industry. On Hollywood Boulevard, we got 'em all: *Curtains, Happy Birthday To Me, Prom Night, Terror Train, Humongous*—all of them. One night there was a premiere of *Scanners* at the Hollywood Pacific Theatre. The director was going to be there, and they were going to show three of his films. It was a packed house. I wasn't too familiar with David Cronenberg yet, but he seemed friendly and very intelligent. He handled the Q & A session well too, as when a woman stood up and said "I know you make films in Canada because it's cheaper. When are you coming down to L.A. to make your movies?" Cronenberg's reply was "I don't make movies in Canada because it's cheaper. I make movies in Canada because that's where I live." That shut her up.

And he was right. These movies didn't cost less than the exploitation flicks made in the States. Usually they cost more. They looked great (Kubrick's cameraman John Alcott shot *Terror Train,* for instance), and had very good performances and scripts. Maybe the scores were a little lacking sometimes, but otherwise these were well-crafted movies that couldn't have been made anywhere but Canada, because few governments outside of Canada had this kind of tax scheme.

The second feature that night was *Rabid*, which I had seen in Portland. At the beginning, with that cool tracking shot that introduces Marilyn Chambers, the audience screamed "Yeah!" She was really great in that movie, and should've had a bigger career. After *Rabid* came *They Came From Within,* Cronenberg's first feature. A hoot! My favourite Cronenberg film. What a night that was. It confirmed that there was a whole world making films I liked, and as a matter of fact, liked maybe a bit more than most of the stuff made in the States. Italy, Spain, Australia and Asia were making amazingly unusual B movies to capitalize on the international market the US had been dominating. Canada's ventures into exploitation filmmaking was particularly interesting to me. Most of these movies tried to be "American" by pretending to be set in the US, and with the Canadian actors trying their best to lose the Canadian accents. (Except *Humongous*— whew!) Usually they cast an American star that was in reality a Canadian national: yes, Glenn Ford is Canadian! Everyone in the movies seemed awfully polite and proper; more British than American. I liked that.

After working as a P.A. for a few years, I started to direct and produce movies myself. In 1986 I made a horror flick called *Dreamaniac,* and I was off and running. I cranked 'em out faster than anyone. My name was listed in numerous directories and industry publications, and I would get occasional phone calls from Canadian producers wondering if I was Canadian because my last name was French. I wasn't, but my grandparents were from Quebec. But the Canadian producers would tell me that, because of Canadian content rules, either the script or the director had to be Canadian, and the scripts were always American. Why? "Because Canadians can't write!" the producers cackled. I thought to myself, I guess you're not looking hard enough.

In 1996, after many years of directing and producing B movies, I got a job making a fairly big budget HBO feature called *Skeletons*. It starred Ron Silver, James Coburn and the absolutely fabulous—and Canadian—Christopher Plummer. Chris only worked for two weeks, but we got on wonderfully. He was friendly, professional and always concerned that I was happy with what we were shooting. I told him I was a fan of his Canadian films, and he was proud. I also told him I was thinking of moving to Canada because work was slowing down in the States, and the calls for a Canadian director were starting to happen more often. He said "Lovey, you should move up there!" So I started the process of emigrating to Canada. I'd been in L.A. for almost 20 years, except for six months living in Romania, where I made 8 movies. I was bored with L.A. and in need of a big change.

It took about 17 months of intense scrutiny from the Canadian government before I was approved and granted Landed Immigrant status, meaning I would qualify as a Canadian for Canadian Content purposes. I was in Vancouver for a while, and then was hired to direct *Wishmaster 3* and *Wishmaster 4*, a pair of horror sequels that were being made as Can-con and needed a Canadian director with horror sequel credits, of which I had a few. Vancouver was busy that summer, and so I suggested the shoots be moved to Winnipeg, Manitoba, smack dab in the middle of Canada. That was fine, but the only slot the shoot could fit into coincided with another job: making *The Brotherhood* back in L.A. I had to leave the *Wishmaster* sequels, but by then I'd scouted Winnipeg and loved it. It was clean, friendly, safe and, well, cheap.

Since the *Wishmaster* experience, I'd decided to start up my own company, Rapid Heart Pictures. Shooting in L.A. had become more costly and difficult, and so I spoke to Leslie Oswald, the line producer of the *Wishmaster* movies, and set up the shooting of one of my Rapid Heart quickies in Winnipeg during the slow season. It was a sequel as well: *The Brotherhood III: Young Demons,* shot in Cinemascope in 5 days on the prairies of Canada in the dead of winter. It turned out to be the most fun I ever had on a movie. The Canadian cast and crew was amazing, the city was very helpful and the movie turned out great. Winnipeg was clearly the place to make my movies—so I moved there! I'd gone from watching work by Canadian horror directors to becoming one myself.

To this day, when I mention those fabulous Canadian tax shelter flicks that were made in the late 70s and early 80s to the locals up here, people usually change the subject. They're still a little proper up here in Canada, and those films are a bit of an embarrassment to most. Not to me! I loved them. I hear our local rep house, the Cinematheque, is going to show a bunch of them soon. I'll be the first in line.

DAVID DECOTEAU
June, 2003
www.rapidheart.com

INTRODUCTION

Terror on the Tundra

I T'S NO EXAGGERATION TO SAY that the history of Canadian fiction filmmaking is, in the main, one of catastrophe, neglect and wasted potential. Cursed projects like *The Viking* (1931), in which the producer and many of the crew were killed in a boat explosion; the costly box-office failure of Canada's flagship big-budget effort *Carry On, Sergeant!* in 1928; a cinema fire in Quebec the previous year which killed a number of children; a string of ill-considered decisions regarding trade and cultural relations with a certain entertainment juggernaut to the south; and much incidental misfortune and poor judgment besides helped create an industry that has grown into something crippled, wary, and dumbly resentful, like a puppy repeatedly kicked as it was learning to walk. The American film industry was most often wearing the boots, but it was Canadians who allowed the booting.

The "documentary tradition" in which our cinema is rooted is itself very well documented, and the curious dearth of feature filmmaking in Canada from the beginning of time up to the late 1960s has been frequently remarked upon. When narrative features were produced in Canada before that time, it was almost invariably by someone who had served out an apprenticeship making documentaries at the National Film Board of

David Cronenberg directs *Shivers* as Dan Goldberg crouches behind

Canada and the end result did not stray far from the usual currency of that venerable institution. Style and subject matter both were heavily under NFB influence in these early days, so straight-ahead drama—the more rooted in everyday reality the better—was the implicit, and sometimes the explicit, order of the day.

When the industry finally did kick in, in the early 1970s, the worth of its product still seemed to be based on how likely it was that a given story might actually have happened. Sure, went the received wisdom of the time, a movie about Maritime chuckleheads trying to make it in Toronto must be worthy of our money and attention: after all, it happens for real all the time. There's nothing wrong with that line of thinking, nor, in theory, with the films that resulted; except that the corollary to it all was, of course, that movies featuring subject matter not so likely to have happened—horror movies, say—were looked upon with a good deal less respect and affection. Federal funding was certainly not easy to get. The very idea of a Canadian horror movie to this day invites one of two responses: either the assumption that you must be talking about David Cronenberg, or simple astonishment that such things even exist. But exist they do, and moreover in a great enough number and variety to validate (or so I assert!) an entire book on the subject.

The question of quality arises pretty quickly in discussing Canadian horror movies. The vast majority of them—as is the case with the vast majority of horror films in general—simply aren't by any objective criteria very good, but the good ones are good enough, or interesting enough or compelling enough, to make up for that. Even many of the bad ones have interesting or compelling or otherwise near-redemptive elements to them. The genre itself has an angry, subversive quality to it: these are not movies intended to comfort or reassure their audiences, or to put a smile on their faces and a song in their hearts, and so from the outset they are greatly at odds with most other genres in popular film. "No horror film is truly mainstream," David Cronenberg has said, and this outsider status means that even the lowliest of them are worth at least some consideration.

I maintain, however, that Canadian horror films—as much because of the pleasurable paradox of the phrase "Canadian horror" as anything—are something much better than run-of-the-mill. Their imperfections often have a gloriously unwitting character, of the sort that makes a subject much more attractive than it would be otherwise: the allure of the underdog, the runt, the deformed cousin living in the attic. They are disparaged, denied or ignored in their own country; they are hatched and just as quickly consigned to a stateless bastardy, wandering the continent looking for an audience and maybe a little respect, and, finding none, they curl up on the bottom shelves of the back rows of the most disreputable video shops in the crummiest quarters of town, or else pop up late at night on one of a dozen theme cable channels. My inclination as a Canadian is to be protective of these misfits and to do what I can to help them along their way. Movies are easy to anthropomorphize: they are complex, with identifiable goals (to be seen and enjoyed by as many people as possible); and they are often draped in the personalities of their creators to some greater or lesser degree. If Canadian horror movies were people at a house party, they'd be the graceless eccentric slouching in the corner of the kitchen and drinking Extra Old Stock, their sodden woolen socks piled at their heels. Who wouldn't want to hang out with a person like that?

Philanthropic urges and personal interest aside, the aim of this book is twofold: to bring to light the curious phenomenon and colourful history of the Canadian horror movie, and to explore any distinctive national qualities they may or may not possess. Questions must be asked if we're to get anywhere: like, is there really anything Canadian about a Canadian horror film? What scares the average Canadian, besides guns, de-socialized medicine, weak beer and Americans? (Or to put it more succinctly: America?) What demons haunt the frozen fringes of our dreams; what do we see when the lights go out? More to the point, what do we in Canada make our horror movies about, and why? One might argue that the same things frighten anyone from anywhere. Put a Tunisian, a Laotian and a Canadian in a room together, for example, and none of them will care much for the idea of being attacked by giant snails. But a mixture of more specific with more ambiguous, primal fears (a giant snail on the one hand, say, and generally being eaten on the other), once brewed up, is frequently

My Bloody Valentine

constrained by borders and formed, or augmented, or brought more sharply into focus, by a national character. The giant snail thus becomes a metaphoric representative of whatever its real-world creators' country-mates feel most immediately threatened by—colonialism perhaps, or despotism; a new technology or an unfamiliar ideology. Take the Japanese: in 1945 they were made the object of the most horrifying bomb attacks in the history of mankind, and ten years later, when the children of those firestorms had grown a little older and some had become professional filmmakers, they were turning out movies in which Tokyo is repeatedly crushed to powder by a two hundred foot, fire-breathing nuclear iguana by the name of Godzilla. Or consider the United States, which spent years—the Fifties, to be precise—expressing on film its terror of the ever-imminent Red Menace, lightly disguised in the movies as an invasion from Mars (cf. *Invaders From Mars, War of the Worlds, Mars Needs Women, The Angry Red Planet*) or an attack from some unnamed galaxy by crafty, relentless alien creatures who sought to pounce upon and absorb unsuspecting Americans, either literally (like that damned hungry pinko *The Blob,* which became a deeper shade of red—get it? get it?—with each hapless small-town Yankee it imbibed), or very slightly less so (as with the *Invasion of the Body Snatchers,* who came smiling and waving, as the Commies no doubt would, in the guise of a husband, a wife, a neighbour, a friend). The 2001 terrorist attacks on New York and Washington did very little to curb the desire of Americans to watch buildings crumble and planes fall from the sky on their movie and television screens—just the opposite, in fact.

The reason for this is elemental: we want to see bright lights shone upon our fears (horror films, generally speaking, begin in darkness and end in light: the cleansing fire, the flashing beacons of police cars, or simply the morning sun), and those fears subsequently dealt with by professionals, whether they be scientist, soldier or a team made up of both. The more difficult questions come when we try to nail down exactly why we fear what we fear and how it came to be that way. The problem will not be made any easier just because it's Canada we're dealing with (because Canada is a nation of contrasts and contradictions, and worse yet, is filled with people endlessly trying to designate and define and glibly self-analyze these contrasts and contradictions, often using a lot of alliteration to do so, and very often doing so to the point where you just want to run around in circles gabbling incoherently and tearing at your hair rather than listen to it for one more single second), but it'll be made substantially more amusing. Canada, David Cronenberg has said, is a country cursed with the ability to see both sides of an issue, so conflict—the essence of drama or so we're told—is not our strong suit. This leaves us with our poor frostbitten insecurities, which, as it happens, are always pretty funny.

And then there's Canuck-O-Vision: that peculiarly Canadian quality which infects so many movies from north of the 49th. Energetic denunciation of this quality—a mixture of slightly fuzzy, hollow sound; a blue cast or, sometimes, a milky fog over the picture; several completely superfluous shots of a flapping American flag; a plaid shirt, the CN Tower or a stray, accidental "Eh?" perhaps, and, often, a musical score by a composer named Paul Zaza—is quick to come up in any informal discussion of Canadian cinema, at least insofar as the discussion is between Canadians. Those from other lands tend not to notice it as much. Whether or not you believe that Canuck-O-Vision exists in great enough quantity to warrant such discussion, it may be worth considering that perhaps having a readily identifiable quality to Canadian films is really not such a bad thing. Perhaps it ought to be cultivated somehow; that is, if the qualities that make it so can be isolated, synthesized and applied to future productions without too much difficulty.

A CENTRAL BUT POTENTIALLY TROUBLESOME CONCEPT ought to be nailed down before we go much farther into the subject of Canadian horror movies. Just what, in this internationalist age of co-productions and foreign investment, constitutes a Canadian film anyway? David Cronenberg's 1986 remake of *The Fly* is an instructive example: the film was shot in Canada (in the famed Kleinburg studios located just north of Toronto) by a Canadian director and by a mostly Canadian crew, but the lead actors, the producers and the bulk of the financing were American. The city in which the film is set goes unnamed, and skyline shots, which would unavoidably include that pesky, phallic CN Tower—the bane of many a Toronto-as-New York production—are noticeably absent. So where does that leave *The Fly*? Cronenberg himself had to address this question during a bar-room scene in which Jeff Goldblum, playing the doomed man-fly, backs up an arm-wrestling challenge with a hundred-dollar bill. Should it be American or Canadian money, the prop man asked? It was decided that the bill would be an old-fashioned American greenback, and not a brown Canadian C-note that might, in the midst of a movie about a hideous man-fly, confuse and disturb U.S. audiences with its alien unfamiliarity. But even this decision does not make *The Fly* an American movie: Cronenberg's thorough rewrite of American screenwriter Charles Edward Pogue's original reworking of the 1958 *Fly* (which, to add to the confusion, was an American film explicitly set in Montreal) thoroughly Canadian-izes the characters and themes with just the sort of details this book is dedicated to exploring. And so, more on that later; suffice it for the moment to conclude, by my perhaps as-yet obscure reasoning, that *The Fly* is every bit as Canadian as the beaver pelts and snowshoes hanging on your wall. Less Canadian, but still enough so to warrant inclusion in this book, is the Golden Retriever-vs.-monster movie *Watchers:* a 1988 film boasting an American producer (Roger Corman) and source novel (by Dean R. Koontz), but British Columbia locations and a largely Canadian cast (yes, Corey Haim was born in Canada). Still, this routine creature feature, with its shaggy monster and reliance on gratuitous boy/dog love scenes, could have been made anywhere by anyone: it just happened to have been made in Canada, because that's where the tax breaks are.

Makeup sketch from *The Fly*

In illustrative contrast sit the seemingly endless horror franchises which have ended up in Canada like draft-dodgers, their true citizenship strictly a matter of opinion. The horrors conjured up by the word "franchise" are usually more fast-food than film oriented, and the cynicism in which the term is rooted when used to describe a film series appears largely to have been forgotten. But there seems no end to the parade of horror sequels which grimly troop their way north, such as the twin grandaddies of slash, *Halloween* (the eighth chapter, *Halloween: Resurrection* (2002) was shot in Vancouver) and *Friday the 13th* (the eighth installment of that one had Vancouver standing in for New York, the tenth, *Jason X,* was shot in Toronto and featured David Cronenberg in an extended cameo, and the epic battle of *Freddy Vs. Jason* (2003) was waged in the streets and sound-stages of Vancouver once again), as well as an episode of *A Nightmare on Elm Street* (the aforementioned battle of the titans), *The Amityville Horror* (a rogue entry in that long-running haunted house series, titled *The Amityville Curse* (1989), was shot in Quebec), *The Omen* (part four, the last in number and by far the least in quality—and that's saying something—was shot in Vancouver), and more than one of the *Wishmasters* (III and IV were shot back-to-back in Winnipeg), the *Xtros* (both sequels to the original British alien picture were shot in B.C.) and the *Urban Legends* (both were shot in Toronto, and number two featured *Terror Train* veteran Hart Bochner as the killer). Still other serial horror stories, such as the *Witchboard, Night of the Demons* and *Brotherhood* tales, have also had installments lensed north of the 49th. There isn't much Canadian about most of these movies besides their locations (as opposed to their settings), many of their actors and much of their crews, and consequently you may not read about every last one of them in this book. Some popular series, however, are homegrown (*Prom Night* and *Ginger Snaps,* for example), and a few, like the *Watchers* franchise, actually began in Canada before drifting south to their spiritual and financial birthplace for subsequent episodes.

The preceding paragraphs may have muddied more than cleared the waters, but the upshot is that the matter of whether a horror film is Canadian or otherwise can only be decided on a case-by-case basis, and for the moment it may as well be done by me.

The defining borders of the horror genre are likewise fuzzy. Horror can mix freely with science fiction, suspense, action and even comedy. Again, David Cronenberg—who appears, like most intelligent people, to regard purity as the least interesting of virtues— provides us with excellent material for defining our territory. *The Fly,* for example, contains all the science and hardware of typical gearhead sci-fi, but also a hideous, rampaging bug monster and a welcome element of Gothic romantic-tragedy, and so on balance seems more of a horror movie. *Scanners* (1981), on the other hand, may deal with evil brain-bursting mutants, but is constructed much more along the lines of a science-adventure story, and as a result neither it nor its innumerable sequels and spin-offs (*Scanner Cop* et al) will see very much ink in this book.

Suspense movies, mysteries and policiers will occasionally intrude into this narrative by virtue of their particular treatment of the suspense scenes, the particularly horrific nature of the threat, or some supernatural element present in the story. *American Nightmare* (1983), *City in Panic* (1987) and *Matinee* (1988) are all good examples of these fine-line treaders. Even the pedigree of the film's makers might occasionally come into play, as in the case of George Mihalka's *The Watchtower* (2001). That picture, while more of a mystery-travelogue than an outright horror movie, was nevertheless directed by Mihalka, one of Canada's premier horror directors (the man behind *My Bloody Valentine,* say no more; though he's made films in almost any genre one could name), and so you may find it mentioned, if not very enthusiastically dissected, in the pages which follow.

Horror is, along with pornography, among the most misbegotten of genres, and this is perhaps triply true in Canada. Directors such as David Cronenberg and William Fruet were practically disowned by the critical community of the nation after releasing their first work in the genre. (Cronenberg has been energetically re-embraced, while Fruet's career, sadly, never really recovered from his Amish-style shunning.) We Canadians lack that conservative, puritanical core and troubled national upbringing which allows Americans to make the most frivolous, exciting (and at times sneakily intelligent and subversive) movies in the world, while at the same time ensuring that not a penny of public money will be spent doing it, lest moral values be corrupted somehow. So while we are freer with our taxpayers' dollars, we have to ensure that what gets put on the screen by their grace is culturally defensible; which means that it has to be "artistic" in some quantifiable way, or at the very least profitable. This means that our genre movies run the risk of stifling themselves with superfluous or misguided conceptualizing on the one hand, or pandering to whatever is—often wrongly—considered the current public vogue on the other. A distinct national cinema has for both better and worse been forged as a result of the situation, and it is in many ways most visible in looking at the horror genre. There are movies in the Canadian horror canon that, in spite of (or perhaps due to) their often desperate attempts to appear American, clearly could only have been made in Canada.

Horror is perceived as dangerous, both because it travels on the dark side of human experience and because, done well, it tends to reveal things about that experience many might prefer to keep hidden. Add public money to the brew and you have a potentially combustive cocktail, whose flashpoint is hit whenever a particularly controversial film is released, like David Cronenberg's first feature, *Shivers*. Robert Fulford, writing in a September, 1975 issue of *Saturday Night* magazine under the pseudonym "Marshall Delaney" (a nom de plume he assumed every week for his movie column) penned a querulous article about that movie entitled "You Should Know How Bad This Film Is. After All, You Paid For It." The article essentially took Cronenberg and the Canadian Film Development Corporation to task for colluding to use taxpayers' money for a film that was, to Fulford, a grotesque and badly-made cavalcade of perversions unbefitting of Canadian cinema. (The CFDC, now called Telefilm, is an organization whose mandate is contributing to the funding of Canadian films.) But as *Shivers* is neither a mindless circus of depravity nor badly made, it seems clear that Fulford's objections to it must have some other source: one very possibly located within Fulford himself. And that's what a good horror movie can do—tap into these secret corners and produce reactions, whether they be unexpected, objectively unsupportable or simply nonsensical.

Robert Silverman as the creepy janitor in *Prom Night*

But within the genre, quality horror movies make up the minority. There are more interesting films than good ones. This goes for Canadian horror films as well, probably even, again, triply so. The factors against which the average Canadian horror movie must struggle as it is conceived and made—principally a shaky sense of national identity; a cinematic, not to say artistic, tradition in diametric opposition to horror; the paradox suggested by those first two components, and a host of economic issues on top of that—insure that most of them founder in their quest for greatness. But that hardly matters in a book like this, as simple Hollywood competence is in my view one of the least important and compelling qualities a Canadian horror film can have. A bald-faced, desperate grab for slickness, doomed to failure from the outset, is very often more interesting than the slickness itself; which is after all something money can readily buy.

Canadian horror cinema is a cinema of moments, rich with unlikely imagery, baffling storylines and bizarre narrative twists. It is the home of defiantly unpredictable confluences (severed heads, disco dancing and Leslie Nielsen all in one movie, for example!) and largely illegible, usually accidental subtext. With careful observation, consistent, if strange, maple leaf-shaped patterns do emerge, but they sink back into the gory mire the moment one's concentration lapses, leaving you to wonder if they were ever there at all. The impression left is of some deeper meaning just out of view, perceivable only if one is willing to put in the work and adopt a mode of thinking that is in equal parts nationalistic, broad-minded, elliptical and clear.

For those unwilling or unable to think in this way, the Canadian horror canon is, simply, a whole lot of fun. Trolling around for those spooky or goofy gems with which the Tundra Terror pond is well stocked is one of the most enjoyable endeavors I've ever undertaken, and it is my hope that in reading this field guide, you'll be inspired to put on your hip waders, jump in your blood canoe and join right in.

T-E-R-R-O-R
BEYOND THE POWER OF PRIEST OR SCIENCE TO EXORCISE !

THEY CAME FROM WITHIN ↑

"THEY CAME FROM WITHIN" starring PAUL HAMPTON • JOE SILVER
LYNN LOWRY • and BARBARA STEELE as "BETTS" • produced by IVAN REITMAN
written and directed by DAVID CRONENBERG • a TRANS-AMERICAN FILMS Release
Color prints by Movielab

R **RESTRICTED**
Under 17 Requires Accompanying
Parent or Adult Guardian

I.

Put on the Mask!

(The Beginning to 1967)

THERE WAS NO SUDDEN BARRAGE of Canadian horror films, crashing down like German Expressionism or the French New Wave to stun, delight and inspire the world. The early history of horror in this country is made up of timid little coughs and half-hearted clearings of the throat, and those belated and infrequent enough as to make anyone who insisted that such productions even existed appear to be a liar or a hallucinating drunk. In fact, movies of almost any identifiable genre were rare in Canada until the late sixties, and movies of any kind at all, aside from National Film Board of Canada documentary productions, were to say the least sporadic. Accordingly, the first part of this horror film history must be a fairly cursory history of why horror films were not made in Canada.

At the time of the invention of motion pictures, in the late nineteenth century, Canada was largely a sparsely populated wilderness in need of workers and citizens who might help it find its place as a world power. Cinema was not primarily seen as a form of entertainment, but rather a handy tool for nation-building. Entertainment could wait: there was work to be done. The Canadian Pacific Railway, a hard-working establishment from way back, jumped on the medium and sponsored dozens of films from adventuresome

Peter Roffman
c. 1960

photography buffs across the country that were designed to attract the immigration needed to fill out the population. James Freer, an immigrant from England who upon his arrival in the young and untamed country became a Brandon, Manitoba-area farmer and die-hard prairie enthusiast, was the first such impressario. These films, with titles like *The Thresher At Work,* were emphatically not dramatic or narrative in nature, nor the slightest bit entertaining to contemporary viewers; but they were determinately propagandistic and even fantastical in their efforts to lure would-be settlers, as much in what they neglected to show (namely, winter) as in what they did (fertile fields, glorious scenery, affordable machinery and an eternal, resplendent summer of limitless opportunity).

The result of this line of film production was a healthy influx of manpower (including a young Boris Karloff, who emigrated to Canada in 1909 to become a farm labourer) and an appreciation for the effectiveness of documentary. So Canada kept its head down and concentrated on the work at hand, while the United States, with its established industry, strong economy and multitudinous cities, set about populating the orange groves of Hollywood and harnessing the more diversionary aspects of cinema, using the local scenery and climate to a perennially world-beating advantage.

There were to be no horror films out of Canada for a very long time. European countries, their strong Gothic and folklore traditions coming quickly to the fore, were producing horror-fantasy films as early as 1896, with the two-minute Georges Méliès film *Le Manoir du Diable* standing as the first horror movie ever made.[1] The U.S. joined in the horror game in 1910 with Thomas Edison's production of *Frankenstein,* and soon screen terrors were flowing from the studios of America, France and Germany, and at least trickling out of Great Britain, Italy, Denmark, Hungary and Japan. But Canada was a land of practical-minded people: the kind who wore animal skins draped over their backs and had to work almost constantly simply to survive the howling, skin-blasting winters. There was no room for fantasy here, and horror, well, horror was thin ice, or snow blindness or a rogue bear. Vampires just didn't do it, and there were in any event no old castles or ruined abbeys for them to live in.

There were the woods, of course, and those who had been living in them for centuries had their own blood-chilling traditions and legends; but the superstitions were not yet rooted as deeply in the European mind as was needed to build the proper cultural foundation. The settlers had been hearing about Native monsters for years: the Wendigo, for example, which was a spirit who could possess some unlucky passing warrior and turn him into a frenzied, flesh-ripping cannibal, was as frightening as any Old World vampire myth, but was not latched onto by the new arrivals. There was too much work to do, perhaps, and still too few people to do it. To this day a richly veined lode of indigenous myth remains largely unexplored by Canadian horror filmmakers, Native or otherwise.

One exception, a small but echoic hiccup in the Dominion's film history, is *The Werewolf* (1913), an eighteen minute long picture thought by many to be the first werewolf movie ever made. The claim seems likely; it's certainly the first werewolf picture made in Canada. (It would remain just about the only werewolf picture made in Canada until *Ginger Snaps,* eighty-seven years later.) The film is reportedly based on indigenous shapeshifter myths, and used the cinematic trickery of the times—that is, simple, abrupt cuts, or quick dissolves—to show a young aboriginal girl, Watuma, transforming into a wolf. A holy man puts an end to this heretical behaviour by waving his cross around. But Watuma returns a century later, as wronged supernatural beings will do, and takes her belated vengeance. Two different actresses played the separate incarnations of Watuma, while a real wolf played her in wolf form. The film was directed by Toronto-born Western picture specialist Henry McRae, and the available information suggests that the film was effectively destroyed in 1924 by a fire.

By the early teens Canada was adequately populated with farmers and labourers from many lands, and ready to produce its first narrative features. These were generally wilderness dramas involving noble savages, crowds of cutely Disney-esque animals, pistol-brandishing foreigners and dogsleds. The seventy-five minute *Evangeline,* filmed in Nova Scotia for $30,000.00, was the first. Others followed, with titles like *Self Defence, The Marriage Trap* and *The Great Shadow.* There were

Secrets of Chinatown

also the Ernest Shipman productions: a series of seven films over a period of four years or so, filmed in cities across the Dominion from 1919 through 1923. "Ten Percent Ernie" was an entrepreneurial producer with a habit of prying back ten percent of his hirelings' wages for supposed re-investment into the movie, and a wife, Nell, who was willing to strip down and do a nude scene for her husband's first big Canadian venture, *Back to God's Country.* The profits from this picture started Shipman off nicely, and he bounced around Canada making wilderness adventure films in cities from Calgary to St. John until the squeeze tactics of the big American companies and the resulting lukewarm box-office forced him more or less out of the business. (Nell, by this time divorced from the old ten percenter, had her own acting and screenwriting career, and had moved to the United States and into film production.)

AMONGST THE WILDERNESS DRAMAS AND WAR FILMS (though not apart from them), a few tremulous, almost unintentional steps towards the shadowy world of horror movies were made by the Canadian motion picture industry. *Satan's Paradise* (1922), a classic 1920s film title if ever there was one, told the story of some fake spiritualists who, through repeated séances, attempted to convince a mother that they could put her in contact with her dead soldier son. The son does indeed materialize (in a scenario prefiguring Bob Clark's *The Night Walk* (1973; a.k.a. *Deathdream*) by several wars and some fifty years), but here he proves not to have been killed but merely shell-shocked. The spiritualists are thereby debunked, and retreat into the shadows never to prey on the helpless war-bereaved again. This film was shot in Toronto for a reported cost of $2000, but suffered from an "unsuccessful release," meaning it probably never even made its paltry budget back.

Another near-horror was *The Devil Bear* (1928). This was not, as one might assume, or hope, a killer bear film along the lines of William Girdler's *Jaws*-inspired *Grizzly* (1976), but rather a strange-sounding drama about a gorilla, kept as a companion by a sea captain, who escapes from a boat docked in Halifax harbour after his owner is thumped on the head, and whom the frightened locals at first take to be some sort of monster. The gorilla wanders around Canada (specifically around the Thunder Bay, Ontario area and the spectacular Kakabeka Falls, where the film was shot) in the company of the dazed, amnesiac sea captain, and the pair have all manner of wilderness adventures before making friends, as the monster in *Frankenstein* (1931) would later do, with a cabin-dwelling hermit. But it was no horror movie; just an adventure-comedy about a stranger in a strange land.

In 1927, a British quota legislation decreeing that a certain percentage of films exhibited in the UK must be of British origin (which is to say, produced in the British Commonwealth, and with a hefty fraction of the salaries going to British subjects, which at the time included Canadians) meant that the industry in Canada was given a small financial shot in the arm. "Quota Quickies," produced mainly in an unheated horse barn in Victoria, British Columbia, included mist-shrouded mysteries like *Secrets of Chinatown* (1934), in which sinister hooded figures, hopped up on opium goofballs, roam the shadowy streets of Vancouver's Chinatown, kidnapping white women and worshipping the devil. Many at the time of the film's release (or rather, many of the very few who actually saw the picture) no doubt took *Secrets of Chinatown* as a horror film, with the Chinese as the monsters, but it was in reality only a pallid and xenophobic detective-mystery. Still, with its clutching hands, shrouded figures and unmotivated drifts of smoke, the film freely employs the style and tone of horror, and so represents one more small step towards the horror genre by Canadian producers, as well as a prophetic indication of the ignominy to come in the tax shelter years of the late 1970s.

The 1930s were, according to Peter Morris's pioneering study of Canadian cinema, *Embattled Shadows,* "a gloomy period… for Canadian film production… Even at their best, the quota quickies are no more than efficient, routine B-movies." By all reports, this may be a generous assessment of the overall quality of these pictures, but they nevertheless represented a film industry, even if a slipshod, faintly sleazy one engineered by foreign interests. As such, the quota quickie machine, if allowed by circumstance to continue, might have provided a foundation for a truly indigenous, self-sustaining cultural industry in Canada much earlier than was the case. But the host of American producers in B.C. fled back to California when the British laws changed, leaving no hint of infrastructure and little in the way of a positive imprint to encourage Canadians to take up the torch; or, to overstretch an analogy, design, construct and light their own all-new torch.

These gasps of activity notwithstanding, Canada was in no position to build a film industry. It was not in Hollywood's interests to allow it, and so, by aggressive acquisition of Canadian exhibition space, the Yankee monopoly over Canadian film production and viewing was assured. The results are still painfully evident today.

Horrific Canucks—Part I

BY THE MID 1930S, without producing a single horror movie of its own, Canada had nonetheless made an impact on the horror movie scene. Halifax-born actor David Manners, a kind of Colin Clive Lite, was acting his heart out in several of the best known of the great Universal Pictures horror cycle; or in other words, several of the most famous horror movies ever made. He was an effete Jonathan Harker in Tod Browning's 1931 *Dracula;*[2] was the highest billed un-bandaged star in Karl Freund's *The Mummy*; and, joining both the respective great top-liners of those two films, Bela Lugosi and Boris Karloff, he played guileless young husband Peter Alison in Edgar Ulmer's excellent *The Black Cat*.[3] He would, moreover, play the eponymous role around whom all the mystery swirls in the 1935 version of Charles Dickens' unfinished novel *The Mystery of Edwin Drood*. Manners' acting style jibes nicely with both his surname and his country of birth: he's generally open, friendly, and very polite. These qualities, notoriously unhelpful when battling monsters, kept him in emasculated, Ralph Bellamy-type roles for most of his short movie career. He retired from the screen at the end of the thirties to write novels, died in 1998 at the age of 97, and was not wrong in predicting to an interviewer that he would probably be best remembered for his horror film roles.

The Bloody Brood

Even more indelible a mark was made by Fay Wray, the girl in the gorilla's paw, who was born in Alberta but raised in Los Angeles. After working in movies for ten years (including stints for both the Vons, Sternberg and Stroheim), *King Kong* (1933) ensured that she, her sheer white dress and her astoundingly powerful screaming lungs, would achieve an iconic cinematic immortality for all time. Her horror career neither began nor ended with *King Kong*, however: at the very same time she was shooting the big monkey movie (which was made over a very long period of time due to the endless, time-consuming special effects involved), her trademark shriek was getting exercise next to Lionel Atwill in the early Technicolor spookshow *Doctor X* (in fact, the very first Technicolor horror film ever made), *Mystery of the Wax Museum* (which was the second) and a monochrome Frankenstein rip-off called *The Vampire Bat*. She therefore stands as perhaps the only Canadian ever to have acted in four horror movies at the same time—

five, if you count *The Most Dangerous Game* (that old chestnut about madman Count Zaroff hunting the most dangerous prey he can think of—humans!—across his private island) as a horror movie, as many do. Wray was the original scream queen, a cinematic trooper whose devotion to both her craft and her shriek set the bar for all who followed.

Another Canadian whose horror work, even though on the other side of the camera, would be the foundation of his eventual wealth and acclaim was Mark Robson, who was born in Montreal and whose trip up the Hollywood ladder began humbly, in a Twentieth Century Fox properties room. After several years, by whatever capricious twists of fate and surges of ambition, cunning or luck the thumbnail biographies of such people usually leave out, he found himself in the cutting rooms of RKO Pictures. There he would assist in the editing of *Citizen Kane* and *The Magnificent Ambersons* before hooking up with RKO's legendary in-house horror producer Val Lewton. After cutting Lewton's production of *Cat People* (1942), directed by Jacques Tourneur,[4] Robson was engaged to direct a fine, spooky thriller called *The Seventh Victim* (1943), which would remain probably the best work Robson ever did as a director. Other Lewton spookfests followed: *The Ghost Ship* (1943) first, and then a moody pair called *Isle of the Dead* (1945) and *Bedlam* (1946), both of which had stories based on scary old paintings and featured David Manners' old co-star—and, briefly, fellow Canadian—Boris Karloff. Robson's career moved uptown after this strong beginning, and he would never again recapture the intensity of *The Seventh Victim,* ending his career by instead churning out entertaining Hollywood tripe like *Valley of the Dolls* (1967) and *Earthquake* (1974). He was certainly well off by retirement time, and whether he knew it or not, he had horror to thank for it.

Known as "Hollywood's most-liked filmmaker" (trust a Canadian to snag that title), John S. Robertson, born in London, Ontario in 1878, made the John Barrymore version of *Dr. Jekyll and Mr. Hyde* in 1920. Forgotten now, he was a big shot in his time, directing such stars as his countrymate Mary Pickford, and working in Britain with Alfred Hitchcock as his art director.

None of these people had much claim on Canada, however, nor Canada on them. Certainly they never identified themselves as Canadians, or even ex-Canadians, as someone like Mike Myers might occasionally do today. But they remain a part of Canadian horror film history nonetheless, even if a tangential and largely uncelebrated one.

There were other actors, more readily identifiable as Canadian, who made appearances in foreign horror films. Raymond Massey (whom I've always thought might have been a horror star to rival Karloff, had chance or inclination taken him further in that direction) made an early appearance in the U.K. crime spook-fest *The Face At the Window* (1932; not the later Tod Slaughter version), and, in the same year, as a David Manners-like foil in James Whale's *The Old Dark House.* (Massey could never muster the reserves of jejune impotence so effortlessly spewed by Manners, however.) Donald Woods, the Brandon, Manitoba-born journeyman actor, appeared in one of the earliest revived-giant-monster pictures, *The Beast from 20,000 Fathoms* (1953), and in 1960 starred in William Castle's "Illusion-O" gimmick film *13 Ghosts.* Glenn Ford was another

Canadian who danced around the genre now and again in his career, appearing in thrillers like Blake Edwards' *Experiment in Terror* (1962) and, later, in one of the more (relatively) high-class examples of the slasher movie cycle, *Happy Birthday To Me* (1981; discussed at greater length in Chapter 4). He also appeared in the hugely expensive Japanese medical thriller *Virus* (1980), playing the President of the United States while shooting on location in Toronto. And Lloyd Bochner, born in Toronto and known from his role as Old Mister Colby on *Dynasty*, showed up in films as diverse as William Castle's

The Night Walker (1964), Daniel Haller's *The Dunwich Horror* (1970), the well-loved TV movie *Satan's School for Girls* (1973) and, more recently, co-starring with Lou Gossett Jr. in a bit of piffle called *Bram Stoker's Legend of the Mummy* (1997). He also contributed to the world of Canadian horror by siring Hart Bochner, who would play a major role in *Terror Train* (1980).

The Mask

Victor Jory, born in Dawson City, Yukon, showed up in an episode of the horror series *Kolchak: The Night Stalker* and in the 1978 Curtis Harrington TV movie *Devil Dog: Hound from Hell,* in both instances playing a Native character, as though being from up north made him more aboriginal by nature. Who knows, maybe it did. Redface is still redface, though, and there've always been plenty of talented Native actors to choose from. But not for such niceties was Hollywood in those less sensitive days. Finally, London, Ontario-born Hume Cronyn appeared in the 1943 version of *Phantom of the Opera,* and then much later in a toxic-waste thriller called *Impulse* (1984). This hardly makes a horror career, of course, but it's all part of the rich tapestry that is Canadian horror history.

IN 1938, AN EMPHATICALLY NON-HORRIFIC PERSON, the Scottish-born administrator John Grierson, was brought over from England to Canada to run the National Film Board of Canada, the very creation of which indicates a decision made as to which direction Canadian film should go. Grierson's appointment sealed the deal: he was very much in favour of the documentary form over made-up drama, which he regarded as useless fakery and flim-flam. (So devoted was Grierson to the form that he had in fact invented the very word "documentary" back in 1926.) "Although he proclaimed a yearning to liberate and extend filmmaking," reads David Thomson's Grierson entry in his *New Biographical Dictionary of Film,* "he evolved a narrow doctrine hostile to many other types of cinema, essentially bigoted and unintelligent and isolated by history."

Certainly insofar as Canadian film is concerned, it cannot be doubted that Grierson's passion for the documentary form (already well-appreciated in Canada) and his concomitant dismissal of staged and performed drama—and especially, one assumes, any attempt at fantasy—was instrumental in shaping the entire nation's policies and attitudes and the directions in which its cinema would travel. These attitudes would live on, as would the National Film Board, long after Grierson's 1945 return to England, making a man who had worked in Canada for barely six years "the single most important figure in the development of a Canadian film culture," according to his biographical entry in *Take One's Essential Guide to Canadian Film.*

The NFB has dipped the occasional toe into horror, though strictly for the purposes of education. The 1950 driver's ed short *Gentleman Jekyll and Driver Hyde* shows us the dire consequences of road rage in the days before road rage had a name. An everyday fellow goes driving, only to sprout horns, fangs and facial hair when faced with common obstacles on the road. (This could be the first special effects monster makeup ever put on film in Canada.) A child on a bicycle invites a growl of "Get out of the way, kid!" from the enraged motorist; a woman barely avoids being run down (though her eggs are not so lucky), and other drivers are invited by the irritable fiend to "go fry your fish!" Luckily he learns the value of patience and calm before there's any real bloodshed. Of course, *Gentleman Jekyll and Driver Hyde* isn't very scary as horror movies go. But it hinted that somewhere in the bowels of the country's most venerable filmmaking institution, there were people with an appreciation for the power of the genre and the will to use its unique grammar.

Spooks Up North

THERE WERE A FEW HORROR FILMS not made by or starring Canadians, not filmed in Canada nor made with Canadian money, that were nevertheless set in Canada. *The Fly* (1958) and its sequels, *Return of the Fly* (1959) and *Curse of the Fly* (1965), were all set in and around Montreal, with a character roll made up entirely of French names. This is strange, particularly given that the remakes, nearly thirty years on, would both be filmed in Canada and set in some North American no-man's land; but, as pointed out in an article by Chris Fujiwara in *Filmfax* magazine, the Quebec location does serve a few useful dramatic purposes. For one, Fujiwara theorizes, the question, potentially and dangerously at the tip of every American audience member's tongue, of why the scientist in the movie doesn't bother reporting his amazing teleportation discoveries to some government body is easily answered by simply saying "Well, it's Canada. Who knows how they do things up there?" In America the lab would most likely be under much greater scrutiny by meddlesome Army brass, as in movies like *Tarantula* (1955). Other troublesome points, like the behavior of the police, which is rather more laid back in *The Fly* than in most American films of the period, may be explained by the same logic. The foreign-sounding names and the slightly formalized, off-kilter manner of the characters is made both explicable and palatable by the Canadian setting. It's foreign, but it's not *too* foreign.

Another recent *Fly* article, titled "The Disintegration of a Canadian Family" (by Erich Kuersten, *Scarlet Street* no. 48), points out:

> That the tale unfolds in Canada is, in itself, telling… Canada's national identity seems a molecular fusion of American, British and French culture, a suitable place to loose the fused fly/man. Canada has the British air of civility, the French sense of culture, and the American "let's split the atom!" enthusiasm. On a purely visual level, Americans may think of Canada as "up there," in a sort of mysterious north, floating above the United States like a buzzing cloud over a picnic.

The Mask

Still, whatever the value of setting the series in Canada, the scientist is teleported from Montreal to London near the end of the third film in the series, *Curse of the Fly,* thereby ensuring that if further sequels were warranted they could be set in a still more familiar and easily recreated location. The audience's taste for flies was well-sated by then, however, and no further fly-films were made until 1986.

Fiend Without a Face (1958), the flying brain picture to beat them all, was exotically set on a rocket base in northern Manitoba. This was a British-made film from ex-cinematographer Arthur Crabtree, the director of the later Anglo-shocker *Horrors of the Black Museum,* and setting it in Canada meant he could use all the British-sounding actors he wanted while still providing a recognizable though remote landscape to the American audiences for whom the picture was intended. On top of that, it's easy to believe that the characters (under attack by grotesque space-brains who jump around the room like ticks and strangle hapless victims with their spinal-column tails) are well and truly far away from any possible aid. The cavalry might possibly make it to, say, northern Montana if the situation demanded it, but they wouldn't have a clue how to find Flin Flon. It's fun, for Canadian audiences at any rate, to witness the conflict between the small-town Manitobans and the American air force brass—the locals initially believe the brain-murders are the work of an insane Yankee G.I.—even though the actual actors were neither Canadian nor American. When the alien nature of the threat is revealed, the Canadians and Americans put aside their differences and work together to fight it, in the process reinforcing the altogether fantastical nature of the plot.

Other ersatz-Canadian locations would come many years down the road. Ed Ragozzino's *Sasquatch* (1977) was filmed entirely by Americans in the Cascade mountains in Oregon, but it was explicitly set in the British Columbia interior. Clive Barker's *Nightbreed* (1990), starring famed Canadian horror director David Cronenberg in full-on creepy-guy mode as a murderous psychiatrist, was filmed in England but for some reason set in Alberta. According to at least one review of *Nightbreed,* the Canadian setting "works against true dementia and crowd frenzy, the Cronenberg tradition notwithstanding… Bloodthirsty vigilantes, brutal sheriffs and deracinated rednecks armed with shotguns seem so… American. They didn't call it 'Alberta Chainsaw Massacre'."[5] True enough, but what the reviewer fails to realize is that they easily could have, for what is Alberta if not Canada's Texas? In any case, this comment demonstrates the common perception of Canada being, quite simply, an un-scary place.

A counterpoint to this attitude came in 1992. In David Lynch's theatrical prequel to his popular television series, *Twin Peaks: Fire Walk With Me,* there is a scene in which some hapless Twin Peaks residents go on an ill-advised trip north of the border, where they find Canada itself—the entire country—to be an horrific, hallucinogenic place, and its residents a pack of slavering lunatics. The barely-subsumed corruption and psychoses of Twin Peaks have erupted into full-blooded everyday life north of the border: to Lynch this is the ultimate reward/punishment for a history of emotional repression, and a warning sign for the residents of his little Washington state mountain town: loosen up or your demons too will come to life and take over, just as they have in Canada.

In the 1950s canada was not an horrific or hallucinogenic place filled with lunatics. In fact it sounds a little boring. The idea of a viable commercial film industry in Canada appears to have been about on par with notions of walking on the moon. At the same time, American companies were churning out low-budget science-fiction and horror as though possessed: the likes of Roger Corman and American International were trotting out wonderful new B flicks on a near-weekly basis. Hammer Films, in England, had tapped a rich vein of Gothic horror. Wonderful, eerie genre flicks were being made in Italy, Germany, France and Mexico, and in Japan the mighty Godzilla was being hatched. In all of these countries the profits were steady as long as the costs were kept low. So where was the Canadian entrepreneurial spirit and vision which had shown itself in so many other areas? Surely there must have been some would-be producers north of the 49th who would like to have joined in on the fun.

Indeed there were, but they were hobbled by the lack of an infrastructure, the paucity of available labour and the prevailing notion that Canada's forté was and ever would be the production of documentaries. But as the National Film Board was turning out its rock-solid documentary shorts and the Canadian Broadcasting Corporation was teaching itself the television ropes, both institutions were providing experience and instruction to technicians and creative personnel alike. Young directors such as Sidney Furie and Harvey Hart were working for the CBC, while Don Haldane was cutting his teeth at the NFB. All of these men were more than a little interested in creating a self-supporting industry in Canada, but for the moment it simply didn't happen.

Furie began his feature career by writing and directing a drama of reckless youth entitled *A Dangerous Age* (1958), which started life as a CBC production but wound up as a theatrical feature instead. The rub for Furie was that it was released in England, but couldn't find distribution in the country in which it had been produced. He tried again, with a cool-daddy-o teen rebellion drama called *A Cool Sound From Hell,* which was received in Canada with even greater indifference than *A Dangerous Age.* Throwing up his hands in frustration, Furie moved to England, where he told reporters "I tried to start a feature film industry in Canada, but nobody cared." His first UK productions were in the horror genre: *Dr. Blood's Coffin* and *The Snake Woman* (both 1960). Moving to the United States in the mid-sixties, he would later make the 1982 ghost-rapist picture *The Entity.*

The Mask

A friend and protégé of Furie's from his CBC days was an aspiring feature film director called Lindsay Shonteff. Shonteff, seeing that Furie was working steadily across the pond, took a page from his book and relocated to England in the early 1960s, where he was hired by producer Richard Gordon to make the cult favourite *The Devil Doll* (1963) after Furie turned down the job in favour of more mainstream work. The result, a moody, effective piece in the "living doll" sub-genre, was nonetheless reportedly made under Furie's close supervision. Shonteff then directed a supernatural jungle-revenge picture called *Curse of the Voodoo* (1964), which was in every respect much less successful than *The Devil Doll.* He went on from there to a string of low-brow espionage thrillers and crime adventures, including one called *The Fast Kill,* which, in a strange bit of circularity, would eventually become a kind of near-scriptural stylistic guide to the iconoclastic Canadian director Guy Maddin during the making of his melodrama *The Saddest Music in the World* (2003).

Harvey Hart and Don Haldane (later to direct, respectively, the Canadian horror features *The Pyx* and *The Reincarnate*) continued slogging it out in Canada, though Hart would soon head to the States, and in the meantime independent production companies were springing up to provide product for the hungry medium of television. In the midst of all this, like some swaggering cowboy emerging from the purple sage to set things right in town, came one of Canada's premier showmen, Julian Roffman.

Born in Montreal in 1915, Roffman began his show business career as a member of McGill University's Red and White Players. He became discouraged with the limitations of theatre upon realizing that you could only play to a limited number of people at any one time. Film, through which you could reach untold thousands with a single production, was to Roffman clearly the way to go. Roffman himself was, in manner if not in physical stature, bigger than life, just like all the classic movie moguls, and the medium of film matched his personality well. Hearing about some film courses in New York, the young go-getter enrolled, picking up the know-how he needed while supporting himself by sweeping floors at various Gotham film studios.

From janitorial duties, Roffman was promoted to assistant cameraman and assistant director positions on a variety of short series made for companies like Universal and Paramount. In 1935, the March of Time newsreel films began production, and Roffman joined the project first as an assistant director and then a director, making documentaries on coal mining, doctors, and U.S. Senator Huey Long to play before the cartoons and features. He produced a popular series of films whose mandate was to reveal misrepresentations by advertisements (as big a problem then as it is now, evidently); based on a book called *One Hundred Million Guinea Pigs,* the movies were released under the blanket title *Getting Your Money's Worth.*

More documentaries followed: movies about art, aviation mechanics, hillbillies, polio. In 1940, Roffman returned to Canada and took up with John Grierson's NFB, then only just entering its terrible twos. "I was already a veteran compared to the neophytes there who had never seen a camera cranked," Roffman remembered. "They were all wildly engaged in making films, but none of them knew which end of the camera took the picture. It was a madhouse with people rushing up and down the corridors."[6] Roffman made a great number of army films through the Film Board, like the psychological study *13 Platoon,* and a zany recruitment film for women called *The Proudest Girl in the World,* which was written by comedy Canucks Frank Schuster and Johnny Wayne, and resembled nothing more than a full-blown Busby Berkeley dance routine. The army, as might be expected, were leery of such an approach for what was supposed to be a standard-issue recruitment film, but Roffman's vision was supported by Grierson, who told the brass "This small young man is an excellent filmmaker. Let him do what he wants." A grateful Roffman would thereafter keep a picture of Grierson hanging in his office right beside one of his own father.

Wounded in the war, Roffman returned to New York and took up the documentary camera once again, winning prizes for such short subjects as the very successful *F.D.R.— Hyde Park.* Television beckoned, and Roffman began making commercials and television drama. In New York he co-founded a company called Pioneer TV Films, which evolved after his tenure into a massive company now known as Screen Gems; and then, returning to Canada once again, he partnered up with an old NFB friend named Ralph Foster to create Meridian Productions. Based in Toronto, Meridian turned out commercials and television programs, and in 1959 became the first Canadian company to move into the new technology of videotape.

Nat Taylor, meanwhile, was an Ontario film exhibitor and general showman who had founded the trade paper *Canadian Film Weekly* in the early 1940s and wrote columns exhorting any and all, especially the federal government, to fully commit to the task of building a Canadian film industry. Taylor was an energetic player in the nascent industry: he'd tried to help Sidney Furie market *A Dangerous Age,* and in 1959 had opened the Kleinburg film studios (officially known as Toronto International Film Studios Inc.) just north of Toronto.[7] Kleinburg was for a long time the only film studio in the area; perhaps even in all of Canada. Taylor and Roffman formed a partnership called, naturally enough, Taylor-Roffman (though the Taylor named on the incorporation documents was, for some obscure business reason, actually Nat Taylor's wife Yvonne), and immediately embarked on their first purely commercial feature project, *The Bloody Brood.*

While not a horror film, *The Bloody Brood* is nonetheless a violent exploitation picture which trades heavily on polite society's profound fear of beatniks. A pre-fame Peter Falk stars as a nasty hep-cat named Nico whose favourite pastime is feeding glass-filled hamburgers to hapless delivery boys. Nico, it turns out, is not a real beatnik but a calculating criminal for whom death is the ultimate thrill show, and he gets his comeuppance at the hands of the slain delivery boy's brother. The film was atmospherically shot by none other than the German special effects and cinematographic pioneer Eugene Shuftan, inventor of the Schufftan Process[8] of matte photography. A year after filming *The Bloody Brood,* Shuftan shot Georges Franju's fright classic *Les Yeux Sans Visage;* and two years after that he won the Academy Award for his work on *The Hustler.*

The Mask

The Bloody Brood was filmed in 16 days for a total budget of $80,000. The budget had come directly from the pockets of Taylor and Roffman themselves ("I nearly hawked our studio to finance it," Roffman claimed), but the film did not make its money back for the partners. "A distributor in New York was living off the revenues, but we didn't find out about it until later," Roffman says. "He was an old man and we let it go. What could we have done?" Nevertheless, this taste of commercial filmmaking was heady and appealing, despite Roffman's loftier inclinations. The school essay *Julian Roffman: Man of Action* informs us of the filmmaker's very Canadian preference for documentary, and the pressures and temptations which led him into a more mercenary arena. "He... like many others, was seduced by a bigger canvas and more money," the essay reports. "He should have continued making documentaries, he feels, but instead he started making 'tripes'... In the future, he hopes to apply himself to the issues of the unemployed, the unwanted, and the elderly." So it goes: the father of Canadian genre filmmaking was, it turns out, among the most committed, socially responsible documentarians Canada ever produced. Such are the wonderful ironies of history. But what, one wonders, did Roffman's hero John Grierson think of his protégé's work in crime and horror movies? In a "minor manifesto" outlining his thoughts on filmmaking, of which documentary was the only valid kind, Grierson asserts that "the young director cannot, in nature, go documentary and go studio both." Roffman was attempting to do just that, and at times, under the great Calvinist administrator's hawk-like gaze, it must have been very hard. But he persisted, and in so doing he made Canada's first real horror film.

It Begins: The Mask

MADE IN AND AROUND TORONTO in the spring and summer of 1961, *The Mask* would in fact set a number of Canadian cinema benchmarks: besides being the first Canadian horror feature, it was Canada's first 3-D movie; the first Canadian movie to make its money back before shooting had even completed; and the first Canadian film to receive wide distribution in the United States (and later, the world).

The financial failure of *The Bloody Brood,* insofar as Taylor and Roffman were concerned at least, was forgotten at some point over the next year or so. Nat Taylor began casting about for what he hoped would be an even more commercial property than the killer beatnik story had been. After considering a number of ideas brought to him, he decided to look into a proposal put forth by a pair of New York advertising men named Frank Taubes and Sandy Haber.

The two men didn't have a script, exactly. It was more like an idea. One can imagine a classic Madison Avenue pitch session: Taylor sitting there as the two excited gray flannel suits spelled out their brilliant brainstorm. "What if, okay, okay, what if… we made a 3-D movie and a regular 2-D movie all at the very same time?"

"What?" Taylor likely would have answered. But Taubes and Haber were ad men after all, and persistent, and they explained that, in their view, making a regular movie with 3-D sequences would be a wonderfully exploitable gimmick, and cheap too! The switch from two to three dimensions could be made an integral part of the story, like dream or fantasy sequences around which the flat-screen drama would revolve. They had gone so far as to make a little 3-D film as a test, and this they screened for Taylor. He wasn't sure what to think, so he brought his partner Roffman in to have a look.

Roffman was profoundly unimpressed by the pair's test footage. Their 3-D effects were, he says, "crap," and he couldn't tell what was going on in the story, of if there even was a story. Besides which, to Roffman, 3-D was "just an exploitation feat that had had its run and nobody wanted to talk about it." The great initial boom of 3-D had peaked in 1953, and two years later was nearly forgotten. As a gimmick it was laughably out-of-date, and doing it badly and only half the time to boot wasn't about to bring it back. Roffman himself had sour memories of the 3-D craze, since the effect had done nothing but give him headaches.

But in the face of Roffman's reluctance, the ad men turned on the waterworks. They begged and pleaded with him to reconsider, saying that they had all sorts of money tied up in the idea already, and if nothing was done about it they'd lose their shirts. Roffman relented, not so much because of the Madison Avenue blubbering, but because he remembered a National Film Board friend of his, the theoretician and technical expert Raymond Spottiswoode, who had developed a three dimensional system some years earlier for Great Britain's National Research Council. In 1953, Spottiswoode had, in fact, literally written the book on 3-D. Roffman was quick to figure this had to be better than the 3-D he'd been shown by the ad men in New York.

Spottiswoode confirmed that indeed it would be, but achieving acceptable results in 3-D was at best difficult, and in his opinion better not tried at all. Still, he told Roffman, he would be able to arrange for the rental of the equipment—which had spent the last decade gathering dust in a warehouse—if indeed Roffman was still determined to go ahead with the project.

He was, so the NRC refurbished the cameras and later sent them over to Toronto, renting them to Taylor-Roffman for the very princely sum of 4,000 pounds a week. But before all this there was the matter of a story and script—just what was this movie going to be about? Taubes and Haber were no help; despite getting screenplay credit on the film, they weren't writers, just idea men, and aside from the 2-D/3-D brainstorm, even their ideas weren't that good. To write the script that became *The Mask,* Roffman hired some writers he knew from his television experience, a couple named Joe and Vicky Morhain. The Morhains turned the notion into a story with which Roffman was perfectly happy, but they proved unable to write the all-important hallucination sequences, which were, after all, the central attraction to the whole concept.

The Mask

The story went as follows: Michael Radin, a high-strung, sweaty archeologist, kills a woman while in the thrall of a possessed tribal mask he'd brought back from South America and subsequently stolen from the museum which had sponsored the dig. He tries to explain the power of the mask to his psychiatrist, Dr. Allan Barnes, but is met with typical headshrinker patronizing and thinly veiled skepticism. (Already we can see that the film contains more than one mask!) The highly excitable Radin storms out and returns to his cluttered garret, where he prepares a package for his landlady to pop in the post for him. After she's taken it away, he shoots himself in the head.

Cops, including the stalwart Lt. Walker, try to puzzle out the strange suicide. Naturally they have some questions for Barnes, but he's remarkably little help. As Walker leaves, Barnes receives the package which, to nobody's surprise, contains the hideous skull-like mask. The disembodied voice of Radin commands Barnes to "Put the mask on now!" Barnes does, and is drawn into the first of the movie's 3-D hallucination sequences.

Like Radin before him, the button-down analyst becomes a sweaty, murderous psychopath as the mask eclipses his far less interesting real personality. Law, personal boundaries, simple decency—all are as nothing compared to the lure of the grotesque visage and the smoky, surreal wonderworld to which it is the passport. Barnes, acting entirely out of character, tries first to have sex with and then to murder both his girlfriend Pamela and his sexy secretary Miss Goodrich. After a chase and a few scenes of jeopardy, Lt. Walker and his men are able to restrain the frenzied shrink, carting him off to the madhouse for the rest of his life. The mask is returned to the museum from which it was stolen, but in the movie's final moments is clearly working its diabolical sorcery on another hapless victim.

Few stories could be more appropriate for Canada's very first horror movie. What could be more terrifying to a Canadian in the fifties (or a Canadian now, for that matter) than an outside force which breaks down the barriers of social propriety, good manners and basic politeness, and brings forth all the repressed demons from within? The xenophobic angle of having the mask come from South America seems borrowed from the American films of the time, but then again, it probably didn't need to be. (Imagine if the mask had been of Native Canadian origin! How Canadian would that have been?) The ethnic background of the mask is in any case secondary to the actual source of the movie's horror—the repressed urges which, to polite society's shock and dismay, bubble and churn within each of us, needing only the turn of some as yet unidentified key to achieve release. The key itself is immaterial: even the science of David Cronenberg is just a vehicle for the director's true interests to make themselves manifest.

Of course, *The Mask* might be an appropriate title for almost any Canadian film. We're a nation of mask-wearers, after all: half British Bulldog, half Uncle Sam, and a thousand other guises besides. We'll wear whatever mask suits the occasion, pacifist, peacekeeper or patsy. Help invade Iraq? No, thanks. Can't see the point. Join a ludicrous, expensive and unworkable space-missile venture? Sure, why not. Sounds great!

But getting back to cases. *The Mask* needed dream sequences, and Roffman hit on the idea of hiring famed montage expert Slavko Vorkapich to write, design and create them. Born in Yugoslavia in 1892, Vorkapich had spent years in Hollywood as an art director and special effects artist, but was most famous for the montage sequences he devised for films such as *The Good Earth* (1937), *Broadway Melody of 1938* (1937), and *Mr. Smith Goes to Washington* (1939). He'd also produced short films, directed a feature called *Hanka* in 1955, and, most recently and relevantly, executed some design work for another atmospheric, low-budget horror picture: Albert Band's spooky *I Bury The Living* (1958).

Roffman's plan was to hire Vorkapich and let the testy Serbian take care of the hallucinations completely so that he, Roffman, like the Griersonite documentarian that he was, could concentrate on the more real world segments. (Though there's nothing all that real about the straight drama sequences in *The Mask,* which are graced with some of the most stilted acting outside of a high school health film.) Roffman was eager to "get the hell out of it and just do the story part, and then edit the whole film and finish it, and go home."

This idyll was not to be, however. As the weeks leading towards the shoot raced on, Roffman was concerned to observe Vorkapich do little besides "just sitting there." This was certainly not the dynamic orgy of cinematic creativity he had hoped for! Vorkapich had a few surprises in him, though: when his ideas for the nightmares did finally come they were extravagant beyond all reason, involving thousands of frogs, mice and iguanas, as well as gigantic and complicated sets decorated with such things as vast pools of black ink. Roffman was startled and dismayed, though he admits he had been warned that something like this might happen.

Vorkapich was fired with little delay. "I'm sorry," Roffman told the profligate Serbian. "If I indulge you we'll be out of business and we'll only have a few feet of film." Vorkapich accepted his dismissal with little more than a wave of the hand and a demand that his name be kept on the credits. Roffman couldn't imagine why—what if the film turned out terribly? (Though Vorkapich lived until the mid-seventies, *The Mask* would be his final screen credit, and as such, whether he knew it or not at the time, would be a lasting legacy.) The montage expert told Roffman simply "I trust you. You are a driven man."

That, then, was that for the great Vorkapich. Roffman found himself about to shoot dream sequences he'd never wanted to go near, and which he had absolutely no taste for or the slightest idea how to do. The solution was to tackle everything as a group effort. It was like the *Magnificent Seven* all of a sudden, with artisans of different but complementary talents all riding in for a common purpose. Roffman picked up a cameraman, Herb Alpert (not the leader of the Tijuana Brass, more's the pity, but he was the brother of Harry Alpert, who had shot several of Roffman's NFB documentaries), some special effects people, principally the Twentieth Century Fox optical effects expert James Gordon—whom Roffman termed "a genius!"— and floor effects people Herman Townsley, "Skin" Schwartz and Dick Williams, and a storyboard artist named Hugo Wuetrich. Everyone contributed ideas, and Wuetrich drew them up as fast as he could. Many of the concepts discussed and drawn were never actually shot: a sequence called "The Tarantula Tunnel" in which giant spiders would swarm the masked dream protagonist, was one such casualty. But in the end, three dream sequences were conceptualized and designed to Roffman's satisfaction. He passed them off to a Toronto psychiatrist and film buff with the idea of having them vetted for some semblance of psychological likelihood. Here again was the NFB professional cramming as much reality and social relevance into the film as he could.

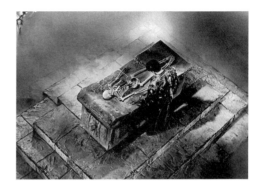

The Mask

In the meantime, Nat Taylor had been working on the picture's financing. This aspect too was to be revolutionary in Canadian film history: the first Canadian film to make money before it was even finished! Roffman had begun shooting the 3-D dream sequences, and as these were processed, Taylor invited executives from both Warner Brothers and Paramount to have a look at the rushes. Initially skeptical about the box-office appeal of 3-D, the studio suits became a good deal more interested upon learning of the audience interaction element, wherein a voice on the soundtrack would instruct the audience to don their tinted glasses at the crucial moments. Perhaps casting an eye over towards Columbia Pictures, which was at this point still making money off its William Castle gimmick pictures, the executives watched the footage and were excited enough to talk terms with Taylor and Roffman. Sweetening the deal from the studios' perspective was the fact that the particular 3-D process in which *The Mask* was being shot did not require all manner of expensive equipment for exhibition, as other systems did. The only extra cost would be the red-and-green glasses themselves. The Paramount executive offered $350,000 for the film, lock, stock and barrel, but Taylor decided to go with the lower Warner Brothers offer on the basis that the Warner people "were nicer guys."

Shooting on the dream sequences continued. Innovative special effects techniques (at least, innovative for Canada) were required at nearly every turn, from the flayed-skin makeup of the corpse-like demons who haunt the netherworld behind the mask, to a snake powered by magnets, to the flames and puffs of smoke that were to leap out into viewers' faces. "Skin" Schwartz was in charge of most of the physical effects, and, Roffman says, "he was just great. Anything I wanted, I'd say ' "Skin", can I do this?' He'd say 'Can do,' and he would do it." A mishap occurred at the end of the dream-sequence shoot, in which the camera, shooting in slow motion, inopportunely ran out of film in the middle of a complicated, one-take special effect involving a collapsing altar made of Fuller's earth. Roffman nearly strangled the camera assistant responsible for the mistake.

But then it was on to the regular drama scenes, and they went as smoothly as silk in comparison. These were done over sixteen days, and were shot in Toronto and at the Kleinburg studio. The museum interiors were done on location at the Royal Ontario Museum. The cast was made up almost completely of Canadians, with the exceptions being Paul Stevens, playing Dr. Barnes, and Claudette Nevins as his girlfriend, Pamela. The mask itself had been commissioned from a Toronto artist by Roffman, who had given her photographs of genuine native facewear upon which to base her work.

When the shooting was completed, Roffman went down to Hollywood with James Gordon to do the optical work on the film. Twentieth Century Fox, it turned out, was looking for some income to balance out their huge expenditures on *Cleopatra*, and was happy to rent the entire optical department out to Roffman. With Gordon at the helm, all manner of flames, spirals, smoke effects and other hypnotic trappings were laid over the hallucination scenes. The opticals took longer than they otherwise would because of the extra dimension involved.

After two months of work, by the end of August, 1961, the optical effects were complete. Louis Applebaum, a Toronto composer who had scored many NFB documentaries in the early years, was writing music. The next thing to worry about was a prologue, since—Roffman's hunger for reality showing itself yet again—it had been decided to tie the movie's mask to real masks which existed in cultures around the world. A promotional trailer would be shot at the same time, and both it and the prologue would feature a real-life mask collector named Jim Moran, who would appear on screen talking about his collection and about how the story told in *The Mask* could easily happen to anyone. Moran, an American, had packed his mask collection in his car in order to drive them up to Toronto for the prologue and trailer shoots, but was stopped at the border by baffled Canadian customs officials, who, after inspecting his cargo, demanded an arbitrary $175.00 in duty. When Moran explained that the masks were going to be used to promote a Canadian film, the guards, their minds broken by the very idea, relented and let him pass through without paying a penny.

Moran's preludial spiel, which emphasized the otherness of the film's central prop and was accompanied by simple shots of him talking along with a few insert shots of his masks, went as follows:

The Mask

> My name is Jim Moran. I've just returned from a trip around the world, collecting strange and unusual masks. I think it's safe to say I'm something of an authority on rare masks—festival masks, drama and religious masks, dance masks and death masks from ancient tombs. Man's desire to change his face—to assume a strange or frightening disguise—to impersonate his gods or to frighten devils—is a desire older than the history of language. I've seen masks unearthed from the ruins of crumbling tombs and masks hanging in exotic temples to ward off evil spirits. But nowhere… in my travels… have I seen anything to compare with the power of this mask and the horrible curse it bears. This is the mask around which the story you're about to see revolves. And I can tell you that even though I am not superstitious, I would not put it on for all the wealth of the Indies. This mask was part of an ancient ritual so unearthly… so terrifying… it has been wiped out of the memory of man. Still it is a thing of evil. Still the dreadful power clings to this mask.
>
> You in this theatre are especially privileged to join in seeing the terrifying sights that can only be seen through the mask. Each of you has been given a mask. When you see the mask put on the picture, you put yours on too. Then, you will share an adventure into the darkest hidden recesses of the human mind. You will see things never before seen on any screen. Soon you will meet Dr. Alan Barnes, who meets his other self when he puts on the mask. Then you will begin to follow the threads that weave themselves into this gripping story. Soon you will see him put on the mask. Remember, when he puts on his mask, you put on yours. It is the beginning of the ancient and forbidden ritual of the mask.

There was thus little chance that audiences would fail to properly react to the movie's interactive element. To promote the film in advance, Warner Brothers put together a trailer also featuring Moran and his masks. From the script, the trailer sounds like something Ed Wood might have used to promote one of his own films, though likely with Criswell performing the monologue instead of Moran.

It began with Moran sitting in a throne, wearing an elaborate mask and saying nothing as the camera dollied in towards him and the lights slowly came up. A narrator intoned:

> Here to tell you more is the supreme authority on all things weird… initiate of the strange and mysterious… the world's greatest connoisseur and collector of masks… Mr. Jim Moran.

During this voice-over, Moran removes his mask, revealing not his face but another mask. By the end of the little introduction he's taken off the second mask as well, and begins to speak a monologue that is, if possible, more purple and hyperbolic than his speech in the prologue:

> I have seen wonders. I have traveled to the remotest corners of the globe… to dead cities… through savage jungles to the inner sanctums of esoteric cults… the temples of exotic rituals… to tombs and caverns and palaces. The result: the most comprehensive collection of masks in the world. Some are works of art; some are astounding and horrifying; some reveal man's highest aspiration; others his unspeakable sins. But nowhere in my travels have I found a mask so absolutely remarkable as this mask… The Miracle Movie Fright Mask… the mask that you will be invited to put on when you see the motion picture called *The Mask!*
>
> This is the mask that will open your eyes to such things as man has never dared to imagine… the mask that will make you part of the sensations of the most staggering experience of your life. But, be warned, the things that you will see when you put on this mask will surely take you to the very limit of your nerves… and to the very boundary line of sanity! Speaking as one who has seen things not granted to most men, I guarantee you that *The Mask* is incredible!

With a come-on like that, how could *The Mask* not be a success? That was the hope, anyway. The film was edited through September and set for release on Halloween, 1961. In its November 1st issue (Vol. 26, No. 42), *Canadian Film Weekly*, the magazine run by Nat Taylor, reported with great excitement and pride that "*The Mask* is the first Canadian feature to get international distribution by a major company."

A premiere of the picture was held in New York City on a morning just a few days before Halloween, and was attended by Roffman, music composer Louis Applebaum, cameraman Herb Alpert, and the two American stars of the picture, Paul Stevens and Claudette Nevins. The film critic for the *Toronto Telegram*, Clyde Gilmour (later a beloved classical music radio host, known for his hearty intonation of the word "Hello!" each week), was also present, reporting afterward that "my initial reaction is that it's a competent, fully professional hunk of horror-movie fiction." Gilmour's review may not quite have been a rave, but that didn't stop him from joining Roffman and the rest for a celebratory luncheon at the Forum Restaurant afterwards. Gilmour later went back to the theatre (the Warner on Broadway) and counted 165 people in line at the box office, presumably having been drawn by the Moran preview or the advertising signs boasting of a new cinematographic process: "Depth Dimension."

With the *Canadian Film Weekly* watching very closely, the American reviews began pouring in. How exciting it must have been for Canadians to see the first American reviews of their film product, and how galling that they were for a cheap horror film! But the reviews were generally positive: "Sharply photographed, and moves rather quickly within a highly melodramatic plot," (Howard Thompson, *New York Times*); "Roffman's direction gives *The Mask* a kind of Ingmar Bergman sort of light-and-shadows effect. The dialogue is good and the players competent." (James Powers, *The Hollywood Reporter*); "If this kind of hair-raising entertainment is your poison I think you'll have fun at it… In the gruesome division, this is really very good." (Ruth Waterbury, *Los Angeles Times*). *The Motion Picture Herald* notice from November 8, 1961, must have been particularly gratifying to Roffman, and indeed to all of Canada: "Producer-director Julian Roffman, former *March of Time* director, gets the maximum effect out of the script by Frank Taubes and Sandy Haber, using a documentary approach which is heightened by a prologue featuring Jim Moran giving a brief history of a number of unusual masks."

John Dunning

On the other side of the coin came comments like this: "Welcome to low-brow Surrealism… *The Mask* has failed in its attempt to imitate what Cocteau did in his Surrealist films like *Blood of a Poet* and *Beauty and the Beast*." (Charles Stinson, also of the *Los Angeles Times*); and Hazel Flynn of the *Beverly Hills Citizen* suggested merely that Canadians "are not quite as hep on special effects as Hollywood."

The *Canadian Film Weekly* review was, of course, a rave, and in their November 22 issue they asserted that "Awareness of Canada as the source of feature films is growing thanks to *The Mask* and Arch Oboler's *One Plus One*."[9] But all was not roses for Taylor-Roffman. According to Roffman's son Peter, some "creative bookkeeping" at Warner Bros. resulted in the Canadian company losing out on profits they should have reaped from the film's million-dollar-plus box-office take in the United States. As if that wasn't enough, almost a decade later the film was apparently picked up for college distribution by Robert Shaye and his newly-formed company, New Line Cinema, who showed it on campuses across America. It proved extremely popular, setting Shaye's company on the road to (eventual) huge success. (New Line stayed in the distribution business for many years, then turned to production and produced hits such as the *Nightmare on Elm Street* and *Lord of the Rings* series.) Warner Brothers re-released it more than once, though under a new title, *Eyes of Hell.* This re-release earned it further critical denigration from the likes of the *Monthly Film Bulletin's* John Gillett, who called it "a thoroughly disagreeable exploitation picture, appallingly acted and haltingly scripted." Gillett was closer to the truth than he knew in adding "Worst of all, one is never convinced that the makers believed a word of it." The film showed up on television ten years after that with the title *The Spooky Movie Show* (during the same early-eighties 3-D boom that saw broadcasts of such lovely dreck as *Gorilla At Large,* and sales of 3-D glasses at the local 7-11), and on video under its original title as part of the Rhino Video series hosted by busty Yvonne DeCarlo wannabe Elvira.

Roffman would never direct another feature film after *The Mask,* though he tried. The experience had certainly soured him on the whole notion of making what he saw as purely commercial products. Some may disagree, but I don't think it's stretching a point to see in Roffman a microcosm of the entire Canadian film industry through the twentieth century. Is that too heavy a metaphoric load to place across the shoulders of one "small young man" (as John Grierson had called him)? Roffman was blessed with a deeply felt social conscience, and it often pained him to work in the beloved, though frequently superficial, medium of film in a corner from which he could discern no social value or help to the needy emanating. He was a practical man and knew the value of a buck, but commercial concerns were in the end secondary. He could have gone on making horror movies, and made a very comfortable living at it—Paramount had apparently offered him a two-picture contract on the strength of *The Mask's* rushes—but he declined. And yet he was not done with the world of horror films. Back and forth it went, this lifelong search for compromise. Clearly, Julian Roffman was a conflicted man, and he very often took a middle ground (as when he tried to plant the fanciful events of *The Mask* into some realistic context) which ultimately satisfied few, least of all himself. Really, how much more Canadian can you get?

❦

As successful as *The Mask* seemed to be from all the coverage in the *CFW,* it would be a full five years before Canadian horror activity would, at least comparatively, heat up once again. In the meantime, the global horror renaissance continued, with great leaps taken in matters of permissiveness and taste over the first half of the 1960s. Roger Corman's celebrated Poe series continued on; financially successful horror films with fairly big budgets, like *The Haunting* (1963), made by Mark Robson's old RKO colleague, Robert Wise, and the influential *Whatever Happened to Baby Jane?*

(1962), directed by Robert Aldrich, which spawned a long and profitable series of batty-old-dame pictures. More important, as far as Canada was concerned, was the emergence of the regional horror film. *Carnival of Souls* (1962), made in Lawrence, Kansas by a company whose regular stock in trade was the production of industrial and classroom pictures, was one of these: a mini-budget film made far outside the Hollywood system in every conceivable way, which relied on elements money couldn't buy, like atmosphere and imagination, for its success. And in Florida, director Herschell Gordon Lewis was pushing boundaries with his gore films. *Blood Feast* (1963), a little splatter classic about a demented Egyptian caterer, made for about $60,000 US, was the first of them. It packed drive-ins across the South, and Lewis, whose previous work had been in charmingly innocuous nudie films like *Lucky Pierre* (1961), knew he was on to a good thing. Bare breasts as marketable selling points were on the verge of being co-opted by Hollywood anyway, and Lewis, a filmmaker with the entrepreneurial spirit of a P.T. Barnum, figured that extreme, if mani-festly fake, violence would be a lucrative back alley down which to wander. He was right. And there was a won-derful little movie made in Long Island, New York, called *The Flesh Eaters* (shot in 1961, released in 1964), which swirled together gore, beatniks, mad Nazi doctors and giant monsters into a bizarre concoction with a regional atmosphere of its very own.

André Link (centre) and friends

European horror cinema was still going strong through the Sixties, with companies like Hammer, Amicus and Tigon prodigiously turning out product in Britain, Antonio Margheriti and the brilliant Mario Bava working out of Italy, and the less obviously brilliant but still intriguing and prolific Jesus Franco making films in Spain, Germany and France. At the same time, wonderfully weird horror cinema was emerging from Mexico (*The Brainiac,* for example, or the loopy Santo films), Brazil (the insanity of José Mojica Marins), Japan (the marvelous *Kwaidan* and *Onibaba,* both from 1964, or the Majin series of 1966[10]) and Argentina.

All this might have given aspiring Canadian film impressarios a hint that it was possible to cobble together a self-sustaining industry out of cheap B pictures, even given the limited resources and infrastructure available to them. But there wasn't a prodigious network of drive-in theatres (the chilly Canadian climate at any rate ensured an abbrevi-ated drive-in season) or skid-row grindhouse cinemas (or the population to support them) to be found in Canada, as there was in the States; nor an endless supply of easily accessible neighboring countries as in Europe or Asia. For several years in the early sixties, Canada would remain a country with the distinction of having turned out exactly one horror film in its entire cinematic history.

Nevertheless, events that would ultimately lead to a later starburst of Canadian horror were taking place, and the 1962 launch of John Dunning and André Link's

Cinépix film distribution company into this nearly barren landscape was chief among them. This company would later be responsible for helping David Cronenberg out of the gate with his first few features, as well as backing early work by William Fruet (*Death Weekend*) and George Mihalka (*My Bloody Valentine*). Other Cinépix productions over the years would include Jean Beaudin's 1972 devil-worship picture *Le Diable est parmi nous* (which Dunning and Link also wrote, though under a pseudonym), Jean Lafleur's *Ilsa, Tigress of Siberia* (1977), the big-budget slasher film *Happy Birthday to Me* (1981), Jean-Claude Lord's robot-Frankenstein picture *The Vindicator* (1986) and the Dean R. Koontz adaptation *Whispers* (1989). In short, their imprint upon the Canadian horror film scene is as vast as a Yeti's.

Dunning, a part-time screenwriter and relatively speaking the more creative-minded of the two, was born into a family of cinema-owners in Montreal in 1927; while Link, the businessman, was born in Budapest, Hungary, five years later. One of Link's early jobs was in the service of a distributor, transporting film cans around his hometown. In his early twenties he moved to Montreal and became a film booker, a profession which led him inevitably to Dunning. Cinépix was strictly a distribution company in its first seven years, only turning to production in 1969, perhaps not coincidentally just around the time of the creation of the federal film production funding body known first as the Canadian Film Development Corporation and later as Telefilm Canada. Cinépix merged with Famous Players in 1989, and the resulting company was named C/FP, and then, in 1994, Cinépix bought back the Famous Players interest and, so as to retain the brand value of their acronym, though minus the slash, renamed the company Cinépix Film Properties. CFP, in turn, was swallowed up in a $36 million sale to a Vancouver investment group in 1997. The company was ultimately appended to the Los Angeles-based Lion's Gate Films.

"They were among the first to prove that it is possible to make movies for international markets and be Canadian," says Serendipity Point Films president (and co-founder of Alliance Entertainment) Robert Lantos, and that is of course true, providing that your definition of "being Canadian" recognizes (as mine emphatically does) such endeavors as kicking off the maple-syrup porn era of the early Seventies with such lyrical T&A pictures as *Valérie*, *L'Initiation* and *Viens, Mon Amour*. In addition, Dunning and Link can claim to have brought over $40 million in production money into their home province of Quebec. In the beginning, though, they stuck with distribution, and the Canadian horror film remained embryonic.

Another critical event not to bear immediate fruit was the signing of Canada's first co-production treaty, with France in October of 1963. This particular partnership—the first such treaty of many with countries all around the world—would later produce Canadian horror pictures like *Cathy's Curse* (1975) and *The Little Girl Who Lived Down the Lane* (1976). For the time being, though nothing much came of either the deal with France or of anything else, Canadian influence on the horror world at large continued.

Horrific Canucks—Part II

LIKE RAYMOND MASSEY, though more than thirty years on, Donald Sutherland began his film career in a horror film or two. *Castle of the Living Dead* (1964), a weird Italian/French co-production reportedly directed to some degree by the prematurely deceased British cult director Michael Reeves, featured Sutherland in a dual role as a haggy old sorceress and an army sergeant; *Dr. Terror's House of Horrors* (1964), the first of the Amicus anthology horror films, in which the Canadian plays a small-town doctor who unwittingly marries a vampire, and *Die! Die! My Darling* (1965), a Hammer whodunit which gave him the role of a retarded gardener.[11] (The film was directed by fellow Canadian Silvio Narizzano, an expatriate like Sidney Furie, who would later return to his home and native land to make *Why Shoot the Teacher?*) Here then, with his hollow eyes and drawn, character-handsome face, was another Canuck horror star in the making: a career direction which was, sadly, cut short by the spectacular success of *M*A*S*H* in 1970. Sutherland would, over the course of

Playgirl Killer

his career, appear in a number of films that rather coyly flirted with the horror genre, including Nicolas Roeg's *Don't Look Now* (1973), Claude Chabrol's Montreal-set mystery *Blood Relatives* (1978), Phillip Kaufman's wonderful 1978 remake of *Invasion of the Body Snatchers,* Bob Clark's Sherlock Holmes-versus-Jack the Ripper thriller *Murder By Decree* (1979), and once more fighting body snatchers in Stuart Orme's *The Puppet Masters* (a passable adaptation of the Robert A. Heinlein alien invasion story, filmed in Canada in 1994); and a crapshow called *Virus* (not the same one that Glenn Ford was in, but rather a useless bit of electro-tripe made in 1998, all too obviously directed by a special effects man out of his depth). But Sutherland never developed into the modern-day John Carradine he might have been; though to be fair neither did Carradine until very late in his career. So for optimists like myself there's still time.

William Shatner, in his final feature before taking off on his three-year mission aboard the starship Enterprise (and years before appearing in the Canuck slasher spectacular *Visiting Hours*), found time to make his own obscure mark on horror cinema history. In 1966 he starred in the world's first and only all-Esperanto horror feature, *Incubus.* Hearing Shatner's familiar cadence intoning reams of synthetic dialogue makes for a curious viewing experience to say the least. Before that, in 1963, he'd played the role of the terrified airplane passenger battling a wing-walking goblin in the *Twilight Zone* episode "Nightmare at 20,000 Feet;" and later in his career he essayed lead roles in *The Devil's Rain* (1976) (which was originally to have been filmed in Canada, but wasn't), *Kingdom of the Spiders* (1977), and the Canadian-shot *American Psycho 2* (2002).

Vancouver-born John Ireland, the star of many Westerns and action pictures throughout the 1950s, and an Oscar nominee for *All the King's Men* (1949), jumped into horror with both feet in the latter third of his career, though strictly speaking it was unlikely a matter of choice. Still, he did so many of them that one might be forgiven for assuming he developed an appreciation, or at least some sympathy, for the genre.

Beginning slowly, with a performance as a murderous psychopath in a William Castle production called *I Saw What You Did* (1965), and playing the first of many horror-movie cops the same year in a strange psychodrama called *Day of the Nightmare,* Ireland went full-out horror-crazy in the Seventies. From an Italian cannibal-comedy set in Vienna called *The Mad Butcher* in 1972, a performance as a horror movie director in the Salt Lake City-shot *House of the Seven Corpses* (1973), and another cop role in Laurence Harvey's directorial effort *Welcome to Arrow Beach* (1974), he descended into ever-cheesier territory in films like *Satan's Cheerleaders* (1977, also starring Canadians Yvonne de Carlo and Jack Kruschen), the Italian curiosity *Miami Golem* (1985), and an American cheapie called *Terror Night* (1987). Ireland's last few roles before his death in 1992 were in Anthony Hickox's zombie-western *Sundown* (1990) and the same director's horror sequel *Waxwork II: Lost in Time* (1992). Along with Glenn Ford he was one of the "secret Canadians" (to use David Cronenberg's phrase) ferreted out by producers looking for a big-ticket star (or at least a once-upon-a-time big-ticket star) to headline their tax-shelter productions; one of the results was the lowbrow demon-rapist film *Incubus* (made in 1981, and not the same *Incubus* as Shatner's gobbledygook Sixties picture).

Yvonne De Carlo, born in Vancouver, played Salomé in the 1945 superproduction *Salomé—Where She Danced,* and so was the poster girl for exotica in Hollywood for many years before taking on the role of the matriarch, Lily, in *The Munsters.* She played the kooky-spooky role from 1964 to 1966. A number of horror roles came her way after that, including *The Power* (1968) and *La Casa de los Sombras* (1977). She appeared with John Ireland in *Satan's Cheerleaders,* in the goofy disco-vampire flick *Nocturna* (1978), the slasher picture *Silent Scream* (1980), a killer-pooch picture called *Play Dead* (1981), the fun monster goof-off *Cellar Dweller* (1988), and was the den-mother to a clan of maniacs in John Hough's British Columbia-shot backwoods-slasher-family picture *American Gothic* (1989).

And then there's Gordon Pinsent, the beloved Newfie thespian who at times seems to define the Canadian film industry all by himself. He was never a horror star (though like Sutherland, there's still time), but he did play the honky cop on the trail of *Blacula* back in 1972—at just about the same time he was acting in the most Pinsentian role of his career: *The Rowdyman.*

Perhaps the most readily identifiable horror personality ever to come out of Canada is Jonathan Frid, the vampire patriarch of the unaccountably popular soap-horror series *Dark Shadows.* Frid joined the series in 1967, expecting to play the role of the urbane hemogobbler Barnabas Collins for only a few weeks. The show became a hit almost instantly, however, and the Hamilton, Ontario-born stage actor was launched into a sudsy superstardom few could have predicted. He spent the next four seasons playing the 175 year-old undead master of Collinwood, wading knee-deep in fog, pushing his way through cobwebs and baring his pearly fangs in greeting. "It had this peculiar never-never land charm to it," Frid recalls of the show that made him famous. "I called it the gothic *Brigadoon.*"

Frid's horror career did not end after his *Dark Shadows* run. He appeared, quite naturally, in the feature-film spin-off *House of Dark Shadows* (though not its sequel), and later in the fairly small role of a butler in a 1972 *Rosemary's Baby* rip-off TV movie called *The Devil's Daughter.* Still later, he played the lead in Oliver Stone's inaugural feature, the Quebec-shot horror film *Seizure,* which will be discussed in the next chapter. Frid, now retired from acting, has kept busy over the last few years maintaining his own web site ("Jonathan Frid: Ongoing Septuagenarian") and, to the delight of thousands of *Dark Shadows* fans, making erudite, befanged appearances at conventions.

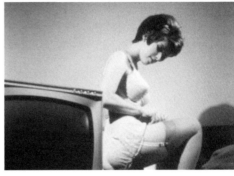

Playgirl Killer

Behind the camera there was director George McCowan, whose experience had come from such work as directing episodes of the big-budget CBC drama *Seaway.* One of McCowan's episodes was the spooky, though ultimately non-horrific "Ghost Ship;" and a multi-part episode called "Don't Forget to Wipe the Blood Off" was repackaged into a feature and released to theatres. His real contribution to the world of horror was a 1972 eco-terror feature called *Frogs,* made in Florida for American-International. Ray Milland, later to travel to Montreal to take part in a killer-kitty thriller called *The Uncanny,* was the star. The movie itself, while not in the least Canadian outside of its director's birthplace, is nevertheless pretty darn special in its own amphibious way.

John Coquillion was an unsung horror star behind the camera. He was a cinematographer, born in Montreal, who lent his considerable talents to British horror pictures like *The Witchfinder General, Curse of the Crimson Altar, The Oblong Box, Scream and Scream Again* and *Cry of the Banshee* before moving up the budgetary ladder to work with Sam Peckinpah on *Straw Dogs, Pat Garrett and Billy the Kid,* and several others. He later returned to both the horror genre and his native land with the spooky haunted-house picture *The Changeling.*

The Vulture

IN 1966 THERE WAS A SORT OF NEAR-MISS: a horror film that was in many ways Canadian, but perhaps not in so many ways as it might have been. *The Vulture* was written and directed by Lawrence Huntington, a Briton who had been making movies since approximately the Iron Age. Huntington's script, then called *Minotaur,* made its way across the Atlantic to a small-time American producer named Jack Lamont, who in turn approached a Toronto outfit called Robert Lawrence Productions. RLP made television commercials, and John Ross, a producer there, and today the chairman of a completion bond company, was intrigued enough with the story to take it on. Ross hooked up with one of his competitors, Dean Peterson, and another friend and investor, Ben Webster, to form Iliad Productions in order to make the film.

The production, which Ross and Peterson originally intended to film in the Kleinburg studios just north of Toronto, was forced, for "financial reasons," to relocate to Pinewood Studios near London, England. Iliad Production was reformed as "Homeric Productions" at some point during the move, and location work was set to take place on the Cornish coastline. Lamont had some kind of deal with Pinewood; the move to England was encouraged partially by this, and also by the limited equipment and personnel then procurable in Canada. Akim Tamiroff, a veteran actor who was to play the movie's mad scientist, had but a small window available for the movie, and this too was a factor in the shift across the pond.

Shooting began in the fall of 1965, with a final budget of US$180,000, or about $200,000 Canadian. Thirty-five thousand of this came from Paramount Pictures in return for the US distribution rights. The cast was a strong one: Robert Hutton (the star and director of *The Slime People,* and a lead in many other genre efforts, from *Invisible Invaders* to *Torture Garden* to *Trog*), Broderick Crawford (an Oscar winner for *All the King's Men* and, prophetically, a co-star to Bela Lugosi in a 1941 comedy version of *The Black Cat*), Tamiroff (who was a Russian, but effective as a Mexican crime boss in Orson Welles' *Touch of Evil,* and at one time or another in the course of his career, every nationality in between), and Diane Clare, who had appeared in Hammer films like *Plague of the Zombies* as well as chillers like *The Haunting, Witchcraft* and *The Hand of Night.* The bright, high-key and generally un-atmospheric cinematography is by Stephen Dade, who had shot Sidney J. Furie's two Anglo shockers in 1960, *Doctor Blood's Coffin* and *The Snake Woman.*

An absolute mind-breaker is *The Vulture,* in its own modest way. Crawford plays a "millionaire newspaperman from Canada" who has set up house in the Cornish countryside. His brother lives nearby and his niece, Trudy, has come for a visit with her nuclear scientist husband (Hutton). Meanwhile a local schoolteacher has been frightened so badly by an encounter with a birdlike apparition bearing a horrible human face that her hair has turned chalk white. As any good nuclear scientist might do when faced with an absolute lack of facts or evidence, Hutton comes up with a hair-brained theory involving "nuclear transmutation" and mounts an immediate investigation, uncovering a local legend involving a Spanish pirate buried alive with his pet vulture and eventually meeting up with a black-cloaked Tamiroff in the Bela Lugosi role of the outwardly affable and grandfatherly, but inwardly vengeful scientist.

Several dizzying and unscientific leaps of logic later, Hutton deduces that a homicidal Iberian man-bird reanimate is targeting members of Crawford's family, whose ancestors had evidently masterminded the premature interment of the pirate many years before. Crawford spends the entire movie grumping and harrumphing in his drawing room; with good reason as it turns out, for the moment he steps outside it he is carried off by a monstrous pair of rubber talons. Eventually Tamiroff flings back his cloak and tosses away his walking stick to reveal that indeed it is he who has been flying around the countryside snatching sheep, rabbits and burly, Academy Award winning actors. Hutton shoots the poor ragged creature, and with a final cry of "Screee!" it tumbles off a cliff and kites down to smash on the rocks below.

Tamiroff appears to be doing the best late-career Lugosi impersonation he can muster up—entirely appropriate to what might, but for colour and locale, be a lost entry in the penurious PRC[12] catalogue. (It must have seemed even more like an old Lugosi vehicle that got re-released by mistake in the U.S., where for some reason it was shown in black and white.) Every scene seems to take place three times, but in spite of this, and such diversions as a creepy verger, an intriguing backstory on the man-bird involving Easter Island, and Hutton's constant, loopy theorizing, nothing at all seems to happen for a great majority of the movie. It's too bad we don't get to see more of the vulture: flapping sounds and loose feathers are about it until the

Playgirl Killer

(anti-) climactic "twist" at the end. At that point all we get is a very funny shot of Tamiroff in bird-boots and cumbersome fake wings. Still, it's just crazy enough and Canadian enough to warrant a look for those who can take it.

Ross and Peterson followed their investment over to Pinewood and Cornwall, where they observed Huntington at work for a few days. Peterson was a cinematographer and had a good deal of production experience, and so, after many frustrating hours of watching Huntington and the crew struggle with the logistics behind a shot of a mechanical vulture flying from a cave, he stepped in (with Huntington's permission) and reconfigured the bit as a hand-held shot from the bird's point of view. "Everybody clapped and cheered," remembers Ross. "Good old Canada taught the Brits a thing or two, even in those early days!"

The Vulture was to be Huntington's final curtain; though his work would live on in the form of the script for the John Coquillion-shot film *The Oblong Box*. But critics were generally unkind to Huntington's directorial swan song: a review in the *Monthly Film Bulletin* describes *The Vulture* as "a pitifully stilted horror film in which the characters stand around either speculating, scoffing or helpfully disbursing yards of background information." Most other critics took the same tack, but a reviewer identified only as "Whit." in the January 25, 1967 issue of *Variety*, gave *The Vulture* a generally positive review, calling it "a well-developed chiller" and asserting that the "technical credits generally are first-rate." None of this is remotely true, and I find myself wondering what film "Whit." actually saw that day, or, if he indeed saw *The Vulture*, just what he was smoking and where I can get me some of that.

Murder on the 'mount: Playgirl Killer

Playgirl Killer, SHOT AROUND THE SAME TIME as *The Vulture,* was in contrast a genuinely Canadian horror movie. Set in an undisguised Montreal (French graffiti and other telltale signs are exotically rampant), the film tells of Bill, a mad artist—few sixties movie artists were not mad—with a thing about twitchy models. Should they so much as wiggle while he's trying to paint them (and they always do), he whines "Don't move! Please don't move," then shows them the business end of a spear gun, or just closes his sweaty palms around their antsy, restless necks. Hitchhiking through the rich Anglo district of Montreal, he hooks up with a spoiled-rotten Westmount debutante, taking a job as her handyman after the deb's sister, the sister's boyfriend (played by none other than Neil Sedaka!) and their father go off to, respectively, college, college, and big-game hunting in Africa.

It's when Bill takes out his sketchpad that all the trouble begins, as it seems he has some issues from a traumatic shipwreck incident to work through. The horrible event is dramatized by Bill's voice speaking over a dreamy, extravagantly fake shot of women cavorting in the sea and a beautiful archer on the rocks above: an image Bill is obsessively dedicated to recreating in his art. The horny deb goes for a nighttime walk in a sheer nightgown and is soon dead, and the demented dabbler with his Green Arrow beard sets up shop in the girl's Westmount mansion (whose interiors are suspiciously downmarket, as though the homeowners who let the film crew on their land were unwilling to extend their hospitality to the interior).

Other victims follow: a francophone chanteuse played by singer and sometime actress Andrée Champagne, a would-be nurse applying for a nonexistent job the artist has planted in the classifieds as bait, and another woman who just happens by on a visit. This last woman is saved by a helpful meter man, who has come to inform Bill that his power has been temporarily shut down for maintenance. This comes as bad news to a man who has carefully arranged a tableau of frozen corpses in the freezer room downstairs as a way to exorcise his maddening shipwreck-inspired visions. Naturally a drawn bow-and-arrow is part of the display, and the poor gibbering madman is shot by his own victim as she thaws and relaxes her grip on the bow. His last words, gasped out through a bright crimson smear, are, of course, 'Don't move! Please don't move!" The horrified, uncomprehending meter man can only gape, stolidly unaware that he's the de facto hero of the piece.

The artist was played by Bill Kerwin, well known for his appearances in the Herschell Gordon Lewis films *Blood Feast, 2000 Maniacs* and *A Taste of Blood* under the moniker "Thomas Wood". Kerwin and his brother Harry wrote the original story, which is hard to imagine being inspired by anything other than H.G. Lewis' own mad-artist picture, *Color Me Blood Red.* Rumour has it that the movie was originally to have been directed by Lewis himself, probably in Florida like any other H.G. Lewis film; but if this ever really was to happen, it did not, and, in the summer of 1965 the production moved north under the direction of Martin Green.

For some reason—rotten dailies, perhaps, or some other sort of "creative differences"—Green was fired after the first few days of shooting. He would go on to make the penultimate Veronica Lake vehicle, *Footsteps in the Snow,* in Montreal the following spring.[13] In the meantime, direction of *Playgirl Killer* fell to the hand of its screenwriter, Erick Santamaria.

Santamaria is truly an international man of mystery. Very little is known about him (by me, anyway), but it's quite possible that he spent the decade after *Playgirl Killer* directing minority-oriented stage plays at New York's New Federal Theatre, and furthermore within the realm of possibility that he's since become a record producer in Panama. Whatever the case, he does a reasonable job of handling the mad-artist action, at the very least accurately emulating the wooden, sun-bleached style of the Lewis pictures, though without the extreme gore. The film opens with a lazily post-dubbed sequence in which Bill, irritated by a model's poorly synched laughter, grabs a spear gun (where did that come from?) and impales her: this is as bloody as the film ever gets. It's violent, yes, but kids' stuff compared to the Lewis norm. If it is indeed true that H.G. Lewis was to have directed *Playgirl Killer,* Bill would likely have followed

Playgirl Killer

up his spear gun volley by smacking his lips and pulling out the girl's innards to fondle in a disgusting close-up. Canadian society in the 60s would have been unlikely to tolerate scenes like this; or perhaps Santamaria was just by nature a more restrained fellow. Maybe he was simply less inventive than Lewis at coming up with creative methods of murder: Santamaria is after all credited with writing the screenplay as well (though it was based on a purportedly original story by the producer, Maxwell A. Sendel).

The appearance of Sedaka ties the film in with the Florida-based Lewis even more, though elliptically. A few years earlier, the doughy singer had made a similar, though strictly off-screen, musical contribution to William Grefé's Florida-lensed jelly-man picture *Sting of Death.* A group of pool-partying youths presciently choose a Sedaka tune called "Do The Jellyfish" to accompany their frenzied boogying, while in the background a big jelly sneaks unseen into the pool. The Sedaka song ends only after the nefarious jelly has stung one young party-nymph nearly to death with its hideous tentacles.

If you've seen *Sting of Death,* the pool party scene in *Playgirl Killer* will come as a rush of pleasurable déja vu, except that this time Sedaka is physically present to sing his song (backed by a band called J.B. and the Playboys, who should have become big stars but didn't), and there's no jellyfish in sight other than Sedaka himself. But Neil is no mere crooner in this one: he plays a dramatic role as the older sister's (somewhat unlikely) object of lust. After flirting with him in the broadest possible way by the pool, she sneaks into his room at night and drops her nightie, which is sheer enough to make the gesture more or less symbolic. Thusly seduced, Neil packs his bags and takes off with the ever-unsuspecting younger sister and the calcified father, none of whom will ever be seen again. (Not through the depredations of the mad artist, but simply because the script is done with them.)

Playgirl Killer is oddly structured and a little slow in places, but it exudes a wonderful lowbrow cocktail vibe, particularly during the scene in which Bill, prowling the lounges of St. Catherine's street in search of victims, comes across Champagne and is immediately beguiled by her beauty and crooning talent. (The singer is bathed by cinematographer Roger Moride in a loving, fuzzy, faux-Technicolor glow, and it's easy to share Bill's attraction to her.) The pool-party sequence near the beginning makes you want to rush off and have a pool party of your own, ideally with JB and the Playboys providing the entertainment. It's a great scene, and might be as close as Canadian cinema ever got to recreating the frothy fun of a Frankie and Annette beach party movie.

Secular, untraditional, populist entertainment that it is, the picture serves very well as the perfect cinematic expression of Quebec's Quiet Revolution, then at its climax. Quebec had thrown off the shackles of the socially conservative, fifteen year-long Duplessis era, and, under Jean Lesage, busied itself through the first half of the Sixties setting up such progressive organizations as the country's first Department of Cultural Affairs. The emergence of the politician/boulevardier Pierre Trudeau onto the provincial scene accelerated the transformation. It may seem strange to link a tawdry, if entertaining, proto-slasher picture to a profound socio-political evolution, but the connection is unmistakable. Films, however fictional, are social documents, and this is perhaps particularly true in Canada.

⁕⁕⁕

THROUGH THE MID SIXTIES, Parliament Hill in Ottawa was the scene of impassioned debates and speeches belatedly declaring the necessity of a feature film industry in Canada. The potential economic value was only partially driving the discussion (the Canadian dollar was strong at the time and there was little reason to believe that Americans would be flooding across the border with hastily-written scripts and suitcases full of Yankee greenbacks), and it was the cultural value of telling Canadian stories which was held up as the primary justification for supporting such an industry with public monies. "It is in cinema today," effused Secretary of State Maurice Lamontagne in one of his speeches on the subject, "that… we find the great questions, the anguish, the problems, as well as the successes of man." Clearly this was an important business to get into if Canada was to express itself on the world stage.

The story has been told elsewhere in plenty, so I'll stick to the main points: in 1967 the Government of Canada, after considerable argument back and forth, formed the Canadian Film Development Corporation, or CFDC, supplying it with a one-time lump sum of ten million dollars. By early 1968, Michael Spencer was installed as "Acting

Secretary" (his title would change to Executive Director a year later, a position he would hold for the next decade) and money was being apportioned to a roster of productions that were intended to give Canada, finally, its voice in the sphere of world entertainment. The goal was, Spencer says, "establishing a commercially viable industry in Canada… supporting all sorts of movies." A laudable enough goal, one might think, and yet it was strongly opposed by a wall of donnish sanctimony and highbrow hand-wringing. "After awhile," admits Spencer, "we found the political heat a little hard to take."

It wasn't just snobbery that fuelled this resistance. Whether or not the United States was waging a deliberate program of cultural imperialism is immaterial, because it certainly felt that way. Efforts had been made for years to reverse or otherwise deal with this pattern: these included the censorship of "excessive displays of American patriotism" from Canadian screens in the 1920s; a program in the 1940s called the Canadian Co-operation Project, which ostensibly aimed to at least get something back from the Hollywood by making its stars into mouthpieces for Canadian tourism but was in reality a weak-kneed capitulation to Yankee interests; and

Playgirl Killer

the Massey Report in the fifties, which declared, apropos of American culture, that "a vast and disproportionate amount of material coming from a single alien source may stifle rather than stimulate our own creative effort."

So, to many, the creation of an office designed to stimulate the creation of commercial work seemed like an insane, "if you can't beat 'em…"-style surrender, reminiscent of the Canadian Co-operation Project. Debate on this matter raged in the halls of the National Film Board as well, with many of the filmmakers there opposed to the idea of a state-supported film industry on the grounds that it would ill behoove a government to get into the business of pure, Hollywood-style, profit-orientated entertainment; or else simply fearful for their jobs. One can easily imagine the disquiet such a proposal would arouse in an establishment devoted to telling the down-and-dirty stories of ordinary, unglamorous Canadians; if they'd been able to look forward a few years and see films like *Goin' Down the Road* (and, ten years on from that, *My Bloody Valentine*), they might not have felt so bad.

II.

I'm Dreaming of a
BLACK CHRISTMAS

(1968—1971)

T IS FITTING THAT THE PROPER BEGINNING of the Canadian feature film industry came in the same year as the election of Pierre Trudeau, a prime minister who seemed as glamourous and dynamic as a movie star himself. Indeed, thanks to one-time horror filmmaker Gerard Ciccoritti, Trudeau's life would become a movie—or, at least, a TV movie—in 2002.

In the world of horror films, and indeed independent film of all stripes, 1968 is a key year. October of that year saw the epoch-making release of Pittsburgh-based industrial filmmaker George Romero's *Night of the Living Dead*, a zombie picture which amply demonstrated once and for all that effective and extremely profitable films could be made for little money far outside the Hollywood sphere.[14] Now, with genre-friendly public funding standing ready and a startlingly successful model as encouragement, surely Canadian filmmakers were ready to begin turning out horror films by the dozen!

No, they were not. The first official CFDC-funded films (which is to say, partially-funded, since the organization was mandated only to provide a percentage of a selected film's budget) included *Act of the Heart*, a Paul Almond-directed melodrama, a mini-budget Francophone picture called *La chambre blanche*; and *Explosion*, an action-drama about American draft-dodgers heading north and causing trouble in the home and native land. Julian Roffman, perennial poster boy of Canadian independent film, was the latter film's producer, and it was made under the combined banner of his new Meridian Films company and, from south of the border (since this was a Canada-US co-production), Bing Crosby's company, BCP.[15]

Cinépix moved from exhibition to production at around this time. The production arm of the company was called DAL, which I'll venture to guess stands for Dunning And Link. Their first efforts were not horror, however, but the highly enjoyable and generally profitable maple-syrup porn pictures, which began in 1969 with a film called *Valerie*. It would be a few years of such productions—and the attendant scorn from critics and clergy—before Dunning and Link would fully assume the crown of "Canada's Roger Corman," as David Cronenberg has called them.

In the meantime, low-budget scare movies emanated from around the world, from the continuing horrors of Hammer and American International, to the sexy vampires of France's Jean Rollin, the bargain-basement efforts of Andy Milligan and Herschell Gordon Lewis, the manly Iberian lycanthropy of Paul Naschy, and a variety of American independent productions, like the New Orleans-shot *Night of Bloody Horror* (1969) or the New England madness of *I Drink Your Blood* (1971). And now, finally, but still very slowly, Canada would begin to take part.

Pure Bunkum

THE FIRST HORROR PICTURE MADE IN CANADA around this time was a highly mysterious production known as *Creature of Comfort*. There's no record of it being produced with CFDC money, which perhaps accounts for the fact that it doesn't ever seem to have been properly finished. The film was directed by Graham Driscoll in Toronto sometime around 1968, and features a performance by Donald Pleasence, the menacing British character actor who had played the cat-loving Bond villain Blofeld the year before in *You Only Live Twice*, and would gain a whole new fan base a decade later as Dr. Loomis in the *Halloween* series.

The story was told in the episodic format that was the mainstay of the British company Amicus (for whom Donald Sutherland had acted in *Dr. Terror's House of Horrors* four years earlier). Pleasence was the owner of a bedding shop who knowingly sells a hungry, amoeba-like comforter to a series of unwitting customers. The poor saps who end up with the killer coverlet are bloodlessly absorbed in the night as they sleep, and the baneful blanket ends up back in Pleasence's shop the very next day, ready to be sold to subsequent victims. In Laird Stuart's script (written under the rather flimsy *nom-de-plume* "Robert Stuart"), all of the victims (a corrupt businessman, say, or a shrewish wife) are morally corrupt or otherwise unpleasant, and therefore fully deserving of their ingurgitation by the deadly duvet. Stuart himself remembers seeing some footage and thinking that the film looked good, but he was never to see the finished product, as the production company ran out of money and the film was seized, apparently, by the bank whose money was invested in it. Subsequently the film disappeared completely, as though swallowed up by the ferocious flannel itself, and has yet to rematerialize.

It may still, however: odder things have happened. One of the odder things to have happened is a movie called *Death Bed: The Bed That Eats*, made in Detroit in 1972 by a grad student named George Barry. Who knew that after *Creature of Comfort* there would ever be another killer bed movie? But there was, and moreover it was made with a strong infusion of Canadian talent, who came down from Toronto to help out on the extremely low-budget picture. One of these was a lighting technician named Jock Brandis, who would later work as the gaffer on a number of David Cronenberg pictures and prove indispensable in helping the giant mechanical snake to work properly on the set of William Fruet's giant snake picture *Spasms*. The soundtrack to *Death Bed* was mixed in Toronto, and then it, like its predecessor, disappeared completely. However, against all odds it has resurfaced, and by April of 2003 it was playing at film festivals and being reviewed in *Variety*, and this was followed by a video release in the fall of the same year. If that can happen, then maybe *Creature of Comfort*—especially considering that, in Donald Pleasence, it features an actual big-name movie star—will someday see the light of day too. But screenwriter Stuart confirms that the producer of the film, Donald Adams, has passed on, and no one seems to know the status of director Graham

Driscoll. It's possible that he's grown a beard and started a new life in film as a Hawaiian cinematographer, but if that is indeed the case, then good for him. I'm not about to go bothering him about his old life as a bedding-horror filmmaker in Toronto.

And that was not it for the Canadian cursed-comforter genre. Not one but two episodes of the Toronto-shot *Friday the 13th* television series, which had nothing to do with Jason Voorhees and everything to do with haunted antiques, featured a bit of killer bedding known as "The Quilt of Hathor." The episodes were directed by Timothy Bond, who would later co-write *Happy Birthday To Me*.

Along with *Creature of Comfort*, another unfinished horror film from the period was *Fiend*, written and produced by Claudio Castravelli and Joel Uman. Uman was also the cinematographer and director of the doomed project. The pair had worked together in 1971 on a comedy called *Up Uranus!* (one of the great titles, but a tough movie to find), and by late 1972 were ready to shoot *Fiend* in Montreal. Though the picture was never completed, Castravelli went on to become a busy producer of all manner of genre fare, and in 1984 directed the killer-judge picture *Evil Judgment*.

Northern Hippie Horror

THE COUNTERCULTURE CAUGHT UP WITH CANADIAN HORROR; or, rather, Canadian horror caught up with the counterculture, in around 1969: a little late, perhaps. Hippie horror had been around for a few years: Michael Reeves' *The Sorcerers* (1967), the acid-flashback killings of *Mantis in Lace* (1968) and *The Curse of the Crimson Altar* (also 1968) all crammed long hair and groovy paisley prints, in spirit if not in fact, alongside their scares.

In the summer of 1969 came the 100% pure Canadian madness of *Flick*, also known as *Dr. Frankenstein On Campus*. The movie starred a very young Robin Ward (later to appear in Bruce Pittman's killer-twin picture *The Mark of Cain*, and perhaps best known for his role as host of the game show *Guess What?*) as a modern-day Dr. Frankenstein, who is booted out of his highbrow European university for dueling (his opponent is National Ballet of Canada dancer Lawrence Adams) and is forced to enroll at the University of Toronto, well known for its lax policies on sword fighting.

Frankenstein's social life in Toronto consists of sitting in way-out clubs with his new friends Susan and Tony, listening to the acid rock of Toronto hitmakers Lighthouse, and making uptight remarks like "Is this what you North Americans mean by 'getting it together'?" Upon being accused of being uptight, he counters with "I am not uptight. I am very *down loose.*" He also complains about people making fun of his name, quotes Milton and Wordsworth a lot, and clearly isn't shy about putting the moves on Susan. The club they're sitting in, meanwhile, is populated by extras culled from the (then) well-known Judy Marsh Modeling Agency.

The club scenes are shot with lots of coloured lights, weird angles, machine-gun editing and tromboning camerawork, some of which comes right before a shot of an actual trombone! The movie calms down a bit when we cut to the lab of Professor Preston, who is Frankenstein's U. of T. mentor and is conducting research on mind-control and the "tri-genital" region of the brain. (Preston is played by Sean Sullivan, some years before David Cronenberg's *The Dead Zone*, in which he appears as Christopher Walken's father.)

As Frankenstein seduces Susan (leading to a very curious topless romp in a muddy stream, intercut with brief flashes of Frankenstein's wide, staring eyes), campus radical Dave Brouwer, who lacks both charisma and the top three buttons of his shirt, stirs up trouble at a student demonstration against computers. (Judy Marsh Agency models fill out the crowd once again.) Professor Preston is singled out by the mob as the campus' leading advocate of dehumanization, a charge which later proves to be absolutely correct.

Frankenstein and Preston both have the same goal: control of other peoples' brains by electronic apparatus. The main difference between the two is that Frankenstein, a little more forward-thinking, believes the process can be made wireless. Inspired by Preston, Frankenstein very quickly works up a remote control and electrode system to effect brain control. He tries it out on his new girlfriend's dog and cat. In a titanic battle, the cat kills the dog, and Frankenstein announces his general policy on experimentation: "If mankind is to progress, the guinea pigs must pay the price, whoever they are! That's how life is!"

This rationalist manifesto stated, it's time for some more Lighthouse at a crazy happening in the student residence, extras courtesy of the Judy Marsh Agency. Pot smoke fills the air and we see shots of model-beautiful hippies freaking out on exercise equipment. "This is really a groove, man!" cries a fellow who's put one of those vibrating belly-shaker belts around his head. Two more hippies don hardhats and engage in a billygoat-style head butting competition. Tony, a tae kwon do expert, tries the game and emerges victorious. At that moment, buzz-killer Frankenstein arrives at the party and is promptly set up on a drug rap, which is reported in the student paper the next day.

The Reincarnate: crowds lining up

In an angry-dean scene right out of *Animal House*, Frankenstein is once again kicked out of school. His response is to take four of the students involved in the set-up to the lab for a beaker-full of pure alcohol, which knocks them out. He implants them all with his electrodes and, when they wake up, takes them to a graveyard and makes Tony kill them with karate chops.

Further murders take place, with the hapless Tony cutting a swath through Frankenstein's enemies with his deadly chopping hands. With one punch he kills the journalism student who wrote the story, and then drowns the photographer who took the incriminating photo in her own chemical bath while strangling her with a film strip for good measure. The grumpy dean is violently bonked with his own cane while on a constitutional down Philosopher's Walk. Susan, waking up in the morning wearing nothing but her sunglasses, is naturally upset by the news that many of her friends and acquaintances are dead; but not so upset that she doesn't rush off to research an article on ancient tapestries for the school paper.

The movie comes to an abrupt climax at the Royal Ontario Museum as Frankenstein attempts to use his kung-fu assassin to take care of the tapestry-gazing Susan. But a rambunctious kid knocks the control box out of his hand and smashes it. "Sorry, mister! I didn't mean to break your radio! I gotta go now!" cries the rapscallion. Tony, coming abruptly to his senses, chases Frankenstein up the stairs and knocks him over a railing. The mad grad student's shirt rips in the fall, and long rows of unraveled stitching are revealed on his body. "He was just a creation, poor guy," says Tony. "But whose creation?" asks Susan. "Who's the real Frankenstein?" As if they couldn't have guessed. We see Professor Preston walking away from the scene, tossing away his own remote control device, disappointed that his creation has burst, certainly, but already planning another. He walks south down Queen's Park Road as a final Lighthouse tune comes up on the soundtrack and tiny credits appear on the screen over him.

Flick's genesis came when young television commercial producers Bill Marshall and Gilbert W. Taylor got the idea, as Nat Taylor and Julian Roffman had done a decade before, to make an utterly and unashamedly commercial film. Says Taylor, "Bill and I said right from the start: 'Well, let's make a B movie.' And that's exactly what we did."

Flick was made on a low budget, half of which ($150,000, to be precise) came from the CFDC. The rest came from Glen Warren Productions, which partnered with Marshall and Taylor's Limelight Productions to form an amalgam called Agincourt Productions. The film was shot over 19 days in August of 1969, coming in $70,000 under budget, and was released in Canada the following April. It's not exactly a good movie, but it's surprisingly slick, with lots of extras and crane shots and other hallmarks of professionalism. Plus, Skip Prokop and Paul Hoffert of the populous Toronto rock band Lighthouse (with future Cronenberg collaborator Howard Shore on sax) provide several groovy tunes—some of them performed onscreen—and a half-decent dramatic score in the bargain.

The film was not received terribly well in Canada. According to CFDC boss Michael Spencer's memoirs, *Hollywood North*, the *Globe and Mail* review of the film, by Martin Knelman, sported the headline "*Flick* Is a Horror, All Right: All Canadian, All Lousy." But Gil Taylor believes that the critical establishment and film community simply weren't yet ready to accept the phenomenon of the Canadian B movie, and the facts bear him out. "When it came out," Taylor recalls in Spencer's book,

> …everybody said 'Oh my God: they've made a B movie.' And we said: 'Yeah, and that's what we told you we were going to do. We were doing a Roger Corman type of deal.' As a matter of fact, Roger Corman said it was as good as anything he'd done. Yet Canada didn't understand at the time that there was a place for B movies.

Variety contradicted the hometown reviews in a notice dated 22 April, 1970, asserting that the film "holds together in what it promises to do. Suited to a double bill, it should break even, and for a first effort by Toronto's Agincourt Productions, *Flick* is a creditable effort." Added the reviewer: "The music is first rate… [but] camerawork is derivative of TV commercials."

Current reviews of the film tend to complain that it's "dated;" but what kind of criticism is that? Certainly it's very much of its time (well, truthfully, a year or two behind), with its student protests and heady hipster vibe, but certainly no less enjoyable for it. Probably it's more enjoyable. (An earlier draft of the script, written before the riots at Columbia and Berkely, had the students throwing buns to express their displeasure—very Canadian, but a little naïve.) The main problem is the shapeless story, which is almost totally devoid of narrative drive, and the equally confused politics. There's a sense of wasted potential walking hand-in-hand with the pleasure in watching this film. It could have been a crazy B-movie Canuck-O-Classic, but it isn't quite. Instead it's an artifact, entertaining enough, but also proof that Canada (or at least Taylor and Marshall, in their early thirties at the time) didn't quite have a handle on the youth market, or any real idea of what was happening with the kids of the time. Considering this in retrospect, box office failure was assured.

A Name For Evil (known also as *The Grove*) was another horror movie influenced by the anti-establishment attitudes of the time. Shot in British Columbia for Penthouse Pictures in 1971, the film follows an architect, played by Robert Culp, who has become monumentally disenchanted with the superficiality of contemporary North American life; so much so that, in a move foreshadowing the opening sequence of the *SCTV* comedy show, he tosses his television off his high-rise apartment balcony. He and his reluctant wife (Samantha Eggar) flee the hurly-burly for a lakeside mansion owned by Culp's deceased grandfather, The Major. The house proves a handyman's delight, to put it mildly, and the renovations are complicated by The Major's continuing, grumpy presence, in spirit form, on the property. It seems he doesn't cotton to strangers, or even his own kinfolk, messing around with his real estate. "I didn't allow The Grove to be changed in my life, so why should I allow it now that I am… dead?" he reasons in an ominous, southern-fried voice-over. The proprietary ghost does take a shine to Eggar, however, and Culp is soon assailed by visions of his wife swooning in the old phantom's embrace. An agitated Culp rides off on a mysterious white horse, which takes him to an orgy in progress at the local watering hole. Here's where the

Le diable est parmi nous

Penthouse angle really comes to the fore, as gyrating rural hippies disrobe and run around the forest like wood nymphs, with Culp tagging along also, unexpectedly, in complete *deshabille*. He and one of the lady hippies break off from the pack and have a romantic interlude by a waterfall. When he gets back to Eggar the next morning, she informs him that, contrary to his memory, he'd been home the whole night, right beside her, masturbating furiously. Naturally, Culp, along with the audience, is confused, and the couple take up their bickering ways anew, except this time it ends with Culp's apparent castration and the subsequent defenestration of Eggar.

A Name For Evil is one perplexing film. It seems to be an elliptical metaphor for the disintegration of Culp and Eggar's marriage (sitting right alongside the plain-as-day narrative fact of their marriage disintegrating), but writer/director Bernard Girard, working from a novel by Andrew Lytle, thankfully declines to make that aspect overly explicit. The ghost angle loses focus in the second half; or rather, since it was never terribly sharp, fails ever to gain any focus. But the movie looks good, with fine photography by Reginald Morris (later to hook up with Bob Clark to shoot the marvelous *Black Christmas*) and a great, huge, spooky-looking house as a main location. Culp is an odd choice for the hero, but he gives a committed performance (letting it all hang out, as it were) and pulls off the middle-age-crazy bit as well as anyone. His commitment led him to become one of the financing partners in the film, and he was soon making artistic suggestions to cinematographer Morris. Eggar is good also as the frustrated wife, and it's nice to see Clarence "Big" Miller in a substantial role (though how could he play anything *but* a substantial role?) many years before his celebrated appearance in *Big Meat Eater*. The film also features an effective score by Dominic Frontiere, later to provide *The Stunt Man* with its memorably eccentric music.

A Name for Evil is something like a horror version of *The Swimmer*, the Burt Lancaster picture in which he wears a Speedo throughout and tries to swim home by way of his well-heeled suburban friends' pools. That comparison may seem a bit of a stretch to some, but John Cheever fans and all those who've run across *The Swimmer* on late-night television and wondered just what the hell was going on are well-advised to seek out a copy of the Culp picture nonetheless. It'll be difficult to locate, but I believe you'll find the effort—and a comparative screening with *The Swimmer*—worthwhile.

The Devil is Among Us: Cloning Rosemary's Baby in Canada

The big scary 1968 hit most aped by Canadian filmmakers in these early days of horror was not *Night of the Living Dead*, but *Rosemary's Baby*. In terms of what Canadian filmmakers could afford to ape, this made no sense. The Polanski picture featured movie stars and was based on a popular novel. Perhaps it was the film's stately European class, its serious-minded approach to the fantastic, which appealed to the Canadians. It was entirely possible for NFB filmmakers like Harvey Hart and Don Haldane to look at Polanski's achievement and think "why, there's a commercial sort of film I wouldn't be scorned for making." Up north, patently trying for a crossover commercial hit was still a hot-button endeavor which, on the Anglo side of things at least, left one's work open to derision and dismissal; and on the Francophone side it was more politicized and angry, but otherwise much the same. The use of such tried-and-true low-budget tropes as sex and gore in a film would have got you booted all the way down the Côte de Liesse. (The crucial exception was Dunning and Link's Cinépix, who were by this time working on the production as well as the distribution end of things, cranking out the hallowed "maple-syrup porn.")

The particular brand of horror in *Rosemary's Baby* had its appeal to the Canadian mind as well. There were almost no special effects and very little on-screen violence. Terror is sensed rather than seen. In a country with no special effects personnel to speak of, this had to have its appeal. The feeling of a greater force at work, rising from its smoky underworld and seeking only to use and then cast away its helpless victims, might also have touched a nerve with Canadians. To be a Canadian is to constantly wonder just what influence and power one really can boast in the wider world; to regularly consider, and occasionally doubt, the value of quiet diplomacy against the might of bombs and guns. It doesn't seem a stretch to draw a line between this state of affairs and a susceptibility to a movie like *Rosemary's Baby*, with its passive, innocent, pixie-cut protagonist battling a shadowy evil she can barely comprehend. As well, the chaos of America in the 1960s—demonstrations, riots, assassinations—had barely touched Canada, and there was no need to allegorize the frenzy on film as Romero had done with his zombie picture. (This would change very shortly, however, with the October Crisis.)

The first diabolical thriller to go before the cameras was Don Haldane's *The Reincarnate*. Haldane, like Julian Roffman, had spent the early days of his career with the National Film Board, and in 1963 directed their first English-language narrative feature, *Drylanders*. It was perhaps for this reason that he was hired to direct *The Reincarnate*, for the film was originally to be a Julian Roffman production, and as Roffman had little desire to direct horror features himself after the ordeal of *The Mask*, he would have been likely to hire someone very like himself, who had proved his allegiance to truth, goodness and honesty in filmmaking by making earnest, heartfelt documentaries. Haldane had certainly done that.

Le diable est parmi nous

Roffman had had a bitter run over the past decade. Thanks to the reported perfidy of Warner Bros., he knew it didn't matter much how popular a film was; you could still walk away with nothing. Roffman turned to higher-brow projects that would at least provide some creative satisfaction. With an old documentary collaborator named Ben Kerner, he wrote a film version of the Sinclair Ross novel *The Well* under the title *Hunger for Loving*, with Melvyn Douglas, fresh off the superficially similar *Hud*, set to play the lead. Roffman intended to direct the picture, but the financiers insisted on hiring Sir Carol Reed, so the feisty Canadian shrugged his shoulders and set about the job of producing. To his great disappointment the whole project fell through while in pre-production. Kerner and Roffman penned another script, something called *Davey and the Man from Zar*, but it never got off the ground. After that, Roffman and Harvey Hart spent a good deal of energy trying to put together a film version of Phillip Roth's 1962 novel *Letting Go*, and this enterprise was proceeding apace when *The Reincarnate* came along.

The film's story came from an American writer named Seeleg Lester, who had been active writing scripts for *The Outer Limits*. Lester, a dapper gentleman who was always nattily dressed and had impeccable manners, was a friend of Roffman's, and so had sent the screenplay his way. Roffman and Nat Taylor were still partners at this point. Taylor loved the script, but Roffman thought it was the worst thing he had ever read. How could he tell his gentle, cultured friend Seeleg? He couldn't, and in any event Lester was touchy and defensive about his work, making confrontation even more difficult. Roffman's only out was the Roth project, but when Roth himself pulled the plug on it, the producer had little choice but to put the horror movie he didn't much want to make on the front burner.

Things didn't get any better for Roffman. He still hated the script, and when the movie was cast he hated the actors too. His devotion to truth and rightness in film was taking a severe pounding, and finally it was too much. Just as the film began shooting, in October of 1970, Roffman walked out on it, dissolving his ten-year partnership with Nat Taylor in the process. Taylor was, of course, terribly upset. All this and the War Measures Act too, what with the other October Crisis in full swing. (This event, in which Pierre Trudeau invoked the War Measures Act to deal with the beginnings of a revolutionary uprising in Quebec, would not find an outlet in the nation's horror cinema until 1977, with the appearance of David Cronenberg's *Rabid*.)

As the one who did the walking, Roffman found himself at a disadvantage when the time came to apportion the partnership's assets, and though he had co-owned the Kleinburg studios and other properties, Roffman got nothing from the bust-up but *The Mask*. Since Robert Shaye was showing the film on campuses across America without sharing the profits, this didn't amount to much in financial terms, and the film itself may just have served as a bitter reminder of what to Roffman was the dark side of movie making. However, he also got the actual mask, which stayed in his daughter's bedroom as she was growing up and gave the poor girl nightmares. The scary prop, a hideous thing bearing what looks like real human teeth in its mouth, is now on display at the Canadian Film Reference Library in Toronto where it greets startled visitors at the front door.

Shooting of *The Reincarnate* proceeded without Julian Roffman. The story of the film runs as follows: A lawyer (played by Jack Creley), who is also a "reincarnate" with 8,000 years worth of past lives, learns that he's about to die, and finds himself a young, fiery sculptor (Jay Reynolds) to become for his next life. The notion of being reborn into a body already well into its twenties and with an established career in sculpture flies in the face of most conceptions of reincarnation that I've ever heard of, but for the most part Lester's script otherwise treats the subject with impressive and indeed persuasive gravity. Perhaps to a fault: at times it seems like the whole film is one endless lecture from Creley to Reynolds (and so to us) about the manifold delights of iterate living.

Reynolds is duly converted by the end, and, aside from the victims of the black-magic pall surrounding Creley and his gang, who could not be? Their power takes the hugely clichéd form of—what else?—a black cat, which engineers the deaths of several people who might potentially be even remotely in the way of the scheme. In one instance, to vanquish the randy boyfriend of a girl who for the purposes of the reincarnates' ceremony must remain a virgin, the yowling cat crashes in through a skylight and implants a shard of glass in the boy's throbbing neck. It also manages to send a car flying off those notorious death-traps, the Scarborough Bluffs. At the end the ritual takes place as planned, and Creley's soul goes into the young sculptor's body.

The picture isn't strictly speaking a devil-cult picture, but it features all the trappings of one (mysterious deaths, robed figures chanting, an altar), and so fits pretty neatly into the genre. Anthony Kramreither, who would later produce Can-horror fare like *Humongous* and *The Brain*, appears as Creley's good old-world buddy, a fellow reincarnate named Van Brock. The film's notion that, like the Satanists in *Rosemary's Baby*, reincarnates have a tight-knit international community and possess cultivated though apparently omnipotent powers, are among its most compelling aspects; and these are almost entirely embodied in Kramreither's courtly, assured performance. The reincarnates seem like they must have a wonderful wood-paneled club somewhere (probably in Vienna or Prague) which serves the finest brandies the world has ever known. Their imperialism is different than what you'd find in a regular gentleman's club: instead of entire countries, these fellows only want to take over one person at a time.

Originally running an epic 122 minutes in length (which no doubt would have made watching it feel like being trapped in an elevator with a reincarnation crackpot in full filibuster), the final version of *The Reincarnate* came in at a streamlined 95. The film was released on April 30th, 1971, and played for six successful weeks at the Uptown 2 in Toronto. Film scholar Gerald Pratley was impressed enough with the public turnout to snap pictures of the long lineups. Filmmaker Gerard Ciccoritti (maker of the *Graveyard Shift* vampire pictures

The Pyx

of the late 1980s) recalls that the film was all the rage around town during its run. "The papers were full of big pictures of the Hollywood-style premiere in Canada, and it was touted as 'We've arrived! We're making a big, classy picture that happens to be a horror movie.' And I went to see it, and it was just some piece of crap."

Ciccoritti's boyhood impression wasn't so far off, at least in purely critical terms. The film is flat and painfully talky, but there's something kind of fun and captivating about it anyway. Creley is an authoritative sort of an actor, and so his lectures don't grate the way they would from the mouth of a lesser talent. (This is no doubt why David Cronenberg hired him to play the Marshall McLuhan stand-in with a similar taste for oratory ten years later in *Videodrome*.) The script, talky as it is, is at least intelligent and assumes its audience is intelligent too. The film is well shot by cinematographer Norman Allin, who, after years of working at the CBC, regarded it as his entry into a life of feature film work. Allin also operated the camera, and stated that his approach to lighting the picture was to keep it as realistic as possible. Well, naturally—it's Canadian! So there's a lot to recommend the picture for Tundra Terror fans even though it isn't by any objective standard a very good movie.

The first Cinépix venture into horror came in 1972 with Jean Beaudin's *Le Diable est parmi nous* (a.k.a. *The Possession of Virginia*). Scripted by André Link and John Dunning under the pseudonym Julian Parnell (though in the English-dubbed television print I saw, also stripped of any sex and violence, there is simply no screenplay credit at all), the film is very like a French-language corollary to *The Reincarnate*.

Dunning and Link mentioned their inaugural horror project to CFDC executive director Michael Spencer. He assured them that the Corporation would very likely approve such a picture, but when the script arrived at the CFDC office, Gratien Gélinas, a well-known playwright and the CFDC board chairman, disliked it and was disinclined to help fund the film. Other board members agreed. Spencer had to go back to Dunning and Link and admit that he'd spoken too soon. The Cinépix producers, bloodied but unbowed, raised the money and made the film anyway. Perhaps this doggedness stemmed from the fact that they'd written the script themselves, but no doubt contributing to it was the lack of success their (inadvertently) Catholic-themed sex films were having in breaking into the American market. The pictures were doing wonderfully in Quebec, but in the U.S. it appeared that genre films—horror, science-fiction, maybe even westerns—were the way to go. Cinépix was more than ready to experiment with the notion, anyway.

The film opens with a troubled-looking, rather fey man named Jack, who is seen wearing a kimono and fondling various pieces of art before leaping out his apartment window. The dead man's friend, reporter Paul Dwyer (played by a very sleepy-looking Daniel Pilon), investigates the case, which is complicated by the jumper's strange will bequeathing all his earthly possessions to his sultry blonde shopgirl Virginia. She appears to be Paul's girlfriend, but this is one of many aspects left unclear by the uncommonly murky script. Matters take a still darker turn when Paul's cat is poisoned and Virginia falls victim to a toxic whiskey. She survives but the cat does not, and one thing is made abundantly clear: Paul is in danger from some mad poisoner. A funny-looking old lady, whose every appearance is heralded by a jaunty tune on the highly eclectic soundtrack, seems to be involved.

At a frankly hilarious early-Seventies love-party, which he attends at the insistence of a co-worker, Paul meets up with a famous and beautiful piano player named Helen Davis (Louise Marleau). Returning to his apartment, he finds it trashed. Virginia is missing and there is a note indicating that, if he wants to find her, he should head to the neighborhood church. He does, and promptly discovers Virginia's bloody corpse hanging in the bell-tower. He shouts "Virginia!" and runs out to summon the police by hurling his flashlight through a shop window.

The police return with Paul to the church but find only blood and a frayed rope. Paul suspects the same funny old lady, since she has left a heel print in the blood very similar to one he saw at the scene of his friend's suicide. Paul tells the story to his stout, Machiavellian publisher, and then, on the pretense of doing a story on her, embarks on a whirlwind courtship with Helen Davis.

After another visit from the old lady and a few more creepy things, Paul comes clean to Helen about the goings-on of the past few days. She tries to dissuade him from any further involvement, but Paul is determined to get to the bottom of the mystery.

He may do so, but we don't, at least not in the English-dubbed television cut of the film. Things get a little confusing at this point in the picture. Paul and Helen go to a strange mansion with a weird, near-dwarf butler, and take part in a mysterious ritual put on by "The Secret Sect of Chanel." The moderator of the ritual has a TV announcer voice and reveals that Helen is destined to take the place of failed Chanel member Jack. The cult is of satanic inclination and the ritual proceeds much as they do in all such films. At one point, Paul calls out "Virginia!" as he had done in the church upon finding her dead. This seems *apropos* of nothing, however.

Halfway through the ritual we cut to a shot of Paul and Helen emerging from the mansion and stopping in the driveway to kiss. A limousine carrying the corpulent publisher zooms out of nowhere and smashes into them, sending the lovers flying in slow motion through the air. But Paul suddenly wakes up and falls off his couch: it's just a horrible dream! He walks into his bedroom and finds the funny old lady lying on his bed. He tries to wake her, but she seems to be dead. As he turns to walk away, she rises, and with a hideous shriek stabs him repeatedly in the back, just as the red raincoat-wearing dwarf would to Donald Sutherland two years later in *Don't Look Now*.

The Pyx

That's it for Paul. A phone call from the publisher's unctuous assistant, Xavier, reports that "Grandma" has taken care of things, and all is once again in balance in the devil-cult world. In the very last scene we see that Helen is now the owner and proprietor of Jack's antique shop.

And so: what? Here is a movie which seems to have great chunks missing, which appears in its English-dubbed version to very likely have a completely different story than in the French original. There is lots in the film to recommend—the amazingly eclectic score, the great early Seventies sets and atmosphere, and the claustrophobic sense of perpetual doom—but the overall feeling is more or less "what the?" Surely the original version offers more, including, perhaps, a little more information as to just what the heck is going on at the end; and until I see it, my inner jury on *Le Diable est parmi nous* will have to remain out. "Out" is where even Quebec audiences stayed when the film was released—it did almost no business, and Cinépix returned to the diminishing maple softcore business.

The short burst of early-Seventies Canadian devil-cult thrillers came to a distinguished, if at times slightly dull climax in 1972 with Harvey Hart's *The Pyx*. Hart, like Sidney Furie and so many others, began his career at the CBC before heading south to make American television shows, among them episodes of *Alfred Hitchcock Presents*. In 1965 he directed a sort of supernatural detective movie for television called *Dark Intruder*, starring fellow Canadian Leslie Nielsen as a proto-Kolchak[16] investigating a demon on the streets of San Francisco. He came home to Canada in 1970 and concentrated on feature films like the prison drama *Fortune and Men's Eyes* (1971) and, a year later, *The Pyx*.

The executive producer of the film was Canadian television maven Maxine Samuels, a hard-drinking party animal with a forceful, Mrs. Robinson-esque personality. She and Hart had acquired the rights to Loyola University professor John Buell's novel, but the project ran out of money while still in development. In the meantime, Julian Roffman had partnered up with Ralph Foster to start Meridian. By the early Seventies he was an old pro at applying for production funding from the CFDC. Hart and Roffman were old friends, and for Hart, Roffman was—on both a professional and personal level—almost a father figure, just as John Grierson had been for Roffman thirty years before.

The horror genre, it seemed, would simply not let Roffman alone, no matter how much he despised it. Hart asked his old friend for help in putting together funding for *The Pyx*, and Roffman, who was heavily connected with the Liberal Party, hooked the production up with a lawyer named Geoffrion, who helped arrange the nearly one million dollars of financing required to make the film. By now Roffman was the producer, and it must have been a little strange after the *Reincarnate* donnybrook to find himself involved in such a very similar film.

The Pyx begins with hooker Elizabeth Lucy, played by Karen Black, dead at the base of a Montreal apartment building, clad only in a sheer gown and clutching a pyx—a container used by Catholic priests to carry the Eucharist on house calls—in one cold, lifeless hand. A police detective (Canadian actor Christopher Plummer in his first ever Canadian role) arrives on the scene and begins his investigation. The rest of the film alternates between scenes of Plummer snooping around and sequences depicting the events which eventually lead Black to her death at the base of the building. Of course it all has to do with the shadowy activities of a devil cult and their lust for demonic power. A brutish handyman, a slimy henchman in a suit and an aging madame, played by stage actor Yvette Brind'Amour in her film debut, all figure in.

The atmosphere on the set during the nine-week shoot was as divided as the film's structure. Karen Black by all accounts didn't win any hearts with her behavior on set, clashing with Hart and sowing discord left and right. She kept cats in her hotel room as well, and after the cats had thoroughly messed it up, Black destroyed the room and was kicked out. By contrast, Plummer was totally professional, and Roffman came to admire him greatly.

Hart was very much the Roffman acolyte in his approach to directing the film. In a *Cinema Canada* interview, he revealed that "To me, the documentary aspect of it was the horror of our everyday lives… To try and outdo that would have been an attempt to top myself with horror, and there are lots of people who are much better at that than I… The attempt was to shock [audiences] philosophically." Of course, William Friedkin said the same sorts of things about *The Exorcist*, but Hart, a good Canadian filmmaker to the core, really meant it.

"I consciously wanted to suck the audience into the immediacy of it so they couldn't cop out and say 'this couldn't happen to me,'" said Hart. To help in this, he interviewed police on the Montreal force to get an idea of how cops behaved and how they felt. He came away from this with the conviction that cops, in the absence of any initiative from church or populace, have come to view themselves as the closest thing to representatives of God himself. "It's like in the States," Hart said. "When you allow Nixon to assume too much power, he starts to believe he should have that power. That's exactly what's happening to the police."

An obnoxious, hotel room-destroying harridan Black may have been during the shoot, but her performance in the film is very good. As a valuable bonus, she composed and performed three songs for the movie's soundtrack: "I Was Touched By Your Passing Through," "It All Turned Out The Way I Planned It" and "Song of Solomon Chapter 3 Verses 1 to 4." These melancholy numbers, produced by Dylan/Cohen collaborator Bob Johnston (credited in the film as "Miss Black's music consultant"), give the film the atmosphere of an urban version of *The Wicker Man*, a similarly folk-song-heavy cult picture with Christopher Lee made in England the same year.

Cannibal Girls

The Pyx was a big deal in Canada at the time: a sophisticated Hollywood-style thriller with an international cast and expansive, wide-screen photography (by René Verzier, fresh off *Le Diable est parmi nous*). In the *Toronto Citizen*, Natalie Edwards enthused "Finally! A dandy commercial movie, well acted, well produced and altogether OK… It is distinctly and delightfully Canadian, yet blessed with a solid American style, pace and slick surface." The picture made $200,000 in its first three weeks of release, $43,000 of which was from Toronto theatres. In the days before the "opening weekend is all" method of calculating a film's success this was perfectly decent, and for a Canadian film exceptional.

Canadian critics had waited a long time for a movie they could lavish with compliments like "altogether OK." And now here it was, a picture with which we could impress our southern neighbors. Of course, its release in America was little more than desultory, and, as an extra insult, it suffered the ignominy of being released on video under the title *The Hooker Cult Murders*, where it sat on shelves right next to Roman Polanski's *The Devil Had Sex With Me And Now I Must Bear His Child*, William Friedkin's *A Little Girl Possessed By Satan Vomits On Some Priests* and Richard Donner's *You Can Tell He's The Devil's Child Because He Dresses Better Than You*.

Of course, next to the excesses of Friedkin's picture, released only a few months after Hart's, *The Pyx* would seem pretty tame, so it's little wonder American audiences ignored it. It's still an enjoyable enough movie though, graced with plenty of Montreal smoked-meat atmosphere, good performances and the same fuzzy solemnity found in many of the best early-'70s pictures. It does, however, demand to be seen in its original wide-screen format, so if you can find it on DVD, all the better.

The Pyx was the end of Julian Roffman's horror career, and thus the end of an era. Roffman was not Canada's first old-style mogul producer (Ernest Shipman was probably that, and Canada had begat Mack Sennett, Jack Warner and Harry Saltzman in the bargain), but, with his devotion to documentary and his commercial pragmatism, he was emblematic of both what Canada was and what it could, and would, be. Cinematographer and director Gary Graver, an American who worked for Roffman in his later producing days and became his friend thereafter, spoke of his friend's "high integrity" and intelligence. "Julian saw through the bullshit of people, and that was what I liked about him," Graver said. "He was a little guy, feisty and wiry. Not everybody liked him, though, because he was opinionated. But I liked him a lot. He was a hands-on producer, a troubleshooter. He knew what was commercial. And he knew what he wanted as a producer."

Whether he had retreated somewhat in his documentary ideals in later days is not certain. Graver only knows that Roffman didn't talk documentaries with him, and appeared fully committed to narrative fiction. But that was probably a show, for Roffman was as Canadian as a filmmaker could get, even more so perhaps than his protégée Hart. Reality was a primary virtue to him, and it would remain so until his death in 2000.

Ontario Gut-Munchers

AROUND THE TIME OF *The Reincarnate*'s release in the early spring of 1971, a couple of young McMaster film students named Ivan Reitman and Dan Goldberg were sitting in an Ontario courthouse under police guard, arrested on charges of obscenity and trembling with the certainty that they were going to spend their next few years in jail. The legal bone of contention was a film called *The Columbus of Sex*—by all reports fairly innocuous,[17] but remember, this is Ontario—which they had produced and John Hofsess had directed. The two were indeed convicted of the offense, but the sentence was suspended and Goldberg and Reitman eventually managed to sell their first feature production.

This hard-won battle led to a new project, *Foxy Lady*, which Goldberg produced and Reitman directed as his feature debut. This film, funded in part by the CFDC, was not a success; its lengthy post-production was something of a chore for the young Reitman, and he and Goldberg decided the best tonic would be to launch into another film as quickly as possible. The smartest thing to do, it seemed to Reitman, would be to make the movie completely on credit; that way they could start immediately. The determined youngsters set about making a plan of action.[18]

Within a day of making this decision, Reitman and Goldberg had convinced the head of the Bellevue Pathé film laboratory (and soon-to-be movie mogul), Harold Greenberg, to give them a 50% break in the cost of processing services in return for a small share in the film and the promise of the other half if their movie—thus far nameless and bereft of even the barest story or script—ever became profitable. On the same day they cadged a truckload of film equipment from a company called Cinevision, also promising a small percentage of the profits. Over the next week, they gathered up a cast and a crew willing to work on a hundred percent deferral basis. Now all they needed was a story.

Over a cup of coffee in Reitman's parents' kitchen, they came up with a tag line for the movie poster: "These girls eat men!" The logical extension of that, clearly, was a sexy cannibal movie, and the title *Cannibal Girls* seemed a good fit. They started up a company, Scary Pictures, and hooked up with their *Foxy Lady* collaborator Bob Sandler, who shaped their rough ideas into the semblance of a story. The actors, including future *SCTV* players Eugene Levy and Andrea Martin in the lead roles of Cliff and Gloria, workshopped the story until they had a feature film's worth of dialogue and plot. For cash, Reitman and Goldberg managed to persuade a handful of people to invest in the movie, netting themselves a total of ten thousand dollars to begin shooting.

Cannibal Girls

The story, which might kindly be described as "loose," tells of Cliff and Gloria, a couple who've only been dating for two weeks but are already taking winter road trips together to strange, snowy, Southern Ontario towns. Arriving in one such place, "Farnhamville," they run across an old lady who tells them the strange legend of the three beautiful girls who once lived in a nearby farmhouse and who regularly lured men to the house, kept them waiting around for a few days, and then cooked them up for dinner. ("They were cannibals!" exclaims the lady, who continues, a bit redundantly, by saying "And they et men!") The infamous farmhouse has become a restaurant owned by the highly eccentric and overbearing Reverend Alex St. John, who wears a top hat and tightly-buttoned mime gloves and also happens to employ three beautiful, sinister girls as waitresses.

We learn, in flashback, the story of the Cannibal Girls, which comes down to a few vignettes of them luring nerdly, tweed jacket wearing men to their farmhouse, seducing them (not difficult), killing them, and then eating them up for dinner. Gloria and Cliff react to this story with a proper amount of awe and then head out to see what Farnhamville has to offer a young Toronto couple like themselves.

Pretty soon, though only after a good deal of bickering, Cliff and Gloria are drawn into the local customs (the whole town, under the Reverend's Manson-like thrall, is happily cannibalistic), and eventually there's something of a twist in which Gloria herself becomes a fourth Cannibal Girl and chows down on the extravagantly afro-ed Cliff after first thumping him in the chest with a medieval mace. Blood sprays from his mouth as though from a fire hose, prefiguring, in spirit at least, the *SCTV* days to come. The movie concludes with the old lady telling her tale—which, with Gloria, now boasts *four* voracious girls—to a new couple. "They were cannibals!" she declares once again. "And they et men!"

There's plenty for the Tundra Terror aficionado to enjoy in *Cannibal Girls*.

The movie opens in comfortably familiar and grimly realistic territory: on a snowy back road with the lead characters suffering car problems. Horror indeed! Levy and Martin provide lots of pre-*SCTV* laughs and are impressive in their largely improvised performances. The gore is messy and unprofessional, as it should be, and there's a butcher character (played by an actor called, simply, "Kingfish") who prefigures the similar meatsman played by *A Name for Evil*'s Clarence "Big" Miller in the later Can-classic *Big Meat Eater* ("Pleased to meet you, meat to please you!"). If Reitman and Goldberg hadn't consciously intended to make their film as diametric a contradiction as possible to sober, grim devil-cult movies like *The Pyx*, well, then, they might as well have.

Over a nine day marathon, Reitman, Goldberg and their crew, including director of photography Robert Saad, shot for sixteen hours a day. The main farmhouse location was provided by May Jarvis (of the wealthy Toronto Jarvises, the ones with the street named after them), who also played the chatty motel owner. Manfred Guthé, today a busy cinematographer but on *Cannibal Girls* a mere camera assistant, remembers the *Cannibal Girls* shoot as "fun but arduous… everybody was working together. It was a good film to work on." For continuity (since there was no real script to speak of), the filmmakers were forced to rent what at the time was known as a VTR machine: a video camera and deck. (This must have seemed very high-tech for a low-budget shoot—video assist systems, now commonplace, were only then first being put into use on large Hollywood projects.) Two special effects men were hired to provide the crude gore carnage, and one of them, happily, was a butcher. Real meat was therefore the main ingredient in the film's cannibal makeup effects.

When the primary chunk of shooting was done, the problems really began. It was quickly determined that more film needed to be shot in order to fill in some story holes. This was done with $5000 secured from an exhibition firm called Premier Operating, run by Barry Allen and Leonard Bernstein. Admits Reitman, "We actually made a big mistake at this point. We lost sight of our original goal, which was to make the thing fast even if it looked like shit. That's the key to making a profit in the exploitation market, but our artistic sensibilities got in the way."

Over the next year or so, using the last of the Premier Operating money and what remained of their tattered credit, Reitman and Goldberg's artistic sensibilities compelled them to shoot a number of extra scenes, which in turn obligated them to spend more time in the editing room and more money at the labs. In all they shot for fifteen days over and above the original nine-day run. Pathé continued to process their film, though Scary Pictures was paying them only a sixth of the bill rather than the half they had promised. Cinevision changed hands, and with that the equipment rental deal changed as well, and Reitman and Goldberg began getting massive bills which they could not pay. They had 75 minutes of film cut together, and in desperation they decided to go to the CFDC for funds to finish the picture and pay their creditors, some of whom were by this time threatening actual violence. Pathé was beginning to talk in terms of seizing the picture. There were other time pressures as well, since the filmmakers wanted to get the film finished for the Cannes market—their best chance to make a profitable sale—which was only two months away. The CFDC screening, Reitman thought, went very well. The CFDC board appeared to enjoy the movie immensely, and the filmmakers celebrated by borrowing $5,000 from Reitman's uncle to shoot the final sequences they needed to put the film together. This was done in the complete confidence that the CFDC would give them the $40,000 they had asked for, a sum that would see the picture finished and their debts paid. "And it was a great shoot," said Goldberg. "We did it all in three or four days and it was well planned out this time."

But when Reitman called Michael Spencer to get the CFDC decision, he told them that they had discussed the matter and come to the conclusion that the film wasn't commercial enough. (Spencer has no recollection of saying or thinking anything remotely like this.) This sentiment, whether real or imagined, bowled Reitman over: he thought he'd made the most commercial film in the history of Canadian cinema. But for whatever reason (the memory of losing money on *Foxy Lady* being perhaps a part of it), the upshot was that the CFDC had declined to take any part in the *Cannibal Girls* financing

Cannibal Girls

picture. "I was really shattered," says Reitman. "We can laugh about it now, but I couldn't talk for about half a day." The youngsters had what they called "a series of showdown meetings" with their creditors and somehow convinced them to hold off for just a little while longer.

In the hunt for money, they met a strip-joint owner who was looking for a tax shelter for his profits. (The 100% Capital Cost Allowance, allowing every penny of a film investment to go untaxed, was still some years away.) They hoped to get the $40,000 they needed from him, but the strip-joint owner's accountant counseled him to invest no more than $15,000. Reitman and Goldberg had no option but to accept.

On the strength of this, the pair borrowed still more money. They printed posters and stills in preparation for Cannes (the market and the competitive festival are coincidental but separate); they had a score written and recorded by their friend Doug Riley, and they prepared the opticals (the titles, dissolves, and so on), and began cutting the negative.

The negative cutting was being done by Pathé, but it was farmed out to a separate organization, and the optical house, Film Effects, was separate from that. Aware that Pathé was still in a position to seize the film if they didn't get paid, Goldberg took on the job of trucking the various reels of negative around from place to place, but he was careful to always keep one reel in his car so that Pathé would never have the whole film in their possession.

Meanwhile, in order to get the strip-joint owner's money, the legal mechanics of the deal required that Pathé, who were by this time *de facto* part owners of the film, give signed approval to the deal. Pathé would therefore need to be guaranteed priority in debt payment, and to that end signatures of permission from every single investor had to be collected. "It was incredible," remembers Goldberg. "We would owe someone five hundred dollars and we were able to get them to sign something saying they wouldn't get their five hundred dollars until Pathé got their money. People went along with it because they wanted the film to be finished—they would never get paid otherwise."

The releases were all signed and delivered as promised to the strip-joint owner's lawyer. It was the day Reitman was supposed to leave for Cannes with the film, and the strip-joint money was needed to finish it off. The strip-joint owner had a cheque for fifteen thousand dollars in his hand. The two youngsters could barely believe that their troubles were nearly over. But then the lawyer started asking for more documents—things that the two youngsters neither had nor could easily get, like waivers from the entire cast and crew, many of whom were out of the province or even the country. The strip-joint owner, despite genuinely wanting to make the deal, folded the cheque and put it back in his pocket.

Reitman, scheduled to leave for France in three hours but without a penny in his pocket or a plane ticket, was, he says, "a broken man. I was crying. It was one of the worst moments of my entire life." He went to his parents' house in this state, where his father, who'd suspected the whole time that the strip-joint deal would go sour, was waiting with a cheque for a thousand dollars. This was salvation, at least temporarily: enough money to get Reitman to Cannes with his publicity materials. The small problem of having no finished film would be Goldberg's to solve.

With Reitman in Cannes, putting up posters, distributing leaflets and hawking the film for all he was worth, Goldberg embarked on a game of chicken with Pathé. He convinced them to make an answer print of the film, but was still careful to always keep a couple of reels of the negative in the trunk of his car so that the film couldn't be seized. There were by this time so many claims and liens against the film that Goldberg had convinced himself that he would toss the reels off the Scarborough Bluffs without hesitation if it looked like they were going to lose control of the movie. This conviction helped his negotiating skills no end, since he operated now like a man with nothing left to lose, "like a crazy man," Goldberg recalls. He could walk into a Pathé office and tell them they could make the print and possibly recoup some money, or not, and be guaranteed to lose it all.

In Cannes, meanwhile, Reitman was making connections. He met Mordecai Richler, who was there to write an article about the festival, and Richler introduced Reitman to an American called Louis Hayward, known informally as Deke. Deke Hayward was vice-president of American International Pictures, Sam Arkoff's legendary and beloved B-movie factory. Hayward allowed that they might be interested in having a look at the picture, and Reitman assured him that it would be screening the next Monday.

But the film was far from being ready to screen on Monday. It was still in Toronto, in the possession of Film Effects, the optical company, who were not going to release the as-yet uncut negative to Goldberg until he came up with at least three thousand dollars.

The frantic producer convinced a friend with some credit to borrow that amount from his bank. He also called Harold Greenberg at a New York hotel, seeking assurance that Pathé would not try to seize the film. Greenberg granted this assurance. Goldberg picked up the negative and took it to the negative cutter, but always kept two reels in his car. As each reel was cut, he would drive it over to Pathé for printing. But now the lab wanted to seize the film after all. Greenberg's assurances meant nothing; he was in New York. The Pathé accountants only knew that Goldberg owed them $20,000, and to them the best way of recouping it was to force him to sign *Cannibal Girls* over to them. Goldberg, now in a state of high hysterics, reminded them that he had the two missing reels in his possession, and would toss them off a cliff at the slightest provocation. Time was running out: the film needed to be on an airplane for France the next day, and it had to leave through the National Film Board in Montreal. In the middle of this standoff, a call came from Harold Greenberg, instructing his accountants to let Goldberg and the film go on their way. Goldberg went out to his car and got the last two reels for printing. The lab staff had meanwhile been working hard to get the first chunk of the film printed and done. It was all finished by one o'clock that morning, and, after borrowing more money in order to pay for the advertising materials, Goldberg was on his way to Montreal. He got lost in the unfamiliar city, but eventually found the NFB building, gave them the print and the advertising materials, and *Cannibal Girls* was on its way to France.

Ivan Reitman

Reitman was having his own panic attacks in Cannes. He was selling the film as enthusiastically as he could, but still with a cautious note in his voice in case the film never showed up. (Goldberg had sent a telegram from Montreal to indicate it was coming, but Reitman never received it.) He was in constant contact with the CFDC office in Cannes, since the organization was doing them the favour of flying the print over and helping it clear customs. This service would prove valuable: the film finally arrived in France on the day before it was scheduled to be screened for Deke Hayward and any other potential buyers. But it was a Sunday, and the customs office was closed on Sunday. So on Monday morning, with the screening set for midday, the CFDC officials helped guide the print through customs and to the movie theatre, where it arrived at ten minutes before noon.

The film played to an audience of nearly a hundred people, including Hayward and André Link. There was, Reitman recalls, "lots of laughing" from the crowd. But at the end of the screening, instead of beleaguering the waiting Reitman with offers, they all piled out into the street and were gone, Hayward included. Link, acquainted with Reitman, offered to help sell the film to the European territories in exchange for a fifteen percent commission. Reitman agreed.

Bumping into Hayward on the street "accidentally on purpose," Reitman was unprepared to hear the producer say "You know, about that film of yours: it's the biggest piece of shit I ever saw." Reitman parried with "That's great. How much you offering?" Hayward told him that Arkoff was coming to town the next week, and that he should probably see the movie because, although it was a piece of shit, Hayward thought it would "probably make a fortune." He advised Reitman to set up an "exclusive screening" for the cigar-chomping mogul. He did, but by the time Arkoff arrived in town, a number of other distributors were interested in seeing the picture too. Reitman sat them downstairs and kept the imposing Arkoff and Hayward up in the balcony by themselves. As the picture unspooled, Reitman recalls that "these other distributors are downstairs laughing away and helping me sell the film to A.I.P."

Hotel-room negotiations with Arkoff followed. He was interested, but not interested enough to make an offer so outrageously lucrative as to wipe away all the debt *Cannibal Girls* had accrued. It was nevertheless a respectable amount of money—a $50,000 advance and a percentage of the gross—and Reitman took it. He and Arkoff shook hands, and the U.S. deal was done. Piecemeal sales to other markets helped to further pay down Pathé and the other creditors.

A.I.P. made a few small changes to the film. They cut out some of the more violent shots to ensure an R rating in the U.S., and they added a William Castle-like sales gimmick. As the advertising copy explained:

> In order not to offend or horrify those in the audience of a squeamish or prudish disposition, the sound of a bell in the theatre will warn you when to close your eyes of turn away so that you may avoid witnessing certain scenes of an especially erotic or gruesome nature.

It wasn't quite a *Tingler* seat buzzer, or a trip down the Yellow Streak to Coward's Corner, but it was close. It certainly amused the film's makers: "The first time we heard it we went crazy laughing," said Goldberg. *Cannibal Girls* did decent business at drive-ins throughout the States, and played up in the home and native land as well, grossing $25,000 in its first week of release in Toronto. Altogether in North America over the first two months, the film made over $300,000. The reviews were not so good. The influential *Variety*—a publication so often referred to as "the show business bible" that one expects to see that in their banner—tarred the picture as "a misguided, amateurish effort which hits upon a gory idea and gets nowhere in the process." *Interview* magazine reviewed the film simply by stating that "*Cannibal Girls* was directed by Ivan Reitman and the screenplay was done by Robert Sandler. As of this writing these two gentlemen were still at large."

Reitman and Goldberg, along with Joe Medjuck, who interviewed them for *Take One*, are still very much at large in Hollywood, producing juvenile comedies like *Road Trip*, *Old School* and *Euro Trip*. After the *Cannibal Girls* experience, Reitman had hooked up with André Link and John Dunning to become part of Cinépix, and as such to co-produce movies like *Shivers, Rabid, Death Weekend* and *Ilsa, Tigress of Siberia.*[19] After that he happened to produce a little movie called *Animal House* and direct one called *Meatballs*, and it was a short step from there to the set of *Ghostbusters*, his second and so far last horror-comedy. In 2003, a couple of years after spending 80 million dollars to make a failed sci-fi comedy called *Evolution*, Reitman returned to Canada in order to address the Canadian Film and Television Production Association, and the country at large, and take us all to task for failing to make sufficiently commercial movies, and to gloat a bit about his own success. "Since 1972, when I produced and directed *Cannibal Girls* for a cash budget of $12,000, I have directed and/or produced twenty-six movies. I was paid a salary on only three of these. Fortunately, these twenty-six movies grossed in excess of three billion dollars… U.S. Let's just say that my risks have been well rewarded."

The Corpse Eaters

But Reitman had a few positive things to say. He was certain that Canadians could make movies that were original, not "obscure, pretentious or dull." To a sea of gaping, doubtful faces, he asked, seemingly rhetorically, "Can a small budget production really find an audience out there?" Reitman himself provided the answer. "Well it absolutely can. It has happened to me a number of times.

"Look within yourselves for stories and ideas that move you," he instructed. "Look outside these borders when you contemplate your potential audience. Countries do not produce Art. It is created in the fertile minds of individuals who must follow their inspiration unfettered by any nationalistic dogma.

"Don't overlook and don't miss the real talent that lies within our borders. Don't be distracted by focusing too much on the wrong stuff. Think positive, think big, think fresh; think about whom you are working for. Think how proud and happy you will be standing at the back of a theatre and watching a film that is wonderful that you've created.

"Surely that is the greatest joy offered by this work."

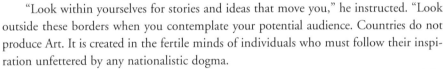

THESE WORDS, OR WORDS MUCH LIKE THEM, rang in the head of Sudbury, Ontario filmmaker Lawrence Zazelenchuk thirty years before they were spoken by Reitman. The "greatest joy" Reitman describes was a constant motivating force to the young horror fan, and he acted on it with an inspiring determination, if not with the greatest resources or results. But he made films, in Sudbury yet, and that in itself is impressive.

Among the most obscure Canadian horror films to have nevertheless had a theatrical release is Zazelenchuck's *The Corpse Eaters*. In fact, aside from *Creature of Comfort*, it just might be the rarest Canadian horror film ever made. But I speak too soon: rarer still, much rarer—lost, probably—are Zazelenchuck's earlier productions, *Attack of the Brain Demon* and *The Mummy's Rampage*. The first of these was a black and white film of about an hour in length, and it reportedly made Zazalenchuk enough money to buy the drive-in movie theatre on Route 69, just outside of Sudbury. Zazalenchuk then made his mummy picture on Super 8mm, but with sync sound. History has not recorded its running time, or many more details about it for that matter. The entrepreneurial film-maker also made a five minute short on the subject of Halloween.

Zazalenchuk was in his late teens at the time he owned the drive-in, and he already had the beginnings of a drinking problem. But he loved movies, and horror movies in particular, and so he set about making what would be his magnum opus: a zombie picture called *The Corpse Eaters*. Zazelenchuck would be the writer and producer of the film, but he wanted a director to handle the nuts and bolts of making the movie. The ultimate authorship of the movie may certainly be ascribed to Zazalenchuk, however.

He was a dreamer, the young Zazalenchuk, and ambitious: he wanted none other than horror icon John Carradine to star in his film. His budget was only $36,000, which was a little low to attract even Carradine (whose late-career work would include *Vampire Hookers*, *Satan's Mistress*, *Evils of the Night* and *Billy the Kid vs. Dracula*, ultra-low budgets all), but it was an awful lot to Zazalenchuk, who had saved the money by working at the local nickel mine, Inco. Shooting began in the summer of 1973, with local actor Edmond LeBreton in the role intended for Carradine, and Zazalenchuk's high school friends filling out the other roles.

The film starts with a warning, much like the one appended by Samuel Arkoff to *Cannibal Girls*: a red spiral discombobulates us as a flat, reedy, slightly nasal voice (dare I guess that it's Zazalenchuk himself?) informs us that the film we are about to see contains scenes that may be too shocking for some. The voice promises that we will be given advance warning of grotesqueries to come: a shot of a man retching and a high-pitched, warbling whistle will tell those of us with shaky constitutions that it's time to turn away. We are given a quick example of what to watch for, and then the movie itself begins.

We're at the Happy Halo Mortuary, where the unctuous, straggle-haired owner is comforting a bereaved couple. Dr. Zaroff from the hospital calls: someone has just died and requires immediate embalming. "Looks like a bear attacked him," we are told. "His face is a mess." Bill, the embalmer on duty, consents to take care of the new client. "Kind of *like* those *hard-core* cases," the agreeable Bill admits. "*Bon appetit*," says the boss. "And Bill… not too much booze!" he adds, waggling a warning finger.

The boss walks through the graveyard, thinking bitter, unkind thoughts about the dead. "If they only knew what they look like!" he marvels about the corpses. "Dead people aren't as sweet as people like to remember them as being." And then, for some reason picking on the special bear attack case of that night, he gloats, "Probably deserved everything he got!"

The boss's musings are periodically interrupted by shots of Bill working on the bear-mauled body, which, far from having a messed-up face, has only a small cut which might easily have been inflicted by a careless razor-stroke. The boss returns to the mortuary, and together he and Bill stick some cotton in the corpse's cheeks. 'Any bastard'd look like an angel when I got through with 'im," brags the boss.

We dissolve to a quartet of young Ontarians driving their outboard boat around a lake as sprightly rock music warbles on the soundtrack. The two couples have a shore lunch and listen to acid rock on their radio. A pair of them start getting it on, and a beefy guy with a moustache who looks like Meathead from *All in the Family* pours Molson Export over his girlfriend's droopy bare breasts. (I happen to know at least one *Corpse Eaters* viewer who has stated that the retching guy and the warning whistle should by rights have shown up just before this scene.)

The Corpse Eaters

After this Sudbury-style soft-core interlude, the gang—Ritchie, his grumpy sister Lisa, her boyfriend Alan and Ritchie's gal Julie—must decide what to do with their evening. Rock and roll concerts are clearly out of the question, since that's all they've been doing for weeks. It's decided that a graveyard would be just the place to hang out. Ritchie, the Meathead figure, pipes up, "I've got some grass! We could really blow our minds there!" How horribly right he is.

By the time they drive to the graveyard, it's nearly dark. (It's actually the same dusky day-for-night as it will be for the rest of the film.) Like any good young Canadians, they keep a Coleman lantern and several sleeping bags rolled up in the trunk, and these are brought out for the trek among the tombstones. It starts to rain. They head for a crypt, the door to which is mysteriously ajar, and take shelter. For entertainment to pass the time while the weather clears up, Ritchie decides they should have a séance. It seems his uncle taught him some special words for raising the dead, shortly before he "disappeared pretty weirdly," according to Lisa.

He bids the other three to hold hands and "concentrate on something," then utters the words—the usual cod-Latin nonsense—and is dismayed when nothing happens. Turning a nearby crucifix upside-down proves the solution. The words are repeated, and this time something disconcerting and weird happens. No one can say just what it was, but all present are deeply unsettled. Ritchie straightens the crucifix and vows "I'll never do *that* again!"

At around this juncture the movie turns to slow motion as zombies burst into the crypt and dogpile all over poor Ritchie. He's badly bitten and the others drag him out and try to make a run to the car. Julie, however, is overwhelmed by the cadavers and is pulled to the floor of the crypt for a good, no-nonsense, European-style gut-munching. The warning buzzer and retching man finally make their first appearance at this point.

Then we are treated to the sight of zombies partaking of a "Sudbury Special"—a pound or two of red-dyed weisswurst consumed off the stomach of a woman blitzed on Molson Ex.

The other three make their way to the car (a sweet '72 Challenger from the looks of it) and peel off. They take the gravely injured Ritchie to the hospital, where doctors are perplexed by the severity and character of his wounds. After letting Ritchie writhe and moan on a gurney for awhile without offering him a painkiller, they attempt to operate and fail miserably. Ritchie dies, or at least appears to. This is too much for Lisa, who falls into a faint.

While in her swoon, Lisa has a terrible dream in which a zombified Ritchie attacks her. She wakes up and hugs Alan, who is still wearing the same blood-soaked shirt he'd had on when they arrived at the hospital. We cut then to Ritchie at the Happy Halo Mortuary, and we realize that in fact most of the movie has been a flashback, and Ritchie was the corpse supposedly mauled by a bear. The bitter mortuary boss is getting drunk and grumping about all the paperwork he has to do. He hears a noise and stumbles downstairs. "Where is everybody?" he slurs, weaving around the empty coffins. The corpses have awoken, of course, and he finds them feasting gruesomely on a body. The movie gets a little confusing here, but the upshot seems to be that the mortuary owner is driven insane by the sight of the walking corpses and has to be incarcerated in the Sudbury Mental Hospital. The film ends with the maniacal laughter of the owner as he tries to persuade the orderlies that he's not crazy.

Donald Passmore and Klaus Vetter share the credit for directing *The Corpse Eaters*. For reasons that are unclear, Passmore was fired after four days of shooting and Vetter, who'd been hired to photograph the film, took over. Zazalenchuk didn't actually like Vetter all that much, but to the young producer he appeared to know what he was doing. The Super 16mm photography turned out to Zazalenchuk's satisfaction, at least. Filming took place in locations all around Sudbury, including Zazalenchuk's parents' bedroom. To their dismay, this was turned into the funeral home chapel in which the final eyeball-munching massacre takes place.

Zazalenchuk himself handled the film's makeup effects. His ghoul makeup is every bit as good as that of any of the Italian zombie pictures it precedes, and indeed is more convincing than the simple blue colouring used by Tom Savini for the background cadavers in *Dawn of the Dead* (1979). Zazalenchuk was particularly proud of one effect: a fake face he'd carved out of a pineapple. The gore effects were something else again— as in *Cannibal Girls*, real meat and animal parts, including sheep eyes, were used whenever possible. To cast the film's zombies, Zazalenchuk went down to what passed for a Skid Row in Sudbury and recruited the local bums. They went along with him happily, performing their roles with utter conviction. The only problems came when the hungry hobos ate up all the animal parts that were being used as gore.

When the shoot was over, like so many filmmakers before and after him, Zazalenchuck found that his paltry budget could not pay the lab costs. Eventually, through his drive-in, he raised the money, and the film enjoyed its world premiere screening at the 69 Drive-In on August 16, 1974, and a healthy run after that. Just as the initial run of George Romero's *Night of the Living Dead* attracted local ticket buyers simply by virtue of being the first movie made in Pittsburgh, so did *The Corpse Eaters* eventually attract almost every Sudburyan of movie-going age.

If Larry Zazalenchuk had one goal, it was for people to see *The Corpse Eaters*. So when some slickly-dressed New York distributors came knocking, offering him $5,000 for the North American rights, he jumped at the chance. But the New Yorkers were just sharpies looking for a tax write-off—they could make more money for themselves keeping *The Corpse Eaters* on the shelf and declaring it as a loss. And that's exactly what they did. Zazalenchuk was heartbroken about this callous eradication of his work, but there was nothing he could do about it. He sold his drive-in and bought a motel in Florida, against the advice of his friends, who knew that the best way to deal with a drinking problem and a broken heart was emphatically *not* to buy and move into a motel with a fully stocked lounge. But Zazalenchuk spent the rest of his short life in that Florida bar, drinking himself to death in short order after the effective disappearance of his film. He died in 1981 at the age of 36.

Seizure

There are further levels of disappearance concerning *The Corpse Eaters*. It seems to have suffered at the hands of the censors, reportedly losing such carnage as a meat cleaver cutting off a face in the climactic mortuary scene. (The film is still extremely gory, however: more so than *Cannibal Girls* and the first three David Cronenberg films combined.) After the cutting was finally done, the film's running time was reduced to a scant 57 minutes.

The film's life has recently been managed by Zazalenchuk's friend, an American video distributor named Dennis Atkinson, who came across the film's workprint at an auction and bought it. Atkinson has copies of the tape to sell, and from his customers has heard comments on the film like "It's a lost classic!" A new life for the picture seems to have begun: in August of 2003, it played to enthusiastic crowds at a small film festival in Gimli, Manitoba, and, just as soon as he can get his hands on the cut scenes, Atkinson plans to release it on DVD. According to Atkinson, the negative was rescued from the lab and now sits in the care of the National Archives of Canada, along with—potentially—the bits and pieces of censored footage, totaling approximately four minutes. I don't generally like to prognosticate on such matters, but in this case I firmly believe that a restored DVD edition of Lawrence Zazalenchuk's *The Corpse Eaters* can't be too far away.

NEXT DOOR TO ALL THIS BELLY-MUNCHING, a young American filmmaker named Oliver Stone was directing his first movie, a moody psychodrama called *Seizure*. Stone was twenty-six, and had already experienced a tour of duty in Vietnam, a stint at NYU film school (where Martin Scorsese was one of his teachers), and the experience of co-producing a New York-shot erotic thriller called *Sugar Cookies* when he and a friend called Jeffrey Kapelman raised the money to make *Seizure*. The pair showed Stone's NYU student work to groups of Canadian investors, and in this way slowly cobbled together $150,000 in cash. With deferments and other investments the final budget was $250,000, and the production set up shop in Val-Morin, Quebec to shoot the film in the fall of 1972.

The story had a successful horror writer suffering from hallucinatory intrusions by three of his own characters into his life. This occurs over a weekend in which he and his family are having guests, most of whom are slaughtered by the unholy fictional trio. The end of the film finds the writer waking up from what has apparently been a long and feverish dream, only to find that he's either still dreaming or he never really was to begin with. The script was written by Stone with Spanish producer, director and screenwriter Santos Alcocer, credited on the film as Edward Mann.

Stone and Kapelman (who produced the film) were beginners, and apparently it showed. "I don't think they had a firm grip on what it was like to run a production from a financial standpoint or a psychological standpoint," recalled Tom Brumberger, the film's New York-based special effects makeup artist. "They particularly didn't know how to handle the French Canadian crew, who were very volatile."

Veteran Quebec cinematographer (and sometime director) Roger Racine was one of these touchy Francophones. According to John Fasano, another American who, fifteen years on, would journey to Quebec to make his first feature film and use Racine's services as director of photography, Racine simply "wouldn't listen to my direction." Fasano reported also that the crew would often refuse to speak English and pretend not to understand his increasingly desperate instructions. Whether this particular sort of trickery was attempted on Stone is not known. In any case, the animosity appears to have gone both ways: Brumberger reports that "I found that Oliver created a certain tension on the set—an atmosphere I thought at first was an adverse environment to work in, and a good many others on the film felt that way. But I saw the film about a year and a half later, and realized that it was that intensity that made it work."

Stone had better luck with his cast, which, for an ultra-low budget horror film is extremely impressive. Jonathan Frid played the tortured writer, and the three homicidal fictions were played by Martine Beswick (a noted scream queen and veteran of several classic James Bond pictures), Hervé Villechaize (another one-time Bond villain, and also the film's still photographer) and Henry Baker, a gentle giant and amateur opera singer who, with Frid, had appeared on *Dark Shadows* several years previously. The cast also included Sixties heartthrob Troy Donahue, future *St. Elsewhere* nurse Christina Pickles, and the woman who will forever be known as Miss Togar from *Rock 'n' Roll High School*, Mary Woronov.[20]

Though he as much as disavows *Seizure* now, preferring to consider *Salvador* as his filmmaking debut, Stone was committed to the movie at the time of its making. "I gave my blood to it, along with every last dime I could raise," he told *Fangoria* magazine in 1981. But this was barely enough to get the film finished: "I cut the film myself, with an assistant, while living in a $40-a-night hotel room," Stone reports. "We eventually got chased out of Canada owing money, and I had to steal the answer print from the lab and run with it over the border to the U.S. in order to sell it."

The lab was Pathé, who by this time must have been getting used to young horror filmmakers covertly running off with prints. Harold Greenberg, Pathé's president, was in fact one of the film's principal investors, and through the parent company of which he was the owner, Astral Bellevue Pathé (later Astral Communications), was the Canadian distributor as well. Relations between the Americans and Canadians were never good, and this was exacerbated first by Stone's flight for the border and then a replay, with nationalities switched, of the events that doomed *The Corpse Eaters*. According to Stone, Astral was unwilling to properly distribute the film beyond using it as a second feature to support other low-budget schlock. "The reason this sort of thing happens," Stone explained to *Fangoria*, "is that these companies are owned by an element in Canada who call themselves 'tax shelter specialists.' They buy films for some ridiculously low figure, never pay, and then own them outright. Because they make their profit by deferring taxes for the year that the film was bought, they have no incentive to make any further profit from it. Now when a guy contacts me about getting the film to show in England, there's nothing I can do about it. I can't even get the Canadian assholes on the phone, or to cooperate in any way. There's nothing I can do—except express my rage."

Black Christmas director Bob Clark

Perhaps the thing to do is make a scathing film exposé about the whole affair. In any case, Stone was greatly dispirited by his *Seizure* experience. He was, he says, "totally disillusioned and spiritually depleted" with the business of directing feature films. He took a job with a sports film company and concentrated on screenwriting, not taking up the bullhorn again until 1981, with another horror film that has since slipped off his resumé, *The Hand*.

❦

THE STATE OF THE CANADIAN FILM INDUSTRY at this point, about six years after the creation of the CFDC, was, if not in outright crisis, certainly imagined to be so by a great percentage of the participants. The influx of government money had not resulted in the string of über-Canadian hits many had hoped for. Dissatisfaction was the prevailing mood, even though by the tax shelter era, only a half-dozen years away, the early Seventies would be regarded as a golden age for Canadian cinema. Summit meetings to address the problem were held in Winnipeg, with the first of them, held in the late winter of 1974, producing the Winnipeg Manifesto. The Manifesto demanded a "public production capacity" that would allow for full financing of Canadian feature films, a public distribution organization to disseminate the film locally and abroad, and quotas on the number of Canadian films shown in Canadian theatres. Denys Arcand, David Acomba (who would later make a not-bad zombie movie called *Night Life*) and Don Shebib were among the signatories.

The next year's Winnipeg meeting would be attended by David Cronenberg, in the period between the shooting and the release of *Shivers*. With such anti-commercial sentiment pervading the events, it's probably lucky that the attending filmmakers would not have known much at that time about the tyro horror director's soon-to-be-contentious first feature. There would have been some drunken name-calling in the Ramada Inn lounge for sure if they did, and maybe even some shoving. Knowing Canadian filmmakers, though, that's certainly as far as it would have gone.

In the wider world through the mid-Seventies, horror movies were experiencing a popularity they never had before. Big-budget movies like *The Exorcist*, *Jaws* and *The Omen* were packing audiences in, and the lower-budget end of things, held up by *It's Alive*, *The Texas Chainsaw Massacre*, *The Wicker Man* and *Suspiria*, was just as profitable, and much more interesting. Canada tried more and more to do its part, and while the results were often charming, they were also decidedly mixed.

Clark and Company

CALLING *The Night Walk* (a.k.a. *Deathdream*, *Dead of Night*, *The Veteran* and *The Night Andy Came Home*[21]) a Canadian film might be stretching a point slightly: after all, it was filmed in Florida by an all-Floridian cast and crew, is explicitly set in America and, at least on the surface, deals with particularly American themes. But the film was made as a three-way co-production between Canada, the United States and Britain (or, if not officially a co-production, then with financing for its approximately $300,000 budget coming from all three countries, but mostly from Canada) by a filmmaker, Bob Clark, who was shortly to become a naturalized Canadian, and is referred to over and over as a Canadian film in almost every book, article and website in which it is mentioned. So, taking the film's central premise to heart—which is to say that if you repeat something over and over enough with sufficient conviction, it simply becomes true—*The Night Walk* is, after *The Corpse Eaters*, the second Canadian zombie picture.

Clark, born in New Orleans in 1941, had in collaboration with writer/actor/special effects man Alan Ormsby made a small, culty picture called *Children Shouldn't Play with Dead Things*. The film was seen and picked up by a Canadian company called Quadrant Releasing (who had made a Florida connection by investing in two of maverick polyga-mist director Ted V. Mikels' films), and they approached Clark soon after with an offer to finance a new horror picture. Ormsby wrote the story and script in three weeks, and the production was soon under way.

The film begins in an unnamed but obvious war zone as a soldier, Andy (Richard Backus), is killed by enemy gunfire. Back home, his unsuspecting family—father Charlie (John Marley), mother Christine (Lynn Carlin) and sister Cathy (Anya Ormsby, Alan Ormsby's wife)—sit around the dinner table as Marley carves the roast. Carlin can't stop talking about her son, with whom she's clearly obsessed, and whom they haven't heard from in months. But Carlin's not worried—after all, Andy had promised he would come home, and Andy, a good, respectful American boy, has always kept his promises. A family friend in full dress uniform brings the bad news before dinner is even finished: Andy has been killed in action. As Marley sobs, Carlin retreats into complete denial. Marley later wakes up to find her in a rocking chair, repeating "You promised, Andy… you promised…"

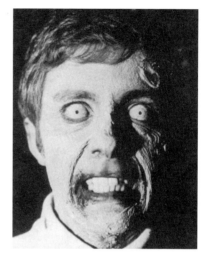

Dead or not, Andy is in the end a product of his family, and so obeys his mother. He hitches a ride with a trucker, who is later found dead, and appears at the family home later that night. Of course everyone is delighted to see him, especially Carlin, and when Backus insists that he has in fact been killed, the others take it as a joke and burst into raucous laughter. Andy isn't joking, though: he is certainly dead, and moreover has become a blood-drinking zombie. He's also become deeply unpleasant: he's rude, uncommunicative and mean (as though returning properly to the teen years his repressive, patriarchal upbringing never allowed him the first time around);

The Night Walk

and at one point he kills the family dog, Butchy, by crushing his throat with one hand.

He takes up hemogobbling again when he murders the family doctor, which is especially exigent because the doctor suspects Andy's involvement in the death of the trucker. Marley also has his suspicions, but he's a weak man and a drinker and is able to do very little about it. Andy takes to wearing sunglasses, black gloves and a nifty, Jim Jones-like outfit, which he dons to go double dating with his old girlfriend, his sister and her boyfriend. They go to a science-fiction double feature at the local drive-in, where Andy kills and drinks the blood of his girlfriend, strangles the sister's boyfriend as he had Butchy, and takes off in the car. By this time his skin has started to rot off, and it's left to a despairing Carlin to drive him, police in hot pursuit, to the grave he has prepared for himself.

The Veteran was Ormsby's original title for the script, but the Canadian producers felt it was too political in its implications. Their counter-suggestion was *The Night Andy Came Home*, which neither Ormsby nor Clark liked much. Then, finally, *Dead of Night* was agreed on, though reluctantly on the part of Ormsby, who remembered the 1945 British anthology film of the same name. *The Night Walk* was another title floating around at the same time, and only later, when the film started playing on television and home video, did the title *Deathdream* figure in the *melange*.

Whatever you want to call it, *The Night Walk* is an extremely good low-budget film. "Low budget" is not here used as a qualifier to the film's excellence; it's simply a fact readily apparent in every frame of the picture. But the imaginative realization of the themes and Clark's simple, intelligent direction resulted in an engaging piece of work that ultimately transcends any thoughts of scale or budget. Critic Robin Wood was much taken with the movie, offering this analysis:

> ...the concept is remarkable and rigorously worked out; the film accumulates tremendous force by the time its climactic sequences are reached... Few horror films have been so explicit about the monstrousness of patriarchal family structures... of Andy the son, the film offers (by presentation and implication) a double image: nice, unremarkable boy and devouring ghoul—a figure quite inadequate to sustain the ideological burden he is meant to carry... The film's ultimate insight is remarkable: that, under patriarchy, the patriarch suffers as much as anyone... The film is also a useful reminder that a radical statement about Vietnam must be a statement about much more.[22]

Wood's comments underline the dual citizenship of *The Night Walk*'s thematics, even if that duality is incidental. Explicitly American concerns, specifically the war in Vietnam, are enacted by very Canadian characters, particularly Marley's weakling father. Backus, in the meantime, is the respectful, deferential son poisoned by what superficially seems like some foreign influence picked up in battle, but in fact had its genesis right there in the home.

The cast helps flesh out the film's subtextual richness a great deal. Marley was an accomplished actor: he'd been nominated for an Academy Award two years before for his role in *Love Story*, he'd survived the experience of working for John Cassavetes in *Faces*, and he was the man who wakes up with the horse's head in *The Godfather*. Later in his career he appeared in the 1977 killer-auto film *The Car*, and Larry Cohen's fine 1978 sequel to his earlier hit *It's Alive*, called, naturally, *It Lives Again*. He looked a little like a short Rory Calhoun. His final role, just before dying during open heart surgery, was in the 1984 Canadian artificial-heart drama *Threshold*. Lynn Carlin, playing his wife, had previously appeared with Marley in Cassavetes' *Faces*, during which shoot the two actors had a remarkably hostile relationship, with Marley repeatedly accusing Carlin of not being able to act. Five years later, they were reunited in *The Night Walk*, hopefully on friendlier terms, but clearly using their former animosity in their scenes together. Veiled resentment is a common currency in any family, after all, so it could only have helped. Backus is good as the boy/ghoul, and Henderson Forsythe likewise competent as the doctor, and though a certain amateurishness pervades the rest of the supporting cast, the performances are nevertheless entirely serviceable.

In addition to writing the script, Alan Ormsby also supervised the film's makeup, assisted by a very young Tom Savini, here working on his first film. Ormsby later wrote films such as *My Bodyguard* and Paul Schrader's remake of *Cat People*, and also authored a book instructing young people on the fine art of movie makeup. Savini, the future special effects superstar (eventually famous enough to play himself in an episode of *The Simpsons*), got to do his very first bullet wound for the film, ultimately excised from the final cut. But Savini's work, along with the undeniable potency of the film as a whole, would lead it to become a beloved cult film in the years to come, with a remake from director Eli Roth, under both the *Dead of Night* and *Deathdream*

Deranged

monickers, announced in 2003, and a restored DVD release of the original film the year after.

Part of the financing deal through Quadrant involved doing all the post-production for the film in Canada. Clark went up to Toronto and instantly fell in love with the city, and indeed the entire country. The energy of Canada, which to Clark made the country feel younger in every respect than the U.S., intoxicated him, and the film industry in particular, suffused with the excitement and verve of youth, drew him in still further. He almost immediately arranged to move to Canada, and there he would stay for ten years. Even after repatriating to the U.S., he continues to work north of the border as much as possible, making talking-baby movies and the like.

Hot on the heels of *The Night Walk*—it was shot only a month or two later, in fact—came *Deranged*. Attending an industry convention in Kansas City called Show-A-Rama '72 in order to promote *Children Shouldn't Play with Dead Things*, Alan Ormsby met a concert promoter named Tom Karr who was eager to get into the film business. Karr had since childhood been fascinated with the story of Ed Gein, the notorious Wisconsin madman upon whom the stories for both *Psycho* and *The Texas Chainsaw Massacre* were based. Ormsby was keen to direct, and he took Karr back to Florida to meet up with Clark and Jeff Gillen, who had been *The Night Walk*'s first assistant director and also wanted to be a full-on director. After viewing *Children Shouldn't Play with Dead Things* and hearing about *The Night Walk*, Karr was sold on the group of filmmakers. Ormsby set about writing the screenplay, which was at first called *Necromania*. (The title was changed to *Deranged* about halfway through the shoot.)

Ormsby stuck closely to the Gein story, but added a strong dose of black humour to the brew. Karr was less than enthusiastic about this, feeling that the horror would thereby be diluted and the subject matter treated less reverentially than he thought appropriate. But Ormsby maintained that the humour was essential: first because telling the story exactly as it was with no leavening at all would simply be too grim, and also because the things Ed Gein had done were so strange and bizarre that, for Ormsby, they were very nearly already in the comedy arena.

Both Ormsby and Gillen were interested in directing the film, so Karr decreed that they could both do it. Clark, the natural choice for director, had only recently finished with *The Night Walk*, and was in no hurry to be typecast as a horror director; or at least not as a director of horror movies costing $200,000 or under. He had his eye on bigger fish, and it was soon to pay off. He remained associated with *Deranged* as a sort of mentor. "Bob was, in essence, the executive producer," Gillen said in a 1994 interview. It was Clark's influence which helped bring the production to Canada. He was in the process of editing *The Night Walk*, and it seemed expedient to try and piggyback the post-production of *Deranged* onto the same editing deal. The story took place in winter, and so the lingering Canadian snows—along with the nascent tax shelter deals—were also a draw.

The story began with a grim-voiced on screen narrator—actor Les Carlson, here in the guise of a newspaper reporter and later to appear in Clark's *Black Christmas* and Cronenberg's *Videodrome*—introducing the story of simple-minded momma's boy Ezra Cobb. "It is a human horror story of ghastly proportions and… profound reverberations," Carlson warns us. Cobb, played by gaunt character actor Roberts Blossom, lives alone with his overbearing momma on an isolated farm. She dies of a massive, hilariously grotesque hemorrhage, but not before instilling in Ezra a profound misogyny and a general policy of isolationism.

Still lonely and pining for momma a year after her death, Ezra trucks down to the graveyard and disinters her. No beauty queen when she was alive, old Mrs. Cobb isn't looking any better for her year underground, and Ezra figures he's got a real job on his hands to fix momma up. According to Carlson's unctuous reporter, who keeps appearing on screen in Ezra's bedroom or just outside his house, Ezra hits on the idea of using real human skin to patch his mother up. He becomes first a body snatcher and then a murderer, graduating to the latter crime when, in a panic of chastity, he kills eccentric widow Marian Waldman after she puts on a séance and then tries to seduce him. Next, Ezra goes to a bar where mournful Stompin' Tom Connors tunes play on the juke box, gets drunk on whiskey sours and manages through subterfuge to bring a waitress to his house, at which point the movie's most terrifying scene occurs.

Ezra promises to drive the waitress home but takes her to his farmhouse instead and disappears inside on the pretext that he's "just gotta go git somethin'." After drumming her fingers on the dashboard for awhile, the impatient waitress ill-advisedly goes inside to find Ezra and discovers herself inside a house of horrors, with corpses, putrefying body parts and macabre items built from human remains littering every surface. Worse, she finds Ezra, by now dolled up in a wig, a shawl and a hideous mask made from a human face. In a scene nearly as intense as anything in *The Texas Chainsaw Massacre* (which, being similarly based on Ed Gein, had the same gruesome set dressing and costume elements), Ezra chases the terrified woman around before sitting her down at the dinner table to meet mother. The waitress keeps her head long enough to buy an opportunity to clobber Ezra on the head, but after she flings momma's corpse around the room, he gets mad enough to beat the poor woman to death with a nearby femur.

Ezra next becomes fixated on the girlfriend of the kid who lives next door. He kidnaps her from the hardware store where she works and, when she jumps from the back of his pick-up truck, chases her through the woods. (These scenes were meant to be intercut with shots of a deer, to show that, in Ezra's view, the humans he killed were little more than wild game. However, neither a real deer nor even stock footage of a deer were within the boundaries of the tight $200,000 budget.) He takes her back to his barn, strings her up and guts her, just as the next-door neighbors and the police arrive to see what's going on. The film ends in a chilling freeze-frame of the completely insane Ezra's laughing face.

Black Christmas

Deranged was shot near Oshawa, Ontario, in the late winter of 1973. Canadian thespians were cast in every role, including the lead, but when producer Karr arrived at the location, he found himself less than satisfied with the actor chosen to play Cobb. A quick casting session was set up in New York, and was reportedly attended by such young hopefuls as Harvey Keitel and Christopher Walken. Blossom was the last to audition, and though he at first seemed too old for the role, his look and sound were perfect, and he was cast. To the disquiet of the crew and the benefit of the film, he proved during shooting to be something of a method actor.

The film is at least as grim and certainly more graphically gruesome than *The Texas Chainsaw Massacre*. Tom Savini, working as the head of makeup now, would see to that. Les Carlson's narrator mitigates the horror somewhat—if you're particularly sensitive, his appearances are almost welcome. But for the most part, *Deranged* is a creepy, top-flight addition to the rural-psycho genre. Blossom's performance is faultless, and the direction by Ormsby and Gillen very effective. Ormsby's script alone was disturbing enough to get the company kicked off one of their rural locations after the devout farm family who owned the property got hold of a copy.

The completed picture was shopped around to a number of potential distributors, all of whom proclaimed it "too rough" for their tastes in exploitation. Eventually American-International, the unheralded and unwitting champions of early-Seventies Canadian horror, picked the film up. To secure an R rating, a scene of graphic excerebration (for which Savini used Jell-O as brains) was cut from the picture, along with bits of the climactic gutting scene. The film premiered in February, 1974, at the Mike Todd Theatre in Chicago and opened strongly, but failed to become the sensation the superficially similar *Texas Chainsaw Massacre* would when it was released in October of the same year. *Deranged* would later be released uncut on Karr's own video label, and in 2002 on DVD by MGM in its trimmed American-International version.

In the late 1960s, a designer-turned-writer called Roy Moore teamed up with a director named Timothy Bond, and together began making short films for the CBC. After making 14 of them, with an eye towards establishing themselves in the feature world—which Bond had earlier approached by writing a movie-of-the-week script for Universal called *She Cried Murder*—the two wrote a horror script called *The Babysitter*. The story was based on an urban legend they'd heard about a babysitter terrified by a series of phone calls later proving to have come from a killer who was inside the same house and calling from a separate line. (This exact concept, a quaint artifact since the invention of call display, eventually became the 1979 film *When A Stranger Calls*.) Financing for the film failed to come through, and the script sat dormant for almost four years. Moore and Bond had printed up two hundred and fifty copies of the script and sent them to every place they could think of, and one of them eventually found its way to the offices of Vision IV, a company run by Harvey Sherman, Dick Schouten and Bob Clark.

In the meantime, after presumably getting a return on their investment in *The Night Walk*, Quadrant Releasing were ready to partner up with Bob Clark on another horror picture. Schouten and Sherman optioned the babysitter script and had Moore rewrite it with sorority girls instead of children as the killer's targets. Moore worked at night on the script and, he says, managed to give himself a serious case of the willies. As there was no longer a babysitter in the story, the project needed a new title, and Moore came up with *Stop Me*.

It was under this title that Clark first read the screenplay. He saw its potential immediately, but reworked it somewhat, adding humour (the foul-mouthed sorority sister played by Margot Kidder is largely his creation, along with the tippling house mother, whose practice of hiding bottles in crafty spots throughout the house was based on Clark's Aunt Mabel) and smoothing out some of the brutality. The story of what would eventually be called *Black Christmas* was simple: A maniac whose face we cannot see (Clark used first-person shooting in the same way but long before John Carpenter used the same technique so successfully in *Halloween*) climbs the trellis of a sorority house and hides in the attic while the sisters are having their last party before Christmas break. We meet sensitive Jess, foul-mouthed alcoholic Barb, sweet-natured Claire, curly-haired Phyl, and Mrs. Mac, the aforementioned house mother. The psychotic makes a rather shockingly obscene phone call to the girls, as he has evidently done before (the sorority sisters call him "the moaner"), and then kills Claire with a plastic dry-cleaning bag as she packs her things for the Christmas break.

We meet more characters as Claire's disappearance becomes an issue: her boyfriend Chris, her prissy father Mr. Harrison, police lieutenant Fuller, a fatuous desk sergeant named Nash, and Jess's high-strung pianist boyfriend Peter. A killer is indeed loose: a little girl has been found murdered in the park. Mrs. Mac is killed by the attic-dwelling intruder, who is given to regular bouts of psychotic rage. The police put a trace on the sorority house phone to find out where the mysterious calls are coming from, and then, that night, the maniac kills first Barb and then Phyl, and Jess is left to face him. Evidence has pointed to Peter, and when he shows up at the house, breaking a window to get into the basement where Jess is hiding from the maniac, she brains him with a poker. The police arrive and take it for granted that Peter was the murderer. Jess is sedated and put to bed, but as soon as she is left alone, the attic door opens and the killer creeps out. Our last image is of the house from the outside as a telephone begins to ring.

Clark had ambitious casting plans. He wanted Bette Davis to play the drunken, cynical house mother, but she was unavailable. Edmond O'Brien, of the film *D.O.A.*, was chosen to play Lt. Fuller; but, tragically, he was in the advanced stages of Alzheimer's disease by the time of *Black Christmas*, and, as Clark has often and touchingly related, he took upwards of forty minutes to button his shirt in preparation for leaving his hotel room after arriving in Toronto to play the role. With a heavy heart, Clark knew he'd have to recast the Lt. Fuller part, and John Saxon (who had in fact been approached earlier to play the role before O'Brien was cast) flew in to take it. Olivia Hussey, winner of a Golden Globe for Most Promising Newcomer—Female, for her role in Franco Zeffirelli's hit *Romeo & Juliet*, was cast as Jess, and *2001: A Space Odyssey* star Keir Dullea came on for less than a week to play the role of the hypersensitive Peter.

Black Christmas

The rest of the cast shaped up like a who's who (or so it seems in retrospect) of Canadian talent. Margot Kidder, who had the year before played a pair of identical French Canadian twins in Brian DePalma's excellent *Sisters*, was perfectly cast as Barb; Andrea Martin, sufficiently recovered from her *Cannibal Girls* experience, was Phyl; Doug McGrath, famed from his role as one of the "beer-swilling proto-hosers"[23] in Don Shebib's archetypal Canadian classic *Goin' Down the Road* played Sergeant Nash; Art Hindle (seen playing hockey and wearing a giant fur coat) was Chris; and Toronto stage actress and Ezra Cobb victim in *Deranged*, Marian Waldman, was a fine replacement for Bette Davis as Mrs. Mac. Les Carlson, the high-comedy narrator in *Deranged*, wore a delightful shirt for his role as the phone company guy who traces the killer's calls.

The shoot went smoothly, though it took place during an unusually cold spell of weather. Art director Karen Bromley recalls that she bought her very first down parka during the making of the film—the night of the search party scene, filmed in Toronto's High Park, was the worst—but since frost, snow and ice played their own small roles in the story, it was not entirely unwelcome by Clark. Canada was a cold place, especially to a Floridian, but it was his new home and he would show it in all its frigid glory. He is helped in this in no small way by cinematographer Reginald Morris, who is somehow able to bleed Christmas lights and burnished oak interiors of all their customary coziness as the film progresses. (Their collaboration on *Black Christmas* inaugurated a working relationship between Clark and Morris that would last for at least fifteen years.)

The film was released in Canada in October of 1974, where it did very well. As they had done with *The Mask*, Warner Brothers picked up the distribution rights to the picture, but had more than a few concerns. "They decided that *Black Christmas* was a bad title, that people would think it was a blaxploitation movie about Santa Claus," claims John Saxon.

The film was held in limbo for almost a year, slapped with the movie-of-the-week title *Stranger in the House*, and finally given a cursory, limited release in the summer of 1975. It tanked. The film underwent more title changes: it was called *Silent Night, Evil Night* for a while, then was re-christened with its original handle. It never, however, became the barn-burner that its makers hoped for. "If it had done as well in the U.S. as it had in Canada, it would have been a huge hit," says Clark, "but it was a modest success at best."

Canadian critics were by and large unimpressed with the picture. Writing in the January, 1975 issue of *Cinema Canada*, Natalie Edwards called Clark's film "a browner's sycophantic effort to sidle up to lower U.S. taste for cheap thrills and fast cash." *Black Christmas* was, to Edwards, nothing more than an "anti-female stock horror caper." (Edwards thereby anticipated the flavour of the not unwarranted criticism that would dog the slasher movie genre in the future.) She was glad at least to note the presence of Doug McGrath in the cast, lauding him as "a man who can literally reek sex;" but she regretted that in Clark's film he was "relegated to a sexless boob-cop role." Nevertheless, "he made it a pleasure anyhow."

Given the open ending, the inadvertent establishment of slasher movie orthodoxy and the modicum of commercial auspice, investors offered Clark the chance to make a sequel. He thought seriously about this idea for a while, even coming up with a story and a title, *Halloween*. At around the same time, Clark was working with a young Kentucky-raised filmmaker named John Carpenter, who asked him if he was intending to make the sequel. Clark, tired of horror movies for the time being and wanting to expand his repertoire, told him no. A few years later, of course, *Halloween* would arrive to become the highest-grossing independent film of all time (when the term "independent" had some shred of meaning). Carpenter's film employed the P.O.V. shots of *Black Christmas* and a number of other stylistic tricks as well, but Clark, who seems an easy-going sort, doesn't feel ripped off or copied. He correctly points out that there are as many or more dissimilarities as similarities between *Halloween* and anything Clark had done or might have done. *Halloween* is a good solid thriller in its own right, of course, and in its time was a phenomenon as much as a movie; and its major connection with Canadian horror films is its co-spawning (with *Friday the 13th*) of the slasher boom of the early eighties. Canada, in the midst of a boom in lowbrow, faux-American production, would churn out many films which owe more to the *Halloween* juggernaut than *Halloween* does to *Black Christmas*. By 2003, there was further talk of a *Black Christmas* remake, as well as Eli Roth's remake of *The Night Walk* and a modern retelling of Clark's all-Florida extrava-ganza *Children Shouldn't Play With Dead Things*.

There were a few dramas to play out on the Canadian horror film scene before all that, however. The arrival of David Cronenberg on the scene would be only the first.

III.

"You should know how bad this movie is; after all, you paid for it"

(1975 –1977)

I N 1973, DAVID CRONENBERG was just another shell-headed youngster with wide lapels and a movie camera in his hand. He'd made several shorts and two very well regarded mid-length pictures, to be sure, but one has to pay the pickle man after all, and art movies like *Stereo* and *Crimes of the Future* just wouldn't do that, even in 1970s Toronto. Cronenberg had made a few short items for the CBC as well, but that wasn't a regular gig and in any case wasn't what he wanted to do with his life. Nor was working on other people's films. "There are a lot of people who say a guy like you should spend ten years carrying around Julian Roffman's film cans," Michael Spencer told him. But Cronenberg had grander plans for himself.

He'd spent the past ten years first observing and then participating in the Toronto film scene. In the mid-sixties he'd been very impressed with David Secter's University of Toronto production *Winter Kept Us Warm*, simply because he'd never really considered that films could be made on that level. They were mysterious things that just happened, like mountains or clouds, but now were being made before his eyes by people like himself; and when he watched Secter's film he was thrilled to see people and places he recognized on screen. "It was stunning to recognize yourself," he recalled to Chris Rodley

David Cronenberg
and his Bolex

in the excellent book-length interview *Cronenberg on Cronenberg*. "Like any minority."

It wasn't long before he picked up the camera. Two short films, *Transfer* and *From the Drain*, were the first results, shot with a Bolex camera on budgets measurable in the low three figures. *From the Drain* contained Cronenberg's first special effects sequence: two men are sitting in a bathtub and after a few minutes of Beckett-like conversation about a mysterious war, a plant creature emerges from the plug hole and strangles one of them. In making these films and showing them in group screenings with other Toronto filmmakers, Cronenberg found himself part of a community for the first time.

Cronenberg's next projects were on the level of the student features he'd admired a few years earlier. *Stereo*, shot less than a year after then-Justice Minister Pierre Trudeau's assertion that "there's no place for the state in the bedrooms of the nation," was a sixty-five minute, 35mm black-and-white opus concerning futuristic sex experiments conducted by the "Canadian Institute for Erotic Inquiry." *Crimes of the Future*, also sixty-five minutes in length but this time in colour, told the story of a cosmetics-provoked epidemic called Rouge's Malady. It was made in 1970, two years after *Stereo*. Both films are visually polished (shot silently on 35mm, a format which Cronenberg, having only the money for one or the other, chose over 16 mm with synchronized sound) and engaging and clever, and may yet remain the purest expressions of Cronenberg's bio-political concerns.

They were far from commercial enterprises, that much was sure, and they certainly weren't horror movies, or even the weird bio-horror-science-action hybrids the director would later make his province. But they were proof that Cronenberg was an honest-to-goodness filmmaker with a unique and intriguing vision, and there was certainly room for that on the Canadian film landscape. At this point, after all, there was still room for just about anything on the Canadian film landscape.

But, as Cronenberg points out, "*Stereo* and *Crimes of the Future* are not films one builds a career on, not in the sense of being a professional who earns a living making films." He was now certainly a filmmaker, if only because he could no longer envision himself doing anything else. He tried other things even so: he moved to France and began writing a novel, and also dabbled in sculpture. But he had a movie camera with him as well, and used it to make short, impressionistic documentaries for the CBC. A trip to Cannes helped settle his mind, even though the sideshow commerciality of feature filmmaking was at first repulsive to him. But Cronenberg didn't want to live in the avant-garde ghetto, and with the arrival of his daughter Cassandra, he now had a family to support. So the repulsion settled into resolution, and in 1972 he returned to Toronto and began writing a script called first *Orgy of the Blood Parasites*, later *The Parasite Murders*, and eventually *Shivers*.

The script was firmly in the arena—or the "drome"—we have come to know as "Cronenbergian." Coming from the pen of David Cronenberg as it did, this is understandable. But the purity of theme in this first feature ought to be enough to shut up critics who have since scorned his work in general as contrived or purposefully weird. Mutations with a purpose and diseases with a will are simply the subjects that interest him.

The *Parasite Murders* script took place in a sterile apartment block, Starliner Towers, which happens to house a mad scientist in the process of creating sentient, organ-like creatures whose jobs include eating the cancer off, say, a diseased liver, and then replacing the organ with its own body, spontaneously adapted to the purpose. But the creatures don't quite work out as planned: they cause homicidal horniness in their hosts, and escape *en masse* into the building, infecting its already hedonistic inhabitants. A doctor and his sexy nurse battle the scourge as best they can, but the story ends with a crowd of infected swingers nosing their cars out of the parking garage and towards the city, leaving the viewer to wonder: "It's the 70s. Will anyone notice?"

Shivers

As the script developed, Cronenberg made more short pieces for the CBC, including one about the Scarborough Bluffs. He was also doing some investigating: just what, Cronenberg wondered, was the state of the nation with regards to "filmmaking of the imagination"? As far as he could tell there was none. But then he found Cinépix, and André Link and John Dunning and was greatly impressed with their commitment to making "very sweet, gentle, lush softcore films with a lot of tits—great tits, actually." He was equally taken with the way Dunning and Link had made Quebec nationalism work for them: by including thematic elements of particular interest to the French Catholic mindset and ignoring any commercial concerns other than the bosoms, they had made their "maple-syrup porn" pictures runaway Quebec hits. Any business they did outside the province was gravy—but they got the gravy too (though mainly from Europe rather than the United States). Clearly, Cronenberg thought, these were the people for him.

In a bid to direct one of the Cinépix softcore epics, Cronenberg ran his avant-garde mini-features for Dunning, the more creative side of the team. Dunning liked the movies, and Cronenberg too, but didn't give him the job. (The film was called *Loving and Laughing*, and was ultimately directed by John Sole.) However, when Cronenberg showed him the *Parasite Murders* script, Dunning responded extremely well, knowing that a horror movie, rather than another Catholic sex farce, would be the best way to get Cinépix products into the puritanical United States. Dunning and Link took the script to the CFDC as the first stop in their funding drive. But there, Cronenberg says, "it was greeted with absolute revulsion and confusion." Michael Spencer, recalling the event, says merely that "We knew from the title that this would be a risky project."

It took nearly three years for the CFDC to agree to fund the picture. The CFDC was under regular attack from conservative columnists and members of the House of Commons for their participation in the Cinépix sex pictures, and now here was a film with at least as much sex and a large helping of grotesque violence on top of it. They also cited "script problems" as a factor. Cronenberg's filmmaking aspirations were not helped by the delay. "It took a lot of endurance to not go do something else," he says.

At a certain point—early 1974, to be precise—the temptation to do it *somewhere* else became overwhelming. Cronenberg sent the *Parasite Murders* script to a number of Hollywood companies, including Roger Corman's New World Pictures. After a while, with great fear and trembling, Cronenberg called up the Hollywood legend to ask if he'd liked it, and if he'd like to talk about making it. Cronenberg didn't speak to Corman himself, but an assistant to the producer responded enthusiastically: "Sure! Come on out! Roger would love to talk to you!"

This was the sun coming out after two years of rain. With his friend Norman Snider (later the co-writer of *Dead Ringers*), Cronenberg flew out to Los Angeles. For a Canadian boy, it was a revelation: "This was my first time there. It was late February, when the weather was absolutely dismal in Toronto. We got off the plane and, my God, the sun was shining and there were palm trees! We rented a Mustang convertible, listened to the Beach Boys and drove on the Santa Monica freeway with the wind in our hair and the music in our ears. We thought 'this is really it!'"

Cronenberg and Snider called up the Canadian creator of *Saturday Night Live*, Lorne Michaels, who was living in the Chateau Marmont, and persuaded him to let them stay there too. Moses Znaimer was in the room also, along with Michaels' wife Roz, and the time was filled with spirited discussions about the state of Canadian filmmaking and Cronenberg's efforts to fit in to it. Michaels made the baleful observation that "We thought we were going to be the first generation that was going to be able to stay home in Canada and do it." The subject turned to Cronenberg's problem in particular. After a long rant from Cronenberg about the bureaucracy of the CFDC and "funding by committee," Znaimer, who'd been putting down Cronenberg, his movie and his filmmaking aspirations in general, suggested that maybe the CFDC were blaming their refusal to participate on parliamentary heat because "they just don't want to hurt your feelings."

Shepherded by Alan Collins, a film editor of Cronenberg's acquaintance (he would later cut *The Brood*), the director made the rounds of low-budget film companies and parties. For this trip, Cronenberg had adopted a new method of self-presentation, which, in an echo of movie themes to come, he called "as without, so within." This basically meant dressing up in the spiffiest clothes he could afford in an attempt to appear professional and competent, and to attempt to reach a perfect equilibrium by matching one's exterior with the interior. Dressed according to this philosophy, he went to New World to see Corman, but the producer was having a root canal and quite literally couldn't talk to the young Canadian. One day, despite (or perhaps because of) their fancy car and clothing, Cronenberg and Snider were stopped by cops who assumed they were drug dealers. The cops looked in Cronenberg's mouth to see if he was "holding," and seemed quite disappointed to find nothing in there but tongue and teeth. (Had this been a scene in a Cronenberg film, the cops would have been stabbed by a penile protrusion emerging from his mouth, or else swallowed by a giant vagina.) At another point, Cronenberg visited and fell in love with Schwab's drugstore, the legendary Hollywood hangout. In the meantime, he enjoyed the parties, the sunshine, and the movie-loving attitude of everyone he met. His desire to live and work in Canada was being sorely tested.

He met Jon Davison, a producer who then worked for Corman, and asked him if it was crazy to want to make a low-budget horror movie. Davison, who would later produce Joe Dante's *Piranha*, said it was not. "What I mainly got from Corman's outfit and other people was interest and excitement and acceptance of this as just business as usual. And that's really what I needed." He also met Barbara Steele, an eerie horror queen who had appeared in the Mario Bava classic *Black Sunday* fourteen years earlier. As it happened, Jonathan Demme was renting Barbara Steele's beach house, and Cronenberg went there to hang out. As Cronenberg, Steele and Demme were sitting on the beach, and Cronenberg was relating the trouble he'd had getting *The Parasite Murders* financed, Demme revealed that he'd not only read the script but had had a visit from a Cinépix representative who had offered it to him to direct. Cronenberg blew his top. "To come 3000 miles to discover this betrayal!" he fumed. In a video interview on the Canadian video release of *Shivers*, Cronenberg assigns the blame for this not to Dunning and Link, but to Alfred Pariser, an associate of Dunning and Link's who would later help produce co-productions like *Full Circle* and *The Little Girl Who Lives Down the Lane*.

Shivers

Cronenberg returned immediately to his hometown ready to confront the Cinépix executives. But they greeted him with the news that the CFDC was ready to fund *Shivers* with Cronenberg as director. "There would likely be questions in the House of Commons," Spencer later wrote about the decision, "but we hoped it would be a profitable artistic investment." With $76,500 from the CFDC in its pockets (for a total budget of $179,000), and still called *The Parasite Murders*, the movie was moved into production. Locations were chosen in Montreal, principally a Nun's Island apartment complex.

"Suddenly I had fifteen days to learn how to make a movie," Cronenberg said. In reality he had much less: he had to figure it out before the film began its fifteen-day production schedule. The Cinépix strategy was to surround their neophyte director with more experienced people. Ivan Reitman, though he had originally found the script "disgusting," was given the job of line producer (the producer who works most closely and directly on the set with the director). Cronenberg was very grateful for this, because Reitman, who understood the hell of making movies, was unceasingly supportive, maintaining faith in the project even as Cronenberg's wavered. Cronenberg's emotions were on a roller coaster as it was: even as he was happy to have found a new direction for his art, he was devastated by his father's concurrent death; even as he was over the moon at having his first feature film see a green light, he was plunged into melancholy at the prospect of relinquishing complete authorship of the work.

Reitman's *Cannibal Girls* cinematographer, Robert Saad, was hired to shoot what was now called *Shivers*. It was the first time Cronenberg had not shot his own film himself; he seems, in fact, to have previously assumed that cinematography was simply a part of the director's job. As there had been few special effects movies made in Canada to this point, there was an understandable dearth of special effects personnel available. But here was a movie that featured monsters and gore, and not only that, but scenes of the monsters moving around beneath the skin of their victims. So the Cinépix people found Joe Blasco, a Los Angeles-based makeup man who had worked for many years doing Lawrence Welk's maquillage (where, Blasco joked, he'd had plenty of practice for horror movies). Blasco was evidently the right man for the job: he knew how to save a penny, yet was clever and artistic. Cronenberg himself designed the creatures (easy enough, since they look more or less like a piece of shit), and Blasco built them in his L.A. shop. In part so that future Canadian productions would have a local special effects person, a makeup artist named Suzanne Riou-Garand was hired for "almost nothing" to apprentice with Blasco.

The film was cast locally for the most part. Exceptions included British-born horror diva Barbara Steele, who was already a part of the film's history having been on the beach hearing the director rant about it, and Lynn Lowry, whom Cronenberg had seen in George Romero's *The Crazies*. Ivan Reitman went down to New York, lunched with Lowry, and brought her back up to Montreal for the shoot. Chicago-born Joe Silver was also recruited, and, partially by delivering many of his lines while eating, proved memorable enough to return in Cronenberg's next movie, *Rabid*. Silver also had the goriest death scene in the movie: set upon by parasites, he attempts to pull them off his increasingly bloody face with pliers.

The crew installed themselves in their Montreal apartment building location. Cronenberg lived in a suite that was also used by the effects team: his bed was often damp with fake blood. It was a giant step forward for Canadian films that a full suite for the special effects was even required—special makeup before this had been the butcher store leavings of *Cannibal Girls*, *Deranged*, *The Corpse Eaters* and the bird boots of *The Vulture*; effective enough, but hardly groundbreaking. Blasco's effects were not only new to the Canadian scene, they were relatively new to the world.[24]

The movie's sound was innovative in Canadian film as well. Dan Goldberg was *Shivers*'s sound supervisor, and for Cronenberg it was another area in which his film could stand apart from its countrymates:

> …we consciously tried to make it very real. We post-synched when we found that relative sound levels weren't right. It's not like other Canadian movies that were influenced by Grierson: the sound is recorded with a shotgun mike and however people do things, for example putting down a glass, then that's how it comes out. Danny had to create ambiance with his special effects. He did all the movement tracks; for example for people putting on coats he used a wet suit. There's a very strong resistance to illusion in Canadian film.[25]

Altogether, the movie was a grotesque and highly sexualized (though not in the least erotic) kick in the pants to Canadian cinema. Nothing like it had been seen before when it was released in October of 1975, and accordingly, nothing like the ensuing media uproar had been seen either. Cronenberg certainly wasn't prepared for it, and even Cinépix, who had weathered no small amount of criticism for their maple-syrup porn pictures, were somewhat taken aback.

It began when Cronenberg invited Robert Fulford, a journalist, film critic and avowed fan of *Stereo* and *Crimes of the Future*, to a screening of the newly finished feature. Fulford had a regular column in *Saturday Night* magazine in which he wrote about movies under the pseudonym "Marshall Delaney." He attended the screening and, diametrically confounding Cronenberg's naïve assumptions, came away aghast at what he considered an "atrocity."

Printed in the September issue of *Saturday Night*, rather unsportingly before the film had even been released, Delaney's reaction to the film went well beyond the territory of the typical film review. He politicized the CFDC's involvement in the picture in calculatedly incendiary, grossly oversimplified, tabloid-depth language, invoking the right-wing grassroots bugaboo of government wasteage to make his argument. *Shivers* was not merely "a repulsive film," it was "a repulsive film Canadians helped pay for." It was not simply "a disgrace," it was "a disgrace to everyone connected with it—including the taxpayers." The article was titled "You Should Know How Bad This Film Is. After All, You Paid For It." Delaney's damning conclusion is that "If using public money to produce films like *The Parasite Murders* is the only way that English Canada can have a film industry, then perhaps English Canada should not have a film industry." At the height of the article's hysteria, he laments that the CFDC was "a fine project betrayed and destroyed" by films like Cronenberg's. (Of course there *were* no films like Cronenberg's at the time, and I can only assume he means any genre project.)

Cronenberg making Shivers

In *The Globe and Mail*, Martin Knelman expressed similar sentiments, if slightly more restrained. He mainly stuck to blasting the film itself. Cronenberg responded to this with a letter to the paper in support of his movie as a work of thoughtful artistry and not just some dunderheaded slime-fest. In response to Delaney's tirade, Cronenberg was, at first, surprisingly sanguine. "Delaney's reaction seems perfectly legitimate: that he found the film repellent. I think he just was not capable of handling his own reaction to it and therefore became very hysterical. Unfortunately he had to bring the CFDC in and get distracted by using my film as a platform for an attack on the CFDC.

"Surely it's obvious that there should be room for every kind of film from every possible country—I mean anything that disturbs you is not Canadian. It should be nice and somewhat serious if it's Canadian; that's the same old bullshit which has produced so many deadly films."

André Link was not so restrained, penning an open letter in *Cinema Canada* titled "Delaney's Dreary Denegration." Speaking as an immigrant, Link expressed surprise at the "Canadian attitude of super criticism of all things Canadian," and branded Delaney's article an "untrue representation of the facts" showing "questionable judgement." It was "vile and vicious, and most of all, very opportunistic." Link boasted of the picture's appearance at the Edinburgh Film Festival (little knowing that this is where influential critic Robin Wood would see the picture and first develop his dislike for Cronenberg and his movies) and of its worldwide sales. "I regret that there are not more films like *The Parasite Murders* being made," he stated, and in conclusion, hinted that the negative publicity may send Cronenberg packing for friendlier climes if we all weren't careful. "Let us not forget that there are a great number of successful Canadians in the film world who are prospering, and it is perhaps no coincidence that they are not in Canada. Do we have to send them all away?"

Not all the Canadian notices were bad. *Cinema Canada*'s Maurice Yacowar thought perhaps that *Shivers* was "Canada's *Exorcist*," and generally cheered its arrival on the scene. *Take One*'s Joe Medjuck put the film on his Ten Best list for 1975. In America, *Variety* published the sort of review that may perhaps be considered a damning by faint praise, but nonetheless helped sell a few tickets: "*Shivers*, a low-budget Canadian production, is a silly but moderately effective chiller about creeping parasites." In Britain, *Time Out* noted that the film was "Misanthropic indeed, but the black humour and general inventiveness place it high above most contemporary horror pictures."

The film is reported to have paid back its CFDC investment handsomely, though it was certainly no *Exorcist* at the box office. Even still, *Cinema Canada* named it "the fastest recouping movie in the history of Canadian Cinema." Only Robert Fulford, who has not seen the picture since his Marshall Delaney days, claims it did not return its federal funding. "Contrary to what was reported, the CFDC received no money back from *Shivers*," he told me in 2003. Fulford's opinion on the picture has not changed in the years since he wrote the article which David Cronenberg estimated took a year off his professional life. Later Cronenberg's reaction to Fulford would mutate from resignation to apoplectic rage. "How dare he!" Cronenberg wrote in a 1977 letter to the *Globe and Mail* after being kicked out of his Kensington apartment as a direct result of Fulford's piece. "This man wanted to take away both my livelihood and the expression of my dreams and nightmares—a clean sweep."

In this Fulford did not succeed, even if that was his goal. (It was not.) Cronenberg would go on from *Shivers* to not only become a filmmaker who would express on film the blood and slime of his native land's subconscious as no one had done before, but also, ultimately, to become a filmmaker who, as he told *Rolling Stone* in 1991, really just does "what I fucking well want."

WILLIAM FRUET WAS A SOLID PART OF CANADIAN FILM HISTORY by the mid-Seventies. His script for Don Shebib's *Goin' Down the Road* alone assured this, but he'd also written Shebib's follow-up *Rip-Off* and David Acomba's *Slipstream*. In 1972, Fruet wrote and directed *Wedding in White*, which was taken by Canadian critics as proof that the nation's cinema had a new superstar whose destiny was quite obviously a career in solemn and serious-minded Canadian kitchen-sink drama. Much celebration was evident in magazines like *Cinema Canada* and *Take One*.

Canada's newest drama champion had been born in Lethbridge, Alberta in 1933. He left Alberta for Toronto at the age of 19 and enrolled in the Canadian Theatre School. His first film work was as an actor in future *Reincarnate* director Don Haldane's 1963 feature *Drylanders*. From Toronto, Fruet decamped to Los Angeles, where he worked on industrial films, attended U.C.L.A. and met Donald Shebib. Fruet lived in a cottage on the beach and passed the time writing and riding around on Shebib's skateboard. His homeland was never far from his thoughts, however: "I really got into Canada in California," he said.

Turd on a wire: the magical creatures of *Shivers*

He returned to Toronto in 1965. A few years later, hooking up with Shebib, he wrote *Goin' Down the Road*, leaping instantly into the CanCon pantheon. He followed this up with an attempt at a script based on a frightening experience he'd endured years before in Alberta. He and another man had been driving along a lonely highway at night, and were somehow caught up in a game of road tag with what appeared to be a carload of deranged rednecks. The thugs pitched stubby beer bottles at them, shouted angrily, and tried to run them off the road. Fruet and his friend barely escaped, and the future director was left wondering what might have happened if he'd been with a woman and the rednecks had caught them.

This horrifying scenario was still with him in the early 1970s, and after the success of *Goin' Down the Road*, he began to shape it into a script called *Death Weekend*. But then, in December of 1971, Sam Peckinpah's *Straw Dogs* had its controversial release, and Fruet could see nothing but the similarities between it and his own story of home invasion, rape and violent revenge. He dropped the idea and concentrated instead on a script called *Wedding in White*.

This movie, Fruet's directorial debut, starred Carol Kane (later to play the terrified babysitter in *When A Stranger Calls*) as a naïve young girl who is raped by her brother's army buddy in 1940s rural Canada, and Donald Pleasance (late of *Creature of Comfort*) as her bull headed father, who forces her to marry the rapist in an attempt to preserve the family from shame. Certainly it was a form of horror movie (and has been listed under that category in some reference sources), but not the sort with which this book is concerned.

The film was a critical success in Canada and Fruet was off to Cannes. But he quickly learned that you can't eat good reviews. "Virtually, I was broke," he recalls. "Here I am on my way to Cannes for the Director's Fortnight, and I don't even own a suitcase. I said 'I've got to do something, and I've got to do something commercial.' I had to make a niche in that market so they knew I could do other things." He dug the *Death Weekend* script out of the drawer, both in spite of and because of its similarities to *Straw Dogs*. "I changed it a little bit, because it was frighteningly close to *Straw Dogs*."

With the script and eighty dollars to his name, Fruet made the rounds to the Canadian companies likely to finance such a picture. This did not take long, since he could only think of two. "I went to Cinépix and Harold Greenberg," he says. "They both wanted it." It ended up as a Cinépix project with a half-million dollar budget, $250,000 of which came from the CFDC, and filming began in and around the Kleinburg studio in December of 1975. Alternate titles considered during the shoot included "Thanksgiving" and "Do or Die." Ivan Reitman, who had entered into a more permanent relationship with Cinépix after *Shivers*, was the producer and second unit director.

Brenda Vaccaro was chosen to play the lead character, a model who, against her better judgement, accepts an invitation for a dirty weekend from a wealthy dentist. The dentist, played by Chuck Shamata, owns a large house by a remote lake, but on the way there, Vaccaro's aggressive driving annoys a carload of thugs led by the intense Don Stroud. The thugs are left in a ditch, but manage to find Shamata's house. From there the weekend is most assuredly spoiled: the thugs wreck the place, rape Vaccaro, and humiliate, torment and finally kill Shamata. Vaccaro takes her revenge on the cretins one by one, slitting the throat of one, burning up another, luring a third to a death-by-quicksand (not a common substance in Ontario during the winter, I'd have thought), and eventually runs Stroud over with a car.

The casting of Vaccaro brought both rewards and problems. She was well-known from many TV and movie appearances, which was good, but in the period leading up to the production of *Death Weekend*, she was first nominated for a Best Supporting Actress Academy Award (for a movie called *Jacqueline Susann's Once Is Not Enough*) and then offered a lead role in a television series with a guaranteed salary even if series tanked. This was not so good. "She wanted out of that picture so bad," remembers Fruet. "Here she is stuck in the middle of this violent horror picture! Brenda Vaccaro became very, very difficult from that point on. I think we had four doubles for her… she wouldn't come out of her trailer half the time. She just tried in every way to sink the movie… which is a horrible experience for your second film."

"Ivan became bad guy, I became good guy, so we handled it that way," Fruet recalls, shaking his head and adding, "Good guy, bad guy, doesn't matter. Tough lady." But Vaccaro was not the only trouble on the *Death Weekend* set. There was a great deal of stunt driving both at the beginning and the end of the film, and part of Fruet's style was to get the camera in as close as he could to the action. Injuries abounded among the stunt and camera crews as well as the actors during the tumultuous final week of the shoot: a broken arm on one stuntman, a broken hand on another, and a third burned during the explosion sequence; a cameraman who barely escaped emasculation when Brenda Vaccaro stomped on the brakes of the car she was driving while he was riding on the hood ("No stuntdriver she," said this technician, an American expat: "I felt safer in Vietnam"); and actors with cracked ribs and faces cut by flying glass. Don Stroud was hit by a runaway car directly in his crotch. Fruet himself escaped more or less unharmed—physically, at least.

When *Death Weekend* was released in late 1975, it was greeted with an extraordinary chorus of what seemed like nothing more than hurt feelings from the small Canadian critical community. The reviews were for the most part vicious and spiteful, and rang with a righteous sense of betrayal. "It got quite a beating when it came out," says Fruet. "Because of course I'd done *Wedding in White* and written *Goin' Down the Road* and those kind of things, which had established me as one kind of filmmaker, and then I came along with this thing."

Death Weekend

Cinema Canada, which had taken on the role of Cronenberg's defender from the Marshall Delaney onslaught, published a review by Clive Denton which called *Death Weekend* "an ugly, vicious, downright shitty movie that will leave you in need of a shower." In daring to make the film, Fruet had "exiled himself from reasonable consideration for a long time to come." In *Take One*, an only slightly less injured reviewer complained that "In any terms other than the crassest economic, *Death Weekend* is almost a complete write-off." The conclusion was that "When the film isn't duplicitous, it is empty."

Piers Handling was one of the few to speak in Fruet's defence, arguing that *Death Weekend* was "all of a piece" with the director's previous work. The film went to the Sitges International Festival of Fantastic and Horror Cinema, where it won the Critic's Award and Fruet won a Best Screenplay award. But it was not enough—Fruet had been shunned, and though *Death Weekend* was financially successful and helped no end in building Fruet's career, he was never again a critical darling of the Canadian film establishment.

❦

DESPITE THE SUCCESS OF PICTURES LIKE *Black Christmas* and *Shivers*, horror was still a rarer sight in Canada than the wild wolverine. Small wonder, since being a Canadian horror filmmaker in the '70s was like being a Kennedy brother in the '60s. Assassins were everywhere, disguised as film critics and self-appointed guardians of the still-lonely redoubt that was Canadian culture, popping up to ladle Griersonite scorn over despised cine-quislings like Cronenberg and Fruet. Why was the negative response and consequent effect so strong, especially in William Fruet's case? The industry in

Canada was still tiny, and, so it seemed to many, the slightest wrong move was to invite disaster and the final cultural victory of the Americans. Playing the Americans' game was not going to carve out a Canadian niche as some argued: it was, rather, courting the invasion, and was only going to hasten a process more and more were seeing as inevitable. It was bad enough to have one of these traitorous abominations made at all; it was far worse when made by a previously loyal cultural mouthpiece like Fruet. So ran one line of thinking anyway.

A few semi-scary movies popped up here and there even so, like, for instance, *The Clown Murders*. This was the first feature by writer/director Martyn Burke, who went on to make such wonder-epics as *The Last Chase*, a post-apocalyptic action picture starring Lee Majors, and the 2002 Sylvester Stallone direct-to-video thriller *Avenging Angelo*. *The Clown Murders* was shot just outside of Toronto in the summer of 1975, cost only $135,000 (in part because it was shot on 16mm), and was released in September of the following year. It's a horror movie only for the last twenty-five minutes or so, but for that time it's an enjoyable pip. Even Clive Denton in *Cinema Canada* didn't mind it all that much, at least compared to *Death Weekend*, calling the clown picture "less repellent because more inept," and reported that "after *The Clown Murders* you only need to wash your hands."

The bulk of the picture concerns a quartet of pals in their forties (prefiguring the very similar quartet which would appear a year later in Peter Carter's *Rituals*, again including actor Gary Reineke) who mount an all-in-fun kidnapping caper of the wife (Susan Keller) of their arrogant, well-to-do buddy Lawrence Dane (also of *Rituals*). The joke goes sour when, to the astonishment of the foursome, the police, led by a determined Al Waxman, take the kidnapping seriously. Eventually the adventure takes them to a deserted farmhouse, where a demented killer in a clown mask decimates the group in classic one-by-one style with a shotgun, an electrified fence and some sharp farm implements. John Candy plays the most likable of the foursome and does an excellent job in the role. His big scene comes near the end, and involves rolling in the dirt and crying while wearing little but his skivvies. Candy was a fine comedian, of course, but for sheer dramatic acting, *The Clown Murders* certainly trumps anything Candy later did outside the comedy sphere, from the tear-stained climax of *Planes, Trains and Automobiles* to the shades-wearing sleazeball he plays in Oliver Stone's *JFK*.

And what about the West? Where were all the sea creature and Sasquatch films that practically demand to be made in such a topographically varied province as British Columbia? One might expect the great forests and mountains of British Columbia to be fertile ground for spooky subject matter. The Sasquatch alone has spawned dozens of films, but legends and stories of all sorts abound in the region. Sea monsters, lake monsters, forest demons, and mountain gods populate the province, and yet horror filmmakers have barely begun to explore its potential.

A Name for Evil had been shot there in 1970, and in Vancouver, in 1973, a horror-porn film called *Sexcula* went before the cameras. Costing something in the neighborhood of $85,000, *Sexcula* was credited to a director named "Bob Hollowich" (actually John

Holbrook, later the cinematographer of *Ghostkeeper*) and a producer named "Clarence Frog" (real name, Clarence Newfeld). Holbrook is co-credited under his real name for the music and the editing of the film, and a cinematographer named John Goode, credited as "Boris von Bonnie," lit and shot the 86 minute, full colour picture. Debbie Collins starred as Sexcula, Jamie Orlando appeared as Fellatingstein, and Tim Lowerie limned the intriguingly-named Orgie. The dual roles of "Gorilla" and "Logger" were played by someone named Bud Coal. Unfortunately, though the film was evidently finished, it was never released, and thirty years on it seems unlikely that it ever will be. That's a shame, since of all the sub-sub-sub genres in the world, Canadian horror porn must be among the most under-represented.

Death Weekend

While *A Name for Evil* and *Sexcula* might have helped the Wet Coast live up to its free-living reputation if the one had been released more widely and the other released at all, this hardly scratched the surface of the area's horror or even its general film production capacities. Vancouver and Victoria, cosmopolitan cities with both mountain and sea within easy reach, had been nearly bereft of any sort of commercial film production since the Quota days of the 1930s. No doubt this paints a rosy picture to present-day Vancouverites, who can't walk to their corner store without taking a three-block detour around the barricades and honeywagons of some American action drama; but in those days there were barely enough experienced people to crew a single feature film, and the sight of a traffic cone could only mean construction.

Vancouver experienced a low-budget production boom in the mid-1970s thanks to a CFDC-sponsored "special investment program" intended to kick-start a home-grown Western film industry. (A Quebec variant on this had in part financed *Shivers*.) The best known of the resulting B.C. mini-budget pictures is probably Zale Dalen's *Skip Tracer* (1977), the well-regarded tale of a Vancouver debt collector finding his humanity. A dearth of crew hobbled all these pictures, but elderly British film personnel, who had finished their careers and retired to British Columbia, were willing to coach the less seasoned Canadians, so when the CFDC opened their wallet to the West the region wasn't caught completely off guard.

A year before *Skip Tracer* came T. Y. Drake's *The Keeper*, the lone horror picture of the mid-70s micro-budget B.C. mini-boom. The film, starring none other than the legendary Hammer stalwart Christopher Lee, tells the tale of a greedy, half-mad asylum doctor known only as "The Keeper;" aptly named, as it turns out, since he *keeps* his patients and all their rich relatives under his mesmeric thrall in an ill-conceived bid to become "the richest and most powerful man in the world." In the meantime, any stray heirs or amateur sleuths who might get in the way are killed off by accidents. The Keeper's ambition is thwarted by a private detective and his undercover partner, a

Runyonesque anachronism of a shoeshine boy, a comedy-relief police inspector and a pair of giants, all of whom emote their screwball-comedy dialogue as though about to break into song. There are lots of scenes involving colourful hypnotic spirals (the best parts of the movie) and innumerable sequences of the tiresome police inspector blowing his stack. Everyone lives happily ever after at the end except The Keeper, who has been driven fully round the bend by his own patients, and one of the giants, who was in on the plot and is arrested by authorities.

Drake, born in 1936, had been a child radio actor for the CBC in Vancouver, and had moved with his family to California at the age of eleven. There he sang in a choir and got work in the movies as an extra. The music business was his next professional venture: Drake hooked up with Bob Shane and wrote songs for Shane's group, The Kingston Trio. Drake produced records, wrote more songs for other groups, spent three years starring on *The Andy Williams Show*, and soon was writing movie and television scripts. He wrote five episodes of the short-lived but well-regarded Michael Parks TV drama *Then Came Bronson*, wrote an award-winning episode of *The Psychiatrist* which was directed by a very young Steven Spielberg, and did some TV work for Gene Roddenberry. But Canada beckoned, and, in 1971, a little like Robert Culp in *A Name For Evil*, Drake retreated from the big city to live the country life on a farm near Nelson, B.C. He still needed to work occasionally, of course, and so periodically he went down to Los Angeles to take a writing job or two.

Several years later the CDFC Special Investment Program was announced, and a couple of would-be filmmakers, David Curnick and Donald Wilson, cooked up a low-budget horror story they intended to film. (Some years earlier, the two had managed to produce a film called *Chester Angus Ramsgood*, which, according to Robert Fothergill, dramatized "the sexual vicissitudes of a nincompoop.") Curnick was to be the director of the nascent horror project. In the final preparation before submitting the script to the CFDC, they gave it to Drake and paid him $500 to polish it up. Drake provided a complete rewrite, starting from the ground up. The application was rejected, so Curnick and Wilson decided that the only thing to do was reapply with Drake listed as the director instead.

They did so, and Drake, with his television writing and performing experience presumably considered a properly professional background, was accepted by the CFDC. But by harkening back to his first job as a child radio actor while rewriting the script, Drake had changed the movie considerably: no longer a simple horror story, it was now an ambitious send-up of 1940s radio drama, complete with intentionally over-the-top dramatics, campy comedy, absurd plotting and funny names. Either Curnick and Wilson didn't mind this, or else they felt they didn't have a choice. Either way, with a budget of $165,000 (from the CFDC and sundry investors) burning a hole in their collective pockets, the project was under way.

Casting was a priority now. Tell Schreiber, an American actor who had moved up to Canada with his family and stayed on after a divorce from his painter wife, was hired as the lead, Dick Driver. (Schreiber's son, Liev, would grow up to become one of the stars of Wes Craven's *Scream* series.) Drake's wife, Sally Gray, who had a good deal of television acting experience, played Mae B. Jones, Driver's undercover partner. Now-veteran Canadian actor Ian Tracey, then eleven years old, snagged his first movie role as the chipper shoeshiner. All this was well and good, but they still had to find a Keeper. Curnick, Wilson and Drake knew they needed a name actor, and to this end they scheduled the film so that the actor playing The Keeper would be required only for a day or two, and had budgeted a generous salary for this short time. Names were bandied about and agents contacted: Christopher Plummer, Ernest Borgnine, Vincent Price and Shelley Winters were all considered and approached, but the scheduling was always wrong. Christopher Lee's name came up. He was lower on the list because, though an accomplished and imposing horror actor, he was more of a cult figure from his Hammer appearances than a main-stream star. (Now, in the new millennium, after participating in both the *Star Wars* and *Lord of the Rings* series, he'd likely be beyond a micro-budget Canadian film's ambitions.) Lee was available and willing to do the part: it would be his first ever North American film appearance.

The Clown Murders

Sets for the film were built in the basement of a furniture store on 4ᵗʰ Avenue in Vancouver's Kitsilano area. The 16mm cinematography was by Doug McKay, at that time one of the more experienced people on the local film scene. (He would later shoot the outrageous sci-fi musical *Big Meat Eater*.) The film's shoot proceeded smoothly over nineteen days in October of 1975, with the reportedly genial Lee coming and going in his scheduled blink of an eye (seven days, to be precise) and greatly impressing Drake and the crew with his sonorous voice and gift for oratory. Lee showed the Canadians what true cinema tech-nique was, providing cutting points by making pauses in his movements and failing to blink in his close-ups. Al Razutis, an experimental filmmaker with a great deal of expe-rience in layering, degrading and otherwise optically transfiguring film footage, was hired to do the special effects, which he worked at in his little studio beneath the Granville Street bridge. Zale Dalen, director of *Skip Tracer*, was the film's sound recordist, and Vancouver animator Marv Newland (who had just completed his classic short *Bambi Meets Godzilla*) did the titles and other animation.

In the film as it exists today, the special effects mainly consist of spinning spirals, flashing lights and Lee's grinning face all sandwiched together, but Drake's visions of the hypnosis sequences were originally much more complex. Upon casting Lee, a horror veteran of countless films, he realized that there were miles of footage of the actor striking menacing poses, baring his teeth and glowering in Gothic surroundings. This could be layered in with the spirals and lights, giving the film production values well beyond its budget. But even getting the rights to use already-shot footage was beyond *The Keeper*'s budget, as it turned out. Also shunted to the sidelines were the wipes and dissolves and other optical tricks Drake intended to make the movie resemble an old

Charlie Chan picture, and the old but recognizable stock film music that would further underline its retro ambitions.

In the editing room, films are roughed out, looked at, re-cut, screened perhaps, re-cut and re-cut again. *The Keeper* was allowed only one or two passes on the editing table. There was simply no more money to continue. To keep their tax shelters intact, the film's investors were disinclined to release any rights to the picture and enable Drake to save up some money and finish it himself. Eventually, in 1982, the picture was released to the voracious home video market. Says Drake, "No one saw a dime."

The Keeper is a Canadian movie through and through: the very first shot is a close-up of a license plate explicitly identifying the locale as British Columbia. And, aside from the accidents to heirs that we only hear about, nobody dies or even gets very badly hurt: a hypnotized policeman who tumbles off the asylum roof while attempting to kill Dick Driver has suffered, we are assured, "only a few broken bones," and will be back on the beat soon. The film has Canuck-O-Vision down in spades: the milky brume over the picture, the hissy sound, the cheap sets. (Of course, defects of the sound and picture can be put down to the unavailability of finishing funds.) A French film-review website calls *The Keeper* "the longest ninety-six minutes I have ever spent in my life," which seems all the more damning given that the movie is only 88 minutes long. If nothing else, the movie helps bridge the twenty-year interregnum, between Julian Roffman's *The Mask* and the double shot of John Huston's *Phobia* and Cronenberg's *The Brood*, in Canadian psychotherapy-gone-wrong thrillers. That nobody asked for this gap to be bridged is wholly beside the point.

The problem, perhaps, is that the film was intended to be at least two things at once. Curnick and Wilson wanted a horror movie, and the presence of Lee in the title role ensured that horror was exactly what audiences would be expecting; whereas Drake was not interested in making a horror movie at all, preferring instead to revisit the spirit of the radio dramas he'd listened to and acted in as a child. And there wouldn't be anything wrong with that, but the friction between the parties involved and the low budget, hardly sufficient for a period production, militated against a satisfactory result. ("On a budget that limited, it's insane, you know?" Drake says of the whole enterprise.) To this day, Drake, denied his Hammer footage and special effects, as well as an opportunity to edit the film properly, calls *The Keeper* "basically an unfinished film from my point of view."

"A COUPLE WEEKS BEFORE WE STARTED SHOOTING *Rabid*," remembers producer Don Carmody, "he came to us, and he had dreamed up *The Brood* over the weekend or something, and had written a treatment. And he basically came to us begging *not* to do *Rabid*, but to do *The Brood* instead. And we all went 'This is crazy! You've got people growing out of shoulders and stuff. No way!'"

The "he" was of course David Cronenberg, and the "we all" were his production manager

Carmody and his producers, John Dunning, André Link and Ivan Reitman, all of whom were committed to the neo-vampire story Cronenberg had brought to them right after *Shivers*. So *Rabid*, Cronenberg's second feature, was a go whether the director wanted it or not. But work was work. After *Shivers* and all its attendant fallout, Cronenberg had faced nearly a year in the wilderness, with the CFDC reluctant to finance another of his films even though the first had become the most profitable film they'd yet been associated with.

Unable to get a feature financed, Cronenberg bided his time making short dramas for the CBC. The best of these, and the closest to his heart, was a comedy called *The Italian Machine*, about a wonderful Ducati motorbike coveted by three motorcycle-loving youths, but owned by a recalcitrant art collector played by Louis Negin. But while Cronenberg could have fun making half-hours for the Mother Corps, he knew that his most fundamental concerns—the politics of rot—would never get an airing outside the R-rated confines of feature films.

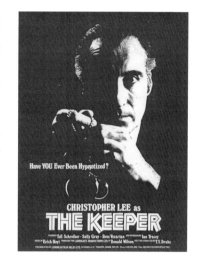

Have YOU Ever Been Hypnotized?

CHRISTOPHER LEE as
THE KEEPER

His association with Cinépix hadn't wavered through this period. He brought them the treatment for *Rabid*—then called "Mosquito"—and began working it into script form at John Dunning's summer house outside Montreal. The story told of a motorcycle crash victim named Rose, who is further victimized by doctors performing experimental surgery on her, and further still by subsequently becoming a vampire-like creature whose unearthly hungers are contagious. She inflicts all of Montreal with her plague before a *Night of the Living Dead* conclusion in which she is killed by an infected man and then dumped unceremoniously into a garbage truck by soldiers. It was essentially an expansion on *Shivers*. But this was the moment of Cronenberg's greatest self-doubt: halfway through the writing of the script, he remembers waking up one morning and telling Dunning "This is nuts! Do you realize what this is about? This woman grows a cock thing in her armpit and sucks people's blood with it! It's ridiculous! I can't do this. It's not going to work."

Cronenberg was, all of a sudden, convinced that audiences would simply laugh at a movie with a story like that. In his own words, like a child giving up her crayons, he'd "lost the magic." It took Dunning to talk him down from the conviction that *Rabid* would be thought absurd even by the most meat-and-potatoes of audiences. "There's something about it," Dunning told him. "It's compelling and weird." Dunning's absolute confidence in the project helped Cronenberg recapture some of the crucial magic, but even then he could bring himself to finish the script only with daily encouragement from Dunning and co-executive producer Ivan Reitman.

When the screenplay was done, Cinépix brought it to the CFDC, but after taking near-nuclear heat for financing a film about slug-like sexual parasites, they were less than eager to take on a project dealing with a woman bearing a phallic, bloodsucking spike in her armpit. But Michael Spencer was still at the helm, and he was not a man to let manifest talent (or proven box-office success) go unrecognized. Eventually the CFDC would put up $200,000 of the film's $530,000 budget, though, according to Cronenberg, "surreptitiously" by "cross-collateralizing it with another."

Casting the lead was now the main issue. Cronenberg had seen Terence Malick's *Badlands* and thought the film's young star, Sissy Spacek, would be good in *Rabid*. But Dunning and Link didn't like her Texan accent, and their exploitation muscles were twitching with the possibility of hiring porno starlet Marilyn Chambers, of the crossover hit *Behind the Green Door*, in her first "legitimate" picture. What press that would make! Besides that, she had a solid fan base, and if mainstream audiences could make a porno movie a hit, surely porn audiences could help make a horror movie go big. Ivan Reitman made the deal with Chambers and her menacing manager/husband Chuck Traynor, and the impending shoot of David Cronenberg's second feature was duly reported in the papers soon after.

This announcement had its down side for the director. Cronenberg's landlady had finally realized that not only was her tenant the notorious "Pasha of Pain" who had unleashed *Shivers* on the world, but he was about to bring a porno actress up to Canada to star in his next depraved production! This was too much for the landlady, and she kicked Cronenberg and his family out of his Kensington apartment and onto the street.

After a pre-production period in which Cronenberg was much more involved than he had been on *Shivers*, shooting on the new picture began in and around Montreal on the 1st of November, 1976. Cronenberg was pleasantly surprised by Chambers's acting skills. "She was a real trooper," he said, "and invented her own version of Method acting… I thought she really had talent, and expected her to go on and do other straight movies." The film's shoot went much as *Shivers* had, except the director had more self-confidence. Everything was on a larger scale than the previous picture: more actors, more action, more locations. Only the special effects were more restrained than before—there were no actual monsters, but there was some blood and the hideous spike in Chambers's armpit. Joe Blasco was again hired to to the special makeup, although this time he just manufactured the latex bits in his Los Angeles studio and sent them up to Montreal, where they were applied by a makeup artist named Byrd Holland.

The large-scale carnage and military presence in *Rabid* has something of an exaggerated October Crisis feel to it, with government officials explicitly condoning gunfire as an acceptable method of dealing with infected crowds. It's a bit like a horror version of Michel Brault's docudrama *Les Ordres*, right down to the occasional news camera feel of René Verzier's shooting. Cinépix, Cronenberg reports, were up to the challenge: "They loved the idea of doing something huge for no money." Don Carmody recalls a lively spirit of cooperation. "We all did everything," he says. "I was one of the producers, the production manager, I helped out in props, I dressed extras… We ended up getting rid of the first A.D. [Assistant Director] on the first or second day, and we couldn't get another one, so I did it for the whole rest of the shoot. I still tease David that I was the best first A.D. he ever had."

Rabid was released in April of 1977 to very profitable box-office and, Cronenberg says, "the usual complement of good and bad reviews." There were no *Saturday Night* articles calling for his head or for the immediate dissolution of the CFDC, but there was still no real sense of appreciation coming from Canada. Cronenberg complained that "When I was poor and esoteric, I was praised by the critics. Now that I'm making films that are a popular success, I'm panned or cast aside. There's a moral in there somewhere." Whatever the moral was, Cronenberg evidently decided to ignore it. His next picture would be in the decidedly un-Canadian drag-racing genre, and after that he would return to horror in the most stylistically traditional example of his career.

In the Woods

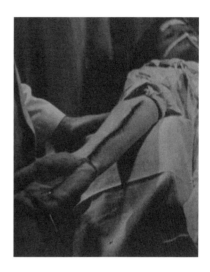

Rabid

THE HORROR POTENTIAL OF CANADA ITSELF, as a vast expanse of wilderness riddled with opportunities for the unwary to meet a violent doom, was finally explored in 1976 in Peter Carter's *Rituals*—called by some the "*Deliverance* of Wawa." Here, a quintet of doctors (Hal Holbrook, Lawrence Dane, Robin Gammell, Ken James and Gary Reineke) on their annual reunion outing are flown into a remote area of wilderness called the Cauldron of the Moon, through which they propose to hike until it's time to meet their plane again six days later.

Trouble first rears its head when the men find their shoes missing from their campsite after the first night in the bush. Reineke, who has organized the outing and made sure to bring extra shoes, dons them and takes off in search of a large dam he's seen on the map. The others wait, but are frightened that night by a deer head on a pole with a snake curling around it: a rough, backwoods approximation of an Aesculapius symbol, which, improbably, the doctors immediately recognize as such. They're encouraged by this discovery to wrap their feet in rags and tramp off in search of Reineke's dam.

Their next misfortune occurs when, in the midst of taking a group photograph, a wasp's nest lands on the ground nearby. They run off, but find themselves tumbling and rolling down a steep, sandy incline. Confusion rules the day, and the men are briefly separated. Collecting themselves, they find James' character, an amiable dope, dead of a broken neck. Did it happen in the fall, or was some force more sinister even than gravity behind it? No one can say, but Gammell claims to have seen a large human figure standing in the brush just before the accident. Unnerved, and already a heavy drinker, he takes to his flask with renewed conviction. The other two cover James with a sleeping bag, eulogizing him as "just a simple, gentle boob."

Using a rope thought to have been left by Reineke to ford a treacherous river, the medicos encounter their next pitfall. A submerged bear trap snaps shut on Gammell's ankle, breaking it and causing him to pull deeply from his bottomless flask in every single shot, rather than merely every second shot as before. Holbrook and Dane set the ankle ("Which way do you want your instep?" asks Holbrook), and fashion a stretcher to lug the alternately babbling and boozing Gammell down the river.

They spend the night at the crest of a hill and awake to find James' head on a pike. The outraged Holbrook flings it off the hill, but not before discovering an X-ray pinned to the pike, which leads him to conclude that the group is being stalked by a mad veteran who had been ill-treated at some point in his past by army doctors. The doctors' constant talk about their own medical blauchups—presumably overheard by the sawbones-hating psychopath—bears this up.

Finally reaching the dam, they find the dying Reineke chained to a chair and impaled by sticks through his legs. Holbrook deduces that this is a back-country replication of the traction suffered by the marauder at the hands of his own doctors. He strangles Reineke to put him out of his misery, and Dane, horrified, runs off. Gammell succumbs either to his wounds or to liver damage, and Holbrook staggers away.

Filthy and exhausted, he arrives at a broken-down cabin and collapses on a bed, believing himself finally safe. He finds an army medal and the missing boots, thinks about it for a minute, and almost immediately figures out just whose cabin he's in. The door opens and who should walk in but an absolutely unrecognizable Jack Creley, the old reincarnate himself, made up with an enormous false beard and milky contact lenses. Holbrook welcomes him to the cabin with an axe to the chest, but it transpires that Creley is not the killer; he has, in fact, been out trying to dissuade the real killer, his deformed brother Matthew, from the doctor-killing spree. Creley advises Holbrook to take off while he still can, then dies from his axe wound.

Holbrook hears stirring outside, and suddenly a knife slides in through the cabin wall and cuts a deep gash in his leg. There is shouting from the woods: it's Dane, captured, tied up and hung from a tree. As Holbrook prepares to cauterize his bleeding leg with a shotgun shell, Dane pleads for someone to come and unstring him, since the demented, grunting veteran is building a fire directly below. Holbrook, on the verge of fainting from blood loss, is in no shape to rescue anybody, and Dane is burned alive. Holbrook crawls to the window and sees a terrifying sight: the twisted madman dancing with joy as the suspended Dane burns in flames.

The murderous veteran tries to make his way into the cabin, and Holbrook blows his hand off with a shotgun. The door swings open, giving us our only good look at the creature, who is strongly reminiscent of the underworld denizen in the classic 1972 British picture *Raw Meat*: bearded, deformed and pitiable, but primal and horribly violent. With his remaining hand, the madman pulls off his dog tags and for some reason offers them to Holbrook, who responds by firing the shotgun. Our last view of Holbrook is as he sits on a deserted highway, waiting to hitch a lift back to civilization. By this time, though, he's sufficiently dirty, wounded, disheveled and crazed, not to mention clutching a shotgun. Frankly, his prospects for a ride look dim.

Rituals is, without a doubt, a classic among Canadian horror films. It's genuinely terrifying at several points and pleasantly homely in others, with all that tramping around the brush. The horror is excruciatingly realistic: since the killer is almost completely unseen for the bulk of the picture—there are a few p.o.v. shots reminiscent of *Black Christmas* and some eerie glimpses of the monster standing in silhouette on a faraway hill—the doctors' main adversary is the wilderness around them. Their shoes are gone, and shoes are well-known symbols, as well as dire necessities, of civilization. With no footwear, they're forced into a contact with nature they never would have asked for: bound by circumstance to evaluate every step of the land they walk over.

The horror in *Rituals* is based on reality, almost obsessively so. Nothing could be more Canadian—it's like a documentary about suffering in the woods. The low budget helps set it apart from its most obvious model, *Deliverance*; since very often a low budget movie is, like a man in the woods with no shoes, forced, willingly or otherwise, into close contact with the banal, the everyday—the real. Ian Sutherland, the film's screenwriter, went with art director Karen Bromley (who had lent her talents for reality to *Black Christmas* as well) to visit a reunion of the Canadian veterans of the Hong Kong defense campaign of 1941. These troops, desperately

Rituals

under-equipped, had been forced to surrender and were among the earliest prisoners of war in the Pacific conflict. They'd not been given an easy time of it. The veterans Sutherland and Bromley met that night in Toronto were old, but they'd gone through hell and it still showed. Some were crippled or disfigured from their illness and torture in the Japanese camps. Sutherland might ask them a question, and they'd respond, but if the question was too personal, too close to home, they answered with a joke. At around midnight Bromley left, but Sutherland stayed to hoist a few more jars with the old vets. Now they were ready to talk, and while little or nothing in particular from those conversations made it into *Rituals*, some flavour of that night with the mistreated veterans made it first into the screenplay and then into the movie.

In the beginning, Dane was set to play the film's lead, but even though he himself was the film's producer, the part was denied him. The executives holding the $660,000 purse strings, Robert Kantor and Harold Greenberg of Astral Films, felt that a recognizable star should be in the film, so Hal Holbrook was brought in and Dane relegated to the second lead, Mitzi. But Holbrook is good in his holier-than-thou role, and Dane well-suited to the part of Mitzi, so it all seems to have worked out for the best.

The film was shot just north of Sault Ste. Marie, Ontario, around Lake Superior's Batchawana Bay, and directed by British-born Peter Carter. Carter had worked for the CBC upon his mid-1950s arrival in Canada, and directed his first feature, *The Rowdyman*, in 1971, produced, like *Rituals*, by Lawrence Dane. Starring Gordon Pinsent as a jocular Newfie, it was a warmly-regarded entry in the Canadian Loser series of pictures typified by *Goin' Down the Road*. Like William Fruet, Carter saw that more broadly commercial work was required if he was to continue directing, and so his next picture, five years later, was *Rituals*. He would stay with genre filmmaking for the rest of his comparatively brief career, next directing a trucker picture with Peter Fonda, called *High-Ballin'*, and later making a made-for-TV *Alien* rip-off entitled *The Intruder Within*, about a slimy monster on board an oil rig. Carter's last movie was a Toronto-set comedy thriller called *Highpoint*; then, in 1982, at the age of forty-eight, he died of a heart attack.

Carter was a tough-minded man, and a yeller, but he was well-respected for his passion. It would certainly take such a man to make a movie like *Rituals*, in which the actors, and the crew along with them, were in real life having exactly as arduous a time as it looks like on screen. After several weeks of location shooting, the company moved to the Kleinburg studios to film the cabin interiors, and Holbrook, exhausted from his rigours, stepped onto the set for a look and promptly lay down on the cot and went to sleep. Art director Bromley, who had worked hard to make the set appear a place of refuge for the harried doctor, remembers this incident fondly as "one of the greatest compliments I ever got about a set from an actor… He thinks he's home, he thinks he's safe."

The film had its premiere screening at the Algoma Theatre in Sault Ste. Marie, Ontario, on the 21ˢᵗ of July, 1977. All the stars and crew attended. After going into wider release later on, *Rituals* got critical notices that went across the spectrum. There were favourable reviews, but it was rare to find one that didn't mention *Deliverance*. Ronald Blumer in *Cinema Canada* dismissed the picture as "not scary." It was re-released in the United States as *The Creeper* and promptly named "Dog of the Week" by TV film critics Siskel and Ebert. But a champion would emerge: none other than the wildly popular horror novelist Stephen King came forward to declare that he found *Rituals* a pretty darn effective scare picture. The film developed a small cult, and they live—or, I should say, *we* live—for the day when it will be once more released in theatres to get its proper due.

Co-prolites

BY THE LATE SEVENTIES, co-production treaties had been signed between Canada and a number of foreign lands, including Germany, Italy, France and Israel. The movies that resulted ran the gamut from some of the best, or at least most intriguing, of Canadian horrors, to some of the very worst.

France was a natural partner for co-productions out of Quebec, and a number of strange movies came of this marriage. *Cathy's Curse*, a sort of *Exorcist-Omen* hybrid financed in the main with francs, was filmed in the fall directly, and no doubt coincidentally, after *The Omen*'s very successful summer 1976 release. The movie, directed and produced mostly by personages of French, as opposed to Quebecois, extraction, was shot in Montreal and features a young girl, Cathy, apparently possessed by the vengeful spirit of her aunt, who had died twenty years earlier in a car wreck. Cathy has a creepy doll which itself seems able to channel some supernatural power or other, and like an evil

Mandrake the Magician, she goes about giving the members of her household traumat... hallucinations which cause violent deaths. The drunken handyman finds himself covered with imaginary spiders and snakes, the girl's anxiety-ridden mother is given food which rots before her eyes, and the nanny is sent flying out the second-story window. Cathy's father, meanwhile, is the sort of movie architect who puts on a construction helmet to hang out at his building site. He can't see anything wrong with Cathy, and is convinced that the numerous deaths and injuries in and around his house are simply a extraordinary run of bad luck. Finally Cathy's face turns bubbly and black and anything made of glass starts exploding. Cathy's mother rips the doll's eyes and everything is fine again. Poorly received, and no barn-burner at the box office, the picture attracted much critical commentary along the lines of this, from *The Aurum Encyclopedia of Horror*: "The uninspired direction and script devote a great deal of footage to showing cars driving up to the house and people getting in or out of them." The director of *Cathy's Curse*, Eddy Matalon, stayed in Montreal to mount his next production: a maniacs-escape-during-a-power-outage thriller called *Blackout*, starring Robert Carradine as one of the psychos and Ray Milland (of *Frogs* and *The Uncanny*) as The Irritable Old Man. It's not really a horror movie, but it's pretty good nonetheless—a good deal better than *Cathy's Curse*, at least.

Behind the scenes on *Rituals*, including Hal Holbrook (second from left), Peter Carter (third from right) and Lawrence Dane (far right)

And then there was *The Little Girl Who Lived Down the Lane*: another Canada/France co-production and another strange evil-little-girl picture. Frenchman Nicholas Gessner directed the movie, and the little girl of the title, Rynn Jacobs, was played by none other than Jodie Foster, shortly after her appearance in *Taxi Driver*. Her performance here is incredibly assured, even if the character is conceptually dubious: Rynn is a preternaturally mature girl who seems to live without parents or guardians of any kind and murders those who come too close to guessing her secret. Her secret, essentially, is that she murders all those who get too close to it—the secret, that is—and soon her cellar is full to bursting with corpses. But the townies keep making trouble. A child molester played by Martin Sheen sees in Rynn a sterling opportunity to ply his terrible trade, and Sheen's mother, the town busybody, is soon on the little girl's hit list as well. Only a magic-loving crippled boy played by Scott Jacoby can get close to her.

Like *The Pyx* and so many other movies in this book, *The Little Girl Who Lives Down the Lane* benefits from the imagery of cameraman René Verzier, and the Quebec locations (representing small-town New England) are properly bleak. 60 percent of the film's 1.1 million dollar budget came from Canada and the balance, like Verzier himself originally had, came from France. The film is slow-moving and odd and not terribly scary, but, mostly due to Foster's intelligently precocious performance and the maritime-autumnal atmosphere, it sticks in the memory.

co-pro, *The Uncanny*, though significantly less compelling than *The Little*
ves Down the Lane, got an awful lot of late-night Canadian airplay in the
made a permanent impression on the minds of the kids who stayed up to
nada/U.K. co-production (70 percent from Canada, 30 from the UK), made
story anthology format best exemplified by the classic *Dead of Night* (1945) and
eight of its popularity in the 1960s, *The Uncanny* begins with a skittish author,
ter Cushing, who is trying to persuade his publisher, Ray Milland, that his
cript proves beyond a shadow of a doubt that the world is secretly run by cats.
meant to illustrate this thesis follow.

The first is a standard-issue EC Comics revenge tale, set in Victorian England, in which a rich old cat lady is murdered by her maid in cahoots with her greedy nephew. Swift retribution at the paws of the cats follows: the maid is attacked before she can get her hands on the all-important will (which leaves everything to the kitties, natch) and driven into the pantry, where she's forced to subsist on stale bread smeared with the most hideous cat food ever shown on film. Tiring of this diet she breaks out, and, finding that the cats have been snacking on her late mistress, is summarily knocked down the stairs and scratched to ribbons by the growly felines. The nephew arrives to check things out, and immediately upon finding the corpses is himself turned into cat chow.

Milland remains unconvinced of Cushing's thesis, so a second tale must be told. The gaunt writer has one ready: some years ago, it seems, in "Quebec Province," a young orphan girl and her cat arrive to live with a heartless foster family. After a good deal of mistreatment, including a buzzing-by-model-airplane, the orphan uses witchcraft to shrink her principal tormentor, another little girl. After the cat has chased the cruel homunculus around for a while—occasioning much shoddy composite photography and a few oversized props—the orphan-girl-slash-sorceress steps on her. I'll always remember the moment when the mother comes in and irately cleans up her daughter's remains, thinking she's a spilled blob of red paint.

With Milland still skeptical even after such compelling proof as this, Cushing relates a final tale, this time set in 1930s Hollywood. A famed horror star, played by famed horror star Donald Pleasance, murders an actress so that his girlfriend (Samantha Eggar) can get a plum role in his latest film. Unfortunately for Pleasance, the murdered actress was very fond of her cat, and less fortunate still that Pleasance decides to drown all her kittens. It's not long before the bereaved momma kitty has her blood vengeance, leading inexorably to the movie's well-remembered climactic *bon mot* (intoned by John Vernon in a heavy accent) "What's the matter? Cat got your tongue?"

In the final segment of the wraparound story, Cushing leaves the house and is set upon by street cats who have been alerted to his whistle-blowing by Milland's prissy-looking white kitty. Milland, meanwhile, succumbs to the hypnotic gaze of the white cat and tosses Cushing's manuscript and all of his research into the fire. (Included among this research is a publicity photograph of Donald Pleasance in the role of Blofeld, posing with his own white cat on his lap in the 1967 James Bond thriller *You Only Live Twice*. It's really quite strange, especially considering that Pleasance's segment is meant to take place in the early 30s.)

The movie was produced by Milton Subotsky, who had produced many anthology films in Britain, none very good but almost all better than *The Uncanny* (the exception being 1980's *The Monster Club*, against which even *The Uncanny* looks like *Citizen Kane*). The film was made under the title *Claws* (*Jaws* was evidently still lingering in more than a few memories at the time), but released as *L'Irréel* in France, *Br-r-r!* in Quebec, and *The Uncanny* everywhere else.

Yet another Canada/U.K. co-production from the period was *Full Circle*, known also as *The Haunting of Julia*. Based on an early book by a pre-fame Peter Straub, the film starred Mia Farrow as a bereaved mother whose daughter chokes to death on an apple, and who is drawn into a shadowy world of ghosts as a result. Keir Dullea returned to the world of Canadian horror to play her husband—a role quite similar to his part in *Black Christmas*—and Tom Conti played a concerned friend. The film was shot in London by British director Richard Loncraine and a mostly British crew. Cinépix under-honcho Alfred Pariser was one of the producers.

Cathy's Curse

Perhaps the most astonishing product of the late-seventies co-production mania was a 1977 Italo-Canuck deal called *Yeti, The Giant of the 20th Century*. Much more Italian than it was Canadian, the picture nevertheless takes place largely in Toronto, featuring, as the title subtly hints, a giant Yeti monster on the rampage. Even the poster is deliriously bizarre, showing the massive snow monster peeking out from between the two curved towers of the new City Hall. The Yeti is captured somewhere in the Arctic by a doddering scientist, Professor Wasserman, and a ruthless businessman named Mr. Hunnicutt, reanimated from his frozen state while suspended in a phone booth hanging in mid-air, and brought to Hogtown for display. Naturally he breaks loose, having taken the time to fall in love with a girl named Jane, and, along with Jane's little brother Herbie and his loveable collie dog, the happy couple hightail it for the wilds of Ontario. But Professor Wasserman, who also happens to be Jane and Herbie's father, is murdered by Hunnicutt's corporate rivals. These nefarious blackguards also take the time to stab Herbie's dog to death (but don't worry: it gets revived later on). The yeti stomps on or otherwise crushes all the bad guys before returning to his home among the snows, but sadly, like so many Toronto tourists in a hurry, he never gets a chance to climb the CN Tower.

As insane as *Yeti, Giant of the 20th Century* is, the Canadian horror film world was about to get a good deal crazier. Here is where the prophesies of the doom-criers from 1968 finally came true, and to a degree never imagined by even the most pessimistic among them. At the same time, dozens of Canadian horror films that never would otherwise have been made, *were* made—for better and, often, for worse.

IV.

Slash for Cash

(1978–1982)

"HOLLYWOOD NORTH TIME," William Fruet calls it without very much affection, "when everybody was making films of every piece of junk that got rejected in the United States." The tax shelters actually began in 1975, when the loophole allowing for a 100% write-off on Canadian film investment was first introduced, but what has become known as the "tax shelter era" only began a few years later, after word of what was also known as the 100% Capital Cost Allowance had spread in the investment community. Doctors, dentists, architects: anyone who had a bit of money they wanted to protect from the greedy fingers of the government would shovel it into a film. The glamour of such an enterprise (as opposed to investing in a building or a widgit factory) made it all the more attractive.

The tax shelter period was a deeply ignoble time in Canadian history. Abuse was rampant; not just of the tax laws, but of cinema itself. Films were made the wrong way by the wrong people for the wrong reasons. As Fruet notes, there was a great deal of talk along the line of "Can't get the money to make Stupid Movie X in the States? Just go to Canada!" What follows in this account of the tax shelter's boom years will, due to the sheer number of movies made during this period, unavoidably come off as a simple, long litany of titles: some good, most bad, but almost all of them managing to have slid

A miner problem
in *My Bloody
Valentine*

a tendril or two into deep corners of the popular consciousness, or at least into my consciousness. These are the movies that helped destroy the 100% Capital Cost Allowance and undermined Canada's position in the film world simply by being so awful, yes, but they're also the films that are still fondly (sometimes over-fondly) remembered on web sites and journals around the world. The posters alone scared the dickens (or the bejeezus, or the crap) out of many. They're overwhelmingly wretched movies: stilted, inept, dramatically insubstantial, silly; ultimately little more than a monotonous succession of tortured *tableaux vivantes*. Why, then, do I love them so?

There's no easy answer. But it's important to step back and look at the bigger picture, and realize that, while films like *Humongous* and *Death Ship* are, not to put too fine a point on it, stink bombs of the very first caliber, they aren't any worse than most of the tax shelter dramas (*Circle of Two*), or comedies *(Crackers)*, or comedy-dramas (*Mr. Patman*) that slouched along beside them. In fact they're often better, have certainly lasted longer, and, very importantly, they're always a good deal more fun.

Equally important are the smaller details. The CCA horror crap-a-thon is not without its moments of arresting imagery: the killer's body plunging from the train trestle onto the ice and snow below in *Terror Train*; the desolate mountainscapes of *Ghostkeeper*; the rampaging wheelchair from *The Changeling*; the boogie van hurtling off the cliff in *Prom Night* and the haunting road-doll of *Curtains* all stick in the memory as much as any bit of film from the period.

But this is not an apologia for the tax shelter years, no matter how much ragged glory we might unearth there. It was not a project tragically poisoned by greed and poor filmmaking; it was a project destined from the outset by its very nature to attract greed and poor filmmaking—pre-poisoned, as it were, and no amount of praise heaped on *Atlantic City* or *The Grey Fox* will retroactively change that. It was really a miracle that any good films came out of it at all. The only possible approach to the tax-shelter movies at this point, twenty-five years later, is to love them as one would a wayward child or a jailbird uncle.

Happily we begin on a high note with David Cronenberg's first venture into tax boom terror, *The Brood*, which was and will probably always remain the director's most purely frightening horror picture, and one of the most personal and deeply felt films in the Tundra Terror canon. Because (by Canadian law, I believe) no discussion of *The Brood* can pass without mentioning this, I'll say right away that the story was born out of Cronenberg's traumatic divorce with his first wife and that the director has very often called it "my version of *Kramer vs. Kramer*."

After *Rabid*, Cronenberg was absent from the director's chair for almost two years. In the summer of 1978, the race-car devotee got a chance to make his dragster picture *Fast Company*, which was shot in Alberta for about $1,200,000, and had a tiny, almost certainly money-losing release in theatres the following May.[26] In the meantime, however, Cronenberg had returned to his pasture of terror, and by November of that year he was at work on *The Brood*.

Fast Company was an extremely important step in Cronenberg's professional development, as it marked his first collaboration with cinematographer Mark Irwin (who would shoot his next five films), editor Ronald Sanders (who has cut every Cronenberg picture since, except *The Brood*), and art director Carol Spier (who would design all his films up to, but not including, 2002's *Spider*). He carried the same crew into *The Brood*, with the crucial addition of composer Howard Shore, who continues to work with Cronenberg to this day while tackling huge assignments like Peter Jackson's *Lord of the Rings* trilogy on the side.

Shore, through his association with fellow Canadian Lorne Michaels, had been the musical director of *Saturday Night Live* in its early years; but before that he'd been one of the saxophone players in the jazz-rock group Lighthouse, and in that capacity had appeared in and so had helped to score *Dr. Frankenstein On Campus* back in 1969.

The Brood, the film Cronenberg wanted to make in 1976 instead of *Rabid*, concerns a divorced man, Frank Carveth (played rather blandly by Art Hindle), whose estranged wife (Samantha Eggar, of *A Name For Evil* and *The Uncanny*) is sequestered at the Somafree Institute, somewhere outside Toronto, and is undergoing a wacky

The Brood

sort of therapy called "Psychoplasmics." This technique has been developed by yet another of Cronenberg's tragically misguided scientists, Dr. Hal Raglan, played by Oliver Reed. Reed's hocus-pocus causes Eggar's rage to take the physical form of a troupe of mutant children in snowsuits. In a series of terrifying scenes, these entities pop out, grab whatever blunt instruments are handy, and hammer to death anyone Eggar hates, principally her parents, her ex-husband, a schoolteacher who is the supposed rival for his affection, and, ultimately, her psychoplasmacist, Reed.

At the subconscious behest of Eggar, the creatures kidnap her daughter, Candy, and sequester her in their quarters at the institute. Hindle drives out to get her back, and is persuaded by Reed to try and keep the increasingly irate Eggar calm while he ventures in to snatch the girl back. Hindle and Eggar engage in what may well be a verbatim recreation of conversations between Cronenberg and his own ex-wife (though probably without the giant embryo-sac and bloody fetus-licking) as the director recalls them. Reed, meanwhile, crashes what appears to be a pajama party in hell (never explained is just where the creatures get their sleepers and snowsuits), and tries to creep out with Candy before the snarling, growling little creatures catch the vibe of upsetness from their mother downstairs.

The background creatures were played by female gymnasts, while the foreground ones were essayed by little people in makeup (including Felix Silla, who had played creatures in *Don't Be Afraid of the Dark*, *Demon Seed* and *The Manitou*, and who was Twiki in the *Buck Rogers* TV series). Reed, by all accounts, very much enjoyed the scene in which the gymnasts pile on top of him and kill him. Makeup sessions for the "broodniks," as they were called by the crew, took upwards of three hours. Veteran makeup artist Jack Young and Canadian Dennis Pike were the artists responsible for the creatures' deeply creepy appearance, along with the carnage they inflict and the tumors and sores of other Psychoplasmics victims.

Anyone wishing to tar Cronenberg as a misogynist may as well start here. *The Brood* arose from a situation not unlike that depicted in the beginning of the movie, except, from the sounds of it, more extreme. Samantha Eggar's character is treated with very little compassion except to imply that her mother was just as bad a parent or worse, and her father was too weak-willed and ineffectual to stop the abuse. This is not used to excuse the Eggar character's behaviour, but what her own sins actually are remain vague, except that she is a woman governed by resentment, jealousy and selfishness rather than love, even, and perhaps especially, when her daughter is concerned.

In my opinion, one viewing of *The Brood* makes it plain that, rather than hating and fearing all women, Cronenberg hates and fears one woman in particular: his ex-wife. But even there, he doesn't allow the film, or his stand-in Carveth, go as far as they might have. When the director's surrogate strangles his hated spouse, for example, it's perhaps the most pathetic strangling ever put on film. There's as little violence as it is possible to have in a physical murder scene, and Hindle's hands seem barely to be in contact with Eggar's throat most of the time. A true woman-hater—and there are plenty of such people making films—would probably have had Hindle perform some graphically orgasmic stabbing or shooting instead. Still, Cronenberg has admitted that "Some of the violence in that movie was very cathartic for me to get on screen... I can't tell you how satisfying the climactic scene is. I wanted to strangle my ex-wife." Eggar, the proxy victim of the director's rage, would later tell Cronenberg she considered the picture to be "the strangest and most repulsive film I've ever done."

The Brood was released in 400 theatres across North America on 25 May, 1979, and in Toronto a week later. This was certainly Cronenberg's widest release yet—courtesy of Roger Corman's New World Pictures—but it came at the price of what to the director seemed a classless and misleading advertising campaign. According to the publicity, *The Brood* was not the complex family psychodrama Cronenberg had intended, but a gross monster movie whose narrative and subtext could be condensed into the tagline "They're Waiting... For You!" Actually the film is both of these things. The picture did well enough, but, as far as Cronenberg was concerned, it was with the wrong audience buying the tickets.

Worse was the treatment of the film at the hands of censors. The film was shorn of several violent moments and a long shot of Eggar licking the blood and slime off a newly-hatched Broodnik. (This was surely one of the moments she was recalling in her later remark to Cronenberg.) The director's glasses steam up to this day in discussing the censorship. "I could kill the censors for their narrow-mindedness and stupidity! Talk about rage!" he told Chris Rodley in *Cronenberg on Cronenberg*. Without happiness but with a certain perverse satisfaction, he notes the irony resulting from the trimmed foetus-licking: "When the censors, those animals, cut it out, the result was that a lot of people thought she was eating her baby. That's much worse than what I was suggesting. What we're talking about here is an image that's not sexual, not violent, just gooey—gooey and disturbing. It's a bitch licking her pups. Why cut it out?... It fucks the whole movie as far as I'm concerned." In a way, of course, it's a tribute to the power of Cronenberg's imagery, but that's of little comfort when nursing an injured movie. Cronenberg was less bloody but unbowed by the experience, his commitment to disturbing imagery defiantly unshaken.

Hell's Swells: High-Toned Horror

The Brood

IN 1970S HOLLYWOOD, horror meant ponderous, big-budget, star-filled terror spectaculars, often with titles beginning with "the." Prefigured by *Rosemary's Baby*, the up-market cycle came to full flower with *The Exorcist* in 1973, and continued with titles like *The Omen* (and its sequels), *Burnt Offerings*, *Audrey Rose*, *The Sentinel*, *The Legacy*, *The Amityville Horror* (written by Canadian Sandor Stern and starring Margot Kidder), and, a little later, Sidney Furie's *The Entity*. Aside from *The Pyx* (which, with its million-dollar budget, barely counts), Canada got into the act only once, right near the end of the trend, with *The Changeling* in 1979.

It's a "that's the one where..." type of movie: the kind people generally remember for one specific moment or image. Your friend may not know the title *The Changeling* (unless he or she is a scholar of Jacobean theatre), and their brow may yet be furrowed even when you mention George C. Scott or Trish Van Devere, but if you say "that's the one where the lady gets chased by that old-fashioned wheelchair," chances are that if they've ever seen it, they'll remember it. Horror starlet Neve Campbell is one who recollects the movie well. Interviewed in the *Ottawa Citizen*, she recalled that "I had a very traumatizing experience when I was 11. I watched a Canadian movie called *The Changeling*—Garth Drabinsky produced it—and it was the scariest thing I'd ever seen in my life. That movie still haunts me and I think part of it is that I believe in ghosts and spirits—after all, I'm Scottish."

Many besides Campbell were frightened by *The Changeling*'s mechanically precise and often routine scare scenes. The film stars George C. Scott as a composer whose wife and daughter are killed before his eyes in a road accident. To get over it he moves into the biggest, creepiest, most-likely-to-be-haunted house he can find. Little surprise registers on his face when the house indeed turns out to be haunted. He teams up with historical society representative Trish Van Devere (Scott's real-life wife at the time) and discovers, through investigative techniques ranging from simple book research to a séance, that the ghost in his house is that of a little crippled boy who was murdered by his father and subsequently replaced by a changeling who has become a rich and powerful senator played by Melvyn Douglas. Meanwhile the banging and whispering continues.

Clues lead Scott and Van Devere to an old well in the ground, where they find the bones of the murdered boy. Scott makes a few overtures to the senator, who assumes that he is being blackmailed and sends hard-ass cop John Colicos (who played an even harder-assed cop the same year in John Huston's *Phobia*) to dissuade Scott from his investigations. However, the ghost causes Colicos to crash his car and die, giving director Peter Medak a chance to pull off a neat shot which begins as a close-up of Colicos' face frozen in a death mask of terror and slowly pulls back and flips over to reveal that the cop's car is sitting upside-down in the middle of the road. Scott does eventually confront Douglas with the true facts of the case, and as the ghost releases his final fury (manifested by the rolling wheelchair, a swinging chandelier and the flaming destruction of the house), Douglas falls victim to a heart attack.

The script was by William Gray (later to write the substantially less swank, but more fun, *Prom Night* and *Humongous*) and Diana Maddox, and was based on a story by Russell Hunter. Not very many Canadians were involved in key positions. Besides the Hungarian-born, British-based Medak, the picture was very effectively designed by Trevor Williams, who created the haunted house by building a false, creepy façade over an existing Vancouver mansion, and it was edited by Lou Lombardo, the skilled cutter who had helped Sam Peckinpah make *The Wild Bunch* an action landmark. The beautiful, wintry photography, however, was by the Montreal-born cameraman John Coquillion.

It's a stodgy sort of picture, too self-consciously "classy" by half, and engineered rather than simply directed, but it does have a few effectively spooky sequences and a likeable central performance by Scott. The picture as a whole strongly recalls *Full Circle*, sharing many general aspects—a recently bereaved central character haunted by the ghost of a child—as well as particular moments. In both films, for example, there are affecting scenes in which the protagonists' agonized weeping for their lost family members are interrupted by mysterious noises from the beyond.

The movie was produced by Joel B. Michaels and, as Neve Campbell correctly points out, Garth Drabinsky. The pair had ventured into film production with *The Disappearance* and *The Silent Partner*; *The Changeling* would be their third major project and only horror film. It seemed a natural project for Drabinsky, who had battled polio as a child and very nearly had to spend his life in a wheelchair, like the vengeful ghost-child of the film. And yet, Drabinsky was able to live the good life like the changeling senator, so he could see both sides of the drama. Small wonder he should be willing to put together a nearly eight million dollar budget to make it into a movie.

A small scandal erupted around the bankrolling of the picture, however. (This is in retrospect a real surprise, since with Drabinsky involved one might reasonably expect the scandal to be huge.) To finance it, Drabinsky sold 264 shares in the film at $25,000 each; a normal enough practice except that some felt the prospectus put together by Drabinsky and Michaels' company had been rushed through its approval process by the

Ontario Securities Commission and not given the same scrutiny as other proposals. It might have been sour grapes which led to the complaints (the offence sounds pretty minor, unless there was actual corruption involved), or it might have been genuine favoritism. After almost a quarter century, with Drabinsky drowning in far more serious trouble, it doesn't really matter.

What we're left with is the movie, which got many good reviews and collected an awful lot of hardware at the first annual Genie awards, as well as the Golden Reel award for the biggest box-office the following year. It's an old-fashioned movie, to be sure, and this term was used both admiringly and pejoratively in various reviews. "Director Medak devotes an unconscionable amount of time to vistas of long, dull corridors and high-angle shots, which prove nothing except that they just don't build 12-foot high ceilings anymore. Too bad they don't revive that lost art and give up on this antique kind of moviemaking," said Richard Schickel in *Time*. *Variety*, however, called it a "superior haunted-house thriller;" and Charles Champlin of the *Los Angeles Times* lauded it as "a highly atmospheric and teasing mystery expertly assembled by

The Changeling

director Peter Medak." The film earned its Golden Reel by performing well in theatres across North America—well enough, in fact, to justify thoughts of a remake, still impending as of this writing.

This, then, would seem to be the crystallization of many Canadian hopes: a "quality" picture made through the tax shelter program, which collected American box-office dollars and good, or at least decent reviews (reviews in the American press at all were good enough for some) in equal measure. Never mind that the movie was set in Seattle (though filmed in and around Vancouver); never mind that its stars were American and its director and other key personnel British. This, after all, was the sort of country Canada was: the world's hostel, a young country with a cultural mosaic that changed as rapidly as one of the multi-screen gimmick films at Expo '67. It was only to be expected that the cast and crew lists of our movies should reflect our society; or so ran some opinions of the day. *The Changeling* certainly served to bolster this line of thought.

At the tail end of 1979, none other than John Huston arrived in Toronto to do the worst work of his career: namely making a gimmicky psycho-thriller called *Phobia*. The picture was co-written by a British writer called Jimmy Sangster, who is best known for his extensive work with Hammer Films in the Sixties. Sangster had written many of the company's Gothic horror outings, but also specialized in their mid-Sixties sub-*Psycho* cycle of films, which included *Paranoiac, Maniac, Nightmare* and *Hysteria*. All of these pictures strongly resemble not just *Psycho* but *Phobia* as well, so much so that Huston's film ends up seeming something of a throwback. The story involves a psychiatrist (played by ex-*Starsky and Hutch* actor and future director Paul Michael Glaser) whose specialty is treating phobias, particularly the phobias of a twitchy group of patients upon which he's testing his new method of therapy. No one should be surprised when the patients start dying at the hands of a maniac who employs methods derived from the patients' own phobias to kill them; nor yet when the maniac turns out to be the doctor himself, who suffers from a murderous phobia of people with phobias.

The film is more or less set in an undisguised Toronto, a fact given away by a scene in which the agoraphobe of the group has a panic attack in the midst of a group of mullet-haired hosers, another in which Glaser plays hockey without a helmet, and one in which the cops discourage one another from shooting a suspect on the run. ("Don't shoot! He's unarmed!" is not a line you typically hear from cops in American movies.) Glaser's character, despite his big sheepskin jacket, is identified as an American, perhaps because the filmmakers considered Toronto far too genteel a place to foster such a dangerous maniac.

For some, the best part of *Phobia* will be the nude scene by Lisa Langlois, one of Canada's minor but talented scream queens, who had acted for Claude Chabrol in *Blood Relatives* and would later appear in *Deadly Eyes* and *Happy Birthday to Me*. She was not terribly thrilled about appearing in her birthday suit: "Doing a nude scene affects the rest of your career," she said. But the self-imposed classiness of the project and the legendary status of its director won her over. "It was a very difficult decision to make, and I wouldn't have done the scene if it hadn't been John Huston directing."

But why did John Huston direct it? The tax shelter era is notorious for wringing the most godawful moviemaking out of generally talented people, and I suppose it's appropriate (and indeed, a testament to the corruptive power of the whole tax shelter phenomenon) that Huston, a master director then in the midst of a creative renaissance with films like *Wise Blood*, *Victory*[27] and *Under The Volcano*, should not fail to escape this curse. Since Toronto was the birthplace of his father Walter, and Huston still had kinfolk there, perhaps the visit to Toronto was more about returning home (a ritual to which Huston was heavily inclined) than about taking the greatest possible advantage of Canadian tax shelter laws by making a corny, old-fashioned psycho thriller.

Bells (released on video in the United States by Warner Bros. under the title *Murder By Phone*) was another kick at the classy horror cat. It was directed by yet another absurdly over-qualified foreigner: Michael Anderson, a veteran Brit whose credits included the original *1984* (featuring John Vernon's sonorous voice as Big Brother), *Around the World in 80 Days*, *The Quiller Memorandum* and the perpetually underrated *Logan's Run*. His last movie before *Bells* was the Canadian-set *Jaws* derivative *Orca*, a picture laden simultaneously with both atmosphere and absurdity. *Bells* tipped the scale on the absurd side, telling the story of a mad telecommunications company employee who has figured out a way to zap people over the telephone. His initial victim, killed randomly at a subway pay phone just to test the device, proves to be an ex-student of renegade science teacher Richard Chamberlain. He journeys to Toronto and becomes embroiled in the case, which is being covered up by the phone company and by

It started as a joke...

THE CLOWN MURDERS

Magnum International Productions Incorporated presents "The Clown Murders"

Starring:
Stephen Young
Susan Keller
Lawrence Dane

Special Guest Appearance By:
Al Waxman

Screenplay by:
Martyn Burke
Music by:
John Mills-Cockell
Directed by:
Martyn Burke

Produced by:
Christopher Dalton
Executive Producer:
J. Stephen Stohn

 An Astral Films Release

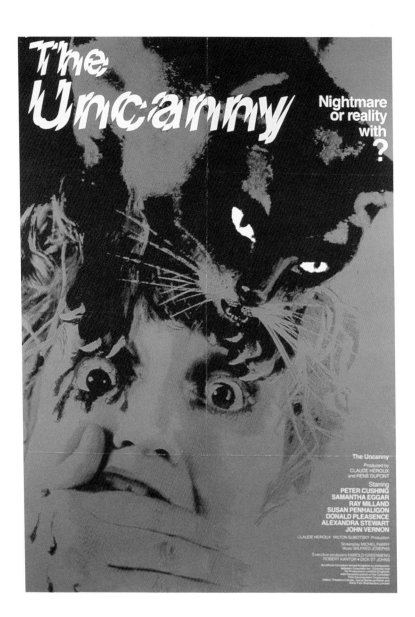

The Uncanny

Nightmare
or reality
with
?

The Uncanny

Produced by
CLAUDE HEROUX
and RENÉ DUPONT

Starring
PETER CUSHING
SAMANTHA EGGAR
RAY MILLAND
SUSAN PENHALIGON
DONALD PLEASENCE
ALEXANDRA STEWART
JOHN VERNON

CLAUDE HEROUX   MILTON SUBOTSKY Production

Screenplay MICHEL PARRY
Music WILFRED JOSEPHS

Executive producers HAROLD GREENBERG
ROBERT KANTOR • DICK ST JOHNS

An official Canadian-United Kingdom co-production
between Cinevideo Inc. (Canada) and
Tor Productions Limited (England)
with the participation of the Canadian
Film Development Corporation
Gibbon Theatres Canada, Astral Bellevue Pathé and
Rank Film Distributors Limited

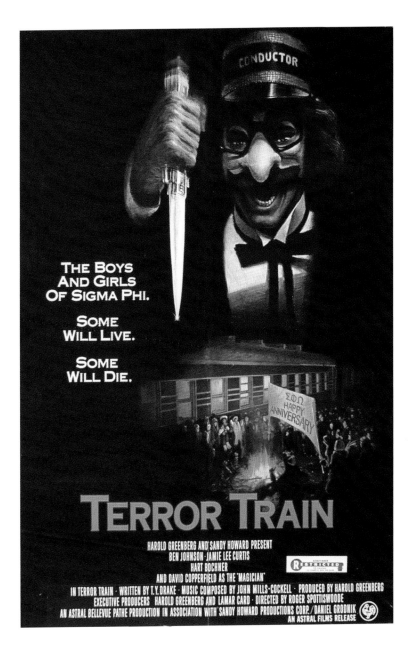

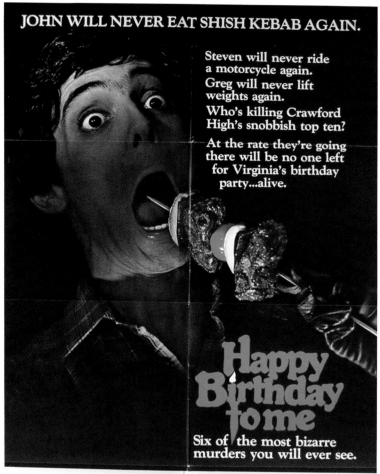

JOHN WILL NEVER EAT SHISH KEBAB AGAIN.

Steven will never ride
a motorcycle again.

Greg will never lift
weights again.

Who's killing Crawford
High's snobbish top ten?

At the rate they're going
there will be no one left
for Virginia's birthday
party...alive.

Happy
Birthday
to me

Six of the most bizarre
murders you will ever see.

COLUMBIA PICTURES PRESENTS
A JOHN DUNNING—ANDRÉ LINK PRODUCTION OF
Starring   A J. LEE THOMPSON FILM "HAPPY BIRTHDAY TO ME"
MELISSA SUE ANDERSON   GLENN FORD   LAWRENCE DANE   SHARON ACKER
FRANCES HYLAND   Introducing TRACY BREGMAN and LISA LANGLOIS
Associate Producer LARRY NESIS   Music by BO HARWOOD and LANCE RUBIN
Production Designer EARL PRESTON   Director of Photography MIKLOS LENTE, C.S.C.
Screenplay by JOHN SAXTON, PETER JOBIN and TIMOTHY BOND   Story by JOHN SAXTON
Line Producer STEWART HARDING   Produced by JOHN DUNNING and ANDRÉ LINK
R RESTRICTED   Directed by J. LEE THOMPSON

WARNING: BECAUSE OF THE BIZARRE NATURE OF THE PARTY,
NO ONE WILL BE SEATED DURING THE LAST TEN MINUTES...
PRAY YOU'RE NOT INVITED.

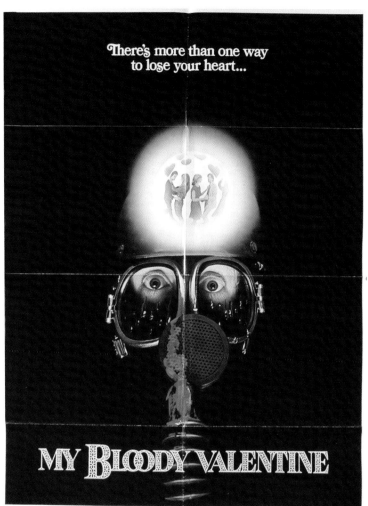

There's more than one way
to lose your heart...

MY BLOODY VALENTINE

PARAMOUNT PICTURES CORPORATION PRESENTS MY BLOODY VALENTINE STARRING PAUL KELMAN LORI HALLIER NEIL AFFLECK MUSIC BY PAUL ZAZA PRODUCTION SUPERVISOR BOB PRESNER ASSOCIATE PRODUCER LAWRENCE NESIS STORY CONCEPT STEPHEN MILLER
WRITTEN BY JOHN BEAIRD PRODUCED BY JOHN DUNNING ANDRE LINK STEPHEN MILLER DIRECTED BY GEORGE MIHALKA   A PARAMOUNT RELEASE
Copyright © MCMLXXXI by Paramount Pictures Corporation. All Rights Reserved.

R RESTRICTED
UNDER 17 REQUIRES ACCOMPANYING
PARENT OR ADULT GUARDIAN

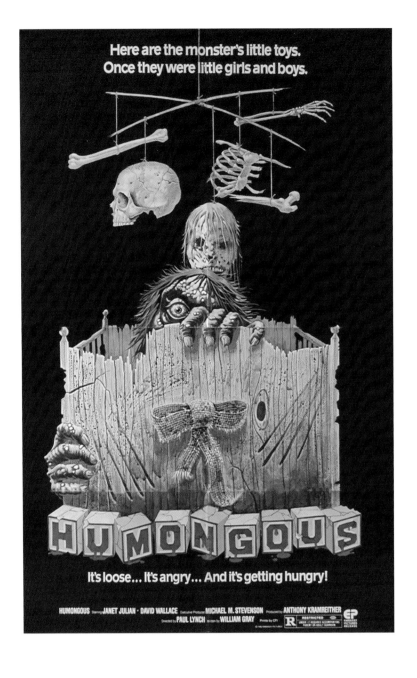

THE DREAMS.
THE NIGHTMARES.
THE DESIRES.
THE FEARS.
THE MYSTERY.
THE REVELATION.
THE WARNING:

The INCUBUS

HE IS THE DESTROYER.

EDWARD L. MONTORO Presents a MARC BOYMAN Production
in association with MARK FILMS and JOHN M. ECKERT PRODUCTIONS Ltd.
JOHN CASSAVETES   KERRIE KEANE   HELEN HUGHES
ERIN FLANNERY   DUNCAN McINTOSH   with JOHN IRELAND
From the novel by RAY RUSSELL   Director of Photography ALBERT J. DUNK csc   Music by STANLEY MYERS
Screenplay by GEORGE FRANKLIN   Produced by MARC BOYMAN and JOHN M. ECKERT
ARTISTS RELEASING CORPORATION   Directed by JOHN HOUGH
FILM FILM VENTURES INTERNATIONAL

YOU SCREAM.
YOU EXPAND.
YOU EXPLODE.

SPASMS

CINEQUITY CORPORATION and MARTIN ERLICHMAN present

PETER FONDA·OLIVER REED in SPASMS with KERRIE KEANE ALSO STARRING AL WAXMAN AS CROWLEY
Executive Producers MARTIN ERLICHMAN · JOHN G. POZHKE · MAURICE SMITH
Produced by JOHN POZHKE · MAURICE SMITH · SPASMS Theme Performed by TANGERINE DREAM
Original Score Composed and Conducted by ERIC N. ROBERTSON
Screenplay by DON ENRIGHT   Director WILLIAM FRUET

© 1983 PRODUCERS DISTRIBUTION COMPANY

PDC
Released through Producers Distribution Company

IF IT CAN'T SCARE
THEM TO DEATH
IT WILL FIND
ANOTHER WAY.

OF
UNKNOWN
ORIGIN

PIERRE DAVID and LAWRENCE NESIS Present
A GEORGE P. COSMATOS FILM
OF UNKNOWN ORIGIN
Starring PETER WELLER, JENNIFER DALE, LAWRENCE DANE,
KENNETH WELSH, LOUIS DEL GRANDE, and introducing SHANNON TWEED
Based upon the book "The Visitor" by CHAUNCEY G. PARKER III Screenplay by BRIAN TAGGERT
Music by KEN WANNBERG Produced by CLAUDE HEROUX Executive Producer PIERRE DAVID
Directed by GEORGE P. COSMATOS
Produced with the participation of the Canadian Film Development Corporation and Famous Players Limited
DISTRIBUTED BY WARNER BROS. Read the Signet Paperback
A BARRIE COMMUNICATIONS COMPANY

R RESTRICTED
UNDER 17 REQUIRES ACCOMPANYING
PARENT OR ADULT GUARDIAN

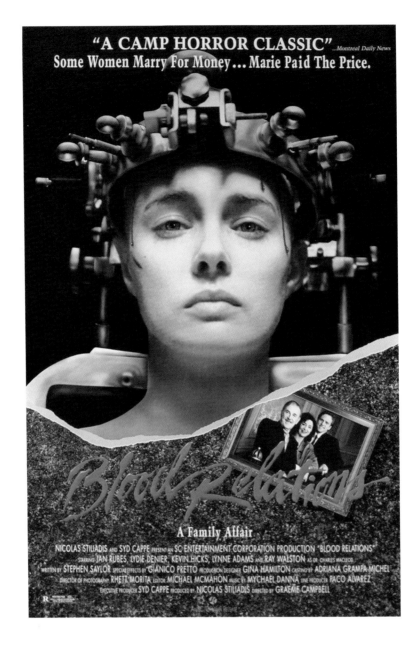

Chamberlain's old mentor, grumpy John Houseman. Romance beckons as well, as Chamberlain finds time to convincingly woo Sara Botsford while still energetically tracing the source of the fatal calls.

The film features photography by Reginald Morris, a score by John Barry and a supporting cast made up largely of actors from *Rituals*. The plot is more than a little ridiculous and the resolution disappointingly small-scale, but the movie still manages to exude a small measure of hocus-pocus enjoyment, which is given extra motive power by the clash between Chamberlain's square-jawed perform-ance and Houseman's amiable slumming. Botsford is caught in the middle, but her manifest talent steers her through. She would exhibit talents of a different sort, if equally compelling, in the dasch-rat epic *Deadly Eyes*.

Getting There is Half the Fun:
Death Ship and *Terror Train*

Death Ship

ANOTHER FILM MADE UNDER the UK/Canada co-production treaty, like *The Uncanny* and *Full Circle*, was *Death Ship* (1980), a poorly-regarded haunted ship movie filmed in Quebec City and in the Gulf of Mexico. The story has the Death Ship (a Nazi "interrogation ship," we are told, but in reality a badly-retrofitted cargo vessel) ramming a cruise ship and then picking up the survivors from their sandbox-style life raft. The sadistic steamer then proceeds to play deadly games with its new passengers, which include cruise ship captain George Kennedy (whose transformation from mildly grumpy to psychotically possessed barely registers as a transformation at all), bearded first mate Richard Crenna, a dashing and intrepid swabby played by Nick Mancuso, eccentric widow Kate Reid, unfunny comedian Saul Rubinek, and a couple of annoying kids. To help fulfill the UK end of things, there are also some British ladies (Sally Ann Howes, Victoria Burgoyne) along for the ride.

The story originated in the mind of producer Sandy Howard of the American pro-duction company Avco Embassy. He took it to Jack Hill, another American, who had previously written the story for the Canadian all-star disaster movie *City on Fire*, which was also produced by Howard and Avco Embassy. Reasoning that a good horror movie needed a more sentient, less purely mechanical antagonist, and unwilling to simply ape the premise of the recent Universal production *The Car* (itself no box-office champ), Hill and his collaborator David Lewis turned it from a simple possessed-boat story into more of a ghost tale, with human possessions a sideline. However (according to Hill), Canadian tax laws in the third proper year of the 100% C.C.A. required that the cred-ited screenwriter be Canadian. To fulfill this, Dominion resident John Robins was hired to do a rewrite, and whether by his own volition or Howard's, returned for the most part to the executive producer's original premise, in which the rusted hulk of a boat does its own terrorizing without the aid of ectoplasmic wraiths. Disembodied voices crying "Achtung!" and "Schnell! Schnell!" echo down the passages, levers pull themselves, steam issues from every pipe and pistons pump endlessly. "They sent me the finished script… and I read the first few pages and I couldn't go beyond that," moaned Hill. "I have never seen the film… but it was a disaster." Hill was reportedly paid not to take a screenplay credit on the film.

Alvin Rakoff, yet another Canadian who had felt the need to move to England in order to start a career, was hired to direct. Born in Toronto in 1937, Rakoff had been a journalist in earlier days, became the first freelance filmmaker employed in British television, had jumped from there into feature films like *Passport to Shame* and *Hoffman*, and had recently wrapped the all-star Montreal-shot disaster epic *City on Fire*. *Death Ship* would be his first and only stab at the horror genre.

Shooting began in Quebec, with a 50 year old Canadian Coast Guard icebreaker, the *N.B. McLean*, used for the Death Ship's interiors. The Chateau Frontenac in Quebec City stood in for the luxury liner interiors seen at the beginning of the movie. The production then moved to the Gulf of Mexico, just off the coast of Alabama, during the summer—which is to say, the hurricane season—of 1979, where a 2080 ton lumber freighter called the *Maurine K.* played the role of the Death Ship's outside. According to Don Carmody, credited as "Production Executive" on the movie, this part of the shoot was to say the least troubled. Sets which had been built on the beach near Mobile, Alabama, were utterly destroyed by Hurricane Bob. The crew found themselves trapped for hours in Chickasaw, Alabama by the wrath of the storm. Even when the weather was fair, the *Maurine K.* was a rusted out hulk with no engine which had to be towed everywhere by tugboats, delaying things further. Carmody was hired on halfway through to try and simply "make sense of it all. It was a clean-up job, basically."

The film was photographed by stalwart tax shelter camera-*artiste* René Verzier in full-on Canuck-O-Vision: all washed-out grays and blues. Verzier, who had a growing reputation as a "human dolly," shot the movie entirely hand-held, which helps give it a few effectively woozy moments. Besides supplying Rubinek with one of his earliest screen credits and providing both Reid and Mancuso spectacular and bizarre death scenes (Reid munches on possessed Nazi mints and transforms into a rotted zombie, while Mancuso drowns in a disgusting corpse-pit), *Death Ship* gives Kennedy the chance to spit out the word "Toronto" with great bitterness. Bemoaning the lot of the cruise ship captain, he complains of "Blue-rinse ladies repeating 'Have a nice day!' over and over again, and then having to have dinner with them so they can go back to Akron or Toronto or wherever and say they ate with the captain." This sort of small acknowledgement of Canadian-ness was usually about as much nationalism as one could expect in a tax shelter film.

The dialogue is atrocious, Rakoff's direction is poor ("He had no idea how to use a camera," maintains Jack Hill), and the sets are unconvincing. There are a few "big" scenes, which, like the abbreviated cruise-ship sinking scene, seem lifted from the disaster films of the decade leading up to *Death Ship*. These give evidence of the sadly misused $4,500,000 budget, decidedly on the generous side for a Canadian production. Choppy editing, in which day and night collide as incongruously as in an Ed Wood production, gives further evidence of *Death Ship*'s production problems. The film could boast of one technological advance: the Heely-Ray Sound System, developed especially for the picture by Toronto sound engineer Ken Heely-Ray. It was a new sort of equalizer, but never caught the public interest the way Universal's Sensurround system had half a decade earlier.

Death Ship's most lasting legacy is the misleadingly evocative poster, which was shamelessly lifted for the similar, but much more expensive, 2002 Warner Brothers production *Ghost Ship*. Certainly the investors, one of whom was my uncle Bob, didn't see any profits on the deal. (Bob, however, was lucky enough to have also invested in *Porky's*.)

Terror Train

Critical reception was not kind. "The viewer has great difficulty in refraining from urging the ship to dispose of its cargo as soon as possible. It is pitiful to see Kennedy and Crenna, accomplished adventure film actors, stranded in such a picture," said *The Aurum Horror Film Encyclopedia*. The review in *Leonard Maltin's Movie and Video Guide* is worth quoting in its entirety: "Luxury liner collides with 'death ship.' Survivors board 'death ship.' 'Death ship' tries to murder survivors. Forget it."

After doing his best to save the floundering *Death Ship*, Carmody moved on to act as "production executive" on another Harold Greenberg/Sandy Howard production, *Terror Train*. The results were far superior to *Death Ship*, though a single, two-hour shot of paint drying would also have been.

Filmed mostly in a warehouse in Montreal, the picture features Western stalwart Ben Johnson as the fatherly conductor of a frat-party excursion train beset by a maniac. The movie begins three years earlier at a different party, where we meet a group of pre-med students (including *Halloween*'s Jamie Lee Curtis as Alana and Lloyd Bochner's son Hart Bochner playing the practical-joke king Doc) whose idea of fun is to lure an irredeemable dweeb called Kenny Hampson into a tryst with a dismembered corpse. Kenny is so distraught as to fail to appreciate the efforts the pranksters (or rather, talented cinematographer John Alcott) have gone to in order to make the gag not only convincing but aesthetically pleasing: the room is hypnotically lit with a series of softly clicking, multi-coloured traffic flashers. No, instead his response to the jape is to descend immediately into untreatable insanity. He stands on the bed clutching a severed arm and spins himself into a frenzy, roaring like a walrus. Then (we later find out) he quits school and spends the next few semesters in the loony bin.

The first hint that the train is in for trouble comes when loveable jokester Ed, dressed up as Groucho Marx and spouting astonishingly poor one-liners as the students prepare to board, is run through with a sword right there on the platform. Everybody assumes it's just another one of his terrific pranks, but the viewers know better as a pair of hands roll the dying Ed onto the tracks and steal his rubber mask and roll-up dickie. He's squished several times over as the train pulls out of the station.

The killer's habit of donning his last victim's costume is one of the film's cleverer conceits. Jock-boy Jackson, dressed as a gill-man, is the next to go, in a scene that appears to have been cut short by censorious clippers. More killings follow, and a great number of magic tricks besides. These are performed by a 23 year-old David Copperfield, playing a grumpy magician ("This is a bad crowd," he growls near the beginning) who pushes cigarettes through quarters, makes cards appear out of thin air, coaxes hot nuts from a machine without paying, and levitates his homely blonde assistant before wooing Jamie Lee Curtis with other, even more romantic tricks.

Johnson is the first to realize that people are being killed, causing him to shake his head and mutter "Damn kids!" Doc's lady friend Mitchy has her throat slit in an upper berth, and Alana's boyfriend Mo is stabbed during one of the magic shows. Doc shows himself to be a craven coward who panics at the slightest hint of trouble, and his panic redoubles when he realizes that the killer is none other than Kenny Hampson out for revenge. The conductor stops the train to search for the killer, but Kenny is nowhere to be found. Suspicion of being Kenny falls upon the magician, since Kenny had been a well-known campus magician himself back before he went insane. In the meantime, Doc's head is cut off, a fresh urn of coffee is made, and a hefty frat boy dressed in Uncle Sam garb helps all the remaining passengers to the back of the train.

The hefty frat boy in *Terror Train* is far and away the most mature of the party animals, which makes an unexpected and happy change from the standard "tubby jokester" character in this kind of film. In fact, the character (played by Greg Swanson) is used to deliver a nicely-performed little speech in a southern-fried senator voice, strictly as entertainment for his fellow passengers, which runs, in part, as follows:

> Ah don't wanna get involved in any contr-versy on th' sitch'ation in th' Middle East, but as senior senator from mah state, Ah think Ah can speak for mah constit-uents, indeed all Amer'cans, when Ah say, fuck 'em!
>
> Y'know, there are ce'tain phrases in Amer'can hist'ry that've caught the fancy of th' Amer'can people. Well, the phrase that's always caught mah fancy, or roused me as't were, is "Let's bomb them suckahs into th' stone age!" Y' know, it wouldn't be like Vietnam. They don't have no jungle to hide undah, jes sand an' rock. To my way o' thinkin', if the U-nited States cav'lry can take care o' Paiutes and Comanches, a B-52 oughta do jes' fine with these ol' camel jockeys.

It's hard to say whether a speech like that would find its way quite so naturally into an

American-made horror film, especially in these post-Iraq days. On the whole, I'd say not.

Kenny skewers a few more people, including Copperfield, and then tries to do the same to Alana, who gives as good as she gets, punching and kicking the hag-mask wearing Kenny and also stabbing him twice: first with a sword and later with one of those paper spike things. Then she knocks him off the train, or so she thinks. Kenny is not so easily gotten rid of! By the end, it is revealed that Kenny had boarded the train in the guise of the magician's ugly assistant. Alana and the conductor team up to push Kenny out of the train for once and for all. He lands with a thump on some snow, slides into an icy river and floats downstream, as much a victim of the harsh Canadian winter, it seems, as the fall or the multitude of injuries he sustained on the train.

Terror Train began life as a notion in the head of producer Daniel Grodnik, who found himself wondering what you'd get if someone mixed *Silver Streak* (1976) with *Halloween* (1978). Sandy Howard, following his usual pattern, made up a poster (with the title "Train of Terror" and a picture of a train emerging terrifyingly out of a face) and began pre-selling the foreign sales while at Cannes flogging *Death Ship*.

Terror Train

Canadian money, as it so often did around this time, flew at the project like bugs at a windshield once a few foreign sheckels were in place. The money came with a need to Canadianize the film with some real Canuck names, so T.Y. Drake, whose sole experience in horror previously had been directing *The Keeper* in 1976, was hired to turn Grodnik's notion into a script. "If I hadn't been broke, I wouldn't have done it," claims Drake, evidently not a horror fan. The enormity of Drake's task as screenwriter is demonstrated by the following promotional synopsis of the story, which is, I think, spuriously inaccurate, pathetically written and generally incompetent enough to print here in full. To preserve the integrity of the document's ineptitude, I have not changed a single wrong-headed word or misplaced comma:

> It was just a "prank". It was all in fun when, on a cold winter day, at the sixth graders graduation picnic, Anna and her sister, Cindy, caught "Little Robbie Firth" (that's what they called him when they teased him) and his best friend Billy, down by the boathouse together. It was all in fun when half a dozen of the boys urged on by Anna and Cindy, stripped Robbie and Billy, tied them together and set them adrift in a rowboat for all at the picnic to see.
>
> It wasn't fun, however, when the rowboat overturned and before everyone's eyes Billy—hands tied—drowned. Robbie couldn't talk after that, so they sent him away and no one ever saw him again.

Six years later—to the day oddly enough—the mid-afternoon celebration finally ended and the super express pulled out of the train depot, the town's heroes on board. The crowd celebrating the departure were proud of the senior class and its award winning band, and the blossoming young Anna and Cindy were ready for a great trip.

What they were not ready for was the night of sheer terror that lay ahead.

The senior class, Anna and Cindy, partied and frolicked promiscuously not knowing that in the second car ahead, silently sat a young woman wearing a veil. It was Robbie, who had escaped the asylum and returned disguised in order to be with all his friends he had not seen in six years on graduation night.

The darkness of night had hardly come when Robbie started with Cindy in the ladies' room. He stuffed her, and her pet cat in the same locker when he was through with his macabre revenge.

Then Anna's new boyfriend, Larry got in the way. Larry Hearst had been drinking and he remained in the dining car. Alone, drowsey, he made his way slowly to the front of the car so he could absorb the fresh air. The countryside swept past swiftly—and he started to come around. And then it happened. A flash in the night. A blade striking Larry's shoulder. He resisted, though badly wounded, as he turned and saw the attacker (camera) and his surprise was mixed with his screams as another strike and yet another send him sprawling into the bushes that line the track.

The band played louder and louder and on into the night. One by one, Robbie—disguised as the woman (and the audience never knows who it really is) picks his way through his/her victims.

Finally it was Cindy—the one he was really after—that notices the girl's little finger of the right hand—missing… it had been a childhood joke… she knew it was Robbie and flees screaming through the train… in the middle of the night… to the last car.

One can easily imagine Drake's dismay upon being handed this document and told to make a script out of it. The depth of his urge to disassociate the final product from this synopsis was such that he even changed all the names. It's hard to blame him. On top of being ridiculous (a sixth-grade graduation picnic by a lake in the middle of winter?) and illogical (Cindy—and her pet cat—are killed and stuffed in a locker, yet she turns up at the end to be chased through the train by "Little Robbie Firth"), the film synopsized here sounds unbelievably stupid. No one in their right mind would help finance a picture like this. But they did—and that was the magic of the tax shelter days.

Without having seen many, if any at all, of the slasher models he was expected to emulate, Drake turned in a draft to Howard. The experienced schlock producer told Drake that he loved it, but that "If this was *Jaws*, there's no shark yet." Howard's specific requests were for more blood, a horrible opening scene (*de rigeur* for the genre after *Halloween*) and an interesting villain. Drake's solution was to give the killer a reason for being a transvestite, and add the notion of him dressing in the costume of his last victim. (This idea was praised in many reviews of the film and copied in some subsequent movies, such as the department store-set slasher *Hide and Go Shriek*.[28]) Drake also brought in the magician character and the tricks with which the film is perhaps over-generously supplied. Howard was more than satisfied with this, and used Drake's script to attract the rest of the nearly $4,000,000 budget used to make the picture.

Roger Spottiswoode, a Canadian national who had worked as an editor for Sam Peckinpah, was chosen to direct. (Spottiswoode's father Raymond was the NFB producer who had provided the 3D cameras for *The Mask* twenty years earlier.) Spottiswoode brought in the famed cameraman John Alcott, who had just completed shooting on Stanley Kubrick's *The Shining*. A train was

Prom Night

hired from a museum in Steamtown, Vermont, and sets were built in a Montreal ware-house by production designer Glenn Bydwell, a Montreal architect who worked on movies only when he felt like it. For the train interiors, in order to help the audience keep track of where the characters were in the train, each car was painted a different colour. It took ten days to paint the complicated floor patterns alone.

In the meantime, much of Drake's dialogue was rewritten by a woman named Caryl Wickman, who was brought in by Spottiswoode and given the credit "director of dialogue." ("Spottiswoode's girlfriend," Drake called her without any evident residual bitterness.) The film began shooting in late November of 1979, during an unwelcome and snowless period of mild weather. This changed on the first night of exterior shooting, when several inches of snow fell and the temperature became cold enough to repeatedly freeze the camera.

Ben Johnson, most famed these days for his role in *The Last Picture Show*, had, according to the *Terror Train* press notes, "devoted most of his life to ranch-style living and starring in western movies." He accepted the role of the engineer based on his admiration for Roger Spottiswoode's editing of the Peckinpah movies. Johnson refused throughout the shoot to go out disco dancing with the rest of the young cast, but did treat everyone involved in the production to a "country-style" evening at Montreal's only bluegrass bar.

Don Carmody relates the story of a visit to the set by the film's completion guarantor, a Londoner named Richard Soames. Soames had recently been involved in a train-bound flop of a picture called *The Cassandra Crossing* (from director George P. Cosmatos, later to direct the Canadian rat-battle picture *Of Unknown Origin*, and later still *Rambo*) and had, in Carmody's words, "taken a bath." For *The Cassandra Crossing*, the train set had been equipped with a heavy-duty, high-tech rocking system to give it some realistic, train-like movement. But this device had been nothing but trouble for the production, breaking down constantly and sending the budget and schedule through the roof. Soames was therefore a little bit compulsive on the subject of train-rocking, and called Carmody on a near-daily basis to find out what was being done to rock the *Terror Train* set. Carmody didn't know, but a quick visit to the set revealed that the train was being quite acceptably rocked by a couple of grips leaning on an iron bar shoved through the springs. Soames was worried enough to book a flight from London to Montreal expressly to see for himself what was being done about it, and Carmody, in a capricious mood, had one of the grips—a husky black man with a sense of humour similar to Carmody's—oiled up by the makeup department and stripped to the waist, and made sure that this man was rocking the train and singing "Ol' Man River" just as the anxious Soames walked by. Laughs Carmody, "He never came back to the set after that! I guess he figured everything was under control!"

Screenwriter Drake had moved on to other things by the time the film was released in October of 1980. The film had been screened for him, and he'd found it violent and unremarkable, then had more or less forgotten about it. He was therefore surprised to hear from a friend that *Terror Train* had debuted at the #2 spot on *Variety*'s weekly box-office chart, and it stayed on the chart for five weeks. Drake says that the film was much bloodier in that first screening than the versions he has seen since, and the film's gore does indeed seem to have been cut in a number of places, with abrupt edits the norm during the murder scenes.

Typically for the slasher sub-genre, at least in the very early eighties, *Terror Train* did well at the box office after its successful first week, providing a hefty return on the $3,500,000 that had been lavished upon it, and the nearly double that figure spent on prints and advertising. It's the kind of movie which attracts the word "competent" in its critical notices; the *Variety* review adds the word "efficient" in describing Drake's script. The *Aurum Horror Encyclopedia* applauds the film's "concise technique," but in the same sentence complains of "thin and contrived plotting" which leads to "a statutory climax." But, like so many other Canadian horror films, it has found a place in the hearts of many contemporary viewers who either remember it fondly from its original release or discovered it later on video. It will have an opportunity to win still more fans through the magic of DVD.

A Franchise is Born: Prom Night

THE CONVERGENCE OF TWO EARTH-SHAKING EVENTS in 1978—the full, furious bloom of the tax shelter era, and the hugely successful release of John Carpenter's *Halloween*—made possible Canada's first homegrown horror franchise: the *Prom Night* movies. Produced by Peter Simpson's Simcom company, the series became less an ongoing narrative than a brand name which, through the 1980s, was attached to any Simcom production even vaguely involving either a prom or a night.

British-born Paul Lynch was the prime mover behind the first of them. Lynch had made a pair of prototypically Canadian pictures involving road-weary losers: a country-music drama called *The Hard Part Begins* (1973) and a wrestling drama entitled *Blood and Guts* (1978). Neither made much money, and Lynch was, like William Fruet before him, hungry for a commercial hit to help stabilize his career, and willing to tackle any genre to do it.

At first he had in mind a children's film, to be called *Catman and the Kid*, but no one was interested. While in Los Angeles trying to drum up speculation in the project, he went to a party and ran into Orval Fruitman, the distributor who had taken on *The Hard Part Begins* back in 1973. Fruitman informed him that Canadian producer/distributor Pierre David, the executive pro-ducer, along with Victor Solnicki, of David Cronenberg's *The Brood* and *Scanners*, was looking to develop a com-mercial genre property (what Canadian producer wasn't

Prom Night

in those heady days?), and Lynch quickly dreamed up a horror film idea he called "Don't Go See The Doctor." Lynch's schooling had been in graphic design, so before going to see David, he drew up a rough poster for the proposed film, complete with the tag line "What happens when your gynecologist cracks? Whatever you do, Don't Go See The Doctor!"

Pierre David, it turned out, was completely repulsed by the idea of an insane gyne-cologist, little knowing that his friend Cronenberg would travel into precisely that territory almost a decade later with *Dead Ringers*, and that he himself would produce the nearly-as-unsavory *Dentist* series in the mid-nineties. So Lynch went back to the drawing board, quite literally, and made a poster out of a notion inspired by a billboard atop his Sunset Boulevard hotel. The billboard was for After Six Formal Wear, and read, in part, "For Prom Night, Think After Six!"

The notion of a prom-themed horror movie had extra appeal for Lynch, since he'd dropped out of high school early and was thereby denied a prom of his own. With his idea in place and a scary poster made, the filmmaker went to a Toronto Film Festival party being held in L.A. and, as fortune would have it, ran into salty-tongued Toronto producer Peter Simpson, who was at the time trying to set up a big-budget co-production with Warner Bros. to be called *The Sea Gypsies*. It's impossible to say whether Pierre David would have accepted *Prom Night* as an idea, because Simpson latched onto it right there and then, and three days later the deal was done. Robert Guza Jr., also the screenwriter of Simpson's *Curtains*, took the concept and shaped it into a story, and then William Gray, the former ad man, music critic and film editor who had worked on *The Changeling* and Lynch's *Blood and Guts*, wrote the final script. After that, with a $1,600,000 budget in place, Lynch and

Simpson began the process of casting their film. Lynch wanted Eve Plumb (Jan from *The Brady Bunch*) in the main role of Kim, but, according to Peter Simpson, Jamie Lee Curtis' agent was lobbying with great intensity for his client, and, after initial resistance,[29] Simpson and Lynch accepted the budding scream queen with the legendary pedigree as their lead. Curtis herself was overjoyed: "I practically would have paid to make that movie—I had only made two movies up to that time, they offered me three times the money I was paid on *The Fog*, and it was the first role that was ever offered to me; I didn't even have to read for it. And they said, 'How would you like to spend six weeks in Toronto?' To me, little insecure Jamie, the idea of making a movie was so exciting, I just went *sigh*!" The rest of the cast was made up of Canadians, including Cronenberg veteran Robert Silverman as a menacing janitor. Silverman, returning to acting after his career was waylaid by a serious injury, came to the set with a "very elaborate biography" of the minor janitor character, after Lynch told the actor "he's got to be scary."

Crewing the film was more difficult than casting had been. This was quite possibly the busiest time in the history of the Canadian film industry—the peak year of the tax shelter boom, when the number of movies made in Canada per capita far outstripped the United States—and crew members with any experience were hard to come by. Lynch wanted Mark Irwin, who had shot *Blood and Guts*, to take the camera on *Prom Night*, but Irwin was off shooting Alfred Sole's ape-love movie *Tanya's Island*. Eventually Robert New—later to shoot the Canadian Dungeons and Dragons horror film *Skullduggery* (1983), and afterwards, upon relocating to the United States, Fred Dekker's delightful *Night of the Creeps* (1986) and some of John McNaughton's *The Borrower* (1991)—was engaged as the film's cinematographer. New had much documentary experience, and *Prom Night* would be his first narrative feature work. The film began shooting at Don Mills Collegiate and locations around Toronto in August of 1979.

The story of *Prom Night* is primal in its simplicity. One day in 1974, four children are running around an abandoned convent, playing a game that seems like a sort of stalk-'n'-slash version of Hide and Seek. Three siblings, older Kim, and ten year-old twins Alex and Robin, happen along, and Robin, wanting to be a part of the game, creeps into the old building. Soon she's being chased by the older kids, who shout "The killer is coming!" at her until she accidentally falls through a window to her death. (20 year-old stunt-woman Karen Pike actually took the plunge.) The kids all swear to keep the cause of the accident a secret, and Robin's death is blamed on a local sicko, Leonard Murch, who is subsequently chased by police and deformed in a road accident. All of the children's performances in this early scene are surprisingly good, it bears remarking, ensuring that, if nothing else, the movie has a relatively strong preamble to set up the by-the-numbers massacre to come.

Six years to the day after Robin's death, it's prom night. Kim, now the prom queen of Alexander Hamilton High and played by Jamie Lee Curtis, is attending with her new boyfriend, prom king and all-around B.M.O.C. Nick. Nick has just broken up with Wendy, whose bitchy character seems modeled on Nancy Allen's from *Carrie*, and her resentment drives her into the arms of Lou (a troublemaking monobrow who is a precise reworking of John Travolta's character in the same Brian DePalma movie) to plot revenge against the new couple. In the meantime, Wendy, Jude and Kelly, who along with Nick were the four older kids involved in Robin's death, are receiving rather less-than-terrifying phone calls from an irritated mystery man with a whispery voice and a good supply of pencils, which he taps endlessly as he sibilates vaguely threatening messages.

Jude, a chipper good-time gal, shrugs off her phone call and takes up with the tubby, boogie van-driving wiseacre Slick on the way to school, while Kelly worries about whether or not to go all the way with her boyfriend Drew, played by Jeff Wincott.[30] Kim and Wendy have a war of words over Nick, and as all this high-school drama unravels, the burned psycho Leonard Murch, blamed, disfigured and incarcerated for Robin's death, manages an escape. Could he be the one making the calls, bent on revenge for having been consigned to a hospital for the criminally insane all these years? Or is it the creepy janitor, Sykes, with his sweaty, leering gaze, hairnet, and easy access to power tools? Or might the proto-human Lou have gone off the deep end? To paraphrase a certain monocular film reviewer, keep a bowl of raw red herrings in the room as you watch *Prom Night* and you'll swear the movie was shot in Smell-O-Vision.[31]

Prom Night

A blast of really, really bad disco music heralds the big night itself. Jamie Lee and Leslie Nielsen bust a few moves on the lighted dance floor. Then comes, quite literally, the showstopper: Jamie Lee and Nick performing a series of ludicrous, robot-like movies for what seems like ten minutes, as the spurned Wendy seethes in the corner with her simian date. Finally, some time thereafter, the killing begins. Kelly, hiding away in a locker room, wards off the amorous advances of Drew, and, after he has left, pays the ultimate price by receiving a mirror shard across the throat. Then come the famous boogie van killings: Jude and Slick, having surrendered their respective virginities to one another in the back of the van, relax with a little maryjane which Slick keeps squirreled away in a stars-and-stripes-emblazoned textbook called "A History of the American People." "I'll remember this night for the rest of my life," murmurs Kelly: not an idle remark, as almost immediately the rear doors of the van fly open and she is stabbed several times in the neck by a balaclava-sporting marauder. Slick tries desperately to drive away, but blunders over the nearby Scarborough Bluffs, his boogie van exploding with what appears to be the force of a thousand-pound bomb.

The actual exploding van was a double for the main picture boogie van which, Lynch reports, one of the transport guys on the movie had found and bought for three thousand dollars. Police later informed the production that this stunt van had been stolen, and that the now-vanished driver had simply pocketed the three grand, but by then the second van was ashes. A stuntman named Terry Martin had packed it with dynamite and gasoline and driven it off the cliff, jumping out just prior to the plummet. Four cameras were set up to record this effect, and Robert New, stationed with one of them at the bottom of the cliff, nearly had his eyebrows burnt off by the force of the blast.

Back at school, Wendy takes a break from the dance floor fun to apply some much-needed mascara. The killer interrupts, and after a long chase through the school, deals a death-chop with his axe. Of the culpable kids, this leaves only Nick. But no one has counted on Lou's plan for revenge, which involves clobbering Nick over the head and taking his place as prom king. With a vengeful axe-murderer on the loose, no more foolish scheme could possibly be imagined, and it ends, quite naturally, with Lou's slope-browed melon tumbling irregularly down the lighted catwalk and into the shrieking crowd of disco revelers. A final fight between the masked killer on the one hand and the still-groggy Nick and Kim on the other concludes with the murderer bopped on the head with his own axe, and, upon losing his now-bloody balaclava, proves to be Kim's little brother Alex, for some reason wearing lipstick and rouge, and who, it transpires, had witnessed the death of his beloved twin oh so many years before. He mumbles as much to Kim and promptly expires on the front stoop of the school. A song of disco commiseration with the pitiable killer is crooned over the end titles: "The night of love has set the stage… to release your hateful rage…"

After the shooting was done, an assembly of the footage showed that something was missing. Peter Simpson in particular felt that the buildup to the prom night action was much too slow. Extra elements of creepiness and plotting were, it seemed, what was required. Several extra days of filming were scheduled, with new scenes involving the phone calls (the tapping pencil, the breathy voice, the shadow on the wall), some scenes with the detective character (named "Detective Teller" because all he does is walk in and tell things to the audience), and the entire subplot involving the deformed maniac red herring added to the mix. These supplements provide sheer eventfulness, it is true, but that doesn't necessarily translate into good dramatic pacing. The additions also displeased its star, Jamie Lee Curtis, who later told *Fangoria* magazine that "all that psychopathic killer stuff was not in the original script, not in the script I agreed to do. They added that after they cut the movie. I'm very angry about that, and I'll always be angry about that because I feel I wouldn't have made the movie had it been a remake of *Halloween*—which is exactly what they were trying to do."

Prom Night was, give or take a few million, pretty near the box-office success Lynch had hoped it would be, and it put his career on a steady if not spectacular track for a good while afterward. But the film itself didn't immediately invite a sequel. For one thing, as Peter Simpson points out, the killer was not a mythical madman like *Friday the 13th*'s Jason or *Halloween*'s Michael Myers, nor a *bon mot*-spewing boogeyman with a pizza for a face like Freddie Krueger, but instead, Simpson complains, "just some fuckin' nerdy brother." This was nothing much to latch a series onto, really. And the reviews were less than enthusiastic: Tom Allen of *The Village Voice* called it "the sorriest rip-off of the year… an all-time bummer." Allen goes on to report that the movie "emanates from Toronto, which is rapidly becoming the clone capital of North America…[*Prom Night*] radiates not so much fear as the insular smugness of a well-made industrial documentary."[32]

These are cruel words indeed when reviewing a Canadian movie intended as pure narrative entertainment. But Lynch was unwavering in his determination to have a career in commercial cinema, and he got right back on the horror horse with his next picture, *Humongous*, whose story he and screenwriter William Gray came up with soon after *Prom Night*'s release. Anthony Kramreither, the movie mogul who had appeared as an actor in *The Reincarnate* ten years earlier, was the producer, and Sandy Howard's Avco Embassy agreed to distribute the picture.

Humongous introduces us to five teens (of the World's Oldest And Most Annoying variety) on a boat trip around what looks like Lake Ontario, or maybe Georgian Bay in Lake Huron. Nick, the most unpleasant of the youngsters, manages by his sheer pigheaded (and contrived) stupidity to blow the boat up, stranding them all, along with a plaid-shirted hoser of a castaway, on spooky Dog Island. This bleak promontory is, naturally, the home of Humongous, the hulking, hairy, cannibal-

Humongous

istic son of a rape victim seen in the movie's "forty-years-earlier" prologue and lyrical, Lynch-designed credit sequence. The Humongous groans loudly throughout his rampage as though stricken with heartburn, and gives deadly bearhugs to most of the cast before being lightly blown up and then impaled on a stick by final survivor Sandy. (Could she have been named for executive producer Sandy Howard? It's entirely possible.)

The cast is a generally competent batch of fresh-faced twenty-somethings. Joy Boushel, who plays the flirty Donna, had been discovered in a Montreal disco called 1234 by Arden Ryshpan, then working as the casting director of George Mihalka's first film, *Pick-Up Summer*. Boushel had also appeared in *Terror Train* and would later show up in *The Fly*. Garry Robbins, the groaning Humongous, would use his experience in the role to great advantage years later in the Toronto-shot *Hills Have Eyes* redux *Wrong Turn*, in which he once again played a murderous, malformed giant.

For all the credit given to the various special effects and make-up artists at the end of *Humongous*, it seems to have been deliberately directed, shot and edited in such a way as to prevent any effects from ever being properly seen. For most of the thing, at least once night falls, you can barely even see the actors. This is likely due to a generally lousy video transfer (or possibly even a purposely darkened print, as was done at the climax of *Taxi Driver* to downplay the violence) rather than incompetence on the part of cinematographer Brian Hebb, who has done much better work elsewhere and is doubtless perfectly capable of reading a light meter. It's still annoying and hard on the eyes, though; it strikes me as unfair to the special effects people whose work has been obliterated. "They got a lot of flak for that," says Garry Robbins of the impenetrable darkness.

Robbins, who stands 7'4" and weighs 425 pounds, was a twenty year-old bouncer in a St. Catherine's watering hole when he was approached by Paul Lynch to play the man-beast. "I'll do it," he told Lynch, "as long as you send a limo to pick me up." When the limousine pulled up in front of his house, Robbins knew the offer was for real, and proceeded to have an (occasionally all-too-literal) blast working on the film. He didn't mind the makeup, which took up to three hours a day to apply ("That's my sweetheart!" Robbins crows affectionately when recalling talented makeup artist Maureen Sweeney), but he did wonder just what he'd got himself into during the dog attack scene. Assured the pooches wouldn't bite, he allowed the wolf-like animals to be thrown at him by trainers. They flew at him jaws first and tore the actor's hand to shreds. Even worse was the exploding boathouse scene, during which Robbins found himself unexpectedly aflame. He jumped in the water, but not before he'd been charred a little; fortunately the next scene involved the creature after his scripted roasting, and so Robbins simply soldiered on with his genuinely burned flesh incorporated into the makeup.

"*'Mungus* is softer than most," Paul Lynch says of his second horror film. "It doesn't have a lot of blood in it." Lynch has indeed avowed that he prefers suspense to violence and bloodletting in his pictures, but this didn't matter much to television virtuoso Norman Lear and producer Jerry Perenchio, who took over Avco Embassy as *Humongous* was being finished. By all reports they hated the horror genre, especially Lear, who is after all most famous for creating *All in the Family*. As a result, Lynch recounts, they first tried to sell the picture to another distributor and, failing, "buried" *Humongous* in the deepest hole they could find. Maybe the poor video transfer can even be blamed on Perenchio and Lear.

An exploding toy boat shot, the aforementioned hoser and the comical moans of the Humongous are entertaining in their way, as is a scene in which Boushel, in one of her meatiest roles, stains her vortex-like cleavage with blueberry juice; but none of this is enough to maintain a discerning viewer's interest throughout the whole interminable 93 minutes. Neither does it offset Lynch's propensity for pointless Dutch tilts and, often, putting the camera all the way on its side, a trick he pulls repeatedly and seemingly for its own sake. It works well exactly once: when Nick, the jerk of the group, is in the boathouse, and in a disorienting sideways shot the Humongous bursts in through the door to crush his head.

"There's naught scary about a giant baked potato with a boiled egg balanced on top," concluded a review of this film on the slasher-loving website *Hysteria*, and I'm inclined to agree. Perhaps one day the film will be released on DVD with a half-decent transfer and reveal itself worthy of reassessment. Or, more likely, not.

WILLIAM FRUET, IN THE MEANTIME, was being drawn into the Canadian horror world once more. After *Death Weekend*, he'd made the Vietnam revenge saga *Search and Destroy* (1979), then did a *Deliverance* riff called *Baker County USA* (also known under the title *The Killer Instinct*), but was expending most of his energy in trying to launch a picture his wife, Ida Nelson, had written, a *My Big Fat Greek Wedding*-style ethnic romantic comedy called *Tony Baloney*. "Everybody loved it, but everybody was afraid of it," Fruet says. "Nobody wanted to talk about hairy legs and Madonnas and things like that." The struggle to fund *Tony Baloney*—which is ongoing as of this writing—nearly led Fruet and his wife to the poorhouse. "Desperation time again," Fruet laughs. "Back to the commercial." In this instance, for Fruet, commercial meant horror, and so Ida Nelson sat down and wrote another script, the Ed Gein-inspired *Cries in the Night* (a.k.a. *Funeral Home*). Filmed for Barry Allen Productions (Allen had invested slightly in *Cannibal Girls* a decade earlier) in the hot summer of 1980, the film was the first and only leading scream-queen role given to one of Canada's busiest horror actresses, Lesleh Donaldson.

Happy Birthday to Me

There are scream queens from all over the globe, with entire magazines devoted to their particular corner of the acting profession. Favourites include Jamie Lee Curtis and Barbara Steele, of course, but also such varied talents as Linnea Quigley (the nude punk zombie from *Return of the Living Dead*), Julie Adams (the girl in the white bathing suit from *Creature from the Black Lagoon*) and Ingrid Pitt (from *Countess Dracula* and many others). In an interview posted on a horror film website called *The Terror Trap*, Donaldson calls her *Cries in the Night* role the most challenging of her horror roles. "I think of it," she says, not inaccurately, "as 'Little Red Riding Hood' meets *Psycho*."

Fruet, on the other hand, has called *Cries in the Night* "my Nancy Drew horror film," and again, it's easy to see why. Here's the story: Perky teen Heather (Donaldson) arrives in a small Ontario town to spend the summer with her weird brawny grand-mother, who, to make ends meet, has reluctantly turned the family funeral home into a guest house. The result is a rustic, moderately friendly place with one small disadvantage in that the guests keep disappearing. But why? Heather teams up with local boy Rick to find out, and Rick's brother, a cop, is meanwhile mounting his own investigation. Eventually, to no one's surprise but Heather's, it transpires that Granny is just as loony as she first appears to be, possesses super strength in the bargain, and that the film is on the whole a rather overly steadfast homage to *Psycho* (1960).

Though shot by the talented Mark Irwin, in a style he referred to as "Ontario Gothic… muted, mellow, contemporary low-key," the film is often as murky as other Canuck-horror of the period, like *Humongous* or *Prom Night*—at least in the lousy video transfers I've seen. Even a freshly minted print probably wouldn't improve the copious creeping through dark corridors, dim barns and gloomy cellars in which the characters constantly engage. Heather, though well-enough played by scream-queen Donaldson, is herself a fairly dim and gloomy presence, proudly exhibiting what must be a real engineering marvel of a bra but not much of a personality beneath it. The most interesting and full-bodied characterization in the entire movie, in fact, belongs to the hoser cop brother, who by the end of the film gets the respect he craves and a last-ten-minutes-of-*Psycho*-type opportunity to explain at length the batty granny's psychotic motivation and superhuman strength. It's a likable little movie for all its faults, with Fruet's usual professional job of direction a great boon. The film garnered favorable reviews in many papers, most of them citing their relief that the film was relatively free of the slasher violence so common at the time. Instead the film seems quaint and old-fashioned, and while a dash of violence or sleaze probably would make the movie a little more entertaining, it remains a pleasant, summery bit of escapism. Its American success—Fruet remembers lines around the block in L.A., and Barry Allen, an exhibitor as well as a producer, claimed that it was the sixth most popular picture of the year on his drive-in circuit—got the director an agent, and overall proved a healthy shot in the arm for his career. The film also became a big cult hit in Mexico, where, according to Michael Ironside, Lesleh Donaldson is regarded by many a swarthy, movie-going *muchacho* as preeminent among horror goddesses.

Blood, Sweat and Beers: Dunning & Link go Kill-Crazy

THE SLASH-FOR-CASH WAVE CONTINUED with two Cinépix productions filmed in the latter half of 1980: the glossy *Happy Birthday to Me* and the more modestly produced but livelier *My Bloody Valentine*. Both of these were produced by the godfathers of Can-schlock, John Dunning and André Link, and both were bought and distributed by major US companies (Columbia and Paramount, respectively).

Happy Birthday to Me, fondly remembered by many, stands as perhaps the most blatant attempt of the immediately post-*Halloween* crop to make a "classy" slasher movie. J. Lee Thompson,[33] the British action specialist who twenty years before had guided such favourites as *The Guns of Navarone* and the original *Cape Fear*, and later ended his career with a seemingly endless parade of Charles Bronson films, was hired to direct, and previously secret Canadian Glenn Ford was cast in a small role as a psychiatrist. The film's sheer length (110 minutes: longer even than *Visiting Hours*, and truly epic for a slasher movie) and fabulous poster art (a terrified young man being shish-kebabbed through the mouth, and the helpful tagline "Six of the most bizarre murders you will ever see") also help it stand out from the crowd.

The setting is a strange sort of boarding school in Quebec whose top ten students (whether tops in grades, scarf length or in simple wealth and snobbery the film never makes clear) have formed an elite group unimaginatively named the Top Ten. Their primary activity is hanging out in a pub called The Silent Woman, where Vlasta Vrana is the bartender, and then drunkenly jumping their cars over a nearby drawbridge. (Demonstrating their signature lack of creativity once again, the group refer to this as

"The Game.") Melissa Sue Anderson plays Virginia, a newcomer to the Top Ten; peppy (and preppie) enough, but suffering, paradoxically, from both traumatic flashbacks and chronic amnesia. It seems she'd been involved in an accident on the very same drawbridge used by the Top Ten for their jumping game, and as a result had lost both her memory and her mother, and furthermore been subjected to experimental brain surgery designed to restore her powers of recall. (The operation is performed very graphically by Louis Del Grande in the days before his own melon exploded in *Scanners* and he subsequently began *Seeing Things*.)

Virginia, therefore, is the chief suspect when the Top Ten begin meeting their bizarre demises. The first of them is Lesleh Donaldson in a substantially smaller part than in *Cries in the Night*, who, not so bizarrely for this kind of movie, has her throat slit in a parking garage. Then comes an objectionable French exchange student, Etienne, whose face is turned into meatloaf after his long, Isadora Duncan-style scarf (which all the Top Ten wear, no matter what they're doing) is tossed into a spinning dirt-bike wheel. (*These* are the smartest kids in school?) Shortly thereafter, weightlifter Steven has his throat crushed by his own barbells after a twenty-five pounder is tossed on his old chap.

My Bloody Valentine

Creepy Alfred, who practices taxidermy and likes to sculpt human heads, is put out of the red-herring business permanently by a workaday graveyard stabbing. Then comes the shish-kebab and a few more stabbings. (The tagline is therefore revealed as a lie: there are in fact more than six murders, but only three qualify as especially bizarre.)

Somewhere along the line, after the killings of superfluous characters played by Lawrence Dane and Glenn Ford, we see that it is in fact Virginia, whom we'd long ago rejected as a suspect for being far too obvious, behind the slayings. Could the filmmakers be sly enough to have anticipated this and therefore gone with the too-obvious suspect? Emphatically not. After more than a few twists, we find that maniacal class envy, of all things, is behind this nasty business. The whole experimental brain surgery/psychiatry subplot was merely a digression, since one of the Top Ten, Ann (Tracy Bregman), had been driven insane years ago when either her mother had an affair with Virginia's father or her father had an affair with Virginia's mother. At any rate, the whole town had been scandalized and Ann was made to feel like an outcast. Thus, her purchase of a Virginia mask and the spate of bizarre murders.

The film ends with the actual birthday party scene, for which Ann has gathered all her victims together, dressed them in party hats and arranged them around a table. She also bakes a cake. A titanic battle ensues between the insane Ann and the merely neurotic Virginia, by the end of which Ann is killed and Virginia left holding the bloody knife as police enter the scene. According to the press notes, several versions of this scene were written and shot, each with a different resolution to the mystery, so that even the cast and crew didn't know who the culprit was until they saw the final film. (If this is true, and if the alternate endings worked every bit as well as the one used, it doesn't say much for the strength and construction of the story.)

Thompson, who had many years earlier worked as a dialogue director for Alfred Hitchcock, appeared happy to be making a "chiller," while doing his part to ensure it rose above the usual slasher tawdriness. "What attracted me to the script was that the young people stood out as vivid, individual characters," he says in the film's press kit. "The difference between a good chiller and exploitive junk—at least in my opinion—is whether or not you care about the characters."

Melissa Sue Anderson, fresh off *Little House on the Prairie*, was for her part relieved to be in something a little more lighthearted than the frontier drama show. Recalling that, in the course of *Little House*, her character had lost two babies, contracted scarlet fever and appendicitis, and gone blind, she remarked that in *Happy Birthday To Me* "it was almost a relief to be chased by a berserk killer." Glenn Ford felt no relief in his small part: he was by all reports a wild prima donna on set, throwing punches at hapless assistant directors and sulking at the slightest perceived insult.

The makeup effects for the film were entrusted to Stéphan (*Visiting Hours*) Dupuis, but for unknown reasons he quit the picture approximately a month before shooting was to begin. Tom Burman, an American special effects artist whose credits included the Sandy Howard production *The Devil's Rain* (1976; starring William Shatner) and the shot-in-B.C. monster thrillers *Food of the Gods* (1976) and *Prophecy* (1979), took over. Burman and his four-person crew had three weeks to construct and build the gruesome results of Ann's handiwork, as well as the mealy corpse of Virginia's mother and the gory brain surgery. According to Lesleh Donaldson, after the group of young actors playing the Top Ten were made up as victims for the final party scene, they got bored waiting for the set to be lit and went for a little stroll around the small Quebec town, giving rise to cries of "*Tábernac!*" and "*Cardinal de banlieu!*" from the astonished locals.

The only parts of the film not shot in Canada were the bridge sequences. A "double bascule" drawbridge was required for the jumping stunts, as well as for the flashback plunge, and the nearest such structure was in Phoenix, New York. The whole town turned out to watch the filming of the jumps, sitting out on lawn chairs and drinking lemonade. Three T-Birds were wrecked in the process, and one driver was hospitalized with two broken ankles—though he showed up later, swathed in bandages, to try the stunt again.

I saw this movie when I was twelve, and must admit that its twists and turns went completely over my head. Seeing it again more recently didn't help much. The convoluted script is credited to John Saxton, Peter Jobin and Timothy Bond (who'd had a part in the genesis of *Black Christmas*, and had directed the well-loved television movie *Deadly Harvest* in 1977 and a supernatural thriller starring Jack Creley called *Till Death Do Us Part* five years later). Columbia Pictures handled the distribution and lavished nearly as much money on the advertising campaign as had been spent on the film itself. When the film was released on May 15th, 1981, it did moderately well but was no box-office smash, and the reviews tended towards the lukewarm (which was, admittedly, a big step up from most tax shelter horrors). In recent years, of course, it has gained a bit of a following, inspired the entire *Scream* series more than any other single film, and fans are now calling for a DVD re-release.

Happy Birthday to Me wrapped in September of 1980, and barely a week later another Dunning/Link kill-fest was under way. This was *My Bloody Valentine*, a film which stands almost without rival as the most Canadian horror movie ever made. Directing the picture was George Mihalka, who, with his sister in 1961, was among the first legal émigrés out of Hungary. Mihalka and his family settled in Quebec, where he grew up, got a degree in English literature and began teaching high school. It was the audio/visual department of the *Cégep* he worked at, along with courses he was taking in educational technology, which helped pique his interest in filmmaking. He began taking courses in fine arts and film, and met a fellow film student named Rodney Gibbons.

My Bloody Valentine

Gibbons was interested in cinematography, and the two teamed up to make educational shorts on a variety of scientific themes. Mihalka told *Fangoria* magazine, "These films were great training on how to express things visually, because it was very difficult to have narration where each scientific term was forty-eight syllables long! We managed to inject these shorts with a certain entertaining quality. They were very watchable."

The next step was an ambitious comedy/fantasy short entitled *Pizza to Go*, which had a "man gets trapped in TV land" plot (as in Peter Hyams' Vancouver-shot bomb *Stay Tuned*) and was promoted as "a Comedy in the Fourth Dimension." The half-hour production was noticed by a veteran Canadian production manager and film executive named Bob Presner. Presner recommended Mihalka and Gibbons to another producer, Jack Murphy. Both men ended up in executive capacities on Mihalka and Gibbons' first feature, *Pick-up Summer*,[34] a frothy, would-be sex comedy in the *Porky's* vein which was shot just outside of Montreal in Quebec's Eastern Townships.

After *Pick-up Summer*, Mihalka and Gibbons began developing another comedy, to be called *Project X*. They had by this time hooked up with Dunning and Link, and were writing the script with some of the many Canadians on the staff of the *National Lampoon* magazine. For whatever reason, the project was stalled, and at this point, in July of 1980, a Montreal repertory theatre owner and producer named Stephen Miller approached Dunning and Link with the treatment for *My Bloody Valentine*, then called *The Secret*. "It grabbed all of us so much that we decided to go head first into production," said Mihalka. "We realized it would be a great opportunity to make a different kind of horror movie whose time had obviously come."

Mihalka quickly joined the Dunning-Link cheerleading team alongside David Cronenberg and William Fruet. "[In Canada] you have a choice: either you make films for the NFB which no one sees, or you make films for someone else. And in Canada, Link and Dunning are the only ones willing to give people a chance to make films."

Dunning and Link's production aptitude almost immediately bore fruit. A distribution deal was quickly set up with Paramount Pictures, who had raked in trash bags full of cash with *Friday the 13ᵗʰ* and were preparing their vaults to take in more with *Friday the 13ᵗʰ Part 2*. Paramount explicitly asked for a film so bloody "it would make *Friday the 13ᵗʰ* look like a Sunday school picnic," and insisted that the movie contain what it called "creative kills" rather than simple stabbings or slit throats. The deal also required that the movie be done and released by Valentine's Day of 1981, not much more than six months hence.

Writer John Beaird was hired to turn Miller's treatment into a screenplay with the least possible delay. Mihalka went scouting for a mining town in which to shoot the film and found himself in Sidney Mines, Nova Scotia, where several years earlier a mine had been closed down and turned into a tourist attraction and museum. Tom Burman, whose work on *Happy Birthday To Me* was nearing an end, was contracted to stay north of the border and do the gruesome special effects.

By the end of September, the cameras were ready to roll. Upon arriving in Sidney Mines, the crew found that the enthusiastic townspeople, ecstatic at the prospect of a movie shooting in their town, had gussied up the pithead with flowers and fresh coats of red and white paint. The art department, under art director Penny Hadfield, thanked the townsfolk for their help and proceeded to break the jaunty mine entrance back down to its dirty old self in an attempt to make it look like a working establishment.

Like *Cannibal Girls* and *Black Christmas* before it, *My Bloody Valentine* sets a high-water mark in Tundra Terror by virtue of its sheer Canadian-ness, *and* functions reasonably well as a regular movie in the bargain. Set in the Cape Breton mining town of Valentine Bluffs, the film gives us at least as enlightening and realistic a portrait of Maritime economic depression as *Goin' Down The Road*, making it perhaps the single most successful synthesis of the Canadian documentary tradition with pure genre cinema.

My Bloody Valentine presents us with local boy TJ's ignominious return to town after a failed Pete-and-Joey style bid to make it in the big city. A love triangle quickly develops between TJ, his old girlfriend Sarah, and Axel, his one-time best buddy, with whom Sarah had taken up during TJ's absence. Meanwhile, the Moosehead-guzzling young miners and their girlfriends are putting together an illicit Valentine's Day dance: a town tradition prohibited since the fateful February years before when a miner, driven mad by a cave-in which might have been prevented but for a pair of negligent supervisors who preferred dancing to monitoring methane levels, vengefully pick-axed all those he held responsible for the disaster. The murders begin anew, of course, each presaged by a threatening quatrain of inept poetry, and eventually intrude upon and finally fully eclipse the kitchen-sink drama established at the beginning of the picture.

As cooked up by the production team and goremeister Burman, the murders are a ghastly lot. The movie opens with a scene in which the killer miner takes a date down into the shafts and, upon noticing a heart-shaped tattoo on her breast, impales her on his pick-axe. (This scene has nothing to do with anything, and seems like something tacked on by producers who wanted the killing to start earlier than it otherwise would.) Then we have an old woman roasted in an industrial clothes dryer, and later in the film we see the requisite old doom-crier, in this case a bartender who delivers the film's backstory while standing before a giant neon Moosehead Beer sign, receive the pick-axe through the bottom of his chin and out his eye. Another fellow, wearing a skinny new-wave tie for the Valentine party, is boiled in a pot of wieners and then stuffed in a freezer, his heart having been removed and cooked up with the dogs. A young partier played by Hélene Udy, temporarily alone while her boyfriend goes to get some more Moosehead Beer, is impaled on a jagged shower pipe so that bloody water sprays out her mouth (this, Mihalka says, was his favourite murder scene to shoot). There are sundry other pick-axings, some drillings, a nail-gunning and a hanging to spice things up still further.

The Incubus

Entertaining, realistic and reasonably atmospheric, the movie is one of the happier products of the tax shelter horror boom, with Gibbons' photography, the novel setting and Paul Zaza's reserved score all nicely supportive to the whole. It is also the longest advertisement for Moosehead Beer ever likely to be filmed—with the aforementioned neon sign, countless shots of people drinking the stuff, and even the prominent use of Moosehead boxes to transport items such as Valentine decorations—and that alone qualifies it as hoser horror of the very first rank. The stubby-'n'-back-bacon accents are thicker than thirty-weight motor oil on a cold morning, and the characters are thoroughly, convincingly and refreshingly provincial. At no time does the cast seem like a bunch of Toronto or Montreal actors in rural drag, even though that's what they were. They seem like genuine small-town hosers, as if Mihalka and his crew had just pulled up in Nova Scotia and cast whoever they found there. To some this is merely bad acting or unfortunate casting; to the more discerning it's quite the opposite.

A Great Canadian Moment occurs early on in the picture when Don Francks, playing the top cop of Valentine Bluffs, receives a gore-drenched heart in a candy box. His response to this is so reserved—he winces as though removing someone else's sliver—that audiences in places like Los Angeles responded with gales of laughter to this respectable display of Canuck underacting.

Unfortunately, despite their orders for bloody and creative kills, most of the more gruesome scenes were heavily cut by the gutless, conservative Paramount Pictures in a bid to avoid the commercially deadly X rating. Their first *Friday the 13th* sequel was just about to be released, and was to suffer nearly as much as *MBV*; and the company was under relentless verbal attack from Gene Siskel, the late movie-review partner of Roger Ebert on their television show *At the Movies*, for making movies like this at all. Siskel in fact had begun a letter-writing campaign against Paramount head cheese Charles Bluhdorn. Over thirty cuts were made in Mihalka's film, totaling several minutes of lost footage, demonstrating that Paramount was evidently as adept with a knife as any psycho. The unforgiving scissors of the censor dilute or outright destroy the effectiveness of Burman's effects, along with any craftsmanship that might have gone into the shooting of the scenes. In one sequence, Mihalka took the time to make an unscheduled shot of a six-pack of Moosehead falling to the ground at the feet of a character who is understandably shocked to find that his girlfriend has been turned into a shower. The director was roundly chastised by his producers for wasting time shooting a six-pack, but after all the gore was trimmed from the scene, the six-pack shot was practically the only one left in the sequence. I ask you: where else could this happen but in the world of Canadian horror films?

Having eviscerated the picture of most of its gore and much of its potency (since the gore was central to the flow of the surrounding suspense scenes), Paramount proceeded to advertise the heck out of it, releasing 1180 prints across North America in time for Valentine's Day. Mihalka remembers being in a cab in Los Angeles when an ad for his film came on the radio. "My god," he thought, "we've really made it!" But though the film "opened strong," it didn't have legs to carry it much past the holiday it was exploiting, on which Mihalka blames the heavy hand of the censor. There have been numerous calls to action on the Internet by fans hoping to somehow pressure Paramount into releasing an uncut DVD of *My Bloody Valentine*—John Dunning apparently has all the missing footage sitting in his office—but it's hard to say if they'll ever go for it. They are apparently planning "special edition" releases of their *Friday the 13th* series, so I suppose anything's possible.

BY THE LATE SUMMER OF 1980, Toronto producer Marc Boyman had a project called *The Incubus* all ready for shooting. A script, based on a novel by Ray Russell, had been written by *Amityville Horror* scribe Sandor Stern (later the writer/director of *Pin*), and Boyman was in the process of rounding up a cast that would eventually include John Cassavetes and Western veteran John Ireland. The natural next step was to entice David Cronenberg into the director's chair, but, despite the project's heavy emphasis on matters gynecological, the "master of venereal horror" wasn't biting. He was in fact working on an anthology film project just around this time, for which he was writing the script and was to direct one of the segments, with John Carpenter and Walter Hill tackling the other two. The project fell through when Carpenter left for Stewart, British Columbia to begin work on his remake of *The Thing*.

So Boyman hired British director John Hough, whose earlier work included the Hammer vampire film *Twins of Evil* and the effective, if overwrought, haunted house picture *The Legend of Hell House*. John Cassavetes, fresh from finishing his lady-gangster picture *Gloria*, and in need of some income as he waited for Columbia to release it, arrived in Toronto to play the lead role of Sam Cordell, a small-town doctor battling the demonic force engaged in raping and killing the locals. John Ireland plays the equally concerned town cop, and Kerrie Keane is the glamorous big-city photojournalist who happens to be visiting.

Meanwhile, a local youth is having dreams of torture chambers, his old grandma is trying to cover some family secret up, and Cassavetes moons after his nubile teenage daughter. The hideous rapes continue, and once we learn that the Incubus requires a human host to hide in when not doing its dirty work, the film becomes a whodunit: which character is unwittingly hiding the Incubus inside him or her?

The film is essentially a supernatural slasher film, with the demonic killer using conventional weapons on the men of the town (a board with a nail in it here, a shovel there) and his enormous phallus on the womenfolk. The *Monthly Film Bulletin*, by way of a *Time Out* capsule review by Chris Peachment, observes that the movie, for all its unsavory content, "chickens out on the central image of Russell's novel—the huge size of the incubus' phallus—and it's a castration that reaches out into the whole film."

Curtains

The climax of the film features a downbeat, perverse and reasonably effective twist, but up until that point the picture is a tough slog: alternately unpleasant and silly, with frequently inane dialogue on the subject of weird sperm. (One such line, occurs when Cassavetes reveals his discovery of "three-pronged sperm" swimming around in the victims' wounds. Cassavetes simply could not say the line without bursting into gales of laughter, thus causing the rest of the cast and crew to laugh too, and the bit was eventually cut from the script.) There's little wonder that Stern tried to hide his authorship behind the pseudonym "George Franklin," but he would more than redeem himself by writing and directing the instant classic *Pin* a few years later.

Peter Simpson's company, Simcom, meanwhile, was not resting on its *Prom Night* laurels. Belgian-born cinematographer Richard Ciupka, a Quebec resident since the age of fourteen, was hired to direct a horror film to be called *Curtains*, which in its original conception was a supernatural slice-and-dicer not all that different from *Incubus*. The monster here was not a sex-crazed demon, however, but a 500 year-old banshee, which was designed by makeup effects man Greg Cannom but never used in the picture.

In the end, as written by *Prom Night* story author Robert Guza, the movie tells the tale of a film director named Jonathan Stryker who is staging a casting session at his country estate. The role up for grabs, we are repeatedly told, is a potential career-maker and award winner: a role very possibly worth killing for. Six actresses show up at the house, including the director's ex-lover, who has escaped from the asylum to which she'd been willingly committed in order to do research for the part. Soon the women are being killed off by a mysterious black-gloved party who wears a creepy old-hag mask not dissimilar to the one seen in *Terror Train*, and who seems to be in cahoots with a creepy doll which appears before each murder. Instead of a supernatural banshee creature, the murderess proves in the end to be the comedienne played by Lynne Griffin (the first victim in *Black Christmas*), and if this twist seems completely arbitrary, that's because it was.

Ciupka, who had done a wonderful job shooting Louis Malle's *Atlantic City* (Pauline Kael had described his cinematography as "extraordinary... his work here suggests [Vittorio] Storaro.") wanted Klaus Kinski for the role of the bombastic Stryker, but ultimately had to settle for Wojeck[35] himself, John Vernon. His intention as a director was to go against the grain of 80s horror, with slow camera movements and a generally European sensibility. This was as antithetic to Simpson's expectations as could possibly be: he wanted a straight and simple horror movie—another *Prom Night*.

In the end, nobody was happy. Ciupka, working with British cinematographer Robert Paynter (who moved on directly after the *Curtains* shoot to film John Landis' *An American Werewolf in London*), delivered the deliberately-paced, distinctly European sort of movie he had intended to make from the start. Simpson, unable to see a money-making franchise there, wasn't too pleased with it, and so, continuing a tradition for which his company was becoming known, he scheduled nearly two weeks of re-shoots which he himself directed and which were shot by *The Pit*'s cameraman, Fred Guthé. This didn't occur until 1982, more than a year after Ciupka's original cut had been delivered, and coincided with the first appearance among Toronto film technicians of T-shirts bearing the legend "Another Simcom Re-shoot!" An entirely new ending and some spiced-up murder scenes were shot and appended to the picture, and it was re-cut into as scrupulous a *Halloween* clone as was possible with the footage Simpson had available. Ciupka had his name removed from the credits, very postmodernly replacing it with that of Vernon's director character, Jonathan Stryker. The two largely different crews responsible for making the picture are divided in the end credits between "act I" (Ciupka's original shoot) and "act II" (Simpson's copious re-shoots).

As is so often the case with films made by several people with diametrically opposed objectives, *Curtains* was a success with neither critics nor audiences when it was finally released in U.S. theatres in March of 1983. (It did not see Canadian screens until September of the following year.) To the *Aurum Encyclopedia of Horror*, the picture was merely "a drearily pedestrian variation on the masked marauder theme" and a "woebegone attempt to ring some changes on the format of *Halloween*." The *Hollywood Reporter*, however, apparently called it classy and chilling, proclaiming it, moreover, "rich in surprises of a gripping, sensuous nature." Audiences evidently were not ready for surprises of that nature in 1983, nor for movies so obviously beset by production problems, and the film made very little box-office impact and spawned no sequels. Peter Simpson retired the company name Simcom shortly afterward, successfully reinventing his decade-old corporation as Norstar Releasing.

Hirsute Horror

DECEMBER, 1980, SAW THE PRODUCTION of what may still be the only horror film ever shot in Lake Louise, Alberta: *Ghostkeeper*. The film's premise is ambitious and welcome: it proposes to concern itself with the fearsome Wendigo of Native legend: a hideous, flesh-eating demon who roams the northern woods in search of people-meat. In fact, however, it follows a trio of unpleasant, snowsuit-wearing snow-mobilers who, one snowy New Year's Eve, find themselves lost and snowbound in an abandoned ski lodge. For what seems an eternity, they wander the halls of the cavernous hotel, peer out the windows at the looming mountains, and sing off-key as they sit around the hearth. Penetrating close-ups of the least objection-

Visiting Hours

able of the three, Jenny (Riva Spier), mark her as the protagonist. Eventually an even less pleasant old lady looms out of the shadows to inform them that they're not wanted at the hotel, but then, after mocking their big-city ways, offers them rooms for the night anyway. From there the mystery deepens: pulchritudinous Chrissy, who looks a little like her *Three's Company* namesake, is grabbed by a bearded man while taking a bath and dragged to the cellar where, behind a wall made of ice blocks, an even more bearded man awaits. Her throat is slit by the first man, the more-bearded man approaches her, slavering and moaning as she lies bleeding on the floor, and then an awkward cut evidently inflicted by censors denies us the dubious satisfaction of seeing what happens next.

Jenny and her jerk-ass boyfriend Marty (played by Murray Ord, who would later make a career change to become Alberta's film commissioner) wake up the next morning to discover Chrissy gone and their snowmobile decommissioned by parties unknown. While Marty pokes around trying to figure out how to fix the sled, Jenny is drugged and then chased around by the chainsaw-wielding first bearded man. She knocks him off the roof to be impaled on an iron fence, and the sight of this so unhinges Marty that he smears grease on his face, delivers a soliloquy about his father and then trudges resolutely off into the woods. (He ends up sitting against a tree, frozen to death just like Jack Nicholson in Stanley Kubrick's superficially similar *The Shining*, which was released only a few months before *Ghostkeeper* went into production.) Jenny finds a shotgun and faces down the old lady, who fakes out the younger woman by taking a page from Darth Vader's book and claiming to be her mother. Jenny blasts her anyway, and then assumes the role she has evidently been destined for from the beginning: that of the new

Ghostkeeper, responsible for the care and feeding of the bearded Wendigo downstairs.

It's hard to imagine how such a delightfully indigenous concept could have been more thoroughly botched in execution. Allusions to the native legend aspects of the story are limited to a couple of shots of totem poles and a book on the subject left lying around for Jenny to peruse, and the Wendigo itself (spelled "Windigo" in the credits of the movie) is nothing more than a portly, hirsute fellow standing mutely in the shadows—hardly the ten-foot tall, toothy, red-eyed demon of lore. On the positive side of the ledger, the movie does work up a little bit of atmosphere, and the acting is not too bad. (This is with the crucial exception of the bland central performance from Riva Spier, who had appeared in a tiny role in *Rabid*, but here is unable to convey the emotions required of her.) The appropriately wintry photography is by none other than John Holbrook, who, under a pseudonym, had directed the lost horror-porn item *Sexcula* in 1974. The director and co-writer of *Ghostkeeper*, James Makichuk, was born and raised in Swan River, Manitoba, worked repeatedly with the well-loved Canadian director Phillip Borsos, and went on to write the story for a female softball team-versus-backwoods rednecks movie called *Blood Games* (1990) and the screenplays for two Winnipeg-shot made-for-cable science fiction pictures, *Roswell: The Aliens Attack* and *Dream House* (both 1998).

The Pit, another movie involving mysterious hairy beings and annoying characters, is a real curiosity, and a lot more fun than *Ghostkeeper*. Twelve year old Jaime is a peeping tom and social outcast (though certainly not, as the press notes label him, "an autistic boy") whose only friends are his talking teddy, the frogs and snakes he keeps in his terrarium, and a clutch of apish troglodyte creatures who live in a large hole in the ground near his home. He's been luring the townspeople he doesn't like (a bully, a nasty old lady in a wheelchair, a football-tossing rival for the affections of his babysitter) to the edge of the pit and then pushing them in since before the movie began, or so the clumsy editing would have us believe; but he's still basically a nice guy—just a little misunderstood. Eventually, with Jaime's help, the creatures climb out of their hole and stage a mini-rampage through the area, munching on topless quarry-swimmers and truck drivers before being driven back to the pit, blasted with shotguns and buried forever by the dumber'n-a-bag-of-hammers townsfolk. Then, finally, in a brief coda, Jaime gets his well-deserved comeuppance at the homicidal hands of a sinister girl named Alicia.

Sammy Snyders, though on the face of things a poor actor, actually does quite a good job of maintaining the fragile balance between likable misfit and insufferable demon child in his performance as Jaime. The troglodyte creatures are another matter: their glowing eyes and fixed, wolfish grins allow them very little emotional latitude. And Sonja Smits, only a year away from hitting the horror big time in David Cronenberg's *Videodrome*, contributes a performance as Jaime's teacher which, while sympathetic, has very little narrative reason for being.

There's nothing particularly Canadian about the movie at first glance, aside from the presence of Smits and another actor, Richard Arlen. The setting is clearly meant to be the United States (the bumbling cops, played by very Canadian actors, wear large American flags on their sleeves), and indeed the movie was shot mostly in Beaver Dam, Wisconsin. But with its pathetic outsider hero, milky cinematography, cheery, tooting musical score and slightly sleazy Afterschool Special patina, *The Pit* otherwise fits snugly into the Can-horror canon. The all-important pit scenes were shot after the fact in a Toronto studio, presumably in a belated attempt to punch up the horror aspects, with the monsters played by midgets in Los Angeles-built suits. Children covered in fake hair had been used in the Wisconsin location, but, all conceded, it looked terrible rather than terrifying, and so the L.A. suits were commissioned and small adult actors put inside them. Whether this was indeed an improvement is debatable (the original outfits can still be seen briefly in the above-ground attack scenes for comparison), but the glowing orange eyes in the new monsters at least provide a nice visual connection with the sentient teddy bear, whose eyes also glow whenever he's aroused. The additional shooting provided an opportunity for extra gore, with big close-ups of the animals nuzzling around at the bloodied flesh of their victims, but it also caused the picture to go $141,000 over its original $900,000 budget.

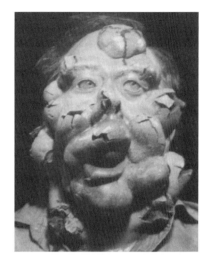

The film was directed by Lew Lehman, whose other contributions to Canadian horror included a draft of the screenplay for John Huston's *Phobia* and an attempt, through his office as the president of the Director's Guild of Canada, to stop the shooting of *Deadly Eyes* in 1982 because they were using an American director. He did some acting in his later years and died in 2000 at the age of sixty-six. *The Pit*, his only directorial effort, was shot in 1979, but not released

Spasms

until two years later. It warn't no barn-burner at the box office, as they sometimes say, and never really attained the cult status it might have. I myself hold a special fondness for the film—for no very good reason, it should be noted—and was cheered to notice it on the DVD release roster for some time in 2004. It's twisted and strange, yet still retains a kind of charming naïveté little seen in horror films of any nation. Oh, Sammy Snyders, where are you today?

Horrific Canucks - Part III

CATCHING UP WITH OUR ROUNDUP OF HORROR HOSERS, we find Michael Ontkean, in the years before *Slap Shot* and his role as Sherrif Harry S. Truman in *Twin Peaks*, starring with none other than Orson Welles in a 1972 Satan-cult thriller by Bert I. Gordon called *Necromancy*. Gordon, renowned for his oversized creature pictures (check out those initials!) would head north to British Columbia a couple of years later to make the giant-critter epic *Food of the Gods*.

In the same year as *Necromancy*, B.C.-born director Edward Dmytryk, with a long

Hollywood career behind him including *Murder My Sweet* (1944) *Back to Bataan* (1945), *The Caine Mutiny* (1954) and *The Young Lions* (1958), and a stint as one of the original Hollywood Ten during the Communist witch hunt (he spent time in jail, then in exile, before finally naming names), made one of his final films, a horror-accented version of *Bluebeard* starring Richard Burton. Dmytryk had only a few films left in him after that, including the Bobby Sherman leper colony drama *He Is My Brother* (1976).

Leslie Nielsen's horror career neither began nor ended with *Prom Night*. He'd played a chemical-addled macho businessman in William Girdler's *Day of the Animals* (1977), and in 1982 he appeared in the "Something to Tide You Over" segment of George Romero's *Creepshow*. Later he appeared as Dracula in Mel Brooks' weak spoof *Dracula: Dead And Loving It*.

James Cameron, a young, bearded go-getter from Kapuskasing, Ontario, threw his hat into the horror ring in the early Eighties. Cameron had moved to Los Angeles at an early age and eventually found employment at Roger Corman's cut-rate dream factory, doing the visual effects and working in the art department on such movies as *Galaxy of Terror* and *Battle Beyond the Stars* (not such a stretch, since any in-house spaceship footage at Corman's company was treated like the town bike: everyone got a ride). Cameron made his directing debut in 1981 with *Piranha II: The Spawning*, the sequel to Joe Dante's entertaining 1978 "homage" to *Jaws*. Cameron's film was no match for its predecessor in any respect, though it upped the ante in giving its eponymous creatures wings, so that they can fly up out of the water and bite the cheeks off of any dumb shlub who happens by. Cameron is naturally a little sheepish about this debut (claiming to have been fired after seven or eight days of shooting), but he would of course make up for it many times over, at least in terms of his own self-esteem, simply by directing *The Terminator* (1984) and *Aliens* (1986). He wouldn't work in Canada until it was time to film the present-day sequences of that dramatically rusty hulk (more so even than *Death Ship*), *Titanic* (1997). Given that his experience in Newfoundland included a messy professional break-up with cinematographer Caleb Deschanel and an incident in which the crew's lunch was spiked with LSD, he's unlikely to return to the country of his cradle days anytime soon.

***

DAVID MAMET OR NEIL LABUTE MIGHT—just might, and still probably not—have been able to tell the tale of a psychopathic misogynist (Michael Ironside) stalking a feminist television commentator (Lee Grant) through a hospital, taking out sundry patients and staff along the way, without falling into the trap of making a rather sick and misogynistic film out of it. A woman filmmaker might have done better still with a story like that; but why would she want to? Screenwriter Brian Taggart (later the writer of the marauding-rat picture *Of Unknown Origin* (1984) and a 1997 Winnipeg-shot cable-TV remake of Stephen King's *Maximum Overdrive* called *Trucks*) very definitely lacks the subtlety and talent required to sidestep this pitfall, and *Visiting Hours*—shot over two months in the fall of 1980 on a budget of $5,500,000 under the working title *The Fright*—lands in the quicksand with an unpleasant "splort."

There is, however, a good deal of effective suspense wrought by Jean-Claude Lord's direction in some of the stalking scenes, and Ironside and Grant, along with Linda Purl as a helpful nurse, all act their roles adeptly. Somehow this doesn't help matters much though, and the overlong running time makes the hurt even worse.

William Shatner plays a character who, lacking any other *raison d'être*, can only be taken for Lord and Taggart's preemptive mouthpiece when he says things like "He's after you because you're a strong woman!" (Just the sort of woman, in fact, whom real-life woman-haters might be happy to see put through just the sort of ordeal Grant endures here.) Grant spends most of her time howling "No! No!" as Ironside trudges relentlessly after her, until she finally gets to stick him with his own switchblade, just as Ironside had earlier done to Purl, to punish her for the crime of being spunky. (Ironside, incidentally, claims to have received "all kinds of marriage proposals in the mail" after the film's release.)

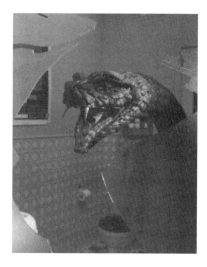

Spasms

On the plus side, we do get to see Neil Affleck, fresh from his role as Axel in *My Bloody Valentine*, essay the small role of a hoser cop, and Michael J. Reynolds—the Man from Glad—as a pompous, patriarchal lawyer. And then there's Shatner, who, despite the bewildering pointlessness of his role and the fact that he's once again simply playing Shatner, looks strangely at home in the slasher *milieu*: he should probably do more of them. Add to that a number of tension-filled sequences and some good photography by the ubiquitous René Verzier, and you have a film which might be worth watching, if you for some reason don't mind being alternately bored and mildly offended for the better part of 105 minutes.

In a review of *Visiting Hours* for *Cinema Canada*, John Harkness made the following observation:

> The crazed killer is an American phenomenon… the fact that these stories are native to the American psychology means that John Carpenter could make art out of *Halloween*… and Tobe Hooper out of *The Texas Chainsaw Massacre* because they felt the stories in their bones. When we try to imitate a foreign genre we wind up with a *Visiting Hours*, a *Terror Train*, a *My Bloody Valentine*… These films are aesthetically unsuccessful because they are not felt by their makers.[36]

Harkness doesn't get into the sorts of films that Canadian filmmakers might "feel in their bones," at least not in that particular article, but it seems likely that sod-tilling, squid-jigging, drunkard-loser movies are what he had in mind. I don't propose that these sorts of movies are any worse for Canada or the Canadian film industry than killer misogynist films might be, but I strongly maintain that they aren't necessarily better. I'm also not convinced that Carpenter or Hooper would take the notion that they can feel knife-wielding maniacs and chainsaw cannibals in their bones as all that much of a compliment, and I am less convinced still that "feeling" a subject or theme to the degree that good art can be made of it is some kind of birthright entirely dependent on the artist's country of origin. There is no invisible wall around our country that keeps out serial killers, nor any special nutrient in the water preventing them from being born and bred here. We can sadly boast of child killers, prostitute killers, sex killers and crazed killers in Canada—horror lives here just as it does anywhere else.

"*Spasms!*" WILLIAM FRUET LAUGHS when the title is mentioned. "That was kind of a silly movie. I was hired, I did the job. That's it." That's as may be, but *Spasms*, for all its silliness, provided Canadian horror cinema with several choice moments, including one that, were it not for the plentiful photographic evidence, might today be difficult to believe ever took place. Also known by the more pedantic handle *Death Bite* (the title of the book upon which it is very loosely based, and which Fruet says was almost unfilmable), the film tells the story of a giant devil-snake reported to live in New Guinea, and an obsessed, cardigan-wearing big game hunter (Oliver Reed) who manages to bring it back to Toronto. Aided by a small-time criminal played by the King of Kensington himself, Al Waxman, the beast escapes, inflicting its toxic "death bite" on anyone it meets. Waxman, it seems, is working for a bald snake cultist played by Canadian director George (*Riel*) Bloomfield. The snake monster meanwhile shows good, solid exploitation-movie sense by first invading a sorority house filled with nubile co-eds (one played by Judy Khaner from *Videodrome*) and then menacing a frisbee-playing babe in a flesh-coloured bikini. The serpent's worst is saved for the nefarious villain Waxman, however: sitting in his van, he gets chomped, blows up like a knotty balloon and splits open into a grotesque, spongy, venomous mass. For fans of *The King of Kensington*, the cheap but beloved little CBC sit-com of which Waxman was the star, or even for *Cagney and Lacey* regulars (Waxman, if you'll recall, played the lady cop duo's gruff chief), his grotesque death scene in *Spasms* must have been more than a little upsetting. For those who thought the CBC show trite and annoying, and Waxman's character too jolly by half, the scene is really quite satisfying.

The climax of the movie has Reed in a gargantuan wrestling match with the demonic serpent. He manages to de-oculate the beast, soiling his white cardigan in the process, but the snake finds the strength for one last death bite before being machine-gunned into bits by Peter Fonda.

The makeup effects for the exploding-Waxman scene were engineered by the legendary Dick Smith, the man who'd transformed Linda Blair into a vomitous demon in *The*

Exorcist, Dustin Hoffman into a hundred-and-seven year-old man in *Little Big Man* and Robert DeNiro into, well, Robert DeNiro in *Taxi Driver*. Smith was at first approached by Fruet and co-producer John Newton only to advise Quebec-based makeup artist Stéphan Dupuis on how to do a bulging, inflating arm. (Smith had done such an effect in *Altered States* the year before, and it bears noting that Joe Blasco had done very similar things in *Shivers* fully six years earlier.)

But it had been decided that a more spectacular effect was required to compete with transformation-heavy productions like *An American Werewolf in London* and *The Howling.* According to Smith, the two men arrived at his upstate New York house in July of 1981 and asked him to think up some sort of effect never before seen. Perhaps he had some trick he'd always wanted to do and never had a chance to try. Smith responded with a lecture along the lines of "Look—you can't come up with some revolutionary new technique at the drop of a hat! It takes a lot of work, a lot of thought, a lot of experimentation…" At around this point, the makeup godfather stopped and smiled, because he'd just had an idea that he realized would be perfect for *Spasms.* "I guess I'll have to eat my words," he told the filmmakers.

Videodrome

Smith's solution was to pump a chemical solvent called trichloroethane up into a foam dummy head, thereby causing an ugly swelling and melting effect which would appear to be coming from inside the body. Fruet and Newton loved the idea and persuaded Smith to come on as the head of the makeup effects department. Stéphan Dupuis became Smith's assistant, and another makeup artist, Carl Fullerton (the young American who had done the makeup effects on *Rituals* several years earlier) was brought in to help as well.

The Waxman explosion is indeed gruesome, despite the fact that Fruet and cinematographer Mark Irwin chose to film the effect at normal speed instead of Smith's recommended slow motion. Also, a green colouring added to the chemical, intended to give the liquid a more poisonous look, stayed at the bottom of the bottle after a neglectful technician failed to shake it up.

Smith was not responsible for the snake monster itself, only the makeup on its victims. "Everything was going fine until the killer snake arrived from New York and it didn't work," remembers Fruet. "They made the skeleton, and it all worked until they put the skin on. Then it didn't work any more."

The snake was built by a naturalist named Ray Mendez, whose experience was in building dioramas for the Museum of Natural History in New York. He was aided in the design by Neal Martz (later to do the makeup effects for *Silence of the Lambs* with Fullerton) and in the robotics by Lew Gluck, whose usual line was in making limbs for handicapped children. Mendez had been brought into the project by Michael Maryk and

Brent Monahan, the authors of the original novel, who wanted a puppet of their snake "just as a plaything." When the book was optioned by the Canadian producers, the authors put them in touch with Mendez.

The screenplay changed the book's large but not monstrous snake into a full-on supernatural devil-creature. But Mendez stuck to his naturalist guns with his design ideas, wanting to keep the snake as realistic as possible. (Here's a little irony for you: an American toning down the fanciful ideas of Canadian filmmakers by his insistence on documentary realism.)

"Producers always want monsters that can come up and shake hands, serve dinner, wear a tuxedo and conquer the world," Mendez remarked. "So we gave them a few modifications on that." Particularly a concern to Mendez and his team were the snake's eyes for a scene in which Reed would be gouging them out. Stated Mendez, "Many scenes in which eyes come out usually don't look right to me. The problem... has always been that when the eye comes out, it comes out like a ball... I wanted Reed to stick his finger into the eye and pop it."

To that end, Mendez made an intricate eye of many layers, which he calculated would react like a real eye when poked. "When Reed's fighting with the monster, he sticks his finger in the eye, the eye collapses, white comes out first, and then you see a spurt of blood, which is very different than just having the eye roll out of the socket; a little bit gorier," Mendez relates. The effects man also recalled that "Oliver Reed [was] a real character. He sprayed the entire camera crew with blood, he drenched them. He really did a number on them."

When the snake failed to perform, Fruet was despondent. "I thought that night, well, that's it. What are we going to do? We don't have this great finale now for this snake to fight Oliver Reed." But everyone's bacon was saved by the film's gaffer, Jock Brandis, who was, Fruet says, "a mechanical genius. He took [the snake] home that night, took apart a crane he was making, put all the motors in, and the next day it worked. I mean, it was a silly thing to begin with, but it actually worked... he virtually saved the movie."

Spraying the crew with blood was only one of Oliver Reed's monkeyshines on the film. He pretended to be black throughout the shooting of the film's New Guinea scenes (actually the Scarborough Bluffs), wore a Labatt's 50 t-shirt at unexpected and inappropriate times, and fell out of a boat during the shooting of a beach sequence. Reed had a bodyguard named Reggie with him, and Reggie was forever admonishing the actor and calling him a "silly sausage." Reggie or not, Reed still made international headlines during the *Spasms* shoot for wandering around downtown Toronto wearing his white cardigan, but, however, no pants. Fruet remembers Reed very fondly, antics and all. "He was a complete professional," says the director.

Spasms was shot from August through October of 1981, and it cost nearly five million dollars. It didn't get a release until 1983, and wasn't very profitable even then. That's likely because it isn't a very good movie: choppy editing of the sort which screams "production problems!" is everywhere, the script is bad and the ending is abrupt and unsatisfying. It's rumored that Fruet and company simply ran out of money, and while that may not be true, judging from the result it certainly may as well be. The most disappointing aspect of the whole thing is that Fruet is such a clean, no-nonsense director, whose movies, good or bad, can usually be counted on for brick-wall neatness of construction. In most of his films he puts together shots like Ernest Hemingway does sentences. In fact, Fruet, a very nice man, looks a bit like a leaner, fitter Hemingway. But in *Spasms*, as in the later Fruet horror *Killer Party*, the Papa-style simplicity is nowhere to be found.

Videodrome

POLL THE HARDCORE DAVID CRONENBERG fans of the world and a not inconsiderable number of them will pick *Videodrome* as their favourite of his films. It's a rare picture to which the "ahead of its time" cliché can legitimately be appended, but *Videodrome* is one of them. *Sui generis* to the max—is it horror? Science-fiction? Mass-media critique? Head trip?—the film perplexed many and ultimately failed at the box-office, but today its fans are legion and its thematic implications, still fantastical in 1983, have become commonplace twenty-first century reality.

Asked in an interview to give a one-sentence description of his movie, Cronenberg responded "The best film you'll ever see in your life." For those who haven't seen it (and equally helpful, perhaps, for those who have), here is a slightly more descriptive plot synopsis: *Videodrome* concerns the exploits of a low-brow cable channel executive named Max Renn, whose in-house technician, Harlan, chances upon an underground snuff-tv show called *Videodrome*, a program which, Harlan tells him, consists of nothing but "torture… murder… mutilation…" Renn (played by the hollow-cheeked James Woods) is captivated by this premise and immediately becomes addicted to the show. In the by-now standard Cronenberg turn of events, he begins experiencing first mental and then physical changes as a result, suffering from violent hallucinations and a vaginal orifice in his belly. Programmed by the shadowy figures behind the show, Max becomes an assassin, murdering, among others, his network partners. (One of these is named Moses, indicating perhaps that Cronenberg well remembered a certain City TV honcho's disparaging remarks in California ten years earlier, and was, as in *The Brood*, again killing his enemies by proxy.) A radio sex columnist played by Blondie singer Debbie Harry, Jack Creley's MacLuhanesque media pundit, Creley's daughter, Sonja Smits, and Les Carlson as a slimy administrator all figure into the complicated plot, which is complicated further by Renn's increasingly frequent hallucinations.

Renn turns out to be a pawn in a vast but vague conspiracy of which *Videodrome* (the show) is but an opening gambit. Its larger goals remain obscure, but world domination may very well be in the cards. Such details are far from Cronenberg's principal preoccupations, however, which is what helps to make his movies—this one in particular—so compelling. Cronenberg is, in my view, above all a humanist, in that he's concerned with the boundaries of humanity: where it begins and, much more so, where it ends. By nailing down that moment, be it in Max Renn, Rose from *Rabid*, Seth Brundle from *The Fly*, or any of a half-dozen others, Cronenberg hopes, as any committed artist does, to unearth clues as to just what it means to be human. Horror is indeed the perfect genre through which to mount such an investigation—exploring aspects of humanity and life by depicting monstrousness and death—but rarely is it done with the conscious concern and intelligence of a film like *Videodrome*.

That said, with its scenes of televised torture, misplaced vaginas and a masochistic Blondie, it's as hard to use *Videodrome* to refute those who accuse Cronenberg of misanthropy and a terrible fear of sex as it is to present the film as an exhibit for the prosecution. It's too impenetrable to use as evidence of anything much, except its own glorious weirdness. But also woven deeply into the picture is a fear of corporate culture and a horrifyingly prescient vision of the future of television.

With the success of the sci-fi action picture *Scanners* having secured the attention of financiers, Cronenberg was able to put projects together much more easily than before, even if they were disturbing and weird. *Videodrome* was made with the tax shelter money still piled in drifts against the buildings of Bay Street. It had been gathered up by Pierre David, Victor Solnicki and Claude Héroux's company Filmplan International,[37] who had also produced *The Brood*. When they asked Cronenberg what he would like to make, the director pulled out an old story called "Network of Blood," installed himself in an office in downtown Toronto and and rewrote it into an extreme, and effects-filled, script he now called *Videodrome*.

The script was filled with strange events: people melting into each other, growing sexual organs everywhere, exploding and mutating in a dozen different ways. Rick Baker, the special effects artist who'd just won an Academy Award for *An American Werewolf in London*, caught wind of it and smelled a challenge. By the time Baker was committed to the picture, however, budget and script revisions had drastically reduced the number and fantastical complexity of the effects sequences, as well as the time available to create them.

There was still plenty of work for ape-loving effects maestro Baker. The portal in Woods's stomach was a major job, necessitating a clever dummy body seamlessly melded to the actor's real head. Later there was the transformation of Woods's hand into a gun—a handgun, get it?—and Les Carlson's exploding head. Gunshot wounds, cigarette burns and breathing videotapes added to the burden of latex.

Any difficulties in realizing this imagery were greatly compounded by Cronenberg's last-minute script revisions. This was a movie he was committed to getting right, but, he says, "It wasn't the kind of film where you just know when you've got it. It was slippery." The director had to stop things periodically to give the crew pep talks, partially in an effort to relieve the freaky tension of working on such a strange film, partially to reassure them that, on some level at least, he knew what he was doing. But as things moved closer to both the end of the shoot and the story—the last scenes would be the last to be shot—Cronenberg felt less and less that he was completely in control of his own story.

One proposed ending to the film depicted an orgy in which the characters would twist and melt into one another, trading flesh and organs and identities in the process. It sounds a little like the climax of a later film, Brian Yuzna's *Society*, in which the grotesque party serves as a metaphor for the class struggle rather than a demonstration of body politics gone haywire and the voraciousness of an insidious technocracy. But that was thrown out in favour of a scene in which Woods shoots himself in the head while hallucinating, and a television explodes with guts. Rancid pig intestines were used for this, and five cameras covered with plastic recorded the stinky effect.

Videodrome

While Cronenberg reports a personal satisfaction with this conclusion, it does seem to undercut his insistance that the film be consistently "first person"—a narrative so devoted to the perspective of its addled protagonist that the audience is completely at his mercy. In the ending of the film as it stands, we go back and forth between Woods's hallucination of having a cross between a pistol and a roast beef instead of his hand, and an outside reality in which we see a simple gun. By this point, according to Cronenberg's conception, both Woods and the audience should be far too gone to glimpse the actual weapon. The inconsistency may be a byproduct of the reshoots required to finally finish the end sequence; it's hard to say for sure. But it does tend to muddy the clarity of vision you can achieve, or think you've achieved, or be tumorously deluded into believing you've achieved, through multiple viewings of the movie, even though clarity was probably never one of Cronenberg's primary concerns.

The picture was released early in February, 1983, by which time Cronenberg was already at work on his next film, *The Dead Zone*. For the first time, the "Sultan of Shock" had a major studio behind him: Universal Pictures, having noted the box-office dollars stirred up by the earlier *Scanners*, had come on with their financing and distribution muscle halfway through the shoot. But they had no idea how to sell the picture. The indecipherable animated trailer alone is proof of this. A disastrous preview screening in Boston, with comments like "I hated your fucking film" scrawled across the cards, foretold *Videodrome*'s prospects in the marketplace.

Indeed the film was a disaster with audiences. Even horror fans generally stayed away. The financial failure of the film was a disappointment for Cronenberg, of course—"I was devastated," he claims—but he tried to look on the bright side. "I'm still gratified that there are 600 prints of my movie sitting around," he told *Fangoria* magazine shortly after the picture's release. "That fact alone makes me feel good, even though they might end up as banjo picks."

IN *Deadly Eyes*—DECIDEDLY LOWER-BROW THAN *Videodrome*—common harbour rats feast on steroid-enhanced corn and transform, as though by magic, into dachshunds wearing fur coats and pointy-nosed Halloween masks. These entities then proceed to gobble up half the population of Toronto—including then-rising star Lisa Langlois and Can-horror perennial Cec Linder—like they were milk bones. Scatman Crothers, fresh from *The Shining*, once more fails to make it through to the end of a film, and his presence is sorely missed in the final reels.

The rodent costumes are actually not too bad—certainly an improvement on those featured in *The Killer Shrews*—but they do give themselves away in shots of the animals hurrying *en masse* down a hallway or a street, in which it's apparent they're expecting kibble more than carrion when they get to the other end. But while this is charming and easily forgiven, one is less disposed to generosity when slogging through the cumbersome sub-plot about the high school teacher (American actor Sam Groom), his smitten student (Langlois) and the attractive, hard-nosed health inspector played by Sara Botsford of *Bells*. Only Scatman Crothers, playing a doomed city worker (he must have considered his death-by-a-thousand-bites scene a birthday present after a year under Stanley Kubrick's thumb), manages to have any real fun with his part.

The budget for the picture was in the neighborhood of 1.6 million, half of which was put up by the Hong Kong based Golden Harvest (maker of many, many popular kung-fu films) and half by Canada's Film Trust Securities. Paul Lynch was originally hired as the director, but three weeks before shooting he opted out, and, as producer Paul Kahnert said, "we had to get a director fast." Golden Harvest had worked with Robert Clouse before with great success on films such as *Enter the Dragon*, so they brought him in. This led to a protest by the Director's Guild of Canada, whose president was Lew Lehman, director of *The Pit*. An American director was contrary to the Canadian Content rules required by the tax shelter laws, especially one who, Lehman argued "had no outstanding international reputation." Clouse of course did have a reputation—you can't make Bruce Lee's biggest hit and not have one—and he also had previous dog-directing experience, having made a killer-pooch picture called *The Pack* back in 1977. The controversy held up *Deadly Eyes*' shooting for two days, but it was ironed out after Kahnert pointed out that 594 of the 606 total cast and crew members were Canadian. The picture began its six-week schedule in late January of 1982.

It has been suggested that director Clouse was having his own brand of fun by including a scene—plucked, almost entirely unaltered beyond the obvious, from *The Blob*—in which a movie theatre is invaded by the shaggy rodents as the patrons are trying to concentrate on none other than one of Clouse's own Bruce Lee movies. My counter-suggestion is that, since both the Lee picture and *Deadly Eyes* are Golden Harvest presentations, the filmmakers simply took what was available and cheap to them to use as the background to yet another ratty slaughter scene. The thirty-eight dogs, which had been brought in from California for the film, apparently were ill with the shits for the entire shoot. One of them, according to Lesleh Donaldson, had even died—suffocated, perhaps, in the suit, or perhaps simply the victim of a heart attack.

The movie is kind of fun in its own way, retaining some of the sleazy energy of James Herbert's book while at the same time providing yet another good argument to the opponents of genetically modified foodstuffs. It also neatly fulfills a glib prediction made in 1976 by a British Columbia director named Peter Bryant, who, in the course of a debate on the future of the Canadian film industry, offered the patronizing (no less so for being accurate) opinion that "I really don't think it is that hard to make a commercial movie. Try rats eating babies." *Deadly Eyes* tries just that, and features in the bargain both a couple who wear loud plaid shirts while snogging and a character named "Hoserman." Add to that some nice photography by the steadfast "human dolly" René Verzier, and plenty of TTC streetcars clanging their way

Deadly Eyes

beneath many a fluttering American flag, and you have one of the most Canadian horror films ever made. It didn't get much of a theatrical release from Warner Bros. before popping up on video, but it can boast a small fellowship of devoted fans.

Another product of the tax-boom era was the gritty mystery-slasher picture *American Nightmare*,[38] executive-produced by Anthony Kramreither and Paul Lynch and boasting the most disarmingly honest title of the whole slash-for-cash cycle. (It was produced under the title *Community Standards*.) Lynch, exercising his talents for graphic design once again, designed the rather nice opening credits, but after they're over the grainy 16mm photography manages to make Toronto look as shabby and sleazy as any urine-soaked Times Square street corner—an accomplishment in itself. The story concerns a rich pianist's hunt for his missing sister, last seen turning tricks in a scummy hotel room before finding herself at the wrong end of a surgical glove-wearing maniac's razor. The pianist immerses himself in his slumming sister's world: an apartment building populated exclusively by amiable strippers, good-hearted prostitutes and sardonic transvestites. The maniac stalks these characters one-by-one in a series of reasonably suspenseful scenes before being revealed as pretty much the person you expected him to be from just about the third scene in the picture.

The film was shot for the bargain price of $200,000, which was in fact a full $70,000 over its original tiny budget. For that amount, we get an effective thriller which appears to have a social conscience, a series of suspenseful stalking sequences, some likeable characters, a seriously scummy Toronto and a killer wearing a beret. That's a lot more than many movies with five times the budget can offer. As a bonus, the film featured an appearance by the late Paul Bradley, of *Goin' Down the Road*, in the role of a hotel clerk. "He's an actor we should see more of," said Lynch at the time, delighted at getting someone of Bradley's calibre to appear in such a small, non-union picture.

American Nightmare, despite (or because of) its sleazy atmosphere and slyly apt title, is one of the better by-products of the tax shelter era. If more like it had been made—that is, more half-decent returns on small cash investments—the whole experiment might not today be regarded as an ill-conceived, greed-fuelled ricochet which sent our whole industry careening off on a course nobody ever planned or wanted, and from which it has yet to recover. Certainly it gave genre filmmaking a bad name in this country, or, rather, an even worse name. Indelible associations were made between cheap, cynical, artless, greedy filmmaking and the types of films that most often resulted. Few of the horror pictures made in Canada over the next decade or two would seriously challenge this assessment.

By 1984 the tax shelter era was over, mortally wounded by the bureaucratic pen stroke decreeing that the 100-percent allowance should be reduced to somewhere in the neighborhood of 65. For the best, perhaps. A debacle the tax shelter era might have been, but it was our debacle. (Unlike the Canadian Co-operation Project, which was, as the name suggests, a collaborative effort.) As such, no matter how many bad films it produced, the era's product is something to which it's legitimate, as a Canadian, to be irrationally attached. It's not an expression of nationalism as much as a simple appreciation of the sometimes shamefully, sometimes hilariously skewed cultural mirror the films hold up to us. And anyway, as terrible as they were, the tax shelter films would have some stiff competition in the movies yet to come: the largely direct-to-video junk of the '80s and '90s.

A killer
waits at the
high school
dance.

If you're not
back by midnight...
you won't be
coming home!

A SIMCOM PRODUCTION
LESLIE NIELSEN · JAMIE LEE CURTIS in "PROM NIGHT"
SCREENPLAY BY WILLIAM GRAY · STORY BY ROBERT GUZA, JR.
PRODUCED BY PETER SIMPSON · DIRECTED BY PAUL LYNCH

AN AVCO EMBASSY PICTURE
Released by BARBER ROSE INTERNATIONAL FILMS LTD.

PROM
NIGHT
X

V.

Monster Chiller Horror Theatre

(1983–1999)

THIS MIGHT SEEM LIKE A GOODLY NUMBER of years to cover in a single, rather thin chapter, but ultimately one must grimly accept that this period was something less than a golden age in Canadian horror movies. Inadvertent mithridatism has led us to accept poor genre product as the norm over the last twenty years, with the tax-shelter pictures bleeding into the direct-to-video years, and not much of it good. The fire of the pioneer days was cooled.

Still, many of the films are of interest for reasons other than quality. Some of them are simply insane. As well, the body of work over these home video-dominated years includes such benchmarks as David Cronenberg's excellent remake of *The Fly*, the box-office hit *The Gate*, and, of course, the towering achievement that is *Pin*. So take my hand and let's stroll awhile through the alien landscape of Canadian horror film in the last two decades of the twentieth century.

Jeff Goldbloom
about to become
The Fly

Horrific Canucks - Part IV

First, however, we ought to visit with a last group of Canadians who've made their mark on horror cinema around the world.

Frances Bay, born in Dauphin, Manitoba, spent much of the nineties playing sinister old ladies in a variety of movies (though she has played goofy old ladies in as many comedies). She appeared in *Die Hard* director John McTiernan's first film, a little spookfest called *Nomads*; she was Aunt Barbara in *Blue Velvet* and Mrs. Tremond in *Twin Peaks: Fire Walk With Me*; she appeared in *Critters 3*, Stuart Gordon's *The Pit and the Pendulum*; and she grew tentacles and carried an axe in John Carpenter's Toronto-shot *In the Mouth of Madness*. She also appeared in the minor Canadian horrors *The Neighbor* and *The Paperboy*.

Dan Aykroyd had apparently wanted to play a monster since his Ottawa childhood, and his dream finally came true on the set of *Twilight Zone: The Movie* (1984). In a short prologue sequence, he plays a mysterious hitchhiker who turns into a blue-faced, fangy creature and mauls Albert Brooks, just after the two have bonded by singing old television theme songs. A year later, he played a sweet-natured parapsychologist in Ivan Reitman's smash hit *Ghostbusters*, and did so again in the inevitable sequel five years on. And in 1991, Aykroyd wrote, directed and starred in a horror spoof called *Nothing But Trouble*, in which he plays an ancient small town justice of the peace who mercilessly torments Chevy Chase and Demi Moore, threatening them with, among other things, a torture device called "Mister Bonestripper." The movie was a terrible stink bomb, and Aykroyd hasn't directed anything since. More recently, though, he made an appearance in *Earth Vs. The Spider* (2001), a strange and terrible direct-to-video clunker.

Neve Campbell, the Guelph-born *Party of Five* star who made an early appearance in a Canadian horror film called *The Dark*, became a genuine horror superstar in Wes Craven's *Scream* trilogy, in which she plays the constantly imperiled heroine Sidney. Campbell also appeared in the teen witch's brew *The Craft* in 1996, right alongside one-time Canadian resident Fairuza Balk.

Another of Campbell's *Craft* co-stars was Helen Shaver, a St. Thomas, Ontario-born actor who played Paul Newman's wife in *The Color of Money*. Besides *The Craft*, Shaver explored the spooky side of things alongside Margot Kidder in *The Amityville Horror*; fell victim to a satanic zit (which explodes and emits spiders) in the Toronto-shot voodoo thriller *The Believers*; and battled giant worms in *Tremors 2: Aftershocks*. She was also a regular on the *Poltergeist* television series.

Keanu Reeves, famed for his roles in *Speed* and *The Matrix*, has made a few horror appearances as well. Besides his manful attempt to take on the part of Jonathan Harker in Francis Coppola's *Dracula*, he battled demonic lawyers in *The Devil's Advocate* (1997), played a serial killer in *The Watcher* (2000) and essayed the role of a loutish husband in Sam Raimi's supernatural thriller *The Gift* (also 2000). As well, it must never be forgotten that, without even taking a credit, Reeves played Ortiz the Dog Boy in the monster comedy *Freaked* (1993).

Later, Canada would produce horror thespians like Laura Regan, the daughter of infamous former Nova Scotia premier Gerald Regan and eventual heroine of the Vancouver-shot *They* (2002, also known, pointlessly, as *Wes Craven Presents: They*). This picture, directed by American Robert Harmon and shot by reliable Canadian cinematographer René Ohashi, is an underdeveloped muddle about the monsters living in children's closets. Regan was also featured in *My Little Eye* (2002), a U.K./Canada/U.S. co-production partially shot in Nova Scotia, which used a security-camera mise-en-scene to delineate the horrific fates awaiting a group of youths foolish enough to participate in a haunted-house reality show. Kris Lemche, from *Ginger Snaps*, also appeared in the spooky, well-loved picture.

Dan Aykroyd

AFTER THE COMPLETION OF *Videodrome* in late 1981, David Cronenberg asserted, he "was ready to do a movie I had not written. I was not ready to write anything, and why that should have been I don't know." But somewhere deep inside he did know: it was to find relief from the unremitting darkness and frustration that was *Videodrome*. The movie would be an adaptation of Stephen King's ESP bestseller *The Dead Zone*, and its relatively light, pulp-ish nature was precisely what appealed. "If you're used to comedy, *The Dead Zone* is a heavy picture," Cronenberg told Chris Rodley, "but if you're used to *Videodrome*, *The Dead Zone* is not."

Another contributing factor might have been that he'd been offered the project once already, three years earlier. King's book had first been optioned by Lorimar Productions and was to be produced by *Tootsie*-meister Sidney Pollack, who had engaged Stanley Donen to direct. A Lorimar executive who didn't know about Donen's participation brought Cronenberg in to have a look, and when the miscommunication was discovered, the Canadian was sent on his way with profuse apologies ringing in his ear. But Donen's *Saturn 3* came out that year and was terrible, and Lorimar, suffering from stinkers of their own like William Friedkin's *Cruising*, closed up their feature film division to concentrate on television, and all this contrived to send the project into hibernation for several years. The shrewd Italian producer Dino De Laurentiis picked it up from Lorimar and hired *Halloween* producer Debra Hill to develop it. Andrei Konchalovsky (*Runaway Train*) was approached to direct, and later Hill and De Laurentiis considered hiring Walter Hill. But Hill was busy with *48 Hours*, so, as far as Debra Hill was concerned at least, that left Canada's "Baron of Blood."

When Cronenberg chanced to meet Hill on a visit to John Landis' office in L.A. and she offered him the job of directing *The Dead Zone*, Cronenberg immediately said yes. Hill, De Laurentiis and Cronenberg met the next day and made the deal. A screenplay existed, written by King himself, which Cronenberg describes as "terrible… a really ugly, unpleasant slasher script." Ultimately the script used for the film was one supervised by Cronenberg and written by Jeffrey Boam, who would go on to have a hand in the scenarios for such films as *The Lost Boys*, *Innerspace* and *Indiana Jones and the Last Crusade* before dying at the untimely age of fifty-one.

The Dead Zone began shooting in various Ontario locations in January of 1983 and lasted through until mid-March. As a result, Cronenberg was almost too busy to notice the poor performance of *Videodrome* when it was released in early February. The crazy little movie was dear to his heart, and so its treatment at the hands of Universal—the bizarrely awful, animated trailer, for example—was wounding. But the *Dead Zone* shoot kept his mind occupied and his spirits reasonably high.

The story finds Johnny Smith, a tweedy high-school teacher, in the throes of a tentative romance with his colleague, Sarah. He drops her off one rainy night and is subsequently involved in an accident with a toppled milk truck. This sends him into a five year coma, and when he emerges, under the care of Dr. Sam Weizak, he's acquired psychic powers (which manifest themselves in visions of the future, the present, or the past), and Sarah has married another man. Johnny experiences a vision of his nurse's house burning down and very quickly acquires a reputation as a man of vision. This leads to his part in the hunt for a serial killer preying on young girls in a neighboring town, and then to an attempt at starting a normal life. But Johnny has never properly recovered from his accident; indeed, he seems to be getting weaker with each psychic event. The film concludes with Johnny seeing a vision of populist politician Greg Stillson becoming President of the United States and starting World War III, and trying, successfully, to prevent this from becoming a reality. He dies in the process, however, marking neither the first time nor the last that a Cronenberg hero would perish in the final reel.

A fine, all-star cast, missing only "Henry Fonda as The President" and "Curt Jurgens as The Kommandant," was rounded up for the picture. Americans filled out most of the larger roles—Christopher Walken in the lead role of Johnny Smith, Martin Sheen as the evil politician, Brooke Adams as Johnny's girlfriend Sarah, Tom Skerritt as the sheriff— but an interesting and talented group of Canadians filled out the supporting roles. There was Sean Sullivan, of *Dr. Frankenstein on Campus*, as Johnny's father, Jackie Burroughs as his mother, Nicholas Campbell as the scissor killer, none other than Colleen Dewhurst as the killer's demented mother, and trusty old Les Carlson as a beleaguered newspaper editor. The great Herbert Lom, originally of Czech origin, famed as Inspector Dreyfuss in the *Pink Panther* movies but also an accomplished horror actor in Hammer and Amicus films, played Johnny's doctor, Sam Weizak.

Producer Debra Hill reports that working with Cronenberg was much different than with her old colleague John Carpenter. Carpenter is quick to make decisions on set, she told *Fangoria* magazine's Uncle Bob Martin, whereas "David likes to take everything into consideration and ponder things a bit, which sometimes frustrates me. But when the time comes, I say, 'Today's the day you have to make a decision,' and he makes it…

David likes to have his options open."

Cronenberg tried some new tricks to help shape Walken's performance. It's been reported that, at the actor's request, Cronenberg kept a .357 Magnum loaded with blanks handy for the scenes in which Walken slips into his psychic visions. Unexpected gunfire caused the sudden flinching in the actor that Cronenberg was after, though it also reportedly gave a camera assistant a temporary hearing impairment. It's been reported too that Walken performed the role entirely while "floating on a haze of marijuana smoke," so the gunshots may have been necessary simply to rouse the actor for the more dramatic scenes. In any case, Walken's performance is excellent, and the film itself is to this day held up as one of the finest of all Stephen King adaptations.

The Dead Zone

It is, at the same time, one of its director's less interesting films, but it's not as bereft of his usual themes and concerns as has often been remarked. Johnny's psychic powers, for example, operate much as any of Cronenberg's progressive maladies, rotting the hero away as surely as a cancer. It's true that here the treatment of medical science is entirely different than in previous films: Herbert Lom's Dr. Weizak is as warm, caring and compassionate as can be, and a far cry from such cold-blooded, progress-obsessed medicos as Dr. Emil Hobbes in *Shivers*, the plastic surgeons in *Rabid* or Oliver Reed in *The Brood*. Even the doctor-hero of *Shivers*, Roger St. Luc, is something less than empathetic: he's a downright chilly fish. But for all of Weizak's caring and concern, he and his science are more or less useless to Johnny. But Cronenberg, recognizing that *The Dead Zone* was the first of his films to feature God-fearing characters, has his own take on the matter: "I think you could make a good case for saying that in *The Dead Zone*, God is the scientist whose experiments are not always working out and that the Johnny Smith character is one of his failed experiments," says the director in Chris Rodley's *Cronenberg on Cronenberg* interview book.

The Dead Zone, though shot in Ontario, was in many ways a Hollywood film: Cronenberg's first. Though *Videodrome* had enjoyed the backing and distributive acumen of a major, if unenthusiastic, studio, *The Dead Zone* was not merely a Paramount Pictures release from the ground up, but was produced by the famed Italian mogul, and human blockbuster, De Laurentiis. Howard Shore, then known only for his scores for *The Brood*, *Scanners* and *Videodrome*, was not contracted to do the music; though the composer who was, Michael Kamen, a neophyte then but since very well established in the industry, was not any better known. Kamen's music was no piece of Hollywood hackwork or beginner's fumble: indeed, even during the process of composition, it was effective enough to have his anguished neighbor appearing at his door and pleading with him to "Please, please stop playing the piano! You're scaring me and my family to death, we're having nightmares, we can't sleep! Please stop!" De Laurentis was dubious about hiring Kamen, opining that "A new composer is like a watermelon—you never know if it's ripe until you open it up." At the premiere, however, the producer followed through on his analogy by declaring the score "ripe, sweet and juicy." Cronenberg himself was well-pleased with the music as well, though neither Kamen nor any composer besides Shore has worked on any of his feature films since. (Like screenwriter Boam, Kamen died young, succumbing to a heart attack in November, 2003, at the age of 55.)

The Dead Zone was a modest hit when it was released in October of 1983, and came at a point when Stephen King's name on a film was losing its automatic-blockbuster veneer. *Cujo* had barked its way onto screens two months before Cronenberg's film, while John Carpenter's *Christine* raced through two months after it. *Children of the Corn* and *Firestarter*, monumental stinkers both, would arrive in the spring of 1984 to tar the Stephen King-feature film connection forever, despite the best efforts of Rob Reiner later on. King himself appeared to appreciate Cronenberg's interpretation of his book, declaring the movie "pretty good," and the concept of sticking Johnny Smith into his own psychic visions "wonderful." For its director, the movie was a giant step out of the Canadian horror movie wasteland. For most, it likely would have been a passport to Hollywood, but Cronenberg was Canadian through and through, and since the dark days before the making of *Shivers* he hadn't wavered in his commitment to live and work north of the 49th.

George P. Cosmatos, Italian-born, of Greek origin, educated in Britain and known to work in Canada, America and all over Europe, is practically a one-man co-production. He'd worked with big actors like Richard Burton, Sophia Loren, Burt Lancaster, David Niven and Roger Moore, but by 1982 he was easy prey to the Canadian tax-shelter trap, as he hadn't worked in features for several years. When he caught wind of Brian Taggart's man-vs.-rat script *Of Unknown Origin*, he enlisted his friend Verna Fields to go to bat for him. Fields, the Oscar-winning editor of *Jaws*, called up the project's producers, Claude Héroux and Pierre David, to recommend Cosmatos for the job.

Taggart's script was an adaptation of a novel called *The Visitor*, by Chauncey G. Parker III. The book was *Moby Dick* in a New York brownstone, with an uptight executive waging war with a large, but not monstrous, rat who has invaded his domain. (Cosmatos pays homage to this conception by using a copy of the Melville epic as a prop in the film.) Taggart's initial pass emphasized the horrific elements of the story, but upon Cosmatos' hiring, the suspense and character aspects were brought to the fore instead. Cosmatos found inspiration in a 1973 National Film Board of Canada documentary called *Ratopolis*, which delves deep into the creatures' uncanny tenacity and knack for survival against all odds.

It was the "story as a metaphor for survival" that appealed to Peter Weller and helped bring him on board the project in the role of Bart Pierce, go-getter businessman and proud homeowner. Weller, later to hit the peak of his fame in the *Robocop* movies, found himself attracted also to a character arc that would see him move from excessive civility—symbolized by his yuppie eyeglasses—to primal barbarism by the end. Weller, too, was taken by *Ratopolis*, as is his character, Bart Pierce, who is seen watching it intently midway through the movie.

The central brownstone location was a difficult thing to find in Montreal. The location eventually secured was an ex-drug rehab house, something very like the setting of the Canadian sitcom *Hangin' In*. The office where Bart Pierce works was in reality the Alcan Aluminum company office, at which the filmmakers could only work on Sundays. René Verzier was hired to shoot *Of Unknown Origin*—"a very good cameraman," Cosmatos calls him. Verzier, living up to his "human dolly" reputation once again, performed long tracking shots without the aid of a Steadicam or other stabilizing rig. "Verzier was steady as a rock," Cosmatos reports.

Of Unknown Origin

A great admirer of *Jaws*, Cosmatos was determined to hold off on shots of the rat until later in the picture. This was undoubtedly the right decision (not just because the rat has a rather puppety countenance), since much of the film's effectiveness comes from the audience's identification with Bart Pierce and his fear and confusion about just what has invaded his house. The producers fought this approach, believing that more monster meant more box office, but on this front Cosmatos prevailed.

The rat was suggested instead by a hilarious shadow seen on the walls (it looks as though the varmint lugs his own spotlight around) and a rather more effective series of extreme close-up shots of twitching whiskers, scampering feet and a heavy, worm-like tail. All of this was shot by a skeleton crew after the main unit had finished its day. The production had forty rats to use, which wasn't always pleasant because, as Cosmatos complains, "rats stink." Furthering the science of using other animals to double for rats, they also used a possum now and again.

The resulting movie has no shortage of admirers, who cite its intensity and allegorical value as primary virtues. To be sure, the movie is at least reasonably effective, and certainly it's different from, and superior to, the usual tax shelter era horror product. Furthermore, for what is essentially a two-hander with one of the hands (or paws) absent for most of the running time, it's a remarkably compelling picture, and it's easily the finest George P. Cosmatos movie I've seen. It's no masterpiece, but it would be a fine complement to *Deadly Eyes* if the two films ever ran in a double feature.

As the tax shelter days receded ever further in the rear-view mirror, horror movies continued to appear, many of them leftover projects from that time. There was Ota Richter's *Skullduggery*, a dull and confusing tale of role-playing games gone wrong, which was apparently shot in 1979 (by *Prom Night* cameraman Robert New) and only released years later to a monumentally lukewarm reception—certainly not with the ticker-tape which greeted *Rona Jaffe's Mazes and Monsters*, a TV movie on the same theme featuring Tom Hanks and also shot in Toronto. Claudio Castravelli's *Evil Judgement*, a dour picture about an insane killer judge, co-photographed by *Seizure's* Roger Racine, was finally released in 1984. It had been shot in 1981 on a budget of just over a million dollars.

City in Panic was a Toronto-set slasher whodunit about a killer stalking the city's gay community who is in turn stalked by a radio talk show host and his policeman friend. The movie was begun in December, 1985 under the title *The Fear Stalker*, with a week of extra shooting done in February, 1986. *Identity Crisis* featured *Flick* star Robin Ward as a set of homicidal twins, one of whom is on a killing spree. It was directed by Bruce Pittman and based on a play by Peter Colley called *The Mark of Cain* (a title by which the film is also known). The picture began for Pittman with a call from Anthony Kramreither, the genteel Austrian-born producer who had appeared as an actor in *The Reincarnate* years before. Kramreither scraped together what Pittman calls a "super low budget" and then stepped back to let Pittman do more or less whatever he wanted with it. Pittman, Colley and John Sheppard (who had authored *American Nightmare*) adapted the play, and Pittman directed the film amid the wintry snowscapes of Ontario. The result is a somewhat overbaked but entertaining psychological thriller with lots of good, chilly Canadian atmosphere. And *Junior*, a slightly more horror-and-prostitute-oriented version of *Deliverance*, featured a pair of working girls who, tired of the street, flee their brutal pimp and buy a houseboat in a small town populated with equally brutal back-woods folk. The biggest, fattest, slobbiest and droolingest of these is Junior, a husky, chainsaw-wielding momma's boy. It goes without saying that he wears filthy overalls. The two prostitutes must pit their Daisy Mae outfits and big-city wits against Junior's over-alls and low country cunning. It's *Straw Dogs* again, but crosses the line into horror by the end, with Junior fully psychotic, disfigured by burns and waving a chainsaw. The ad copy played up the horror angle: "First you saw *The Texas Chainsaw Massacre*... Then you met Freddy in *Nightmare on Elm Street*... Now meet... *Junior!*"

Junior was made for a quickly-scrounged $350,000 and shot in Hudson, Quebec. It was, says producer and co-writer Don Carmody, "an afterthought," which had been cooked up on the set of *Meatballs III*. Carmody and John Dunning, who had produced the sequel, were sitting on the set bemoaning that "wasn't it a shame that we had this wonderful set and didn't blow it up. So we sat there over a few drinks and wrote the treatment for *Junior* that afternoon." Carmody and another writer turned the treatment into a script in a matter of days. Carmody was busy producing both the *Meatballs* sequel and *The Vindicator* at the time, so he brought in Jim Hanley, who had been running Carmody's television company, to direct. The *Junior* shoot took place at night while the *Meatballs* crew was still working during the day. When *Meatballs III* was done, and the *Junior* folks had all they needed, it all ended with a mighty conflagration which razed the boathouse set to the ground.

ONE MIGHT LEGITIMATELY PREDICT GREAT THINGS to ensue from the director who brought us *My Bloody Valentine*, especially when he's teamed with the star of *The Pyx*. Sadly, George Mihalka's *The Blue Man* (released on video as *Eternal Evil*) must be rated a disappointment. It shares a number of story points with *The Reincarnate*—at times feeling almost like a remake, or, if you like, a reincarnation of that picture—but like *The Reincarnate*, it sorely lacks the *joie de vivre* that might have lodged it high up in the Canuck-o-Canon with the likes of Mihalka's earlier horror triumph.

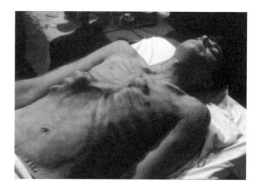

The Blue Man:
too festive?

We are introduced to Paul Sharpe (Winston Rekert), an unpleasant director of TV commercials whose unhappiness about his picture-perfect life is difficult to sympathize with. Rekert already owns a sports car, so his mid-life crisis leads him to indulge in astral projection, which he learns from elusive guest star Karen Black and which he may inadvertently be using to kill anyone with whom he has the slightest grievance (his psychiatrist, his father-in-law, and so on). Sharpe's projection, which we never actually see, is the Blue Man of the title. A mustachioed police detective who looks like a refugee from a porno shoot suspects that the deaths—which involve massive contusions of the victims' ribs and the disintegration of every major organ—may not, in fact, be the heart attacks the coroner's initial diagnosis claims they are. It turns out that Rekert, like the young sculptor of *The Reincarnate*, has been targeted by a body-swapper whose current vessel looks much like a forty-three year-old Karen Black. A weak and (in the context of the film's take on astral projection and soul-trading) fairly illogical twist brings the story to a close after eighty-five reasonably eventful but somehow still molasses-slow minutes. By the end, Rekert (having perhaps gained some crucial strength of character through his absolute loss of it at the hands of the malicious reincarnate) is finally directing the feature film he's been dreaming about making for years.

If only we'd been treated to a glimpse of the Blue Man—potentially an eerie and disconcerting image—the movie might have had some impact. As it is, we are left with the age-old device of seeing the monster only through the crayon scribblings of a child actor, and a number of impressive P.O.V. camera movements courtesy of camera operator Christian Duguay (later the director of *Scanners II*, *Scanners III* and *Screamers*). Special effects man Ed French, an American whose credits include *Sleepaway Camp* and the Montreal-shot Dunning/Link production *Whispers*, had been hired in New York by *The Blue Man*'s "Executive in Charge of Production," Buck Houghton, to build the misshapen corpses of the Blue Man's victims. Houghton, however, found the resulting bodies "too festive." Whatever that might have meant, the effects were not used in the final print and the movie suffers for it. French, with pyrotechnician Matt Vogel, also contributed some gunshot wounds for the film's climax, in which the mustachioed policeman shotguns many of the cast members. These effects more or less made the final cut, but neither Vogel nor French were given credit in the film.

The movie isn't bad, exactly—the relative serious-mindedness of the project, considering when it was made, is welcome, and the similarities to *The Reincarnate* along with the presence of Karen Black breed a fuzzy nostalgia for the early Seventies, even if you weren't there—but one is left with the overwhelming feeling that the film is, for no very good reason, not what it might have been. The film misses out completely on the potential for sexual confusion in its premise, with Rekert exhibiting little of the curiosity, repulsion, or perturbing mix of both one might reasonably expect from a straight man who's just found out he's been sleeping with a millenia-old male consciousness, albeit packaged in a slightly younger female body. With Vlasta Vrana appearing as a gay man who succumbs to Black's charms too, the movie seems to be taking a step in that direction, but the macho hero is never allowed to exhibit the engaging mixture of delight and bewilderment seen in Vrana's character. This lack of thematic fortitude helps keep *The Blue Man* in a corral with all the other seems-like-a-TV-movie wimps.

William Fruet returned to the horror genre around this time with a movie he'd rather forget, a curious item called *Killer Party*. The movie began as a straight-up slasher script from writer Barney Cohen, who had started out as an advertising copywriter and evolved into a screenwriter of sufficient versatility that he could be hired to pen *The Happy Hooker Goes to Washington* on the one hand and several After School Specials on the other. It was one of these latter projects which got him the job of writing *Friday the 13th part 4,* and *Friday the 13th* in turn secured him the task of writing *Killer Party* (known variously during its gestation as *Fool's Party* and *The April Fool*).

The producers of the film, a passel of New Yorkers who both Fruet and Cohen referred to as "inexperienced," were all for creating another entry in the now-tired slasher sweepstakes. But, says Fruet, Warner Bros., who had signed on to distribute the film and provided advance money to make it, "finally looked at the script that they'd put the money up for, and they said 'Whoa! We don't do these kind of movies!'" Fruet was caught in the middle of "this movie that doesn't quite know how far it wants to go with things."

Cohen's original script, Fruet reports, was "pretty vicious." After a convoluted opening, the film seems to be treading well-worn slasher territory—the sorority house, the prank-gone-wrong, the vengeful pledge—but eventually, after much prankage (some by *Terror Train*'s Howard Busgang, who played Ed the ill-fated jokester) and a special-guest-star appearance by Paul Bartel, a party starts up in the abandoned frat house on "Goat Night," and we get some off-screen killings and a demonic possession.

"We were very much on the same wavelength," Cohen says of his relationship with Fruet, "I had a certain amount of problems with the producers who hadn't made a horror film before and were nervous. Fruet made them unnervous." At Fruet's behest, more and more comedy was added to the script, along with the supernatural happenings of the climax. "We eventually went for the all-out approach," Cohen says.

The producers brought in cinematographer John Lindley to shoot the picture, which went before the cameras in Toronto in the summer of 1984. Lindley would later become an A-list Hollywood artisan, shooting movies like *The Stepfather*, *The Serpent and the Rainbow*, *Field of Dreams* and *Pleasantville*. Fruet remembers him as being "certainly in the wrong place on the wrong sort of picture… we both did it for the same reason: we thought we were getting Warner Bros. and we'd get a big release." Fruet bemoans Lindley's extravagant lighting methods, which involved setting up a multitude of lights and then sculpting the shadows with flags, cookies and other tools of gripology. "I'd never seen anybody light like this…You're going crazy, because you're doing a simple shot and waiting half an hour. Unfortunately John and I didn't get along well because I had a job to do, and he was going to do it his way because he wanted the look. But I think he's a very fine DP; it's just too bad we didn't meet under different circumstances."

Killer Party

The movie's violence and makeup effects mayhem, orchestrated by Gordon Smith, seems mostly to have been cut. Fruet doesn't remember shooting much gore at all since it didn't interest him particularly, though production stills show such tidbits as severed hands and torsos impaled by tridents. None of that is in the movie. There was evidently too much ketchup for the timid Warner Bros., who shelved the project for nearly two years before selling it to Metro Goldwyn Mayer. The new company gave the picture a cursory release in the spring of 1986, and it thereafter crawled its way onto the video shelves, from whence it occasionally springs out to variously annoy, delight or baffle unwary viewers with its po-mo opening, crude humour and bloodless, multiple-personality approach to horror.

Blood on a Blue Collar: Gerard Ciccoritti's Vampire Travails

IN THE MID-1980S, YOUNG TORONTONIANS Gerard Ciccoritti and Robert Bergman were working for a production company called PF Productions, which made advertising and promotional films for a variety of clients. Both of them wanted nothing more than to be film directors, and to this end, after working for PF for a year, they quit and opened an even smaller commercial production house of their own, which they called Lightshow Communications. Their plan was simple: spend four years learning the business side of things: how to put on a suit and impress people in meetings, how to manage a business, how to stick to a budget and all that sort of thing, and then make the leap to feature films.

Lightshow grew to four partners in total and became successful very quickly, so that after only two years in business they felt ready to tackle a feature. Short-form drama was still the realm in which they felt safest, however, and so their first feature film idea took the form of a four-part anthology horror film to be called *Night Screams*. Ciccoritti would direct the picture, and, between him, the other partners and an outside writer friend, the four episodes were written. "This was the mid-Eighties," remembers Ciccoritti. "The video boom was huge! If you shot the phone book and kept it in focus, someone would buy it from you. They were so hungry for product. And horror, action and sex were at the top of the list."

Bergman and one of the other partners kept the day-to-day business of Lightshow Communications going while Ciccoritti and Michael Bockner attempted to raise the money for *Night Screams*. This involved much flying back and forth to Los Angeles and other cities, much impressing of potential investors with expensive dinners and nights out on the town, and the depletion of their company bank account inside of eight months.

They kept going on the hope that *Night Screams* would come together and bring in some cash, but it never did. "The whole thing fell apart, and we got kicked out of our swanky offices… the four of us actually had to sneak out at four in the morning with our furniture and equipment, because we were five months behind on the rent." The partners set up new digs in "a shitbox house in Chinatown" and tried to lure back their clients, but no dice. The clients had all found new companies to deal with. It seemed like the end: no money was coming in and they couldn't even afford the rent on their modest new office space.

One particularly depressing Friday afternoon, as the four were discussing which of them should call his father to borrow rent money, Ciccoritti looked at Bergman, the most technically adept of the four, and asked how much unexposed film was sitting in the company fridge. "About ten thousand feet," Bergman answered. "Is that enough to make a feature?" Ciccoritti wanted to know.

Bergman told him that ten thousand feet might itself be a good length for the final film, but taking into account mistakes, accidents and otherwise wasted film, it would take a lot more than that, double or triple that amount at least, to comfortably start shooting. Ciccoritti stood up, told the group "Okay. We're going to make a feature next week," and left for home, where he spent the weekend writing a movie called *Psycho Girls*. The script involved twin sisters, one of them (naturally) insane. She poisons the parents, but the other one is blamed and thrown into the bughouse. Years later she escapes, having by now been driven mad by her unjust incarceration, and, with some equally insane goons along to help out, takes revenge by kidnapping, torturing and murdering the now-sane sister's family and friends.

On Monday Ciccoritti came into the office with his script, and they calculated that if they could put together enough money to buy another ten or twenty thousand feet of film, and then persuade everybody they knew to work for free, then they could make a feature film. The partners agreed, and they spent the next five days casting, crewing and preparing their small horror picture.

It was almost precisely the scenario from a dozen years earlier when Ivan Reitman and Daniel Goldberg had their own brainstorm. Things were different now, though:

Canada had a genre movie history, and there were people around who had made money on horror films. One would think the process could only have become easier.

The film was shot over a nine day stretch in December of 1985, with hard cash costs taken care of by fifteen thousand dollars borrowed from friends and family. There were the usual low budget problems along with the usual creative solutions. Relates Ciccoritti: "One day when we were halfway through killing everybody, the actress phoned in and said 'I'm gonna be three hours late.' Okay, on a low-budget film, what do you do? There was nothing else to shoot. So we invented a new scene." The new scene was a Tarantino-esque break from the action in which the two helper psychos order pizza (Ciccoritti himself plays the delivery boy) and sit around talking about movies they like. Everyone was pleased with the addition, and Ciccoritti notes with pleasure that "Years before Quentin Tarantino, we have the first appearance of a post-modern moment in cinema... it's of a piece, because the whole film is, like, 'anything can happen.'" Ciccoritti took plenty of visual inspiration from existing cinema as well. He laced the first half of his film with Hitchcock-inspired suspense scenes, and the second half was influenced more by the Italian *giallo* pictures and by Pier Paolo Pasolini's *Salo*. "I took the ritual aspect of slaughter and just made it a gore-fest," he says.

Psycho Girls

They spent January editing the picture on a flatbed editing machine in the kitchen of their house, and were just about done when Michael Bockner's father called them up. The elder Bockner was retired now, but he'd been a film distributor back in the day, bringing horror and art house pictures alike up to Canada. He'd been friends with John Cassavetes and had been the first to screen the maverick director's movies north of the border. "Very, very cool guy, a great man... A wonderful inspirational guy for us, me especially." Martin Bockner still had some connections in Hollywood, and he was going down there to visit friends. If the four Lightshow partners had a tape of their film, maybe they'd like him to shop it around on their behalf while he was down there?

They all thought this was a wonderful idea, and made a "poor man's transfer" by pointing a video camera at the editing machine's grainy, underlit monitor. Bockner Senior took the tape with him, and forty-eight hours later, the four got a call from him. He was in the offices of Cannon Films, and they had watched *Psycho Girls* and now wanted to buy it. "They just want to know, how much do you want for it?" Martin Bockner said. The four partners hadn't even thought of this, and after some scrambled calculations decided that paying all their outstanding costs would take somewhere around $120,000. "$250,000," they told the elder Bockner. "Okay," he said, and passed the figure on to the Cannon bigwigs.

Muffled swearing and excited negotiations could be heard from the three-thousand mile distant Cannon offices. Bockner came back on to report that their price could be met, but that was that. No rights, no residuals, two hundred and fifty thousand dollars and goodbye. The four Lightshow partners could hardly believe it: their movie wasn't even finished and it had been sold for a massive profit. "This movie business is easy," they decided.

Cannon had one other condition, though: a new scene, involving either sex or violence or both, had to be shot and inserted into the first five minutes of the movie. Having no choice, the partners readily agreed. "So we looked at the movie again and we though 'boy, we've killed everybody off in this movie. Who's left to kill?'" The answer was to slaughter an initially marginal psychiatrist whose initial function had been purely expository, like Detective Teller in *Prom Night*. To spice it up further, a stripper was hired for the extra shooting, just to get a bit of sex in there too.

Ciccoritti and his friends were enchanted with the feature film business, and clearly horror was the way to go. As it happened, Ciccoritti and Alliance honcho Robert Lantos had mutual friends, and through Lantos (who had seen and liked *Psycho Girls*), Ciccoritti met two New York-based stockbrokers who had a "relationship," as they said in the Eighties, with the Hungaro-Canadian mogul. The two brokers, who had invested in and otherwise financed films through Lantos, decided that it was their time for a little glamour, and they would produce a film themselves. They flew to Toronto and called up their friend Lantos and asked if he knew someone who could make films well and on the cheap. Lantos suggested Ciccoritti and his company.

The two investors, Stephen Flaks and Arnold Bruck, met with the lads of Lightshow Communications. Ciccoritti was the only one of the four who had a completed script: *Graveyard Shift*, the story of a vampire cab driver in New York. It was a very romantic, Anne Rice conception of vampires, "based on an ancient Greek play," Ciccoritti reports, but married to the idea that even a vampire has to make money, and what better job than one at night in which prospective victims would call him? It was a clever idea, and the two stockbrokers saw this immediately. If Ciccoritti could do it for under a half-million bucks, they were in.

The actual process of making the film went "very smoothly," Ciccoritti says. "It was run more like a real movie." Bergman was once again the cinematographer, and Michael Bockner was the producer. The problems, the director reports, only arose at the end. About two weeks before going to camera, Ciccoritti had a small anxiety attack upon realizing that *Graveyard Shift* was not shaping up as a particularly gory or exploitable movie. "There's a lot of sex, but not a lot of blood, because I was more influenced by trying to do something like *The Hunger*," the director says. He knew this wasn't what the investors expected, so he called a meeting with them, "and I laid it on the line. I said 'listen, I don't know if you two guys get it, but we're making an art movie here, an art vampire movie." For two hours, Ciccoritti and the partners went through the script and pointed out all the subtleties and nuances of his script. "At the end of it they said 'That's fuckin' great!'" But Ciccoritti wanted absolute clarity: if they didn't like it, they should say so now, so that he could rewrite it and juice up the gore and the sex or whatever might be needed. "They said 'Don't touch it!'" Ciccoritti avows. "So we shot it and I cut it and it was an art film. They said 'What have you done here? This is an art film!'"

Days of fighting followed. Finally the two producers told Ciccoritti that they were friends with Ralph Rosenblum, the film editor who had cut *Annie Hall* and several other Woody Allen films. The deal was that Rosenblum, retired now, would fly up, look at the film, and decide if it worked or not. All involved would abide by his decision. Ciccoritti, well knowing Rosenblum's credentials, agreed. He and the other Lightshow partners frantically did all they could to get the film ready: they booked a theatre at the lab, put on the best temp effects and music they could, perfected all the dissolves, and made it as nice as possible for Ralph. For Ciccoritti, everything was at stake.

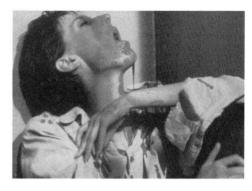

The husky, bearded Rosenblum arrived, shook everyone's hand, and asked to watch the film alone. The two investors went across the street to a bar, while Ciccoritti, terrified and shaking, was up in the projection booth peering out through the little window at Rosenblum and his notebook.

At the end of the screening, everyone gathered around to wait for the editor's pronouncement. Rosenblum pulled out his book and looked up at the group. "Ten minutes in?" he said. "When you see the girl and you go back to her and back to the thing, then back to her and back to the thing, then back to her again?" The Lightshow partners nodded mutely. Rosenblum said, "Only go back to her twice." Then he closed his book.

Graveyard Shift

The New York partners demanded an expansion on this criticism. At this point, Ciccoritti claims, "and I've got witnesses," Rosenblum said something like "In the twenty years I've been doing this kind of favour for people, this is the tightest and best fine cut I've ever seen." While the Lightshow partners cheered, the two producers muttered amongst themselves and said "Thanks, Ralph," and drove the venerable editor to the airport. Upon returning, they told the quartet, "You know, Ralph's an old guy, and he doesn't know what the fuck we're talking about. We're going to recut it anyway."

Graveyard Shift was remade into what Ciccoritti calls "a bit of a mess" by the two Americans. "That's what's available today," he laments. But the film did very well on video, returning something like five million dollars on a $400,000 investment.

Two years later, the two New Yorkers returned to Toronto. In the meantime, the Lightshow fellowship had broken up. Flaks and Bruck told Ciccoritti, "If you do a *Graveyard Shift II*, we will not touch it." So Ciccoritti put together a script for a second vampire movie. This one had the same vampire, played by Silvio Oliviero, having retired his hack and taken up film acting. Luckily there is a vampire movie that he can audition for, and, more fortunately still, they only shoot at night. "So we shot *Graveyard Shift II*," reports Ciccoritti, laughing incredulously at the memory, "and the fuckers did it to me again! At that point it's like 'okay, good lessons to learn, but I wish they would stop. I got it!'"

Ciccoritti's intention had been to make a vampire version of Michael Powell and Emeric Pressberger's *The Red Shoes*. This was the lure with which he had snagged his cast, who were at the time considered real up-and-comers, but it was not to be. The new cut emphasized such gore as there was (the film can boast a decapitiation-by-pool cue) and shots of the vampire's fangs in favour of the atmosphere Ciccoritti had hoped to muster. And so, when the New Yorkers once again interfered with his vision, he felt badly not only for himself but for all the cast and crew who had trusted him. "Maybe it's the Catholic in me, but I still feel guilty," he says.

The movie was released to the same video label as the previous *Graveyard Shift* picture under the title *The Understudy: Graveyard Shift II*. It received some good notices, not least from the tough-to-please *Aurum Film Encyclopedia*, which called it "one of the better horror films about making a horror film." It did well enough on video, but Ciccoritti was not to fall for the stockbrokers' lure again. He didn't need to. By this time he had carved out a career for himself on the Canadian film scene, and now bounces between large-scale television films like the CBC miniseries *Trudeau* and the occasional feature. But, always remembering the genre in which he started, and which he still professes to love, he's got a new horror script ready to shoot.

Buzz, Buzz, Buzz

IN THE SUMMER OF 1986, David Cronenberg finally collided with the mainstream audience that had eluded him thus far. *The Fly* was a legitimate box-office hit, providing Twentieth Century Fox with another big summer science-fiction moneymaker alongside fellow Canadian James Cameron's *Aliens*. (The two films were in fact re-released as a double bill later in the season to wring even more moolah out of them: a tactic which was all the more effective because the two movies were complementary in their tonal opposition. One was a deliberately-paced, almost tender three-handed sci-fi-horror-romance about a giant bug creature with corrosive vomit; the other a nitro-fuelled sci-fi-horror-action film with a large cast battling a great number of giant bug creatures with corrosive vomit.)

The Fly begins with a tall super-nerd called Seth Brundle, played by tall super-nerd Jeff Goldblum, trying to impress freelance writer Veronica Quaife (the almost-as-tall Geena Davis) with his geek wit and weird science. He's invented nothing less than a tele-portation device, with which he proposes to "change the world as we know it… end all concept of transport, of borders and frontiers, of time and space." Intrigued, Davis follows him back to his lab, which is in a Toronto warehouse space (interiors were built at the Kleinburg studios) and is duly impressed by his telepods, which she calls "designer phone booths," but look much more like inverted Ducati motorcycle cylinder heads (the cycle-loving Cronenberg's inspiration for their design). The journalist/subject relation-ship quickly becomes something more, and, eventually, in a drunken fit of jealousy, thinking his new girlfriend must be sleeping with her editor, Seth transports himself through space. There's a pesky fly in there with him, though, unnoticed by the geeky brain wizard through his drunken haze. Oldest story in the world!

In the film's major innovation from its 1958 predecessor, introduced by initial screen-writer Charles Edward Pogue, Seth changes only gradually. (This is the alteration which piqued Cronenberg's interest in the project.) He gets aggressive, mean and unkempt, and in a rare outing from his loft he first meets Joy Boushel, the blueberry gatherer from *Humongous*, and then gives one-time Canadian heavyweight champion George Chuvalo the worst arm-wrestling injury ever. Things get worse: Seth becomes all lumpy and his skin darkens to a rich, burnished amber. Bits of him fall off, to become exhibits in the "Brundle Museum of Natural History." The nerdy researcher finally become something entirely new and dif-ferent: Brundlefly, and through this stretch the movie is powered by a rich, unusual and particularly Cronenbergian confluence of emotions, whereby Brundle is at once fright-ened and repulsed by his new evolution while ever retaining his scientific fascination and childlike delight.

The Fly: telepod under construction

Veronica's editor, Stathis Borans (John Getz), thinking back about four Cronenberg movies, worries that Seth's malformation "could be contagious. It might turn into an epidemic." But this is not *Shivers* or *Rabid*: Cronenberg is here concerned about the politic body on a much more intimate level. Veronica is of course pregnant with Seth's baby (a fact over-heard by the Brundlefly as he lurks like Quasimodo behind the crenellated parapets of his warehouse building); and who knows how a baby like that might turn out? Could be a big fly. Cronenberg himself appears as an obstetrician who delivers a hideous slimy maggot from a shrieking Davis, but it's just a bad dream. (Cronenberg says he played the role because he figured he'd be better able to manipulate the maggot puppet to his own directorial satisfaction than any actor he might hire.)

We never find out what the baby really is, because though the Brundlefly kidnaps Davis and attempts to infringe, Republican Party-style, upon her basic rights as a woman, his plan to create "the ultimate family, all in one body" is interfered with by the meddling Borans, who loses a hand and a foot to the creature's corrosive upchuck in the process, but still manages to save Veronica from the fly-man and his grim dedication to family values.

The Fly was produced by funnyman Mel Brooks' company, Brooksfilms. Chris Walas, who had devised the exploding Louis Del Grande head in *Scanners*, was hired to create the extensive effects. The rest of the crew were Cronenberg regulars, with Carol Spier designing the sets, Ronald Sanders cutting the film, Howard Shore providing an excellent score, and, for the last time before his expatriation to Hollywood, Mark Irwin behind the camera. It would be Cronenberg's last proper horror movie for at least the next twenty years.

FIVE YEARS ON FROM *Visiting Hours*, Jean-Claude Lord unleashed another Cinépix production. *The Vindicator* is a science-fiction/horror story about a scientist who, having died in a lab explosion engineered by his crooked science cronies, is turned for no very good reason into a powerful robot (decorated with a melancholy cast-iron frown on one end and bulbous metallic buttocks on the other) by those same moronic cronies.

Clearly an attempt to cash in on the success of fellow Canuck James Cameron's *The Terminator*, the movie tops its model only in using an actor even less personable and articulate than Arnold Schwarzenegger to play the central automaton. The Vindicator, or "Frankenstein," as he is idiotically referred to in the script, isn't evil like the Terminator, though. He's Canadian, and so he doesn't really want to hurt anyone, but he's saddled with a violence chip (probably of American military-industrial manufacture) which emits a beep like a garbage truck in reverse whenever someone touches him. So we get scenes of the robot tossing around that very particular brand of fake bikers who wear droopy headbands around their wet-look permanents (it was shot in Montreal—couldn't they find some real bikers?) and defenestrating the lab-coated bad guys. Meanwhile, the melancholy 'droid is holding conversations with his wife though a midi keyboard and bench-pressing cars for the entertainment of moon-faced young urchins. Pam Grier, of all people, is on his tail, playing an assassin in the pay of the baddies, and Maury Chaykin sashays around as a perfidious fat-buddy sidekick named, of course, "Bert".

Doesn't sound much like a horror movie, you say? Well, you haven't seen it. But if you ever do, you might notice the following exchange of dialogue:

SCIENTIST: It operates by servomotors of significant yet undetermined strength.
PAM GRIER: What do you mean by 'undetermined strength'?
SCIENTIST: Well, we're not quite sure.

That pretty much says it all.

The year after that saw William Fruet's next, and to date last, dip into the horror well, notable in that it neatly caps a horror career that parallels that of David Cronenberg in a number of small ways. Both began in controversy and ended in bugs, and both utilized the services of Mark Irwin and Oliver Reed along the way. Fruet's insect adventure came in the form of 1987's *Blue Monkey*, a monster movie originally titled *Green Monkey* and which features no apes or gorillas of any colour whatever. Instead it tells the tale of a group of hospital patients, staff and visitors terrorized by an enormous doodlebug. Fruet remembers this one as "not a bad little film… done for two cents, done for so cheap, that movie, you can't believe it."

The script, by American writer George Goldsmith (responsible for the screenplay of the first *Children of the Corn* movie), began as more of an ape story though, inspired by the then-accepted link between the genesis of AIDS and a diseased monkey somewhere in Africa. The scenario fell into the hands of producer Sandy Howard, who got his old colleague Fruet involved and moved the whole production to Canada. Along the way, the script's confused pseudo-science evolved into different confused pseudo-science, namely the story of a rampaging insect inadvertently imported from South America. This was in part due to Fruet's involvement: fascinated by the insect world, he believes that "if you want horror, start with bugs." The success of *The Fly* couldn't have hurt either.

The *Monkey* title stuck, however, even as the giant insect was being built in a Los Angeles special effects warehouse. In Toronto, the crew found a perfect location in an abandoned psychiatric hospital, building one set—a laser laboratory, which, though nonsensical, figures heavily in the climactic destruction of the bug—in the hospital gymnasium, under the art direction of Reuben (*Prom Night*) Freed. All the creepy tunnels and crumbling basement rooms were already there, requiring only slight dressing, some smoke, and lots of flashing blue lights. Production started up in March of 1987.

Mark Williams and his pal, the *Blue Monkey*

The film was the feature debt of cinematographer Brenton Spencer, who was, Fruet says, "eager... he would invent, and he made things work... [His approach was] 'Let's do everything that we shouldn't do,' and it worked." Spencer has since moved into directing, with one of his first credits being the almost-a-*Prom Night*-sequel from 1994 called *The Club*. Spencer and Fruet keep the creature's appearances brief and incomplete for most of the film. "We give hints, like a puzzle," Spencer says. "We hold it really close to the camera. You see it in silhouette, in really low light, through smoke, in strobe light or with backlighting... Only in one scene do we pan down the whole monster and show you every last bit of detail." If this sounds like the approach taken in *Alien*, well, it is, but surely that's only a coincidence.

When we do finally see the mandibled beast, it's one of the more impressive monsters in Canadian horror film history. Designed mainly by Mark Williams (an American who had gained insect experience through his work on *The Fly*), it is, relatively speaking, a fairly realistic-looking hybrid of a wasp, a preying mantis and a dragonfly. It was worn by actor Ivan Roth, with its mouth parts, limbs and stingers all operated by remote control. Williams, who died of a pulmonary infection in 1998 at the age of 39, worked on *The Fly*, *Aliens* and many other monster pictures, but was most proud of his work on *Blue Monkey*. "That's one of the better creatures I've done," he said of the bug.

Between the hideous bug, the enthusiastic 50s throwback atmosphere, Fruet's Gibtaltar-like direction and a good cast (with Americans Steve Railsback and Susan Anspach in the leads, ably supported by a Canadian cast that includes Gwynyth Walsh, Joe Flaherty, Robin Duke, John Vernon and, in one of her earliest roles, Sarah Polley as the little kid who pours growth hormone on the bug to make it big), *Blue Monkey* is a fine and fun, if ultimately inconsequential, addition to the genre. It seems like a remake but isn't, which in this realm of moviemaking is assuredly a compliment.

The same year came more 1950s nostalgia in the belated but, in retrospect, inevitable *Prom Night II*. Frustrated in his attempt to sequel-ize the first film right away, by the simple fact that absolutely nothing about it suggested any compelling way to continue the story, Peter Simpson had let the series lie as the slasher craze sputtered out and faded to nearly nothing in the mid-Eighties. There were other titles lying around the Norstar[39] offices, though, and one of them was a spooky high-school idea called *The Haunting of Hamilton High*, the initial draft of which had been written by John Sheppard.

The project found its ultimate form when a magician-turned-screenwriter named Ron Oliver, who had attracted Norstar's attention with a script based on his experience as a magician at the Bahamian Club Med, was hired to rewrite the *Hamilton High* script. Oliver, a longtime horror fan, remembers being amazed and delighted to find none other than Ray Sager, the actor who had played the eponymous wizard in Herchel Gordon Lewis' 1970 gorefest *The Wizard of Gore*, working in the Norstar office as an in-house producer and assistant director. Oliver took on the project, but, he says, "I couldn't seem to crack it. Too many good ideas. I recall one draft was very *Suspiria*[40] oriented, but it didn't work. It wasn't until we were throwing ideas around one afternoon, and I think *Peggy Sue Got Married* had just come out... I'd always liked 50's stuff as a motif, so it seemed like a good direction to take."

The direction suggested by the Francis Coppola film was, specifically, to bridge the present day high school world with that of the 1950s, though in a horrific rather than a romantically comedic vein. Oliver wrote a script based on this formula, and it was duly sent off to Telefilm. Oliver remembers getting a letter back from them "saying it was exceedingly well-written and suspenseful, and one of the best things they'd seen in the office in years. But of course they didn't finance the movie, as it was horror and Canadian tax dollars couldn't possibly be used for something so 'gauche.'"

Partnering up with an Edmonton-based outfit called Allarcom to make the picture, Peter Simpson sold the *Hamilton High* distribution rights to the Samuel Goldwyn Company, which, Simpson says, was at that time "looking for its *Elm Street*." Using the proven *Prom Night* brand name instead was a condition of the deal. Simpson was happy to comply. The pre-sale was one of the biggest in Canadian film history and neatly trumped any need for a Telefilm cash infusion.

Bruce Pittman was hired to direct the film. Pittman had begun his career apprenticing with directors such as John Frankenheimer (on *99 44/100% Dead*) and John Badham (on the Canadian-shot *Reflections of Fear*). He'd also worked in television, interviewing many movie stars for the program *Killer Bs*, had directed award winning (and Oscar-nominated) short films, and had made the low-budget horror feature *The Mark of Cain*. Simpson had called him up and offered three different scripts, of which Pittman was to choose one. He chose *The Haunting of Hamilton High*, requested a few minor changes in the script, and now he was on his way to Edmonton to make it into a film under its new title: *Hello Mary Lou: Prom Night II*.

Oliver's script began with a fifties prologue in which a bitchy prom queen, Mary

Lou, humiliates her milquetoast boyfriend, Bill. His revenge comes when he tosses a stink bomb at her as she's up on stage receiving her crown. The gag goes a little too far, however, as the stink bomb ignites Mary Lou's prom dress and she bursts into flames.

Bill grows up to be a school principal played by Michael Ironside. Bill, his son Craig (Justin Louis) and Craig's girlfriend Vicki (Wendy Lyons) are all put in jeopardy when Vicki inadvertently releases the vengeful spirit of Mary Lou. A potpourri of moments from films like *Carrie*, *A Nightmare on Elm Street* and *Halloween* ensue.

The Edmonton location had its ups and downs. Sandy Kybartas, the production designer, had to import items as basic as floor tiles because she couldn't find what she needed in the northern Alberta city. There was no adequate lab in the city at the time, so it took several days for the rushes to come back, leaving everyone in constant frustrated suspense. On the other hand, according to cinematographer John Herzog (the gaffer on *Humongous* and D.P. on Pittman's *The Mark of Cain*), the local beer was very good. The crew also enjoyed eating schnizel at the Schnizel Palace across the street from their hotel.

Hello Mary Lou: Prom Night II

The Alberta portion of the shoot lasted six weeks over the summer of 1986. The ambitious special effects for the picture were engineered by Jim Doyle, who had done the same job on the first *Nightmare on Elm Street* picture. Doyle, an accomplished mechanical illusionist with a theme-park background, was still unused to the "now, now, now" time frame of the movies, and so a good deal of the time was spent waiting for his effects to be readied. When they were done, however, they looked very good. Makeup effects on the picture were done by Nancy Howe, who had performed the same task on *The Mark of Cain* and a made-on-video clownshow called *Blue Murder*. Howe's work included the burned-up visage of Mary Lou, a puppet of the character for a climactic transformation scene, and a few gory moments sprinkled throughout.

Oliver had written a locker-room chase scene into the picture, and he remembers being surprised to see that the scene was shot with the actress doing the stalking, Wendy Lyons, totally naked. "Very brave of her," Oliver says, and recalls that Robert Rodriguez once told him that the nude locker-room stalking sequence in his film *The Faculty* was included as a tribute to *Prom Night II*.

When the shoot was done, and a rough assembly screened for Peter Simpson and Ilana Frank (another Norstar producer), they decided, in the classic Simpson tradition, that the film was too slow and psychological and would require substantial reshooting. "The movie just didn't work," recalls Ron Oliver. "What came back from Edmonton was a rather well-acted, cleanly shot, methodically-paced drama with a few eerie moments and a gory ending. Given that the horror market at the time was filled with *Nightmare on Elm Street* and the like, everybody involved agreed that the movie just wasn't scary or gory or fast-paced enough."

Editor Nick Rotundo and Oliver recut the picture with "only the stuff that worked." The resulting film ran about an hour in length, and the *Prom Night* brain trust—Oliver, Rotundo, Simpson and Frank, but not Pittman—sat down to figure out what new elements should be added. The re-editing process, Oliver says, "taught me more about writing and directing than anything else before or since." Old scenes were re-worked and new scenes were conceived, particularly for the picture's third act.

Pittman was never called to do any of this reshooting, though he did have a conversation with Oliver in which he requested that the writer do his best to "keep an eye on the performances and make sure the movie still felt 'real'." Pittman appears to bear no ill will to anyone involved; "very professional of him," Oliver says. The reshoots were done in an abandoned Toronto factory in December of 1986.[41] Brenton Spencer was the cameraman, with Peter Simpson, Nick Rotundo and Ron Oliver all taking part in the directing. Jim Doyle had been brought back up from Los Angeles to supervise the additional effects and make sure they were shot properly. A few extra death scenes, an exploding tombstone, and lots of sparks for the climactic sequence was only some of the new material shot over the ten-day period. "I remember tempers getting pretty frayed here and there, as there was a lot riding on these reshoots," says Ron Oliver. "The movie cost about four million to make, and we had about a hundred grand in the reshoot budget."

Enough reshooting was done to successfully reinvent the picture. Surprisingly, the stiching between old scenes and new isn't all that apparent in the final piece. The movie premiered at Toronto's Uptown theatre, and a prom-themed party was held for the cast and crew afterward. But the next morning the local reviews came out, and they were, Oliver remembers, "scathing. I mean really nasty. It was as if we'd shot a dog and filmed it dying." Oliver, for one, was convinced his career was over.

But then the movie opened in Los Angeles, and the *L.A. Times* review was extremely positive. Both Oliver and Pittman were a little shocked ("Who is this guy? What was he on?" Pittman remembers thinking), and all the more so when the film's box-office was sufficiently bolstered by the notice to break into *Variety's* list of the week's top ten earners. This didn't last, of course, but the pleasant glow provided by quotable bits from the *Times* review, like "*Prom Night II* is the *Blue Velvet* of high school movies!" lived on for quite a while. It also, naturally, indicated the urgent need for a second sequel.

Through The Gate

The Fly AND *Prom Night II* WEREN'T THE ONLY mid-Eighties Canadian horror hits. Hungarian-born director Tibor Takacs' teen-oriented demon-fest *The Gate*, released in May of 1987, delighted many a thirteen year-old headbanger with its stop-motion monsters, sub-Spielberg suburban setting (try saying *that* three times fast) and feisty outsider heroes Glen and Terry, played by Stephen Dorff and Louis Tripp. The movie introduces us to a pair of heavy metal-loving outcast nerds, of the sort who became substantially more sinister after the Columbine High School massacre, who inadvertently discover that playing a certain record backwards actually will open the doorway to hell, and moreover that the doorway is in Dorff's back yard. "We've got demons," intones Tripp grimly, peering into the hole left by a fallen tree. Luckily the formula for getting rid of the demons can be found in the record's fantastically comprehensive liner notes.

The demonic phenomena takes many forms. Both Dorff and Tripp suffer from disturbing dreams. Tripp, sleeping over, imagines that he's getting a visit from his deceased mother, but wakes up to find himself embracing a dead sheepdog instead. Dorff sees something moving behind the walls of his charmless tract house: could it be the ghost of a dead workman left there years before? And Dorff's older sister, played by Christa Denton, feels the stirrings of her budding sexuality. With the folks out of town for the weekend (a relief to all, since they're the worst actors in the movie, worse even than the stuffed sheepdog), the time is ripe for an invasion by the stop-motion demonic minions who emerge from the hole.

Dorff, who has since gone on to be a mid-level star with a knack for picking the wrong projects, sports a bowl cut and looks younger than his years. He gives a solid performance, crying at the frightening things and generally acting like a real kid. Tripp's character is more contrived, and it's hard to believe he's meant to be boiling with anti-social rage inside. Nor does he seem like much of a metalhead, a suspicion confirmed by the denim Killer Dwarfs vest he sports. But at least he's not annoying. Christa Denton is also quite passable as Al, the older sister, who wears a pair of tight mauve jeans for most of the movie.

The Gate

The movie gets off to a slow start, but at about the fifty minute mark, Randall William Cook's fantastic stop-motion effects start up. Cook, who had previously animated monsters for John Carpenter (*The Thing*), Larry Cohen (*Q*) and Ivan Reitman (*Ghostbusters*), and has since won an Academy Award for his participation in the visual effects and monsters of *The Lord Of The Rings: The Two Towers*, creates a whole legion of play-dough demonspawn who are infinitely preferable to the computer-generated crap of low-budget movie making today. Other fine effects for the film are contributed by Craig Reardon, who had done the special makeup for *Poltergeist* and *The Funhouse*, and by Syd Dutton, Bill Taylor and the legendary Albert Whitlock, who all contributed to the matte paintings of the besieged neighborhood and the demonic underworld. All this in a cheap Canadian horror picture!

It's safe to say that the special effects are the best part of *The Gate*. Otherwise, the film is another pale entry in what the *Aurum Film Encyclopedia* has categorized as the mid-Eighties "safe horror" trend, where it joins such milquetoast hits as *House*, *Critters* and *The Lost Boys*. It also edges into another category in the mid-Eighties horror taxonomy: the heavy-metal horror movie. Others in this group include *Trick or Treat*, *Hard Rock*

Zombies, Slaughterhouse Rock, and two other films soon to be discussed in these pages: John Fasano's *Rock 'n' Roll Nightmare* and *Black Roses*.

But in this crowded field *The Gate* held its own, grossing a tidy sum at the box office, and it was therefore deemed necessary to make a sequel two years later. Dorff and Denton's characters had moved to another neighborhood, but Takacs was back, as were screenwriter Michael Nankin, star Louis Tripp, producer Andras Hamori and, crucially, effects artists Craig Reardon and Randall William Cook. Cook had worked with Takacs for a second time on *I, Madman*, a horror film made in Los Angeles between the two *Gate* movies.

"I wanted to get a better story instead of just booga-booga," declared Hamori. "The problem with the first movie was that it was very claustrophobic, kids running around and digging a hole." This film has, in contrast, slightly older kids running around casting spells, with Tripp's character opening the gate to hell in an effort to help out his depressed, alcoholic dad. Needless to say, things go terribly wrong with his plan, and the suburbs of Kleinburg, Ontario are once again crawling with stop-motion goblins, wish-granting devils, ballerinas in monster suits and cascades of fake hell-shit created out of chocolate pudding by special effects man Frank Carere.

The Gate had spent a year or so ripening on the shelf before its release, and the new movie rested up for a full two calendar years before seeing the light of a screen in 1992. By then the eighties horror appeal that had made the first one a hit was of far less value, but the movie still made a few bucks, and, I suspect, did fairly well on video. Thus was the bar set for Canadian horror in the nineties.

A Real Rock & Roll Nightmare: John Fasano Heads North

IN THE MID EIGHTIES, Long Island native John Fasano was just out of college and doing the ad campaigns for the grindhouse product that was at that point finding less and less screen time in the big old scum palaces of 42nd Street in New York. Fasano happened to do the poster art for a film by Roberta Findlay called *Tenement*.[42] Findlay and her producing partner Walter Sear were just about to embark on a ghost/slasher project to be called *Blood Sisters*, but were unhappy with the script that Findlay had written.

Having written plays and magazine articles, Fasano jumped in and offered to rewrite the haunted-bordello picture. Findlay and Sear were sufficiently pleased with the result that they made Fasano the assistant director and gave him the important role of "Larry." Through Findlay and Sear (who had done their share of work in the porn field), Fasano met Jack Bravman, a porn impresario who had dropped out of hardcore when the industry standard switched from film to video. Bravman wanted to direct a horror movie, and when he heard about Fasano's work on *Blood Sisters*, he asked the young go-getter to write the script, further offering Fasano a position as some sort of uncredited co-director.

Fasano came up with a story of undead revenge he called *Zombie Nightmare*. In it, a kindly bodybuilding youth is run down by rich amoral punks, and a voodoo priestess/family friend is called upon to reanimate him so he can exact a little blood vengeance. The cop on the case proves to have been a gang member once himself, in which capacity he had, many years before, knifed the bodybuilder's father after a baseball game. The father reappears at the end of the picture to pull his murderer into the grave. All the main characters, except the dastardly punks, were written as black, and had been given what Fasano reckoned were good black names: Leon, Leroy, Lester and so on. He'd written it with the locations and talent pool of his home town, Port Washington, New York, in mind, and went as far as to offer specific parts to the local actors he knew could do the job.

Bravman soon discovered that his investors thought they wouldn't be able to sell a black-centric movie to the all-important foreign markets. (The black horror cycle had lain dormant since the days of *Blacula* and would not revive itself until the late 1990s.) So Fasano, having written the entire screenplay on his beloved IBM Selectric II, was forced to type out new, whiter names (the lead character became Tony), cut them out with a knife and glue them into the appropriate places in the script. (It was shortly thereafter, exhausted, that he invested in a word processor.) But the investors were mollified, and a total budget of almost $200,000 was amassed.

Casting began. To the delight of all, Bravman managed to get Adam West, the former Batman with a more stilted, idiosyncratic acting style even than William Shatner, to play a crooked cop, and he hired a very young Tia Carrere, later to play in *Wayne's World* and as the lead on the television show *Relic Hunter*, to play one of the punks. (Leslie Nielsen was apparently considered for the West part, but a minor skiing injury took him out of the running.) A bodybuilder named PeeWee Piemonte was hired on as the lead zombie, and a boyhood hero of Fasano's, wrestler Superstar Billy Graham, was cast as the zombie's equally zombified father. All seemed well, and Fasano was overjoyed at the prospect of making—or at least co-making—his first movie. It was decided that Bravman would direct all the scenes with Adam West and Tia Carrere—the more actor-oriented sequences—and Fasano would tackle the rest. In fact, Fasano says, he ended up directing the bulk of the film, with Bravman taking the credit because he figured it might be his only legit directing job ever.

Mere days before shooting was to begin, Bravman learned that the local unions were not going to give them a deal or a permit to make the movie in New York. Undaunted, Bravman contacted a producer friend from his porn days who was based in Montreal. Quickly a deal was set up, and the *Zombie Nightmare* production moved north. Fasano, of course, had to renege on the promises he'd made to all the Port Washington actors who'd been expecting to play in the film, but there wasn't much he could do but apologize to them and wave goodbye as he headed for Quebec.

The Gate II

The Americans (including Carrere, fellow actor Frank Dietz—a childhood friend of Fasano's making his movie debut as West's cop partner—and the makeup effects crew) were put up in a seedy airport hotel, where almost every available television channel played exclusively porn. They were astonished to discover the name of their ostensible director, Jack Bravman, scattered generously throughout the credits of many of the movies.

The first problem the crew faced upon arriving in Montreal was the astounding appetite of Pee Wee Piemonte. His voraciousness routinely cleared the craft services table of any scrap of food, and every day at lunch, the crew would arrive to find their meals already within Piemonte's all-consuming belly. After a few days of this, Bravman fired him. The central part of the bodybuilder had to be recast, and this is where the legendary heavy-metal strongman Jon-Mikl Thor comes in. Thor, fronting his band of the same name, is a Vancouver-born hair-metal singer still active on the rock circuit, who thrills his headbanger audiences with feats of strength, such as inflating a hot water bottle with only his bare lungs. He'd had a minor hit or two in the early-to-mid eighties with *Keep the Dogs Away* and *Knock Them Down*, but by 1987 his hits were mostly behind him, and he was eager to take on the role of the nice-guy zombie who smashes his murderers with a baseball bat.

There were still problems, however. The Canadian crew didn't understand Fasano's position on the film, thinking at first that he was the assistant director (the person on a crew in charge of logistical things such as schedules, and also the moment-to-moment running of the set). As a result, if Bravman was to leave the set, as he often did, no one would listen to Fasano's directions. Roger Racine, the cinematographer who, fifteen years earlier, had shot Oliver Stone's *Seizure*, was particularly resistant to the young screen-writer's presence. Fasano found himself begging and pleading with the crew to do every shot. The language barrier—largely fabricated, since the Quebec crew could speak English perfectly well—was a handy tool often used to ignore Fasano's orders. Listening to Racine's impenetrably Gallic screams one day, Fasano was forced to conclude that "Either he needs a key light set up or he wants a croissant."

The catastrophes continued. Billy Graham, the wrestler who was to play the zombie father, flew up to Montreal as he was supposed to, but nobody bothered to pick him up. Learning this, Fasano sped to Mirabel airport, ran full tilt into the terminal, and, making inquiries, was told that indeed a very large man had disembarked, but after waiting ten hours in the terminal, turning progressively more purple with rage as each minute passed, he'd gotten back on a plane and flown home. Fasano was naturally crushed to hear this, and further dismayed that his wrestling hero was not going to be in the film. He ended up playing the role of the murdered father-zombie himself.

The makeup effects for *Zombie Nightmare* were engineered by two of Fasano's college chums, Tony Bua and Andy Clement (or possibly Clemens, as it's spelled in the untrust-worthy credits of the film). Their work consisted mainly of a few zombie masks and some wildly spraying blood, and it's kind of sad that they didn't include a few more of the flesh-ripping zombie gore staples of the genre, since if any movie could use a little extra tomato paste, it's *Zombie Nightmare*. But the film is resolutely and disappointingly dry when it comes to *Corpse Eaters*-style gut-munching. The true test of Bua and Clement's aptitude came when they had to restyle the zombie get-up, which had been tailored in New York for Superstar Billy Graham, to fit the smaller Fasano for the climactic scene where the undead father (called William Washington; obviously a name Fasano couldn't find the energy to replace during his emergency script-bleaching) pops out of his grave and grabs Adam West. Fasano was shaved and crammed into the head-and-shoulders costume, only to find that there were no eye holes. Upon being lowered into the hole from which he was to pop, Fasano found himself uncomfortably close—in fact, right up against— a red light meant to simulate the ghastly glow of hell.

Zombie Nightmare

With the scent of his own searing flesh in his nostrils, Fasano called for action, springing from the hole with what must have seemed superhuman speed and hauling West back in with him. West, bitten a thousand times over by the mosquitoes which were by all accounts especially voracious that night, was probably only partially acting when he pleads for Dietz's character to shoot him as he's being dragged under. But there, beneath the sod, Fasano felt entirely redeemed for all the trouble, pain and heartache he'd been through: after all, he'd just accomplished what even the likes of Burgess Meredith and Frank Gorshin had failed to do—he'd killed Batman!

Fasano has nothing but praise for West, who was remarkably cooperative during the making of the film. Fasano had regretted not writing more scenes between West and his co-star, Dietz, the movie's cops, which took place outside the police station environment, in a bar or a restaurant perhaps. West simply told Fasano to go ahead and write it instead of moaning about it, and so he did, redressing a corner of the police station to be a bistro and giving the actors reams of hastily-written dialogue. For much of West's performance, owing to the short time (two days) he was on set, the former Batman kept his script nearby, stealing glances when he could. Fasano assumed that the editors would cut away from West during these moments, but, to his everlasting fury and disappointment, they didn't. (In an email, he raged about the "first-time moron Montreal editors" who had ruined his film.)

Curiously, the (American) video box for *Zombie Nightmare*, released by a post Roger Corman New World Video, lists Fasano as the writer, while the actual credits list David Wellington (soon to be the director of *The Carpenter* (1987), and later of classier fare like *I Love A Man in Uniform* and *Long Day's Journey Into Night*) in that position. It seems at first that this must have been the result of the same gross post-production incompetence that led to this gem of a closing-credits disclaimer: "Any similarities between persons or events herein depicted is purely coincidental," but in fact it was reportedly, and unsurprisingly, a requirement of the tax credit regulations that a Canadian screenwriter be credited. Fasano claims that Wellington was in fact the editor of *Zombie Nightmare*. The credits list a "David Franko" in that position, and to add to the confusion, the name of the cinematographer on Wellington's first feature, *The Carpenter*, is David Franco. Fasano further charges that Wellington, cutting, for some reason, from the film's original negative, had used all the best shots of the film for the trailer, leaving rejected takes for the actual movie. (This could explain why it's so dry in the gore department.)

An advantage to the film's hemoglobic aridity is that, as a movie with very little on-screen violence or other potentially offensive elements, it was eligible for treatment by the robots of *Mystery Science Theatre 3000*, the 1990s-era television show in which movies deemed to be sufficiently horrible are verbally torn apart in real time by two wisecracking robots and their jumpsuit-wearing human friend. *Zombie Nightmare* received just such a pasting, and acquired a new life and many new fans in the process.[43] Reviews of the film were not kind: *Fangoria* magazine complained about the lack of gore, and Toronto author L.A. Morse's *Video Trash & Treasures* guide remarked that:

> Someone must have figured there was an audience for a voodoo-zombie-revenge movie with a heavy metal soundtrack and ten minutes of Adam West smoking a cigar. Assuming there is an audience that's been keenly anticipating this particular combination of elements, it's doubtful that this discriminating group would be satisfied with this effort.

Rock and Roll Nightmare came next. This film is, if possible, even more notorious for its all-embracing badness than *Zombie Nightmare*, and it's probably only the picture's occasional nudity and gore scenes that have kept it off of *Mystery Science Theatre* this long. It's the bewildering tale of a rock band called The Tritonz, led by the heavy-metal body-builder Jon-Mikl Thor, who arrive at a haunted farmhouse to record their new record. We know the farm is haunted from a prefatory sequence in which a hapless family is wiped out by the resident demons. After this, and a Sam Raimi-inspired credits sequence (in which the shadow of the camera is almost constantly visible), we see the Tritonz drive (and drive, and drive) to the farmhouse in a boogie van bearing both prominent Ontario license plates and an extra plate reading "USA 1". Shots of the boogie van are intercut with pointless and bewildering crane shots of the house.

When they finally get to their farmhouse/recording studio, the band members and their girlfriends wonder aloud why it is they're in Canada to do their album. "Because Toronto is where it's happening, man!" enthuses a chipper Thor. "The music! The film industry! The arts!" Thus inspired, the band sets to work creating the "ten minutes of new, good material" required by the record company.

The balance of the movie is concerned with the one-by-one decimation of the group at the hands of small rubber puppets. Eventually Thor begins to notice the disappearance of his friends, and in a truly mind-numbing twist, he reveals himself to be a heavenly emissary sent expressly to do battle with the evil forces (represented in the climax by none other than Satan) who had for whatever reason taken up residence in that particular southern Ontario farmhouse. The rest of the band had merely been specters created by Thor to trick the evil into revealing itself. There is a battle to the death between Thor and Satan, who is played by a somewhat larger rubber puppet. For a few moments it looks bad for the heavy-metal archangel, as the hellish mannequin flings starfish at him, but he rallies and manages to wrestle it to the ground.

As *Zombie Nightmare* was "being butchered by the neophyte editing team in Montreal," Fasano was back in New York with Roberta Findlay and Walter Sear. Leonard Shapiro, of the Los Angeles-based company Shapiro Entertainment, had flown into town and was in the process of offering Sear and Findlay a deal in which they would make a horror feature for $100,000. Shapiro would put up half, Reeltime (Sear and Findlay's company) would put up half, and then they would split the net profits fifty-fifty. Sear's non-negotiable counterproposal was to split the gross instead. Shapiro wasn't interested, and prepared to return to L.A. the next day.

Fasano called him at his hotel and said that, if Shapiro was to give him 50,000 dollars, then Fasano would make a movie and they could split the net. Shapiro agreed to the proposition, but issued some conditions: the movie had to be shot on 35mm, it had to have a marketable soundtrack album, contain a certain number of monsters and no less than eight naked breasts. "Can do!" Fasano told him.

Zombie Nightmare

Fasano's plan was to take the fifty grand and make the movie without raising the other half of the budget. He figured that he could write, produce, direct and edit the film himself for free, and shoot the film in Canada where a budget could be stretched like rubber, then Shapiro's fifty grand should take care of all the remaining hard costs. Fasano's first call was to Thor, whom he convinced to star in the film and supply an album's worth of songs for half of Fasano's half of the net. Thor, sensing another opportunity to flex his pecs on camera, heartily agreed. It is Thor who receives credit in the film for both writing and producing it, but this was likely just for the same Can-con reasons Wellington got the *Zombie Nightmare* screenplay credit. Then again, you never know; maybe Thor did write it. A man with the ability to blow up hot water bottles with his own mighty lungs might be capable of anything.

To gather a crew, Fasano simply rounded up the very same technicians who'd recently worked on Thor's video for his other near-hit, *Knock Them Down*, offering them $10,000 to supply all the equipment and bodies that would be needed. He then recruited a cast by offering his friends a $150 apiece to act in the picture for ten days; and finally he set up a special effects shop in the basement of his Bronxville, New York home, where he and effects man Arnold Gargiulo began making the many rubber puppets that were required to kill off his fifteen-dollar-a-day-and-dinner cast. Frank Dietz, who, like Thor, had made his film debut in *Zombie Nightmare*, was cast as a band member named "Roger Eburt."

The film was shot in Markham, Ontario, just a little north of Toronto, under the working title *The Edge of Hell*. The shoot was scheduled for ten days, but on the seventh day, cinematographer Mark Mackay (who had also shot *City in Panic*) heard that his spiritual guru had died, and, as Fasano relates it, "he had to go sit on a mountain somewhere." The three final scheduled days of shooting were all packed into one to accommodate Mackay's pilgrimage, and, as Fasano readily admits, the film shows it.

Nevertheless, *Rock 'n' Roll Nightmare* made something on the order of $400,000 in sales for Shapiro, and he was ready for another horror picture from Fasano. Shapiro Entertainment had in the meantime become Shapiro-Glickenhaus Entertainment (Shapiro's new partner, James Glickenhaus, was the prime mover behind revenge epics like *The Exterminator* and the Toronto-made *The Protector*, starring Jackie Chan and shot by Mark Irwin). They offered Fasano a budget of $450,000 to make the new movie.

All Fasano knew was that the movie should have lots of music so he could tie in a soundtrack album, as he had done with his previous pictures. He and his wife, Cindy Sorrell, came up with a storyline inspired by Tipper Gore's quixotic battle against rock lyrics, as well as, it would seem, the mid-Eighties spate of devil-rock pictures like *The Gate*. The crucial difference between these pictures and other heavy-metal themed horror, like *Rock 'n' Roll Nightmare* for instance, is that the warnings of the fundamentalist crackpot antagonists turn out to be absolutely true—heavy metal is the devil's music and bad things will happen if you listen to it. It's a simple plot device rather than an expression of conservative ideology, of course, but the reactionary message, inadvertent or otherwise, does seem at odds with the spirit of both rock music and horror movies.

Black Roses is nevertheless a very natural follow-up to *Rock 'n' Roll Nightmare*; so much so that it's a little disconcerting, not to mention disappointing, to see that Jon Mikl Thor is nowhere to be found in the cast list. (According to Fasano, Thor was angling to be the director by this time, so he cast someone else in what would otherwise seem the likely Thor role.) The movie proceeds with the same dogged dumbness and reliance on dreadful, bloodless heavy metal as its predecessor. Nevertheless, one can see a progression in Fasano's directing talents and, crucially, a marked improvement in his casting skills.

The picture tells the story of a hugely popular headbanging rock outfit called Black Roses who are on an improbable cross-country tour of middle-American school gymnasiums. While the teens of Mill Basin eagerly await the hard-rock heroes, the town's conservative Mrs. Grundys plot to prevent the big show, citing Satanic influences and filthy lyrics. The band arrive in shiny sports cars and, after first fooling the town elders with tootling synth music and lab coats over their leather, indeed prove to be emissaries of the devil, showing their true forms (beefy and with monstrous latex heads) in a climactic concert. A heroic, mustachioed English teacher battles the rock group for the prize of his students' souls.

Julie Adams, the white bathing-suited beauty from 1954's *Creature From the Black Lagoon*, was Fasano's biggest casting coup (*Creature* had been the first horror movie Fasano had ever seen). She played the Tipper Gore-like anti-heavy metal activist. The mayor of the town was none other than Ken Swofford of *Fame* fame, and Lou Ferrigno's wife Carla played his daughter. Fasano wanted Gedde Watanabe (Long Duk Dong from *Sixteen Candles*) to play the heroic teacher, but Watanabe's agent "thought the movie was beneath him," says Fasano with regret. Instead he cast rugged soap opera actor John Martin, who recalls the Marlboro Man so strongly because he *was* the Marlboro Man. Other roles were filled out by such actors as Vincent Pastore (famous from his endless mobster roles, most notably in *The Sopranos*, and his part in *Return to Sleepaway Camp*) and Paul Kelman (T.J. from *My Bloody Valentine* making a welcome return to the screen). Broadway and soap actor Sal Viviano played the lead Satanic rocker, former Vanilla Fudge drummer Carmine Appice was the devil's own timekeeper, and Fasano standby Frank Dietz played "Johnny Pratt," local hooligan.

Fasano and a new cinematographer, B.C.-based Paul Mitchnik, went looking for locations. Mitchnik showed him Hamilton, Ontario, which struck the director as "a town which still had the innocence of America's heartland." That was just what he needed; that and a car dealer willing to lend two Lamborghinis to the production. Hamilton had that too. In the meantime, on the advice of makeup man Tony Bua, Fasano hired Richard Alonzo to design and build the monsters required for the movie. Bua and several others would also help tackle the special effects.

Zombie Nightmare

The shoot lasted twenty days, and went mostly without incident, except for an impromptu fire and the last-minute refusal by some of the actresses to doff their shirts for the all-important topless shots. "Stunt breasts" saved the day here, as they did when it was discovered that the female lead didn't quite have the measurements required for maximum international sales. Otherwise, Fasano's extensive preparation—every shot was storyboarded—meant smooth sailing and finishing $20,000 under budget.

However, when the movie was cut together, James Glickenhaus pointed out that it was lame and boring. Fasano had to admit he was right. All the killings were off screen and there was way too much talk. The chastened director quickly came up with five monster scenes and shot them with the leftover twenty grand in and around his New York house. These included the scene in which Pastore tells his son that "only two kinds of people wear earrings—pirates and faggots. And I don't see no ship in our driveway!" before being sucked into a speaker by a rubber spider-monster. Fasano also added more breasts, specifically the infamous, extended "tit-rubbing" scene.

While putting the finishing touches on *Black Roses*, Fasano received a call from the

Japanese company Gaga Communications, which had distributed his previous work in Asia. They wanted a North American version of the Chinese "hopping vampire" legend, which had been dramatized in Hong Kong movies like the popular *Mr. Vampire* series. Fasano had seen clips from these films and was also a big fan of John Carpenter's *Big Trouble in Little China*, so the idea of such a re-working appealed to him. Gaga representative Sonoko Sakai and her assistant Jeff McKay had written a script which was, Fasano says, "very traditional, haunted houses and all." Fasano refocused it as a *Romeo and Juliet* story set on the mean streets of Toronto. "As usual I tried to do too much," he says. "Too many characters, too many fights." The film would be called *The Jitters*.

Black Roses head devil Sal Viviano was cast as the button-down hero, with Marilyn Tokuda as his girlfriend and Frank Dietz as a hooligan once again, this time named "Rat." A veteran of *Big Trouble in Little China*, James Hong, played the evil gang boss. The plot concerns the murder of Tokuda's shopkeeper grandfather by the Chinatown street gangs, and his subsequent resurrection as a pogoing hemogobbler by traditional Oriental means. The makeup for the vampire was created by a returning Richard Alonzo, with effects veteran Steve Wang providing a climactic creature.

Gaga Communications had promised Fasano a budget of $750,000, his biggest yet. But halfway through the shoot he was told that his budget was in fact $550,000. The film would suffer in post-production as a result: cheap sound effects, a bad mix, a "quickie, tinny synthesizer score." Fasano was crushed by the end product, particularly since he felt the movie could have really been good if he'd been able to finish it properly. (Fasano and Tom Drake would have a lot to talk about.)

The movie itself is fairly silly, though it features some nice shots of Toronto streetcars and makes the most of the joke that, an hour after a Chinese vampire bites you, he's hungry again. James Hong is his usual fabulous self, though, and raises the movie high above the level its crappy sound and score would otherwise keep it.

The *Jitters* experience left Fasano disenchanted with low-budget horror filmmaking and determined to move up to bigger things. He took a 35mm print of *Black Roses*, his slickest picture, to Los Angeles. Finding that there were few jobs available for directors with his particular experience, he turned to screenwriting, and sold a script to Morgan Creek (the company who made *Nightbreed*) for more than the entire budget of the movie he had brought along to impress the producers. He stuck with writing after that, penning the sequel to *48 Hours*, working on the third *Alien* picture, co-producing *Tombstone*, and more recently writing such films as *Darkness Falls* and *Saving Jessica Lynch*. The Canadian horror parts of the John Fasano saga aren't over, though: he's got a script called *The Screaming Dead* which he hopes to shoot in Vancouver, and in late 2003, B.C.-based horror filmmaker Ed Brisson announced his plans to shoot *Rock 'n' Roll Nightmare II: The Intercessor*, with Thor returning to play himself.

Hide the Body In the Woodpile: *Pin*

AND THEN CAME *Pin*. It's difficult to know where to start with this film. It's achieved a certain cult status, but its very nature, along with its weird, unsettling tone, guarantees that the cult will, hopefully, never get very big. It should be noted that I am a member in good standing.

Pin begins with a sequence showing a group of boys sneaking up to a house where a mysterious, inert figure is seen sitting in a second-story window. One of the lads boldly climbs a trellis to peek in and is startled when the dummy-like figure hisses at him. It's a good, creepy opening made all the better by Guy Dufaux's rich, autumnal photography.

Pin: the Three Ages of Leon

We jump backward twenty years to find a family of obssessives led by Dr. Linden, a cold and clinical small-town pediatrician played by American actor Terry O'Quinn, known for his intense performance in *The Stepfather*. Linden's wife is a neat freak, and his kids, Leon and Ursula, are overdressed misfits. Leon's best friend is Pin, a medical dummy who lives at the doctor's clinic. O'Quinn, an accomplished ventriloquist, uses Pin as a mouthpiece to talk with sick kids and to tell his own children about the birds and the bees and such. Only Ursula has twigged to the fact that the doctor is behind Pin's lecturing. Leon, who has witnessed things like the clinic nurse getting it on with Pin (one of the most discomforting scenes in Canadian cinema), believes the dummy to be alive.

He still believes this after we've jumped forward several years. Leon is now played by David Hewlett (later of *Cube*), and Cyndy Preston, of *The Brain* and *Prom Night III*, plays Ursula. Preston has tried to escape the smothering confines of her family by becoming the easiest girl in school (or so the graffiti would have Leon believe), while Leon himself has grown into a tightly-wound repressive geek who wears a suit all the time and is maniacally protective of his sister.

When she admits to Leon that she's become pregnant, he insists they ask Pin for advice. Ursula learns that Leon has picked up his father's talent for ventriloquism, and has mastered the Pin voice perfectly. Pin's advice is to ask the doctor for an abortion, which O'Quinn grumpily grants. (Another disquieting scene.) In the meantime, the doctor is finally realizing the depth of Leon's devotion to Pin, and decides to get rid of the spooky, skinless dummy. But Pin has his own ideas about it and causes a car crash which kills both the parents.

As an orphan, Leon becomes more devoted to Pin than ever. He uses the horrific mannequin to frighten a busybody aunt to death, sets about spooking a potential love interest played by Hèlene Udy, and plots to murder Ursula's new boyfriend. "Hide the body in the woodpile, Leon," Pin advises sagely. The murder doesn't go off as well as it should, and Ursula, finally having had her fill of Leon's mania, chops Pin up with an axe. The shock of witnessing this drives Leon into a near-catatonic state, and it is he who spends his days sitting motionless by the window. Pin himself, in pieces now, is consigned to the woodpile.

Pin was written and directed by Sandor Stern, who had penned the script for *The Amityville Horror*, *The Incubus* (under a pseudonym), and many, many made-for-television movies. Stern, born in Timmins, Ontario, had resolved at age 15 to become a writer, but ended up in medical school instead. This led to a job writing scripts for a never-produced CBC drama called *Emergency Ward 10*. Many more writing jobs followed, along with much television directing. His script for *The Amityville Horror* gave him horror credentials which he wasn't particularly quick to cash in on. But when he came across a book called *Pin* by Andrew Neiderman, he optioned it and wrote a script. Stern met former Cronenberg associate Pierre David on an airplane and told him about the project. David was interested and took the project to Universal Pictures, who were not. Later on Stern gave the script to René Malo, another Canadian producer. Malo and David, as it happened, had just partnered up to form a company, and with both these go-getters on board, *Pin* came that much closer to becoming a film.

The two producers made up a poster for the movie which featured the words "From the author of *The Amityville Horror!*" in large print, and took it to Cannes to raise money. They did so in short order, and the film was a go. The budget was about 3.5 million dollars, and locations were found in Saint-Lambert and Iberville, Quebec, just outside Montreal. A large portion of the budget—$80,000—was spent on the movie's real star, Pin, which was specially made in time for the kickoff to the 31-day shoot.

Disagreement reared its head a week into the shoot. Pierre David took a look at some of the rushes and declared them not nearly scary enough. He'd sold something else at Cannes, he told Stern; something scary and campy and gruesome. "I can't help what you sold," Stern told him. "This is a psychological thriller and it always was." To mollify the producer, Stern reshot a scene in which Pin, sitting in a motorized wheelchair, chases Hèlene Udy through the house. The scene had originally been short and filmed in fairly normal house lighting, but now it was extended, with scary music and lots of running around corners and through doors, and a good deal of screaming and crying for Udy (who remembers the Pin dummy as "exceedingly creepy in real life"). The lighting was now a dark blue chiaroscuro for no very good reason, except to persuade investors that they had indeed invested in a horror movie.

Stern may also have been feeling the pressure to endow his film with more commercial elements when he made Udy take her top off in a seduction scene with Hewlett. Stern feels badly about it now and wishes he hadn't shot it, but it may have been a matter of give-and-take: "I'll include some breasts if you let me retain the subtle psychodramatics of my film," or something of that nature. Or perhaps Stern (who seems a sensitive gent) really thought at the time the movie would be better with Udy's breasts than without. At any rate, whether she was a bargaining chip or not, Udy doesn't remember the experience very fondly. "Right up until the day, I thought I might convince Sandor Stern to let me keep my top on. Obviously I was deluded. Sandor insisted I play the scene as written." The tax shelter boom had waned, and Udy remembers that "Canadians didn't have much choice in those days. There was very little work and lots and lots of talented people. There was never much room to negotiate. Nudity of some kind was just part of the deal." Still, Stern filmed the scene in as tasteful and matter-of-fact way as he could, successfully undercutting the exploitive element the producers may have been looking for.

Pin is an effective thriller with strong echoes of *Psycho*. It's one of the few Canadian horror movies which takes on repression as a theme (though this is common enough in Canadian dramas) and attempts to make a virtue of subtlety. It's a high point in the Can-horror canon as a whole, and in the wasteland of the eighties it rises like the CN Tower above most others. Of course, it's for the best that *Pin* is what it is, but it's still fun to imagine what it might be like if it had been produced by Peter Simpson instead of David and Malo. It would probably include several scenes of Leon and Pin carrying

Pin

on with strippers, nightmare sequences with a lip-smacking Pin walking around dispensing quips, and a stitched-on climax in which Pin really does come to life and rip arms and heads off of minor cast members. There would also, I imagine, be far less dialogue. I almost wish that version existed. Maybe it's time for *Pin II: Pin At the Prom*.

<hr />

The Kiss WAS A BIG-BUDGET cross between a vampire movie and the cukoo-in-the-nest genre still, in 1988, yet to fully hatch north of the border. Directed by British-born Pen Densham, the movie features exotic beauty Joanna Pacula (*Gorky Park*) as Aunt Felice, who is possessed by some kind of ancient, eel-like supernatural creature which can only live on if passed by a special hocus-pocus kiss to a younger female relative. It's a bit like *The Reincarnate* or *The Blue Man*, but with higher production values and more monsters and gore courtesy of *The Fly* effects man Chris Walas. Faces familiar from the Can-horror canon include Vlasta Vrana (*Rabid*), Peter Dvorsky (*Videodrome*) and Jan Rubes (*Dead of Winter*). It was shot in Montreal but set in an Albany, New York, and they can have it as far as I'm concerned.

Jan Rubes also appeared in a small psychodrama called *Blood Relations*, but in a much meatier role. In that film he's a rich brain surgeon who enjoys playing sadistic practical joke games with his adult son. The son has brought back his new wife Marie to meet the family, and she proves to be not above some scheming herself. But she's picked the wrong family to scheme against, as Rubes is on the hunt for a new brain for his own wife.

Poor Marie ends up clamped in a chair, a brainless husk thanks to Rubes' nimble hands.

Rubes, a Czech opera singer who had emigrated to Canada in the forties and is still most famous for his role as the Amish elder in *Witness*, is at his best in this movie. He's not required to be a stern but good-hearted beard-without-moustache grandpa as in the Harrison Ford hit, nor the jolly Santa Claus he was two years later in Philip Borsos' *One Magic Christmas*. Instead he's sardonic and mean, not to mention homicidal, much as he is in Arthur Penn's horror-mystery *Dead of Winter* (shot in Canada and released in 1987). His grim-to-grandfatherly range has kept him busy in both family pictures and Canadian horror to this day, and *Blood Relations* is one of the best.

1988 was also the year of *Watchers*, the Dean R. Koontz adaptation shot in B.C. The movie details the adventures of a super-intelligent Golden Retriever and the lab-created monster who wants to eat both the dog any anyone who gets in the way. Corey Haim and Michael Ironside contribute to the Roger Corman-financed fun. The film was directed by Jon Hess, a young American whose only previous credit was an action picture shot in Chile called *The Lawless Land*. Hess had worked as a producer on *Food of the Gods II*, directed by Damian Lee in Toronto the year before, and for *Watchers* their positions were reversed.

Also made in B.C. that year was an interesting item called *Matinee*, written and directed by Richard Martin. In this film, a small-town horror movie film festival is the occasion for murder and mayhem, not to mention a good deal of soap operatic drama. The films-within-the-film are enjoyable and the movie as a whole is a minor horror-who-dunit gem, much better than much of the contemporary Canadian product being released.

Ed Hunt was an eccentric American who regularly made the trek north of the border to direct his movies. Maris Jansons, a technician who worked with him, affectionately remembers the burly, bearded Hunt as "a madman!" At first, Hunt made softcore pictures like *Pleasure Palace* and *Diary of a Sinner* for Benett Fode's Phoenix Pictures, which had noted the profits of the Cinépix maple-syrup porn line and wanted to follow suit. Hunt then made an action picture, *Point of No Return*; the Robert Vaughn/Christopher Lee alien picture *Starship Invasions* (shot in Canada by Mark Irwin); and an American-made killer kids epic called *Bloody Birthday*. From the evidence provided by on-set production photographs, while working in Canada he showed good grace and "when-in-Rome" consideration by wearing a large plaid shirt on set. He made horror movies and he made Canadian movies, but ultimately, Ed Hunt's only Canadian horror movie was *The Brain*, shot in Toronto and released in 1988.

A lively pace, an energetic if goofy monster and a self-aware sense of humour are of immense help to *The Brain*, which is otherwise a generally dumb attempt at lowbrow, poor-person's Cronenberg. Ultimately nothing can save it from the direct-to-video grave-yard for which it was evidently intended all along, but if you liked *Videodrome* enough to want to see its basic plot redone by people whose cinematic and intellectual ambitions extend no further than lines like "Now that's food for thought!" to accompany a shot of a giant brain eating a blonde in a lab coat, you could do worse.

The movie concerns a prank-loving pseudo-rebel named Jim (Tom Breznahan), his girlfriend Janet (*Pin*'s Cyndy Preston) and their battle against a mad scientist (played by that lovable talking head from *Re-Animator*, David Gale) who has developed a giant ambulatory brain with goggle eyes and flapping, rather than gnashing, teeth. Gale has a TV show, *Independent Thinking*, with which he controls the minds of his viewers and arranges the death of those who dare to tune out. In the meantime the Brain grows to the size of an old VW bug and begins using a more direct means of control: ingestion. Of course it ends with Gale losing his head once again, but *The Brain* is no *Re-Animator*, and, let there be no mistake, it certainly isn't a *Videodrome* either. (A sense of social responsibility is nonetheless demonstrated by an emphatic end credit warning that one of Jim's pranks, involving sodium and school plumbing, is not to be attempted at home or by laymen.)

The Brain

One cast standout, aside from Gale, is big George Buza, who plays a burly orderly under the Brain's thrall and becomes a head-chopping axe-murderer late in the picture. Buza had worked with David Cronenberg years earlier, playing "Meatball" in *Fast Company*. Another is the Brain itself, which looks like a big meatball even more than Buza does. It was built by *Blue Monkey* veteran Mark Williams in his Los Angeles shop and shipped piece-by-piece to Toronto. Williams declared *The Brain* another of his favourite projects, telling *Fangoria* magazine about the excitement of watching the dailies. "There's this great shot where the creature comes around a corner and bites this kid's head off," he said. "When I saw that, well, it was better than sex. Almost."

Yet another franchise to make its way north was the *Amityville Horror* series. In 1989's *The Amityville Curse*, five uptight hosers buy a house in "Amityville, Long Island" (though not the same distinctive fan-windowed house seen in the previous movies) and soon learn the true price of a foolish impulse purchase. A series of minor accidents (cut hands, sprained ankles) dampens their enthusiasm for pointless renovations not a whit, while the horrific dreams of the mildly psychic Debbie (Dawna Wightman) are merely scoffed at by her tubby, pretentious husband Marvin (David Stein) and ignored by everyone else. Things soon begin to go bump and booga-booga, the sinister old lady from *The Incubus* shows up, and all the trouble is eventually traced to a possessed confessional in the basement, but none of it is very scary. Much of the action, moreover, occurs under a very familiar blue lighting scheme—Canadian Blue, it's been called, not to be confused with a brand or two of beer—provided by cinematographer Rodney Gibbons, whose work in the Can-classic *My Bloody Valentine* is immeasurably superior.

The performances, however, range from serviceable to genuinely good, with Jan Rubes demonstrating once again that he could easily become Canada's answer to John

Carradine instead of taking the easy road and simply remaining Canada's Max Von Sydow. Curly-topped Kim Coates (Canada's Wings Hauser, even as the real Wings Hauser came to Canada to star in *The Carpenter*) once again plays an intense weirdo who ends up with goopy makeup all over his face at the climax of the film.

A thin story, predictable surprises and lifeless, or at least not very horror-oriented direction sadly overwhelm the game cast, and after this entry the Amityville franchise crept back to its original home south of the border, to be continued in films like *Amityville 1990: It's About Time* (no house, just a haunted clock) and *Amityville: Dollhouse* (no explanation necessary). Few in Canada mourned its departure. The director, Tom Berry, had just come off the whimsical Cape Breton father-and-son story *Something About Love* (also starring Rubes), and from the looks of things his heart just wasn't in doing the umpteenth installment of a moribund series whose capacity to frighten had run dry before the first sequel.

Berry would go on to produce a number of Quebec-shot horror/suspense films in the early 1990s, including many of the cuckoo-in-the-nest pictures so popular, or at least so numerous, at the time. Preceding these, however, but not terribly unlike them, was David Wellington's feature debut *The Carpenter* (1989).

Wellington had received (stolen! John Fasano might say) the screenwriting credit on *Zombie Nightmare*, and after his directing debut would go on to quite legitimately have his name on prestigious Canadian films like *I Love A Man In Uniform* and *Long Day's Journey Into Night*. *The Carpenter* features Lynne Adams (who also appeared in *Blood Relations*) as a woman who has just recovered from a nervous breakdown and has returned with her philandering asshole husband to the house they are having renovated. The workers on the job are, almost to a man, lazy and corrupt, and soon a phantom carpenter—the ghost of the fellow who originally built the house—is using power tools in an unsafe manner on anyone in the vicinity with a poor work ethic or lousy attitude.

The carpenter is played by Wings Hauser (America's Kim Coates), known best for his performance as the psychotic pimp in *Vice Squad*, and also a veteran of horror movies such as *Night Shadows*, *The Wind* and *Watchers 3*. Hauser is a well-known hambone, but in *The Carpenter* he's quite restrained and a perfect gentleman, except when he's slaughtering careless construction workers and perfidious husbands. The film works quite well as a little psychodrama (is the Carpenter real, or just a figment of Adams's madness?) and as one of the more intelligent of the late-period, pre-irony slasher pictures.

The *Prom Night* movies are sort of the anti-*Degrassi Junior High* of Canadian pop culture. The third installment, *Prom Night III: The Last Kiss*, follows the adventures of Alex, a goony Hamilton High senior who can't decide whether to spend his summer on the farm with his cute girlfriend Sarah (played by Cyndy Preston of *The Brain* and *Pin*) or on the road with his buddy Shane. A good deal of the movie is devoted to depicting a series of arguments about this quandary, recorded in real time or so it often seems.

The problem is settled by the appearance of charred, demonic Mary Lou, who escapes from some purgatorial aerobics gym, flies up to Hamilton High, and immediately and inexplicably falls in love with the dorky Alex. He halfheartedly reciprocates her feelings and soon finds himself clearing up the corpses of students and faculty she has offed in grisly-burlesque fashion. (Sweaty teacher George Chuvalo, for example, is impaled by ice-cream cones and made into a giant, bloody sundae—but, as witty as Ron Oliver's script often is, it misses this chance for a "Sundae, Bloody Sundae" gag.) Eventually Mary Lou is defeated once again and Alex heads off to the farm with his true lady love.

Cinematographer Rhett Morita (*Blood Relations*) shoots these antics in deep-blue Eighties Canuck-O-Vision, and though Oliver's script is not without moments of cleverness, the movie tries a little too hard to be a jokey camp-fest. Like the previous *Prom Nights*, it suffered from a bifurcated shooting schedule, and this time the seams show. There are also an awful lot of American flags on view, even for a Canadian film (two characters have sex on one, which is subsequently used as a toga, and later a victim is wrapped in one for burial); and snippets of "The Stars and Stripes Forever" and "Yankee Doodle" pop up on the soundtrack. All of this might, to a gen-

Watchers

erous person, seem like an attempt at satire of the typical, blue-mailbox-strewn made-in-Canada production, or maybe some obscure potshots at American patriotism.

But Oliver's explanation for the excessive Americana is interesting. "It was for a very specific reason," he says. "The flag love making scene. Basically, Canadian patriotism doesn't exist, so having them screw on a Canadian flag doesn't mean anything. It wouldn't get a rise out of the audience, Canadian or otherwise, because who really cares what happens on a Canadian flag?" Oliver adds that, with the pervasive fear of American cultural imperialism he detected in Canada at the time, "it seemed to me to be a bit of a satiric poke to watch a 'Canadian' boy in this movie be seduced by a deadly 'American' girl. I'm not sure anyone else got it, but..." If they didn't, an end-credits rap song sampling the Guess Who's *American Woman* might have helped.

The movie was shot for around a million and a half dollars during "the most frigid autumn in Toronto history," according to Ron Oliver. Peter Simpson, perhaps wishing to avoid weeks of reshoots this time, was very present on the set; so much so that he ended up taking co-director credit with Oliver, whose solo feature debut this was intended to be. "I think when Peter was getting financing for the film, to make the money people comfortable he said he'd be on set with me to guide my first directing job to a successful finish," says Oliver. "It was a bit tough, because Peter's personality is bigger than life, and I think some people find it hard to work with him... Peter and I were and are friends, but you simply cannot have two alpha wolves in one pack, you know?

"The stuff that was not so great [in the movie] tended to be material we discussed or argued about on set... I compromised us out of a lot of things, but it wasn't anybody's fault but my own." Oliver managed to pull off a few slick moments, however, like a long crane down from a wide shot of a school gymnasium down to a close-up of a principal having his finger severed. "All in one shot," remembers Oliver proudly. "It was my Dario Argento homage because I wanted the audience to be shocked by it—no cutaways, nothing. It just happens. But nobody ever mentioned it! Kinda makes a director feel like a putz for bothering!"

Whatever Oliver's dissatisfaction with his first movie may be, and whatever the low points of any of the movies chronicled above, none of them approaches the depths of a movie which came along soon after: a movie so heinously awful, so vile and stupid, so inept and punishingly brainless, that it quite easily captures the title of Worst Canadian Horror Film Ever Made: *Things*.

Made sometime in the late Eighties, *Things* is an ultra low-budget grain-fest which not only wanted to seem American, it wanted to seem like a particular American movie, namely Sam Raimi's 1982 Spam-in-a-cabin classic *The Evil Dead*.[44] *Things* shares much with the Raimi picture: a dirty DIY look, a remote cabin setting, and scenes of over-the-top gore. What it doesn't share is far more significant: energy, charm, inventiveness, intelligence, humour and even the barest sense of how best to turn its lack of resources to its advantage.

The movie begins with a dream sequence involving a portly guy named Doug and a naked woman in a mask, from which we gather that Doug and his wife want to have children but cannot, and that Doug wants the dream-woman to be a surrogate mother. A bassinette full of toothy monsters is the unfortunate result, and Doug wakes up from his dream in a terrified sweat.

Meanwhile Doug's hosehead brother Don and his bearded buddy Fred are making their way to Doug's house, which is off in the woods somewhere. They arrive and help themselves to a couple of brewskis, discovering in the process that Doug keeps a tape deck and a book called "Horror of a Thousand Ugly Brutal Cuts" in his freezer. The two buddies shrug and poke around Doug's house for awhile, questioning his taste in knick-knacks and appraising his art collection. Observing one particular piece of pseudo-Surrealist van-art, Fred muses "Isn't this Salvador Dali's famous 'Devil's Daughter' painting? It was thought to be burned years ago! How did Doug get ahold of it?" After a little more art criticism, Don and Fred switch on the TV and watch a movie called *Ground-Hogs Day Massacre*. These scenes are broken up by shots of former porn star Amber Lynn pretending to be a newscaster and reading from cue cards held far off to the side somewhere, and scenes of a scientist and his assistant performing gory experiments on some poor slob.

Doug finally appears, acting all grumpy. It transpires that his wife is sick and consigned to her bed in the next room. Doug has a beer and makes some sandwiches, sneaking a cockroach into his brother's. The Casio theme music rises to a dramatic crescendo as Don bites into his buggy lunch.

In the next room, Mrs. Doug begins screaming and disgorging rubber monsters from her abdomen. Watching his wife's torso explode in a fountain of blood, Doug shouts the understatement of the century: "Don! Fred! Come quick! Susan's sick!" The hosers can only stand there, mullets agape, as the stiff monsters jerk slowly away.

Doug explains that Susan had been artificially impregnated by a certain Dr. Lucas. "That guy should be locked up!" declares Don. He then proceeds to tell a completely irrelevant story he'd read once in a novel, about a luckless boy named Harold, and is soundly berated by Doug for straying off the subject at hand. Fred suddenly vanishes, leaving only a welter of blood behind. Don claims to have seen his buddy pulled into a mousehole, and Doug theorizes he must have been "sucked into the third, fourth and fifth dimension!" Finally they decide that it must have been a simple case of spontaneous combustion.

Doug and Don resolve to take care of the monsters, but later on. "Get me a couple of beers," demands Don. "There ain't no beers, dumbbell," replies Doug. "Everyone alive in this house knows there ain't no beers." There is, however, whiskey, and the two brothers sit around drinking it and telling jokes. Then they begin battling the monsters, which look like large, rigid styrofoam ants. Doug is attacked by one and Don accidentally

Tim conlon as alex in *Prom Night III*, flanked by Peter Simpson (left) and Ron Oliver (right)

hits him on the head with a sledge hammer. Doug survives this only to have his hand bitten off after returning to the kitchen table for more whiskey. This is enough to kill him. Don carries the body to a closet and then arms himself with a drill and continues trying to exterminate the monsters. Fred, previously thought to be at best dimension-hopping against his will and at worst dead, pops out of the bathroom with a small electric chainsaw and helps out, but he is soon torn to shreds by the hideous critters. In the end Dr. Lucas appears at the cabin and loudly assumes that Don is responsible for the carnage. In response, Don shoves the doctor into a room teeming with the creatures and locks the door. Then he runs away and hitches a ride into town. There's a confusing coda wherein a few of the characters return and Don is attacked by yet another creature. The film ends with a long string of made-up credits.

"Directed" with jaw-dropping ineptitude by Andrew Jordan, and written by Jordan and Barry J. Gillis (who also plays Don), the film was financed with money cadged from Jordan's parents and an evidently gullible Toronto distributor named Mel. Upwards of $30,000 was eventually lavished on this picture, but it hardly looks it. The Super-8 photography hurts the eyes even as the script, acting and non-direction hurts the brain.

<hr/>

SOMEWHAT BETTER THAN *Things* is a modern-day vampire picture called *Red Blooded American Girl* (1990), which despite its title is very definitely a Canadian movie, even if one directed by a New Zealander. The movie features a nicely Canadian cast, including Christopher Plummer as the head of a research company trying to find a way to extend life, and Kim Coates, who plays his assistant, Dennis. American TV actors Andrew Stevens and Heather Thomas are the scientists unraveling the mystery.

The movie was written by Allan Moyle, who had played a small role in *Rabid* many years earlier, then lost his hair and became a well regarded director with one foot in the Hollywood mainstream (*Pump Up the Volume*, *Empire Records*) and the other in smaller, regional Canadian work (*New Waterford Girl*). Moyle's script is reasonably interesting, but doesn't manage to successfully negotiate or follow through on its own themes. It's nevertheless very nice to see Plummer doing his urbane bad-guy thing once again.

George Mihalka returned to the genre the same year with *Psychic*, starring Zach Galligan as an e.s.p.-addled student whose visions predict imminent murders by a local psychopath. Naturally the police assume Galligan to be the murderer, so the former *Gremlins* star must take matters into his own hands. The picture is somewhat livelier than Mihalka's previous excursion into the supernatural, but it still can't touch *My Bloody Valentine*.

Happy Hell Night, made by Canadians in Yugoslavia, is also known as *Frat Fright*, and under that title it has a whole different set of crew credits. Why? I don't know. Who really made it? I can't say. Otherwise the two versions are just about identical: badly directed slasher movies with practically the same plot as *Prom Night IV* and a promisingly creepy, though ill-used villain.

After a "25 years earlier" prologue in which a devilish, blank-eyed priest is discovered to have slaughtered a half-dozen fraternity brothers and one girl on the night of the big annual Halloween hazing, the story fast-forwards to 1991 and spends a good deal of time setting up a love triangle between two brothers (jock-ish Eric and motorcycle riding faux-rebel Sonny) and a pointy-nosed girl named Liz. For Sonny and co-pledge Ralph, this leads to a trip to the local asylum with orders to bring back a photograph of the notorious killer priest, who has been languishing in a Gothic cell eating bugs all this time. The priest naturally escapes (though not before posing for a snapshot and making short work of the foolish Ralph), makes his way to the frat house and begins a campaign of slaughter. Eventually Darren McGavin, the Night Stalker himself, arrives to provide a good deal of deeply unhelpful exposition before getting killed twice. McGavin's presence is, if possible, even more wasted than that of the Nosferatu-esque killer.

There's a jolly spirit of nostalgia about this little throwback of a movie. It's got plenty of sex and gore, and in general seems like it must have been made fully ten years before it actually was. Otherwise, it's just another entry in the stalk 'n' slash sweepstakes, notable only for its confusing authorship and wasted spook potential.

Eerily similar in many of its story points was the fourth (and so far the final) installment in the *Prom Night* series, *Prom Night IV: Deliver Us From Evil*. Mary Lou is nowhere to be found in this third sequel, which would be refreshing if the filmmakers had chosen to replace her with almost anything besides a possessed monk terrorizing a group of kids in a remote Toronto house. But that, oddly, is what they settled on.

There isn't much else to the story besides some of those boring murders which require only that the makeup department uncork another small bottle of blood. Since the day forty years ago when he went berserk and chopped up a couple of godless fornicators in the back seat of their Studebaker, the monk in question has been kept sedated in a small basement cell, where by some unremarked-upon miracle, he's failed to age a single day. He wakes up, of course, apropos of nothing in particular, and returns to his old monastery, which is naturally the location four unlucky new fornicators have chosen for their fornicating.

The movie was written by Richard Beattie in an effort, Peter Simpson says, to be "intellectual and sardonic," but this proved not to be a style with which director Clay Borris was comfortable. Borris' usual territory, when he strays from episodic television, is the lowbrow but sanctimonious end of the action genre, and so whatever profundities might have been laid into Beattie's script were as lost on him as they were on me.

Prom Night III

The connection to previous *Prom Night* films is a little obscure, but at least Paul Zaza—the James Horner[45] of tax shelter horror—returns with another of his comfortingly familiar scores. Plus we get a limo ride down Yonge Street, complete with a *Goin' Down The Road*-style glimpse of Sam the Record Man. Oh how hypnotic, those spinning neon records, and how Canadian! The snow on the ground is nice and Canadian as well, though its presence is sort of puzzling, given that it's supposed to be prom night, and, even in Canada, prom night is in June.

These benefits aside, *Prom Night IV* is at best boringly competent and nonsensical, and at worst simply boring. If the series is ever to be taken up anew, I recommend a thorough overhaul and a complete re-thinking. A return to the old characters and story might be nice too. Why, I'm sure Jamie Lee Curtis and Leslie Nielsen would waste no time in flying to Don Mills to take up their old characters again.

The early nineties saw the long-time-coming release of the first Maurice Devereaux joint, *Blood Symbol*. Devereaux, a Montreal-based filmmaker and horror fan, co-directed the film with Tony Morello, and was also the star, the editor and the producer. Co-director Morello doubled as the cinematographer. The picture began shooting in 1985 on a budget in the neighborhood of, one assumes, approximately naught, and as a result took six full years to complete. Was it worth it? I myself haven't seen the movie, but on the website for one of his later works, *laher$*, Devereaux says of this first effort, "Trust me, you don't want to buy that one. It's my first student film and really amateurish." Devereaux was not one to give up, however, and on the completion of *Blood Symbol*, launched himself immediately into another six year project, a tale of zombies and medieval romance called *Lady of the Lake*—a movie which isn't exactly good, but is certainly a testament to its director's determination. It contains a number of arresting visual moments, a nice musical score and a lead actor who looks a little like my brother. There's also a zombie dead ringer for Bruno Gerussi.

This picture, when it was finally done, was distributed by the video branch of *Fangoria* magazine. It did well enough for the same company to pick up Devereaux's next picture, which was *laher$*. This was a stalk-'n'-slash take on reality-tv, which was begun before the genre hit it big in North America with *Survivor* in the early days of the millenium. *laher$* was apparently conceived after Devereaux watched a videotape of the Japanese game show *Endurance*, which featured contestants stuck in heat booths, attacked by lizards and generally abused. Devereaux conceived of a show in which contestants would be chased by homicidal maniacs loosely based on horror heroes like Jason, Freddy and Leatherface.

He made the film—which is set in Japan but was filmed in Montreal—on a tiny budget, but once again snagged Adrien Morot to do the makeup effects. Shot on digital video, the picture is made up of long single takes in which the actors run screaming from the frenzied maniacs through a tarted-up warehouse. If it's time for a commercial, by the rules of the game everyone, killers and victims alike, has to stand stock still no matter how immediate the jeopardy or how close the kill. The gory film was released intact in the United States, but the Canadian video distributors reportedly butchered it: cutting out the gore, but also interfering with the stylistic device Devereaux had set himself.

Home is Where the Horror is

Two American movies from 1987, *Fatal Attraction* and *The Stepfather*, set the path for a certain branch of home-based Canadian horror filmmaking. Hollywood itself enthusiastically took up this strain of moviemaking, characterized most often by a threat to a traditional family posed by an outside element which should be benign but is most definitely not. Thus came movies like *The Hand that Rocks the Cradle* (psychotic nanny), *The Good Son* (psychotic adoptee), *Pacific Heights* (psychotic tenant), *Unlawful Entry* (psychotic cop) and *Single White Female* (psychotic roommate), all from the early 1990s. Canadians, led by producers Tom Berry and Stefan Wodoslawsky, jumped on the train with much less money to spend but as least as much gusto. The movies are part of the horror genre more by implication than by what actually happens on screen: there typically isn't much physical violence, at least compared to a regular slasher movie, and the body count can usually be made quite easily on one hand.

The fifth-column home-invasion theme—attack from within by the last person you'd suspect—seems particularly well-suited to the Canadian mindset, or at least the mindset of Berry, Wodoslawsky, and their frequent collaborators, producer Pierre David, cinematographer/director Rodney Gibbons, screenwriter Kurt Wimmer and director George Mihalka. Perhaps this is the kind of horror movie Canadians can "feel in their bones," as John Harkness put it in his *Visiting Hours* review. One hopes not, since it must be among the most boring run of motion pictures ever made in Canada or anywhere else.

The sub-genre was prefigured in the mid-eighties by such Canadian pictures as *The*

Housekeeper (in which Rita Tushingham plays a dyslexic servant whose inability to read leads to murderous rages) and *Honeymoon*, a Canada-France co-production in which Nathalie Baye is menaced by her new husband, an American stranger whom she'd married to get a green card. David Wellington's *The Carpenter* might also be considered part of the same family, though a it was good deal livelier than the others. This creaky corner of Canadiana came to full flower in 1993 with the release of *The Neighbor*, the directing debut of *My Bloody Valentine* cinematographer Rodney Gibbons.

This film concerned the psychotic obsession of next-door neighbor and retired doctor Rod Steiger for a woman played by Linda Kozlowski, who—as luck and Wimmer would have it— looks just like Steiger's long-dead but no less beloved mother. Kozlowski is pregnant, which makes Stieger's attentions all the more sinister. He manages to get Kozlowski's husband (Ron Lea) out of the way by framing him for a murder, but is foiled in the final minutes by her (not entirely unexpected) plucky resistance.

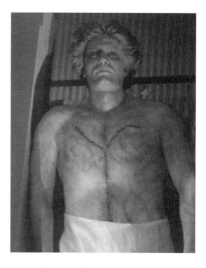

Whispers

Other, similar films followed. There was *The Child* (released also as *Relative Fear*), directed by George Mihalka and concerning the psychotic behaviour of a changeling who inadvertently invades the family of new mother Darlanne Fluegel; *Stalked*, in which waitress and single mother Maryam D'Abo is, uh, stalked by a psychotic admirer; and, believe it or not, one called *The Paperboy*, wherein a maniacal newsie (not unlike the hellish paperboy from the John Cusack comedy *Better Off Dead*) terrorizes a neighborhood inhabited by Alexandra Paul (of *American Nightmare*, the Stephen King vehicle *Christine*, and *Baywatch*) and her family.

All of these films were scored by *Reincarnate* composer Milan Kymlicka, produced by Berry and Wodoslawsky, and either directed or photographed by Rodney Gibbons. Kurt Wimmer (now a big-time Hollywood screenwriter) wrote both *The Neighbor* and *The Child*, and Douglas Jackson directed *The Paperboy* and *Stalked*, along with a late entry in the cycle called *Someone is Watching* (1998). This latter film featured Stephanie Powers, once famed as Mrs. Hart, as a single mom plagued by dreams, flashbacks and strange noises in her new suburban duplex. Her young son claims to have made a new friend: a man who lives in the closet of his room. Strange phone calls, faces at the window and creaky noises trouble both Powers and her wacky neighbor played by Margot Kidder. There are a few killings—Kidder fares no better here than in *Black Christmas*—before the killer is revealed to be not Powers' red-herring boyfriend, but the supposedly dead son of the duplex owner, who has taken it upon himself to recruit Powers and the little boy to be his new family.

"Run of the mill" doesn't begin to describe movies like this: they go the direct-to-video designation one better by appearing to have been direct-to-direct-to-video, if you know what I mean: in other words, movies that couldn't possibly have been intended for anything else (except low-brow cable channels like USA Network or TMN), and whose video boxes seem pre-layered with the dust of neglect before they even hit the shelves. The films are interchangeably available in both the "Horror" and "Mystery" sections of your local video store, and if you should for some reason get a sudden yen to see them, don't worry—they'll be there waiting for you.

❦

For several weeks in the summer of 1993, twenty-four year old screenwriter Robert Cooper must have been over the moon with joy, as it was his lot to have not one but two horror movies from his own original scripts shooting in and around Toronto at the same moment. Both were produced by Peter Simpson's Norstar Entertainment company on budgets hovering somewhere between one and one-and-a-half million dollars, and were released simultaneously (as a double-bill in some parts) in 1994.

The Club, with its prom night setting, was originally considered by Simpson as a possible *Prom Night V*, but, believing that the brand name's drawing power had more or less run its course by then, Simpson allowed the project to revert back to Cooper's original conception and title and hired *Blue Monkey* cameraman Brenton Spencer to direct. A *Fangoria* on-set report of the film's production noted a measure of guardedness among the cast and crew whenever the words "prom night" were mentioned, and quoted actor Rino Romano as saying, rather defensively, "It just *happens to be* a prom night."

The story finds a group of prom-goers enjoying a medieval theme party in Toronto's Casa Loma tourist attraction (famous also as the Elsinore Brewery exterior in the Bob & Doug McKenzie feature film *Strange Brew*). We know something strange is afoot from the leering glances school principal Carver (Kim Coates: who else?) is giving to pretty Amy (Andrea Roth), and the strange manner of handsome, charismatic loner John, played by Joel Wyner (who replaced Corey Haim in the part a day or two into the beginning of the shoot). Supernatural happenings, in the form of apparent hallucinations and random time/space manipulations, plague the group, who spend much of the movie running up and down the halls of the famed Toronto landmark, shrieking. John, it turns out, is some kind of satanic agent whose job is to collect the souls of high-school age suicides. Kim Coates plays the school's twisted sex-murderer principal, who's got his sights set on Roth, but is blown up by Romano before he can get his sweaty hands on her.

The film's makeup effects—devil faces, burn makeup, a severed hand or two—were executed by Francois Dagenais and supervised by Gordon Smith, who was taking time out from the Oliver Stone movies which had been his bread and butter since *Platoon*. For a Canadian makeup artist, Smith has actually worked on very few Canadian horror movies aside from this: just his curious credit on *Humongous* ("Special Effects Apparatus by Gordon Smith and the Gore Boys"), and the mostly excised effects of *Killer Party*. He supplied body parts for the Toronto-shot *Body Parts* (1991) and nightmare prosthetics for Cronenberg's *Dead Ringers* (1988), and has made a bit of a career out of the Vancouver-shot *X-Men* movies. Otherwise he's left the Tundra Terror makeup effects field open to the likes of Stéphan Dupuis (*eXistenZ*), Adrian Morot (*Bleeders*) and Bill Terezakis (*House of the Dead*, *Freddy Vs. Jason*).

Cooper's other horror script was *The Dark*, directed by Craig Pryce and featuring a cast that included Nova Soctia-born Stephen McHattie (the psycho from *Death Valley*), the late Yankee thespian Brion James (the comically dumb android from *Blade Runner*), and Canadians Jaimz Woolvett (Clint Eastwood's young cohort in *Unforgiven*) as a gravedigger and Neve Campbell in an early role as a deputy. All of these actors and several more spend the duration of the picture running around a graveyard in search of a shaggy rat creature—a close cousin to the denizens of *The Pit*—which is in most respects an ordinary flesh-eating monster, but also secretes a healing enzyme. McHattie is a motorbike-riding scientist who wants to preserve the creature for medical use, and perennial bad guy James is the government hard case who wants to kill it. Woolvett, Campbell and the rest are townsfolk who get in the way.

The Club

The Club and *The Dark* are not what you'd call really good movies, and they didn't revitalize the Canadian horror film scene as they might have if they were. They're nonetheless very interesting additions to the canon, since they both harken back to cinematic traditions Canada just doesn't have. *The Club* tries for Hammer Gothic with a twist of metaphysics, while *The Dark* is a more straight-ahead monster picture, garnished with a morality-play aspect. At heart, they're B movies and seem pleased to be so. My own impression of the two films as throwbacks to a golden age in low-budget horror comes not just from the films themselves, but from my fond recollection of catching them as a double feature during their week-long run at Winnipeg's now-closed Northstar Cinema. There might have been two other people in the audience. I enjoyed the night out nevertheless, but didn't realize until years later how rare and special an experience it was: going to the local theatre for a double shot of sex, blood and horror, all cheap and cheesy and gloriously Canadian. It was, I see now, a last hurrah.

AS THE DECADE CONTINUED, Canadian horror cinema dug itself deeper into a pit of mediocrity. Though Canada was finally in lockstep with the rest of the horror world, it was for the least interesting part of the march. Films like *Witchboard: The Possession* (the third installment in an American-bred series about demonic Ouija boards) and *Night of the Demons 3* (another third part of another undistinguished American franchise) provided product for the video shelves and ninety minutes of diversion to the highly undiscriminating, but that was about all.

Both the *Witchboard* and *Night of the Demons* series began as low-budget horror pictures written and directed in the late 1980s by an American named Kevin S. Tenney. By the third episode of each, they were still scripted by Tenney, but were being made in Quebec by Canadian directors. Hungarian-born Peter Svatek, co-director of *The Mystery of the Million-Dollar Hockey Puck* (an iconic slice of mid-Seventies Canadiana) made the *Witchboard* picture in and around a Montreal apartment block which very much resembles the one used in *Of Unknown Origin*. An actor called David Nerman plays a frustrated, unemployed stockbroker whose landlord turns him on to the supernatural assistance of a haunted Ouija board. The landlord is dying of cancer and pitches himself out a window, but he leaves Nerman the legacy of his ring, his Ouija board and his case of demonic possession. Nerman uses the board to make profitable investments, but when he becomes fully demonized and his soul is trapped in a fireplace shovel, it's up to his wife to bust up what the video box refers to as "a deadly ménage à trois."

The movie features a few interesting moments, notably a scene in which a menacing loan shark is pin-cushioned by his butterfly collection, and the conceptually ambitious, though modestly realized, effect-filled climax in which the escaped demon lumbers around Nerman's apartment and puts the moves on his wife. Ultimately, however, this, like any Ouija-board movie, is hobbled by the necessity of scenes involving communication with the Ouija-board itself, o…n…e… l…e…t…t…e…r… a…t… a… t…i…m…e. A duller and less cinematic method of supernatural contact could scarcely be imagined.

Night of the Demons 3, directed in and around Montreal by veteran assistant director and television stalwart Jimmy Kaufman, is a bit livelier. This is likely because the device by which the characters are possessed by demons is an entire haunted house, usually full of party-maddened teens, instead of a boring old Ouija board. Otherwise there's not much to recommend the film, except an appearance by Canadian horror stalwart Vlasta Vrana as a concerned cop who gets his heart ripped out.

Blood & Donuts (1995), the first feature made through the Canadian Film Centre's Feature Film Project, was a vampire yarn that wanted badly to be the modestly genre-busting sensation that *Ginger Snaps* was five years later. Being a vampire movie in which the vampire hardly ever bites anyone, and indeed a horror movie exhibiting very little sense that anyone connected to it had any love for or understanding of the genre (David Cronenberg excepted), it failed.

Directing her first narrative feature was Holly Dale, who with Janis Cole had established a long and impressive list of documentary credits, including *P4W (Prison for Women)*, *Hookers on Davie* and *Calling the Shots*. Upon joining the Norman Jewison-founded Canadian Film Centre, she made a short called *Dead Meat*. But all of this experience can't help the fact that *Blood & Donuts* is a horror film in name only, sorely lacking the energy and passion required to mount a successful genre film.

Boya, played by Gordon Currie like a cross between Eddie Vedder and Relic from *The Beachcombers*, is a vampire who sews himself into a bag as man is first landing on the moon back in '69. Twenty-five years later he is awoken by a golf ball and cast rudely from his burlap refuge into a strange world where people type on "personal computers" and listen to "grunge music." He falls in love with a night-shift doughnut shop waitress and runs afoul of some non-threatening gangsters led by Cronenberg, and somewhere near the end the sun comes up and reduces him to ashes.

The opening scene in which Boya is resurrected is very nice and there's an inventive if unlikely scene involving a resurrection by car battery, but most of this chat-filled picture runs like molasses in January. Very little actually happens, and when it does it has all the impact of a trip to Value Village in a brown Cutlass Sierra. Moreover, while the vampire's charm *might* be measurable under strict laboratory conditions, it isn't noticeable on the movie screen. That'll cripple a vampire movie every time, and it does so here. A poor effort, and, I'm sad to say, Canadian in the very worst sense of the word.

Branded by its producers as "A Violent Clowntasy in Three Acts," *The Clown At Midnight* (1998) takes its title from Lon Chaney's assertion that while a clown may be delightful in a circus, if that same clown were to appear on your doorstep at midnight it's likely to be a good deal less enchanting. The film was shot mainly in Winnipeg's storied Walker Theatre, which operated as the Odeon Theatre for many years and was the scene of many happy hours of moviegoing for the author; it's now a live venue called The Burton Cummings Centre for the Performing Arts. The script, by Florida-born filmmaker and special effects man Kenneth J. Hall (responsible for, among others, a 1987 bargain-basement horror thriller called *Evil Spawn*), concerns the homicidal activities of a cuckolded actor who, during a run of *Il Pagliacci* years before, had killed his wife and her lover while in full Harlequin regalia. Years later, the old theatre is reopened as a school project headed by Margot Kidder as Miss Gibby, the drama teacher of Churchill High (an actual Winnipeg high school). The students involved are a cross-section worthy of *The Breakfast Club*: dour good-girl Kate, leather jacketed rebel George, snobby cheerleader Ashley, jock/bag-of-hammers Taylor, bespectacled goofy-gal Walnut, Kate's good-natured pal Monica and the flamboyant Marty, who, the script makes excessively clear at every opportunity, "goes up the down staircase." Christopher Plummer plays the owner of the theatre, a Basil Exposition type who takes several minutes of screen time to explain the building's history. Kate, it transpires, is the daughter of the since-vanished harlequin, and it comes as absolutely no surprise when he shows up again with a little bit of killing in mind.

The Dark

The film is a perfectly acceptable throwback to the slasher era, though unremarkable in almost every respect, the near-cameo appearances of Plummer and Kidder notwithstanding. It's neither the best Canadian killer-clown movie ever made (*The Clown Murders* beats it out for that title, just), nor the worst (as a quick look at *Blue Murder*, a 1985 video-shot opus about a fed-up clown killing off porn filmmakers, will attest).

A movie in which the monsters are inbred Dutch royalty can't be all bad, and *Bleeders* (1999) certainly isn't. It's at least a marked improvement over director Peter Svatek's previous horror outing, *Witchboard: The Possession*. In *Bleeders*, Roy Dupuis plays the pale descendent of a brother-loving queen seen in a prologue; curious about his weak constitution and uncanny cravings, he and his girlfriend arrive on an island off the coast of New Brunswick in search of answers. They find Rutger Hauer wearing a small bow tie and enjoying himself in the role of the island community's eccentric doctor, Jackie Burroughs as a gun-toting old crackpot, and a band of misshapen, carnivorous troll people—the Dupuis character's long-lost cousins—who have run out of corpses to eat and have emerged from their hobbit-holes to chew on the island folk. The whole thing comes to a reasonably lively climax set first in a lighthouse and then, after the lighthouse floor collapses, in the troll family's underground warren of caves.

Similar to 1994's *The Dark*, but with more monsters and thicker atmosphere, *Bleeders* isn't actually very good on a purely objective level, but it's certainly odd, and sometimes odd's enough. The troll people are indiscriminate in their victims, dragging kids, mothers, deaf-mutes and crippled old people alike into their little subterranean grottos. One wonders if writers Dan O'Bannon and Ron Shusett came up with this one before or after they wrote *Alien*—there's something at once nasty and at the same time quaint and a little old-timey about it, like it was dreamt up by teenagers writing their very first movie script. (Of course, the same might be said, though in a more enthusiastic timbre, of O'Bannon's 1985 directorial debut *Return of the Living Dead*.) It's no classic, but, with its island setting and good monsters by Adrien Morot, *Bleeders* is a bit of a tent pole in the ragged canvas of the Canadian direct-to-video horror movie scene.

Shot in Quebec but set in Maine, *Believe* is like an absurdly overextended After School Special with the addition of a ghost. A prankster kid named Ben (Ricky Mabe) is kicked out of school for his prankishness (by headmaster Vlasta Vrana) and sent by his absentee parents to live with his grumpy, cadaverous grandfather Jan Rubes (here in late-period Karloff mode). Fans of *Blood Relations* will be on the edge of their seats, expecting Rubes at any moment to clamp Ben to a chair and gruesomely pull out his brain. Their waiting will be in vain. Instead, the kid hooks up with Katherine, the girl across the street, to solve the not-very-compelling mystery of the ghost lady in red who haunts Rubes' estate. The solution has to do with a stray deer, a truck rented from some Quebec vintage automobile club or other, and Ben Gazzara.

The movie was directed by Virginia-born Robert Tinnell, who had made the kiddie-horror movie *Frankenstein and Me*, starring Burt Reynolds and *Believe* star Mabe, three years earlier. The cast in the newer movie is impressive, the production values seem high, and the movie is, in general, competently made. However, an outrageously long digression from the plot, in which the kid uses his prankster talents to take vengeance on a pair of bullies named Frank, shows up a plot thinner than donut shop coffee and a story that would have a tough time filling out a half-hour episode of *Goosebumps*. The kid actors are not bad, and even the slushy-voiced, tow-headed lead is not as annoying as he might easily be, but that the adults overshadow them while patently not even trying very hard to makes everyone in the cast look pretty sorry. Altogether a mediocre if heartfelt effort which seems to take a very long time to end.

The dismal parade of direct-to-video horror movies made in Canada, on the other hand, is showing no sign of ending. The years between the end of the tax shelter period and the end of the twentieth century were spent honing the Canadian horror movie into something altogether less distinguishable from American ones than even something like *Prom Night* managed to be. There were high points to come, however, and a chance for Canadian horror to reassert itself more significantly than at any point since David Cronenberg's *The Fly*.

Gordon Currie and
Holly Dale on
the set of
Blood & Donuts

VI.

It Takes a Nation of Hosers to Hold Us Back

(2000 and onward)

Guy Maddin's
*Dracula: Pages from
a Virgin's Diary*

CANADIAN HORROR FILMS ENJOYED A VIOLENT UPSWING in esteem in the year 2000, and the credit for this can more or less all be deposited at the doorstep of John Fawcett's "period picture," *Ginger Snaps* (2000), a werewolf film for which lycanthrope-starved audiences seemed to have been lying in wait whether they knew it or not. Something of a renaissance for Canadian horror (as Vincente Natali's *Cube* (1997) was for Canadian science-fiction), *Ginger Snaps* caused a perhaps inordinate amount of good cheer among the legions of horror fans who had evidently been desperate for a clever, half-decent werewolf movie to come along. (*Bad Moon*, an American stinkbomb starring Eric Roberts as a fur-bearing uncle, filmed in B.C. in 1996, apparently just didn't do it.) It would be churlish, less than accurate and beside the point to label *Ginger Snaps* "overrated," for after all it isn't the movie's fault. There hasn't been a horror movie yet made that deserves the fulsome praise lavished on it by starved werewolf fans.

The movie is good, solid, intelligent entertainment. It's the story of the Fitzgerald sisters—creepy, Wednesday Addams-type Goth outcasts—and the results of sixteen year-old (though still pre-menstrual) Ginger's encounter with the neighborhood werewolf.

The crystalline expression of the movie's conceit comes when, after discovering blood on her daughter's clothes, Ginger's mother (Mimi Rogers) comes to her own conclusions, baking a large red cake, and chirpily announcing "Our little girl has become a woman!" (The same thematic device is articulated in the movie's clever tag line—"They don't call it the curse for nothing!"—which was used everywhere but the United States, where a deep-rooted, literally puritanical fear of women's sexuality among the white male ruling class demanded that the menstruation angle be toned down.)

The rest of the film charts the growing distance between Ginger and Brigitte, who begin as best friends with a mutual death pact, and grow apart as Ginger becomes a sexualized, popularity-seeking were-woman. Brigitte teams up with the local drug dealer (Kris Lemche) to try and return Ginger to normal, but in vain. The film ends with a slightly disappointing climax set in the girls' house, with a rampaging Ginger, now played by a manifestly fake latex werewolf, trying to kill her sister and Lemche.

Ginger Snaps goes a slight distance in redressing the vast gender imbalance in the Canadian horror field. Women are not terribly well represented so far, as even a quick scan of this book will reveal. There are increasingly generous numbers of female film-makers in Canada, but none of them seem terribly interested in making a horror movie. Horror has always been, to say the least, a problematic area where feminism and gender politics are concerned, and it would be no surprise to find women feeling a little unwelcome by the adolescent-boy miasma surrounding the genre. With *Ginger Snaps*, which was directed by John Fawcett, a man, but written by Karen Walton, a woman, at least a strong female point of view is getting a look in.

The movie didn't break any box-office records—certainly not during its brief theatrical run in Canada—but it got uniformly positive reviews, quickly gained a cult following, and did very well on its video release. In addition to being the first decent werewolf movie in quite a while, it is, in comparison with most recent examples of Canadian horror, extremely encouraging. The words "Canadian horror movies" were given some twenty-first century relevance, and it was badly needed.

The parade of duds continued, however, with one case in point being a shot-on-video mess called *Massacre Up North*. Made by an Ontarian named Paul Stoichevski, the movie tells the tale of a vengeful maniac played by the director himself. On a camping trip with his family, young Leslie is trapped in a burning tent and doomed forever after to wear random lumps of putty on his face. He grows into a sullen, pony-tailed, putty-faced loser, resentful of the highly debatable beauty of those around him, and bent on ridding the world of anyone inconsiderate enough to walk around without the curse of putty on their faces. He's tracked by a pair of stupid cops (one of whom is constantly bothered by his cell phone, which rings by playing "O Canada") and his own brother, who has grown up to be the town coroner and is far and away the best actor in the movie.

This cheap and juvenile attempt at psychological horror suffers from abominable acting, poor special effects, criminal overlength, the drab work of the aptly-named video-grapher, Geoff Bland, and the kind of lazy, misanthropic world view, masquerading as a cry for tolerance, that can only be formed after years of living in the comfort of your parents' basement. A sadistic torture scene involving bolt cutters and lots of crimson corn syrup, and the monotone uttering of lines like "Bring your puke-bag!" hardly improve matters in a movie that might as well be the nineties' answer to *Things*.

The film is also a close relative to the absolutely bargain-basement amateur productions, often well below feature length, which surface now and again thanks to the miracle of home video. *Attack of the Flesh-Eating Tree* and *Attack of the Killer Squirrel*, both shot somewhere in Ontario on Super-8, are two of these, and *Transcendental Hopheads*, made in Manitoba, is another. The first is pretty much exactly what it sounds like; the second an energetic, *Attack of the Killer Tomatoes*-type spoof which manages a *Bugsy Malone* brand of surrealism by putting its teenaged cast in cheap suits and homburgs; and the last, shot poorly on video, is the strange and gory tale of a group of misfits corrupted and killed by yet another group of misfits, who are evidently new arrivals in town and part of some ill-defined supernatural cult. The movie is interrupted three-quarters of the way through by a pair of campy movie reviewers in sunglasses and blazers, who harshly criticize the movie—which they've evidently been watching along with us— and then proceed to give away the ending so we don't have to endure it. None of these films are ever likely to be seen outside of the social groups surrounding the actual filmmakers, but they are nevertheless a part of the rich tapestry that is Tundra Terror.

Ginger Snaps

Highly regional horror cinema gained an oddity in the form of a Winnipeg-shot short called *Micro-Nice*. Unclassifiable in almost every respect, this ultra-low budget curiosity is based on a comic book written by the Langlois brothers of Brandon, Manitoba; the pair of artists who between them also wrote, produced, designed and directed the film. The story concerns a coven of witches whose stated purpose is to corrupt the souls of whatever pure-hearted innocents may wander along; to this end, they kidnap a raincoat-wearing naïf called Kipp Jerli, whom they keep tied to a chair in their headquarters while boss witch Petrolia goes out shopping for a crucial missing ingredient to the evil-making potion: venom from Medusa's head snakes.

This should be a simple errand, but Medusa has just accidentally killed her nice new boyfriend, Theobald, and demands that Petrolia use her powers to reanimate him in exchange for some venom. They sneak into the morgue (calcifying a lascivious security guard along the way) and raise Theobald from the dead, but, still infected by the venom, he has become not merely evil but unpleasant as well, rejecting his girlfriend Medusa and embarking on a gory killing spree.

There's a good deal more packed into an eventful 37 minutes, including a creature named Charcater, a show-stopping appearance by a barber named Old Al Mano, a witch-vs.-witch donnybrook and a good deal of strange and wonderful humour. The look of the film, or at least the scenes in the witch headquarters, strongly recalls the old Canadian Sunday morning TV show *Hilarious House of Frightenstein*, though without the periodic poetry readings by Vincent Price. As much a piece of art as a film (like a Winnipeg version of Matthew Barney's *Cremaster* films, perhaps), the movie was first screened near Halloween, 2002, in a home-built cinema, constructed by an all-female art collective, that was itself a piece of art. *Micro-Nice* will doubtless prove difficult to find for the average Tundra Terror fan, but those who happen across it will be rewarded with a brief but entertaining viewing experience.

There is a whole world of short Canadian horror films, which, as befits the form, I'll discuss only briefly. The Winnipeg Film Group, long heralded for its inventively weird output, has produced more than a few of them, including Steve Hegyi's ambitious 1988 werewolf picture *Howling Nightmare*. While at best an equivocal success as a horror movie, it does contain one of the most archetypically Canadian horror moments ever put on screen: a plaid-jacketed would-be werewolf hunter, played by filmmaker John Kozak, pauses to gulp back a beer, when from the blue darkness the lycanthrope strikes, opening the hapless boob's outstretched throat to release both the blood and the brew within. Another Winnipegger, Cindy Murdoch, has dedicated herself to making short, gory zombie movies, and one of the great, but destined-never-to-be-seen short horror triumphs is yet another Winnipeg film, *The Pug-Dog Crisis*, featuring the special-effects transformation of an ordinary poodle (who has foolishly drunk toxic waste) into a heavily jowled, man-eating Pug-Dog. Gory hijinks ensue.

There are short horror films from other parts of the country as well, of course, but space limitations prohibit a comprehensive list. Suffice it to say that the dark undercurrents of our national consciousness are running strong in unseen rivulets and streams as well as in *Ginger Snaps*-sized torrents.

THE DIRECT-TO-VIDEO WORLD SWELLED EARLY in the current millennium with pictures like the Quebec-shot *Island of the Dead* (2000), a movie about vengeful killer flies whose bite causes quick decomposition and death. Malcolm McDowell plays a rich New York developer intent on a profiteering venture involving nearby Hart Island, where, we are told, New York's unclaimed dead have been buried since 1869. Hopes for a good old-fashioned zombie picture are dashed by the appearance of the flies, with McDowell's performance left as the movie's sole pleasure. A heavy Val Lewton-style atmosphere (as in Mark Robson's somewhat similar *Isle of the Dead*) is also missed. Director Tim Southam left the horror field after this for his next seaside picture, a self-consciously classier work called *Bay of Love and Sorrows* (2002), based on a story by Maritime novelist David Adams Richards.

Guy Maddin's classy art-house credentials, unlike Southam's, come un-asked for and more or less unwanted. Maddin is a director who has never shied away from horrific imagery, gory deaths and other genre tropes in his films, and has often professed his love for horror movies, from favourites like Tod Browning's *Devil Doll* (1936) through to the Hammer films that thrilled and aroused him as a moviegoing child. Until *Dracula: Pages From a Virgin's Diary* (2001), Maddin had never made a proper horror movie, and maybe he still hasn't. It is, after all, a ballet picture as much as it is anything else, and made for television to boot, though this didn't stop it from winning Best Film in the "Fantastic" competitive section of the Sitges International Festival of Cinema in 2002, besting David Cronenberg's *Spider* and Vincenzo Natali's *Cypher* among many others.

Maddin has fun injecting the movie with the spooky Gothic atmosphere he loves, and amplifying the xenophobia of Bram Stoker's book and the earlier movie versions of same. To this end it helps that his dancing Dracula is Asian, and therefore even more exotically alien than the standard-issue urbane Transylvanian. With its canny depiction of the simultaneous attraction-repulsion dynamic of Anglo-Saxons to newly-arrived foreigners, the movie anticipates the very Canadian multiculturalism of Maddin's next feature, the depression-era musical *The Saddest Music in the World* (2003).

Transcendental Hopheads

When I watched John Eyres' B.C.-shot *Ripper: Letter From Hell* (2001), I thought it was 1981 again and I was watching *Happy Birthday To Me*. Maybe it was the school setting, or the creative murders of a bickering group of students, or the convoluted plot, or the extreme length (at 114 minutes, *Ripper* beats out *H.B.T.M.* by a good, or rather, a fairly mediocre, three minutes); but very little about the movie, besides the silly, square-filmmaker's-idea-of-what-the-kids-are-into costume design and music choices, locate it in the twenty-first century as opposed to twenty years ago.

The story introduces us to Molly (A.J. Cook), an extremely unpleasant person who had survived a massacre on an island five years earlier and now has enrolled in a college course on serial killers taught by creepy Professor Kane (Bruce Payne). Her fellow students include all the usual suspects, speaking in the broad range of accents found only in co-productions. Meanwhile, a cop, played by *Das Boot kapitan* Jurgen Prochnow as an even creepier red herring than the professor, prowls around the campus wearing a long black coat and eating apples off the point of his hunting knife. As with its 1981 predecessor, the film had a number of possible conclusions its makers could choose from, though these were not different endings written and shot, as in *H.B.T.M.*, but a denouement constructed in the editing room from existing footage.

Another faded star who's made his way north of the 49th to make a horror movie or two is Lance Henriksen, famed for his role in several James Cameron movies and the serial killer television series *Millennium*. He played a grumpy school principal who becomes a grumpy man-machine in *The Mangler 2*, a name-only sequel to a terrible 1995

Tobe Hooper movie. *The Mangler 2* has some pretty stiff competition (cf. *Lawnmower Man 2*), but, being, as it is, a sequel that has very little to do with a movie based loosely on the title of a short story by Stephen King, it could in fact hold the title of the loosest King adaptation ever. The picture was shot over twenty days in the late spring of 2001, in and around an abandoned army base in Chilliwack, British Columbia.

Producer Glen Tedham and writer/director Michael Hamilton-Wright, partners in a company called Banana Brothers Entertainment, were casting about for the most commercial project possible, and decided that nothing could be a surer bet than a Stephen King title. A little research revealed to the Canadians that the sequel rights to Hooper's killer washing-machine movie were available—who would have thought?—and Hamilton-Wright slapped together a screenplay in something like eight days. Having gone to a private school, and evidently having some issues yet to work out about it, he set the story in the same sort of place and had it terrorized and destroyed by a runaway computer program. Dominique Swain's sister Chelse is the star of this very poor, blatantly mercenary film, whose story and setting seem closely modeled on those of *Halloween H2O*, except with a killer computer instead of simply a killer.

The computer somehow controls such things as the temperature of the water in the sprinkler system and the rollers of an old-fashioned laundry wringer, this latter device used as the filmmakers' "homage" to the Hooper film. A better, or at least more entertaining homage might have been to employ the buckets of sloppy gore with which the first *Mangler* was generously supplied. The murders in *Mangler 2*, like the film itself, are entirely without the peppy *joie-de-vivre* extreme gore tends to contribute to otherwise lackadaisical pictures like this. However, though the movie has the requisite large American flag in the background of every possible shot, the filmmakers were canny enough to include a cantankerous Quebecois chef, played by Phillippe Bergeron, who says "tabernac!" a lot and decorates his kitchen and himself with as many fleur-de-lis as space will allow. It was nice to be reminded that I was indeed watching a Canadian horror movie, even if it wasn't such a good one.

And then there was *Sasquatch*. It was, I must admit, quite thrilling to learn that a new Bigfoot picture was in the offing, and a Canadian one yet! There is a common feeling in Canada, or at least among my circle of friends, that the massive biped known as Sasquatch, especially under that name, is more a Canadian citizen than an American one; so, after years of such Yankee Doodle product as *Bigfoot* (1971), the 1977 version of *Sasquatch* (which was set, but not filmed, in Canada), the gory and hilarious, but inept, *Night of the Demon* (1980) and the sappy *Harry and the Hendersons* (1987), it felt a bit like a prodigal son returning to his rightful home.

Sasquatch (2002; filmed as *The Untold*), is therefore the sort of disappointment that makes you wince visibly and repeatedly, and vow to make your own, much better Sasquatch picture right away, just to show that it can be done right. On the commentary track of the Columbia Pictures DVD release of the film, director Jonas Quastel and producer Rob Clark repeatedly assert that the movie was made in twelve days, and moreover was written to be made in that sort of time frame. I think that's where they went wrong: lack of ambition. Fine movies have been made in twelve days and even less, but intending from the get-go to do it that way means that the script will be limited, compromised and essentially censored from the beginning. That's no way to make a film, as the results here irrefutably demonstrate.

After a preface showing the crash of a small plane somewhere in the middle of a mountainous nowhere, and a young woman being chased by something suffering from the same sort of vision impairment as Arnold Schwarzenegger's adversary in *Predator* (1987), the story proper begins: the young woman's father is a rich industrialist named Harlan Knowles, and, two months after her disappearance has organized an expedition—evidently made up of the least competent people he could find on such short notice— to trek into the Pacific northwest to find her. "Twists" in the plot reveal that Knowles' search for his daughter is an afterthought, and his true goal is some one-of-a-kind hunk of technological junk, to which no plans or blueprints exist—yeah, right—that was on the plane with her. One of the party is revealed (in more ways than one, since the scene occurs in a sort of hot tub in the middle of the forest) as an industrial spy mandated to steal the piece of junk. However, a Sasquatch whose mate was apparently hit by the plane as it was crash-landing busts up the party, upset over his wife's unlikely demise. Blinded by rage and grief as he is, the big mangy biped still manages to target only the characters deemed by the simple-minded script to be bad guys. Why should he care to make

Brotherhood III: Young Demons

any distinction? For that matter, why should we? It's really too bad this wasn't a better movie. The great Sasquatch picture has yet to be made, but when it finally is, I fully expect it will be made in Canada.

Absent from this narrative thus far is any mention of Saskatchewan's contributions to the Tundra Terror canon. There isn't much to mention, it's true, but just so those in the Land of Living Skies don't feel left out, I'll bring up *The Wisher* (2002), shot in Regina and Moose Jaw and directed by the man who brought us *Christina's House*. The newer film is an improvement on *Christina's House* in that it's shorter. The movie tells the story of a horror fan called Mary, played by Liane Balaban from *New Waterford Girl*. Balaban is a good actor, but with her ripped jeans and the DVD of *Christina's House* visible in her bedroom, she makes the least convincing horror fan ever put on screen. (Balaban earns her acting stripes just for uttering lines like "Don't go out alone unless Mom or I are with you" without cracking up.) Mary loves horror movies to a point of near-erotic release (a fact she confesses, in the film's most disturbing scene, to a high school shrink played by Ron Silver), but has become unhinged by them to the point of suffering nightmares and bouts of sleepwalking almost nightly. Her hard-ass father quite correctly prohibits her from seeing any more scary movies, but this wise bit of parenting marks him as a bad guy by the dumb and lazy script.

Wouldn't you know it, a horror movie called *The Wisher* is just opening at the local googleplex (which is itself a pretty scary edifice called The Galaxy). *The Wisher* is getting a *Blair Witch*-level of national buzz: it's the movie all the kids in Regina have to see. Naturally Mary is intrigued. She defies her dad and sneaks off to the movie, but is laid low by an attack of nausea ten minutes into the picture. The film-within-the-film *Wisher* looks nearly as crappy as the film-we're-actually-watching *Wisher*, but still, it's hard to fathom why a supposedly seasoned horror fan like Mary would be so affected. She rushes out of the theatre and collapses in a chair.

Things go downhill from there. The hard-ass dad is killed in a car accident (possibly the most spectacular stunt yet filmed in downtown Regina), and Mary barely has time to recover from this when her friends start getting mutilated by a mysterious prowler. It all seems tied in to contrived wishes uttered casually by Mary: "I wish you'd shut up," for example, cried in anger at a blabbermouth pal, results in the friend losing her tongue. Mary starts to suspect that the wish-granting prowler in the movie-within-the-movie has been released into the world for some reason; indeed, we do catch glimpses of a figure fitting that description (the spectre sports a black cloak, a pasty face and a Freddy Krueger-style knife-glove, though with the very minor innovation of shards of glass instead of blades). The Wisher has not come to life, however: it's only a local epileptic nerd who has become obssessed with both the movie and Mary, and stalks her when he's not too busy having seizures. His homicidal mania is cut short by the sound bonk on the head which has been standard treatment for Canadian psychos since *Prom Night*.

Samhain is, like *Bleeders*, nothing if not a celebration of the elaborate, grotesque effects work of Adrien Morot. It goes back to the source of Wes Craven's *The Hills Have Eyes*: a gang of teens and porn stars go on a school trip to Ireland where they run afoul of the remnants of the Sawney Bean family. The Beans were a real-life cannibal clan who, in 17th century Scotland, waylaid and murdered travelers to keep their stew pots full. They were tracked down and hanged by authorities, but, per *Samhain*, some of them apparently survived and carried on through successive inbred generations, by now more latex lump than human. The film was shot in Quebec, and suffered a delayed release because the picture required re-cutting by a real editor after the director, Christian Viel, initially tried to do it himself. With rubbery monsters that are only slightly less convincing than the equally rubbery breasts on abundant display, the picture is a bit of a throwback to the glory days of John Fasano; though even Fasano never dared to coax Irish accents out of inexperienced Quebecois thespians.

In the spring of 2003, two back-to-back sequels (well, a sequel and a prequel, to be more precise) to *Ginger Snaps* were shot in Edmonton, Alberta. KNB, the American makeup effects company who've had a hand in almost any horror series one could name, agreed to tackle the effects, supposedly—according to the films' publicist—because they'd never had the chance to do werewolf effects before. The sequel was directed by Brett Sullivan (the editor of the first *Ginger Snaps* as well as *Blood & Donuts*), and the prequel by Grant Harvey, who'd done second unit directing duties on the first of the werewolf series.

The production of these two films represents some sort of benchmark in the history of Canadian horror films—whether it's a positive or negative one has yet to be seen. Will they retain all that was peculiar and gloriously Canadian about the first movie, or will they be generic, anonymously North American direct-to-video sequels? The mere fact of shooting back-to-back sequels—*The Matrix* excepted, perhaps—tends to undermine the notion that the people making them have any confidence whatever in the staying power of the story. "Get a couple out at once before people realize just how far down the tubes this series has gone" is the usual philosophy. Often it's like hammering in two coffin nails with one blow: for an enlightening example, look at the two Toronto-shot sequels to Sam Raimi's *Darkman*.

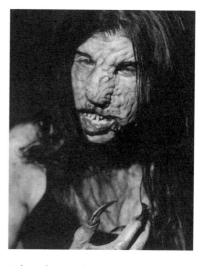

The werewolf sequel, produced as *Ginger Snaps: The Sequel* and released as *Ginger Snaps: Unleashed*, takes place in a drug rehab center into which the unfortunate Brigitte has been tossed. Wounded by her late sister, who returns periodically in dream form, Brigitte is now a werewolf, and she, and the doctors, creepy orderlies and other residents of the rehab, have more to worry about than medication schedules or bedpan privileges. Altogether, it sounds like a blandly typical direct-to-video-level story: nothing special, and an underwhelming follow-up to one of the most successful Canadian horror movies ever made. In practice, it's a little better than expected.

Ginger Snaps 2

The prequel will surely be more interesting. Set in a Canadian fur trading post some time in the nineteenth century, it sounds like a long overdue attempt to use the history of the country as a backdrop to a horror story, and will almost certainly represent the first film ever to feature both werewolves and voyageurs. This is encouraging on many levels. If it works, we might finally start seeing all the Sasquatch and Windigo movies we've been deprived of all these years, or at least more genre movies which actually take place in Canada and use Canadian settings to profitably exotic effect.

For all the talk in this book, and in many others, about questions of national identity as reflected in commercial films, quality really is the bottom line. A national cinema of lasting value is the one which encourages comments like "Those Canadian films are damn good," whereas "Those Canadian films are damn Canadian" is good too, but—for all the praise I've heaped upon *My Bloody Valentine* for its strong hoser flavour—nevertheless thoroughly subordinate. Quality can become a national characteristic as valid as any other and with a better return than most. To my way of thinking if that had been the general opinion of Canadian policymakers, industry people and society at large from the early days of Canadian film, we, and our horror movies and our very station in the world entertainment arena, might be a great deal changed from what it is today. Ideally, the excellence of our films would be inextricably linked to our national character by a hundred years of reinforcing the equation Canadian Film = Superior Quality. Of course, quality itself is a tricky proposition and always has been: any time it approaches a happy state of objectivity, it gets tripped up by some dissenting opinion and returned to the subjective.

People who ask how we are to get audiences in to the cinemas to watch Canadian films are asking the wrong question. A dozen really, really good Canadian films in a row, even if they themselves are of only moderate profile, will help clear the horizon for those that follow. It's that simple: stop making mediocre films for just a little while and start making good ones, because quality, like murder, will out. (Look at Hollywood: still trading on the glory of 1939, the year in which the popular conception of quality intersected with the sort of movies they were actually making. They've been dining on *Gone With the Wind* and *The Wizard of Oz* for decades now!) It's easy to say "make good films" and harder to do it, of course—it's not easy to make films at all—but that doesn't mean we shouldn't try.

Issues of quality aside, it should simply be noted that, unacknowledged and unappreciated as the fact might be, Canada has done very well by horror movies, and horror conversely has done very well by Canada. There's a great partnership there, hallowed by usage and consecrated by time, and it ought to be kept up. The days of Canadians thinking that horror movies are simplistic, lowbrow, meaningless entertainments that can say nothing about Canada nor contribute to its cultural makeup must come to an end; and the days of Canadians making lousy, generically-set horror movies without conviction or care must die as well. The Canadian film industry is in crisis: media giant Alliance Atlantis has drastically clipped its filmmaking wing, our most expensive commercial ventures are flopping at the box office, and Toronto's Uptown Theatre—premiere venue for *The Reincarnate* and who knows how many others—has fallen down. Something must be done, and embracing our ability to make genre films is surely a step in the right direction.

Horror movies may not single-handedly turn things around, but they can help, and it must be recognized that these films are a part of the national cinema whether some in the critical community like it or not. *Cannibal Girls*, for example, is as Canadian a film as *Goin' Down the Road*, perhaps more so since it has rarely been recognized as such; and it is every bit as valuable a brick in the foundation of the house we are still slowly building. So it is with all the misbegotten horror movies in our crazy-quilt cinema history. The genre is an excellent showcase for all the cowards, bullies and clowns which make up our gallery of heroes: really a natural place to express all our national anxieties. It's too bad these same national anxieties make it so hard to express ourselves in horror films, which, as David Cronenberg has said, are after all "films of confrontation." Our own horror movies, absorbed by enough of us, might serve as a psychiatrist's couch on national scale, forcing us to finally confront our chronic inability to confront. At the very least we might get a few respectable films out of it.

Baby steps towards this oddly comforting reality are being taken. Carleton University professor André Loiselle taught a summer credit course in Canadian horror movies in the summer of 2000; in 2003, *Take One* magazine printed Paul Corupe's article on the work of Julian Roffman and other unheralded pioneers; and in the same year *CineAction* mounted a scholarly argument for academic appraisal of the Tundra Terror pictures. Corupe's *Canuxploitation!* website is gaining fans all the time; articles on Hoser Horror pop up here and there, and several other books besides this one are reportedly in the works. Horror film festivals play to enthusiastic crowds in cities across the Dominion, from Fantasia in Montreal to Cinemuerte in Vancouver. Big-ticket or otherwise interesting horror movies, like the *Dawn of the Dead* remake, the third installment of the *Blade* action-vampire series, Lucky McKee's *The Woods* and the Stephen King projects *Secret Window* and *Riding the Bullet*, continue to be filmed north of the 49th parallel.

Ginger Snaps 2

All of this is not yet much to hang a renaissance on, but it's something. More encouraging still are the go-getters of Montreal, who have banded together to try and make their town Canada's horror capital of the new millennium by turning out promising fare like *Sur le Seuil* (Éric Tessier, 2003), *Graveyard Alive: A Zombie Nurse in Love* (Elza Kephart, 2003) and *Le Diable Dedans* (Éric Desgagnés, 2003) among others. On top of this there are scores of young filmmakers across Canada energetically trying their hand at a genre once considered so lowbrow as to not be considered at all.

Canada may one day be counted as one of the great horror-film producing countries or it may not, but after forty-five years of malevolent masks, cannibals, creatures, ghosts, diabolists, maniacs and mutations, it cannot be denied that the country has a genuine horror movie history. For a nation of beer-swilling, hockey-playing, poetry-spouting, pot-smoking, documentary-loving hosers, well, hey—that's not too shabby.

Footnotes

1 According to Phil Hardy (ed.), *The Aurum Film Encyclopedia*, Aurum Press, 1996.

2 This role would be played again sixty years later by another Canadian, Keanu Reeves. In an honourably self-sacrificial move, Reeves evidently made the decision to play the role in the established Manners style, only more so. Perhaps there's something inherently Canadian about the character, who serves, after all, as little more than a stooge for the charismatic foreign bloodsucker to whom he naïvely tries to sell real estate.

While on the subject of *Dracula*, it should be noted that the Spanish language version of same (shot at night on the same sets as Browning's) was directed by American-born but Montreal-educated George Melford, who also directed the dramatic scenes (as opposed to the purely scenic sequences) in one of Canada's most prestigious films of the 1930s, *The Viking*.

3 Ulmer would travel up to Montreal in 1936 to make a quota thriller called *From Nine to Nine*.

4 Tourneur's stellar Lewton horror *I Walked With A Zombie* (1943), incidentally, featured a Canadian nurse, played by Frances Dee, as the lead character.

5 From Thomas Doherty's review of *Nightbreed* in the July, 1990 issue of *Cinefantastique*.

6 Quoted in *Julian Roffman: Man of Action*, an unpublished essay written by Ella Schwarzman in early 1984. Schwarzman was evidently a student in a course called Media Management (though at what institution remains unclear), and her instructor, a Mr. Twomey, was impressed enough by *Julian Roffman: Man of Action* to give her a perfect score of 30/30 for it—a rock-solid A. The original source of the quote was Marjorie McKay's *History of the National Film Board of Canada*.

7 Kleinburg today is known as Cinesite, and, in a strangely resonant turn of fate, boasts a standing White House set that is maintained by Warner Bros. and available for use to any production that needs it. No more perfect symbol of cultural annexation could be imagined. Kleinburg is, incidentally, also "Home of the Binder Twine Festival."

8 Schuftan developed the process before moving to North America and dropping an F from his name.

9 Oboler, an American who was originally a radio dramatist, was a maker of eccentric films like *The Twonky*, and had made *One Plus One* in Toronto. He was, like Roffman, a pioneer in the world of 3-D, having made the killer-lion adventure *Bwana Devil*, which had kicked off the original craze in 1953.

10 The Majin, in case you were wondering, is like a sort of giant Golem monster; which is to say a statue come to life to take revenge on behalf of an oppressed or otherwise victimized group.

11 Amicus and Hammer were British film studios specializing in horror.

12 Otherwise known as Producer's Releasing Corporation, a company famous for its catalogue of incredibly low budget spookshows starring Bela Lugosi or George Zucco, including *The Devil Bat* (1941), *The Mad Monster* (1942) and *The Flying Serpent* (1946).

13 Lake's very last film would be the Nazis-and-maggots horror potboiler *Flesh Feast*, which is sometimes identified as Canadian (probably in confusion with *Footsteps in the Snow*) but was in fact shot in Florida.

14 Romero resisted all offers to make his films in Hollywood or even New York for years. When he finally did make a movie somewhere other than his beloved Pennsylvania—his poorly-received 2000 film *Bruiser*—it was in Toronto.

15 BCP would hit the horror jackpot a year later with *Willard*, a killer rat movie that would be remade in Canada by Americans more than thirty years later.

16 *Kolchak* was a wonderful early-Seventies horror-detective show starring Darren McGavin as a grumpy reporter who was always on the trail of some crazy monster or another, always while wearing the same seersucker suit and battered straw hat. Upon the show's cancellation, McGavin traveled to Nova Scotia to direct a strange horror thriller called *Run Stranger Run* (a.k.a. *Happy Mother's Day...Love George*), starring Ron Howard, Patricia Neal,

Cloris Leachman and Bobby Darin. He also apparently tried to open his own movie studio in Gimli, Manitoba.

17 According to writer Peter Morris, *The Columbus of Sex* was "a lusciously beautiful, sophisticated, almost meditative work. Although replete with erotic imagery, it was totally unexploitative." (Morris, *A Delicate Balance*, page 37.)

18 The story of the making and selling of *Cannibal Girls* is told in its nail-biting entirety in the July, 1973 issue of *Take One* magazine, in an extensive interview with Reitman and Goldberg conducted by fellow future-producer Joe Medjuck. Most of the quotes and the story told in the following paragraphs are taken from this interview.

19 *Ilsa* was produced by Reitman under the Cinépix house pseudonym "Julian Parnell."

20 Woronov was married to *Sugar Cookies* director Theodore Gershuny, and had appeared in the bizarre thriller as well. Other *Sugar Cookies* alumni involved in *Seizure* included Jeffrey Kapelman, co-producer Garrard Glenn, and costumer Linda Coleman. The star of *Sugar Cookies*, Lynn Lowry, would herself travel up to Quebec the next year to take part in David Cronenberg's debut *Shivers*.

21 I've chosen to refer to it by the title I like best; but this is also the title under which the film was originally made.

22 Wood, *Hollywood From Vietnam to Reagan*, 133-134.

23 Thanks to Geoff Pevere for that designation, used in an article he wrote on *Goin' Down the Road* for *Take One*.

24 Not as new as some believe, however, including the film's director: Cronenberg claims the complicated bladder work was invented by Blasco at the same time as Dick Smith was inventing it for *The Exorcist*; but Friedkin's devil movie came out eight months before *Shivers* began shooting. As well, Jack Pierce had used bladder-like contrivances for his work on *Monster On The Campus* (1958).

25 As quoted in Chesley, *Cinema Canada* #16, p. 25.

26 Once, in the very early days of home video recording, my friends and I noticed that *Shivers* was scheduled to play on late-night television. None of us had seen the film, though its gruesome content was legendary in our circle. A plan was quickly formulated: Dave Binding, the only one among us with a VCR, would set the timer on his humidifier-sized machine and tape the movie, and then we would all thrill to a clandestine after-school viewing the next day.

The next afternoon finally came, and we settled down to watch what was certain to be a mind-breaking experience in cinematic depravity. The tape was rewound, "play" was pressed…and on came the credits for something called *Fast Company*. It sure didn't look like a horror movie, but wait a minute—there was David Cronenberg's name! But what was with all the racing cars? We couldn't figure it out. Had Dave Binding screwed up? Had the television listings lied to us? All we really knew was that we'd been deprived instead of depraved, and we were all terribly disappointed. More than twenty years later, however, this strange blauchup remains the only opportunity I've had to see *Fast Company*.

27 I realize that *Victory* is not normally counted among John Huston's creative triumphs, but a surprising number of people, most of them Britons, love the movie beyond all proportion or reason.

28 *Hide and Go Shriek*, come to think of it, also had its psycho in drag when he wasn't wearing a costume. *Terror Train* should sue!

29 Based on what, I'd like to know: Curtis was both talented and famous as the lead in what was at the time the most profitable independent film ever made, *Halloween*.

30 Jeff Wincott is the brother of the somewhat more famous Michael Wincott, who, aside from starring in *The Crow* and numerous Oliver Stone movies, appeared in the Simcom production *Curtains* (1983).

31 Jibe courtesy of Dr. Cyclops from *Fangoria*.

32 *The Village Voice*, August 27-September 2, 1980. Page 40.

33 Thompson's horror experience included a 1966 picture called *Eye of the Devil*, which

could boast a wonderful cast that included David Niven, Deborah Kerr, *Creature of Comfort*'s Donald Pleasance, Sharon Tate, Devid Hemmings and Edward Mulhare. Thompson later made the Charles Bronson-vs.- nude-slasher movie *10 to Midnight* (1983).

34 For a film entirely hinging on the subject of pinball, advertised with poster art of pinball machines and prominently featuring a theme song called "Pinball Summer," *Pick-up Summer* is indeed an unexpected title.

35 Wojeck being a proto-Quincy investigative coroner character on the fine 1960s CBC show of the same name.

36 Harkness, *Cinema Canada # 86*, July, 1982. Page 86.

37 *Videodrome* would be Filmplan's last hurrah, with the partnership breaking up and Pierre David heading to Los Angeles in order to produce and sometimes direct movies like *Scanner Cop*.

38 "The American Nightmare" was also the name given a horror retrospective mounted by the Toronto Film Festival in 1979, and curated by Cronenberg-hating critic Robin Wood. Wood also gave this title to a series of essays exploring horror films of the 1970s.

39 Simpson's company, Simcom, had at a certain point changed its name to Norstar.

40 *Suspiria* is Dario Argento's 1977 thriller about a girls' school overrun by witches.

41 "All those places used to be disgusting," Oliver says of the typical Toronto shooting location. "Then the production companies from the USA started coming up to shoot, and they insisted on cleaning them all up."

42 Findlay, in collaboration with her late husband Michael, had made the notorious *Flesh* series in the 1960s, as well as such Seventies trash classics as *Shriek of the Mutilated* and *Snuff*.

43 Other films with Canadian connections to get the *Mystery Science Theatre 3000* treatment are a Yukon-shot bit of madness called *The Pod People* (a delirious rip-off of *E.T.* from J. Piqeur Simon, the director of *Slugs* and *Pieces*), and *The Final Sacrifice*, an inept but hilarious lost-

city adventure made in Alberta.

44 Thanks are due to to Joe Bob Briggs for the "Spam-in-a-cabin" term.

45 James Horner is a big-time American composer whose original ideas appeared to run out somewhere around 1986, after he did the score for James Cameron's *Aliens*. He collected one of those Oscars, as well as a Grammy and other assorted hardware, some years later when he scored Cameron's *Titanic*.

Bibliography and References

I. BOOKS

Beattie, Eleanor. *A Handbook of Canadian Film.* Toronto: Peter Martin Associates Limited, 1973.

Dorland, Michael. *So Close to the State/s: The Emergence of a Canadian Feature Film Policy.* Toronto, Buffalo, London: University of Toronto Press, 1998.

Elder, R. Bruce. *Image and Identity: Reflections on Canadian Film and Culture.* Waterloo: Wilfred Laurier University Press, 1989.

Gittings, Christopher E. *Canadian National Cinema.* London, New York: Routledge, 2002.

Handling, Piers (ed.). *The Shape of Rage: The Films of David Cronenberg.* Toronto: Academy of Canadian Cinema; General, 1983.

Hardy, Phil (ed.). *Horror.* London: Aurum, 1996.

Hardy, Phil (ed.). *Science Fiction.* London: Overlook, 1994.

Horsting, Jesse. *Stephen King at the Movies.* New York: Starlog Press, 1986.

Katz, Ephraim. *The Macmillan International Film Encyclopedia.* London: Macmillan, 1994.

Monk, Katherine. *Weird Sex and Snowshoes.* Vancouver: Raincoast Books, 2001.

Morris, Peter. *David Cronenberg: A Delicate Balance.* Toronto: ECW Press, 1994.

Morris, Peter. *Embattled Shadows: A History of Canadian Cinema 1895 - 1939.* Montreal: McGill-Queen's University Press, 1978.

Morris, Peter. *The Film Companion.* Toronto: Irwin, 1984.

Morse, L.A. *Video Trash and Treasures.* Toronto: Harper & Collins, 1989.

Pratley, Gerald. *A Century of Canadian Cinema.* Toronto: Lynx Images, 2003.

Rigby, Jonathan. *English Gothic: A Century of Horror Cinema.* London: Reynolds & Hearn Ltd., 2000.

Rockoff, Adam. *Going to Pieces: The Rise and Fall of the Slasher Film, 1978-1986.* Jefferson, London: McFarland & Company, 2002.

Rodley, Chris (ed.). *Cronenberg on Cronenberg.* Toronto: Alfred A. Knopf, 1992.

Savini, Tom. *Bizarro!* New York: Harmony Books, 1983.

Schneider, Steven Jay (ed.) *Fear Without Frontiers.* FAB Press, 2003.

Spencer, Michael, with Suzan Ayscough. *Hollywood North.* Cantos International Publishing Inc., 2003.

Stanley, John. *The Creature Features Movie Guide.* New York: Warner Books, 1984.

Thomson, David. *The New Biographical Dictionary of Film.* New York: Alfred A. Knopf, 2002.

Tombs, Pete. *Mondo Macabro: Weird and Wonderful Cinema Around the World.* New York: St. Martin's Griffin, 1998.

Turner, D. John. *Canadian Feature Film Index 1913-1985.* Ottawa: Public Archives Canada, 1987.

Whitehead, Mark. *Slasher Movies.* Pocket Essentials, 2000.

Wise, Wyndham (ed.). *Take One's Essential Guide to Canadian Film.* Toronto: University of Toronto Press, 2001.

Wood, Robin. *Hollywood from Vietnam to Reagan.* New York: Columbia University Press, 1986.

II. ARTICLES

Acheson, Keith, and Christopher Maule. "It Seemed Like a Good Idea at the Time." *Canadian Journal of Communications* Volume 16, Number 2 (1991).

Anonymous. "Frankenstein in Toronto: The Making of *Flick.*" *Toronto Life.* (October, 1969): 36-39.

Anonymous. "Quirky Sex Thriller in Toronto." *Cinema Canada #81* (February 1982): 8.

Axmaker, Sean. "Jack Hill: Exploitation Genius." *Psychotronic # 13* (Summer 1992): 32-43.

Bearden, Keith. "I'm Dreaming of a *Black Christmas.*" *Fangoria # 159* (January 1997): 13-16, 18-19.

Breskin, David. "David Cronenberg." *Rolling Stone, Issue 623* (February 6, 1992): 66-70, 96.

Burns, James H. "*My Bloody Valentine.*" *Fangoria # 11* (February 1981): 54-56, 64-66.

Carlomango, Ellen. "The Burman Studio." *Fangoria # 14* (August, 1981): 20-24.

Chartrand, Harvey and Peter Ford. "Glenn Ford: The Multi-Purpose Star!" *Filmfax # 95* (February/March 2003): 36-41, 74-76.

Chesley, Stephen. "It'll Bug You." *Cinema Canada #16* (October 1975): 23-25.

Clement, Brian. "Eating Flesh and Getting Naked." *Fangoria #227* (October 2003): 56-59.

Corupe, Paul. "Taking Off the Mask." *Take One* Volume 12, Number 44 (December 2003—March 2004): 17-21.

Dancyger, Kenneth. "Ed Hunt." *Cinema Canada # 17* (December/January 1975): 46-47.

Delaney, Marshall [Robert Fulford]. "You Should Know How Bad This Movie Is. After All, You Paid For It." *Saturday Night,* Volume 90, Number 4 (September 1975): 83-85.

Doherty, Thomas. "Showcases the 'Breed and the bleed,' but doesn't quite succeed." *Cinefantastique,* Volume 21, Number 1 (July 1990): 56.

Dowler, Andrew. "In Progress…Cries in the Night." *Cinema Canada # 58* (September 1979): 6-7.

Edwards, Natalie. "Black Christmas." *Cinema Canada #17* (December/January 1975): 78.

Edwards, Natalie. "Reg Morris C.S.C. past, present and future: a conversation." *Cinema Canada #25* (February 1976): 28, 31.

Eisenthal, Bram. "You'll Eat Up *Samhain.*" *Fangoria #218* (November 2002): 40-44, 82.

Everitt, David. "Of Roaches and Snakes." *Fangoria #20* (July 1982): 13-16.

Everitt, David. "Videodrome: David Cronenberg Talks About His Latest and Most Bizarre Feature." *Fangoria #25* (February 1983): 46-50.

Everitt, David. "Slasher Writer." *Fangoria #45* (June 1985): 50-53.

Fothergill, Robert A. "Being Canadian Means Always Having To Say You're Sorry." *Take One,* Volume 4, Number 3 (1973): 24-30.

Fujiwara, Chris. "The Black Comedy of *The Fly.*" *Filmfax #91* (June/July 2002): 68-74.

Gault, John. "Now, the schlock of your life." *Macleans* Volume 93, No. 10 (13 October 1980): 71.

Gravestock, Steve. "Welcome to their Nightmare; or, to Live and Die in Suburbia." *Take One* (Spring, 2001): 7-12.

Grove, David. "*The Untold.*" *Fangoria #218* (November 2002): 18.

Hamilton, Craig. "Canada's First 3-D Horror: *The Mask.*" *Filmfax # 25:* 83-88.

Harkness, John. "*Visiting Hours.*" *Cinema Canada # 86* (July 1982): 27.

Ibrányi-Kiss, Ági. "Harvey Hart's Back in Town." *Cinema Canada # 10/11* (October 1972/January 1973): 56-59.

Ibrányi-Kiss, Ági. "Winnipeg Symposium: The Turning Point." *Cinema Canada #14* (April, 1974): 14-16.

Isaac, Doug. "In Progress…*Train to Terror.*" *Cinema Canada #63* (March 1980): 3-4.

Kimber, Gary. "*Hello Mary Lou: Prom Night II.*" *Cinefantastique,* Volume 18, Number 1 (December 1987): 40-41.

Klady, Leonard. "Cannes-ada." *Cinema Canada #20* (July-August 1975): 28-29.

Kuersten, Erich. "The Disintegration of a Canadian Family: The Delambres/Brundles in the films of *The Fly.*" *Scarlet Street,* No. 48: 32-35, 43-44, 51-55, 68-71.

Larsen, John and Joanne Larsen-Verducci. "*Dark Shadows* Lives." *Fangoria #58* (October 1986): 12.

Lehti, Steven J. "*The Amityville Curse.*" *Cinefantastique,* Volume 21, Number 1 (July 1990): 14.

Lucas, Tim. "David Cronenberg's *Dead Ringers.*" *Fangoria #79* (December 1988): 26-29, 67.

Magder, Ted. *Canada's Hollywood: The Canadian State and Feature Films.* Toronto: The University of Toronto Press, 1993.

Martin, Bob. "Oliver Stone and *The Hand.*" *Fangoria #12* (April, 1981): 10-11, 44-45.

Martin, Bob. "Jamie Lee Curtis." *Fangoria #15* (October 1981): 20-25.

Martin, Bob. "Tom Brumberger." *Fangoria #27* (May, 1983): 49-51.

Martin, Bob. "On The Set of *The Dead Zone* —Part 1." *Fangoria #28* (July 1983): 42-44.

Martin, Bob. "On The Set of *The Dead Zone* —Part 2." *Fangoria #29* (September 1983): 14-17.

Martin, Bob. "On The Set of *The Dead Zone* —Part 3." *Fangoria #31* (December 1983): 47-50.

McCallum, Gary J. "The Leopard is Loose." *Take One,* Volume 5, Number 6 (January 1977): 38-40.

McDonagh, Maitland. *Filmmaking on the Fringe.* New York: Citadel Press, 1995.

Medjuck, Joe. "The Makers of *Cannibal Girls.*" *Take One,* Volume 3, Number 10 (1973): 23-29.

Medjuck, Joe. "The Further Adventures of Ivan Reitman." *Take One,* Volume 6, Number 8 (July 1978): 20-22.

Newton, Steve. "Waiting for *Watchers.*" *Fangoria #79* (December 1988): 45-47.

Pirie, David. "The Reincarnate." *Monthly Film Bulletin #467* (December 1972): 258.

Pugliese, David. "Who Was That *Mask* Man?" *The Dark Side #72* (1998): 6-9.

Razutis, Al. "Nothing Personal." *Independent Eye* (Mike Holboom, editor). 1989.

Rice-Barker, Leo. "André Link & John Dunning: filmmaking's 'Odd Couple' celebrates 40." *Playback* (February 4, 2002): 15.

Rollans, Scott. "Howling for More." *Fangoria #230* (March 2004): 40 45, 80

Rowe, Michael. "*The Club*—For Dismembers Only." *Fangoria #131* (April 1994): 62-67.

Schwarzman, Ella. "Julian Roffman: Man of Action." Unpublished school essay for Mr. Twomey, dated February 24, 1984.

Sharpe, David. "A Mean Appetite." *Cinema Canada #80* (December 1981—January 1982): 33.

Snider, Norman. "Just Two Innocent Canadian Boys in Wicked Hollywood." *Saturday Night,* Volume 81, Number 7 (July 1974): 17-22.

Sotiron, Minko. "Schlock but Slick." *Cinema Canada #82* (March, 1982): 24-25.

Szulkin, David. "Home on *Deranged.*" *Fangoria #131* (April 1994): 48-55.

Taylor, Aaron. "Blood in the Maple Syrup." *CineAction #61* (2003): 18-28.

Testa, Bart. "Once More, With Ketchup." *Macleans* Volume 94, Number 10 (9 March, 1982).

Timpone, Anthony. "Three days with David Cronenberg's *The Fly.*" *Fangoria #55* (July 1986): 27-30, 65.

Townend, Paul. "*The Brain.*" *Cinema Canada #166* (September 1989): 35.

Waddell, Calum. "Horror Hill!" *The Dark Side #107* (2004): 6-10.

West, Linda. "*Black Christmas* Scripter." *That's Showbusiness* Volume 3, Number 10-11 (May 22, 1974): 13, 15.

Wooley, John. "Workin' the *Graveyard Shift.*" *Fangoria #69* (December 1987): 20-23.

Wooley, John and Michael H. Price. "Forgotten Horrors: *Terror Train.*" *Fangoria #222* (May 2003): 38-39.

III. ON LINE

www.canuxploitation.com is a site run by Paul Corupe, a devoted fan and student of Canadian B cinema. Contains reviews, articles, links, remarks from Canada's favourite cannibal Ezra Cobb, and more. Long may it live.

http://www.encorehomevideo.com/features/corpse_eaters.html is where you can find a copy of The Corpse Eaters if you feel like buying one. I think you do.

www.hysteria-lives.co.uk features detailed reviews of many Canadian slasher films, and moreover displays as robust an enthusiasm for them as you'll find anywhere.

www.imdb.com is of course an indispensable tool in researching any movie project. You wouldn't want to rely on it as a single or even primary source, though, and accordingly I have taken care to get my information elsewhere whenever possible, using the database only to remind myself of things I already knew or to back up assertions from other fairly reliable sources.

www.terrortrap.com contains many interesting, if slightly underdeveloped interviews, including one with Canadian scream queen Lesleh Donaldson; and there are reviews of a number of Canadian horror pictures here as well. They seem to have a fondness for Canadian horror movies, and that makes them all right in my book.

IV. DVD COMMENTARY TRACKS AND INTERVIEWS

Black Christmas (commentary features Bob Clark, John Saxon, Keir Dullea)

Ginger Snaps (commentary features John Fawcett, Karen Walton)

Mangler 2 (commentary features Michael Hamilton-Wright, Glen Tedham, Philipe Bergeron)

Of Unknown Origin (commentary features George P. Cosmatos, Peter Weller)

Pin (commentary features Sandor Stern with moderator Ted Newsome)

Rabid (interview with David Cronenberg)

Ripper: Letter From Hell (commentary features John Eyres)

Shivers (interview with David Cronenberg)

The Untold (a.k.a. *Sasquatch*) (commentary features Jonas Quastel, Rob Clark, Russell Ferrier, Phil Grainger)

Appendix: Films

American Nightmare (1983)
Colour, 90 minutes.
Director: Don McBrearty. Producer: Ray Sager. Screenplay: John Shepperd. Photography: Daniel Hainey. Art Director: Andrew Deskin. Editor: Ian McBride. Music: Paul Zaza.
Cast: Lawrence. S. Day (Eric), Lara Staley (Louise), Neil Dainard (Tony), Lenore Zann (Tina), Mike [Michael] Ironside (Sgt. Skylar), Paul Bradley (Motel Manager).
A maniac stalks exotic dancers on the seamy streets of Toronto. This would appear to have something to do with the disappearance of a young woman and the tension between her brother Eric and their extremely rich father.

The Amityville Curse (1989)
Colour, 91 minutes.
Director: Tom Berry. Producer: Franco Battista. Screenplay: Michael Krueger, Norvell Rose. Photography: Rodney Gibbons. Production Designer: Richard Tassé. Editor: Franco Battista. Music: Milan Kymlicka. Special Makeup Effects: Patrick Shearn. Prosthetic Makeup Effects: R.S. Cole.
Cast: Kim Coates (Frank), Dawna Wightman (Debbie), Helen Hughes (Mrs. Moriarty), Antony Dean Rubes (Bill), Cassandra Gava (Abigail), David Stein (Marvin), Jan Rubes (Priest).
Hauntings and horrors continue unabated in Amityville as a quintet of yuppies attempt some ill-advised renovations on their newest real estate purchase.

Believe (1999)
Colour, 96 minutes.
Director: Robert Tinnell. Producer: Richard Goudreau. Screenplay: Richard Goudreau, Roc Lafortune. Photography: Pierre Jodoin. Production Designer: Jules Ricard. Editor: Gaëtan Huot. Music: Jerry de Villiers Jr. Special Effects: Ryal Cosgrove, Cineffects.
Cast: Jan Rubes (Jason Stiles), Ricky Mabe (Benjamin Stiles), Elisha Cuthbert (Katherine Winslowe), Andrea Martin (Muriel Tatran), Ben Gazzara (Ellicott Winslowe).
A troubled youngster staying with his gruff grandfather unravels the mystery of a ghost who haunts the family estate.

Bells (1981)
a.k.a. Murder By Phone, The Calling
Colour, 94 minutes.
Director: Michael Anderson. Producer: Robert Cooper. Screenplay: Michael Butler, Dennis Shryack, John Kent Harrison. Photography: Reginald Morris. Production Designer: Seamus Flannery. Editor: Martin Pepler. Music: John Barry. Special Effects: Bill Myatt, Henry Piersig, Ken Estes, Dick Taylor.
Cast: Richard Chamberlain (Nat Bridger), John Houseman (Stanley Markowitz), Sara Botsford (Ridley Taylor), Robin Gammell (Noah Taylor), Gary Reineke (Lieutenant Mears), Barry Morse (Fred Waites).
A maniac sends high frequencies through the phone lines to kill his enemies, and it's up to a science teacher/activist to save the day.

Black Christmas (1974)
a.k.a. Silent Night, Evil Night, Stranger in the House
Colour, 98 minutes.
Director/Producer: Bob Clark. Screenplay: Roy Moore. Photography: Reginald Morris. Art Director: Karen Bromley. Editor: Stan Cole. Music: Carl Zittrer.
Cast: Olivia Hussey (Jess), Keir Dullea (Peter), Margot Kidder (Barb), John Saxon (Lt. Fuller), Art Hindle (Chris), Andrea Martin (Phyl), Marian Waldman (Mrs. Mac), Lynne Griffin (Clare), Doug McGrath (Sergeant Nash), Les Carlson (Graham).
A psychotic killer terrorizes sorority girls over the Christmas vacation.

Black Roses (1988)
Colour, 83 minutes.
Director: John Fasano. Screenplay: Cindy Sorrell. Producers: John Fasano, Ray Van Doorn. Photography: Paul Mitchnick. Art Director: Nick White. Editors: John Fasano, Ray Van Doorn, James K. Ruxin. Music: Elliot Solomon. Special Makeup Effects: Richard Alonzo, Bill Basso, Anthony C. Bua, Arnold Gargiulo, Dan Platt.
Cast: John Martin (Matthew Moorhouse), Ken Swafford (Mayor Farnsworth), Sal Viviano (Damien), Julie Adams (Mrs. Miller), Carla Ferrigno (Priscilla Farnsworth), Frank Dietz (Johnny Pratt).
A death-metal band are revealed to be the devil's emissaries when they transform into rubber puppets and terrorize a town.

Bleeders (1999)
Colour, 91 minutes.
Director: Peter Svatek. Producers: Pieter Kroonenburg, Julie Allan. Screenplay: Charles Adair, Dan O'Bannon, Ron Shusett. Photography: Barry Gravelle. Production Design: Michel Proulx. Editor: Heidi Haines. Music: Alan Reeves. Creatures and Special Makeup Effects by Adrien Morot. Special Effects Coordinator: Pierre "Bill" Rivard.
Cast: Rutger Hauer (Dr. Marlowe), Roy Dupuis (John), Kristin Lehman (Kathleen), Jackie Burroughs (Lexie), John Dunn-Hill (Hank), Joanna Noyes (Byrdie).
A man suffering from anemia discovers himself to be the descendant of a monstrous family of Dutch inbreeds, who continue to terrorize a New Brunswick island.

Blood & Donuts (1995)
Colour, 88 minutes.
Director: Holly Dale. Producer: Steve Hoban. Screenplay: Andrew Rai Berzins. Photography: Paul Sarossy. Production Design: David Mo. Editors: Stephen Fanfara, Brett C. Sullivan. Music: Nash the Slash. Special Effects Makeup: Randy Daudlin.
Cast: Gordon Currie (Boya), Justin Louis (Earl), Helene Clarkson (Molly), Fiona Reid (Rita), David Cronenberg (Crime Boss).
A vampire wakes up in Toronto after a twenty-five year nap and battles gangsters while falling in love with a donut-shop waitress.

Blood Clan (1990)
Colour, 87 minutes.
Director: Charles Wilkinson. Producer/Screenplay: Glynis Whiting. Photography: Kenneth Hewlett. Editor: Alan Lee.
Cast: Michelle Little, Gordon Pinsent, Robert Wisden.

Blood Relations (1987)
Colour, 90 minutes.
Director: Graeme Campbell. Producer: Nicolas Stilliadis. Screenplay: Stephen Saylor. Photography: Rhett Morita. Art Director: Gina Hamilton. Editor: Michael McMahon. Music: Mychael Danna. Special Effects Makeup: Gianico Pretto. Mechanical Special Effects: Brock Jolliffe.
Cast: Jan Rubes (Andreas), Lydie Denier (Marie), Kevin Hicks (Thomas), Lynne

Adams (Sharon), Ray Walston (Dr. Charles McLeod), Stephen Saylor (Jack).
Twisted familial relationships are laid bare when Marie accompanies her fiancée Thomas back to the home of his widowed surgeon father Andreas and his even stranger grandfather Charles. Marie learns the hard way not to get involved in family squabbles.

Blood Symbol (1994)
Colour, 87 minutes.
Directors: Maurice Devereaux, Tony Morello. Producers: Maurice Devereaux, Jean-Marc Félio, Tony Morello. Screenplay: Maurice Devereaux. Photography: Tony Morello. Editor: Maurice Devereaux. Music: Brent Holland. Special Effects Makeup: Adrien Morot, Luke Pourdrier.
Cast: Micheline Richard (Tracy), Richard Labelle (Olam), Nadine Fournelle (Brenda), Luke Pourdrier (Luke), Maurice Devereaux (Steve), Trilby Jeeves (Sacrifice Victim).
Diabolists harass a young student, whom they take to be the "chosen one" required for their rituals.

The Blue Man (1985)
a.k.a. Eternal Evil
Colour, 85 minutes.
Director: George Mihalka. Producer: Pieter Kroonenburg. Screenplay: Robert Geoffrion. Director of Photography: Paul Van Der Linden. Art Director: John Meighen. Editors: Yves Langlois, Nick Rotundo. Music: Marvin Dolgay. [Special Makeup Effects: Ed French.]
Cast: Winston Rekert (Paul Sharpe), Karen Black (Janus), John Novak (Detective Sgt. Kauffman), Patty Talbot (Jennifer Sharpe), Vlasta Vrana (Scott), Lois Maxwell (Monica Duval).
A director of television commercials is drawn into the world of astral projection and reincarnation.

Blue Monkey (1987)
Colour, 93 minutes.
Director: William Fruet. Producer: Martin Walters. Screenplay: George Goldsmith, Chris Koseluk. Photography: Brenton Spencer. Art Director: Reuben Freed. Editor: Michael Fruet. Music: Patrick Coleman, Paul Novotny. Creature and Makeup Effects by Steve Neill and Mark Williams.
Cast: Steve Railsback (Jim Bishop), Susan Anspach ((Dr. Judith Glass), Joe Flaherty (George Baker), Robin Duke (Mrs. Baker).
A giant insect terrorizes the staff and patients of a large hospital. Only the tried-and-true combination of a rogue cop and a giant laser beam can defeat the beast.

The Brain (1988)
Colour, 91 minutes.
Director: Edward Hunt. Producer: Anthony Kramreither. Screenplay: Barry Pearson. Photography: Gilles Corbeil. Art Director: Byron Patchett. Editor: David Nicholson. Creature and Makeup Effects: Mark Williams. Special Effects: Danny White, Craig Williams.
Cast: Tom Breznahan (Jim), Cyndy Preston (Janet), David Gale (Dr. Blake), George Buza (Varna), Christine Kossack (Vivian).
A self-help television show proves to be the conduit by which an extra-terrestrial brain monster intends to take over the world.

The Brood (1979)
Colour, 91 minutes.
Director/Screenplay: David Cronenberg. Producer: Claude Héroux. Photography: Mark Irwin. Art Director: Carol Spier. Editor: Alan Collins. Music: Howard Shore. Special Makeup: Jack Young, Dennis Pike. Special Effects: Allan Kotter.
Cast: Oliver Reed (Dr. Hal Raglan), Samantha Eggar (Nola Carveth), Art Hindle (Frank Carveth), Cindy Hinds (Candice Carveth), Henry Beckman (Barton Kelly).
A scientist develops a procedure by which patients manifest their innermost feelings in physical form. A troop of rampaging murderous dwarves is the inevitable result.

The Brotherhood III: Young Demons
Colour, 80 minutes.
Director/Producer: David DeCoteau. Screenplay: Matthew Jason Walsh. Photography: Paul Suderman. Editor: Bruce Little. Special Makeup Effects: Doug Morrow.
Cast: William Gregory Lee (Jeff), Kristopher Turner (Lex), Paul Andrich (Ramsay), Elisa Donovan (Annie), Ellen Weiser (Megan).
A group of youngsters tempt the forces of evil by breaking into their school to play fantasy games.

Cannibal Girls (1973)
Colour, 83 minutes.
Director: Ivan Reitman. Producer: Daniel Goldberg. Screenplay: Robert Sandler, based on a story by Ivan Reitman and Danny Goldberg and on improvisations by the actors. Director of Photography: Robert Saad. Editor:

Daniel Goldberg. Music: Doug Riley. Special Effects: Richard Whyte, Michael Lotosky.
Cast: Eugene Levy (Cliff), Andrea Martin (Gloria), Ronald Ulrich (Reverend Alex St. John), Randall Carpenter, Bonnie Neilson, Mira Pawluk (Cannibal Girls), Kingfish (Butcher), and Bunker as himself.
Innocent Toronto lovebirds Cliff and Gloria find themselves trapped in a small town whose main tourist attraction is a farmhouse-restaurant run by a cannibalistic mesmerist and his three beautiful assistants.

The Carpenter (1987)
Colour, 87 minutes.
Director: David Wellington. Producer: Pierre Grisé. Screenplay: Doug Taylor. Photography: David Franco. Art Director: Sylvain Gingras. Editor: Roland Pollak. Music: Pierre Bundock. Special Effects Makeup: Michel Bougie. Special Effects: Andrew Campbell.
Cast: Wings Hauser (Carpenter), Lynne Adams (Alice Jarett), Pierre Lenoir (Martin Jarette), Barbara-Ann James (Rachael), Beverly Murphy (Crazy Woman).
A mysterious, possibly undead carpenter comes to the aid of a put-upon woman, saving her from other carpenters and her perfidious husband.

Cathy's Curse (1976)
a.k.a. Cauchemars
Director: Eddy Matalon. Producer: Nicole Mathieu Boisvert. Screenplay: Eddy Matalon, Myra Clement, Alain Sens-Cazanave. Photography: Jean-Jacques Tarbès. Editor: Laurent Quaglio. Music: Didier Vasseur. Makeup: Julia Grundy. Special Effects: Eurocitel.
Cast: Alan Scarfe (George), Randi Allen (Cathy), Beverly Murray (Vivian), Dorothy Davis (Mary), Roy Witham (Paul), Mary Morter (Medium).
A young girl living in Montreal is possessed by the evil spirit of her aunt. Family members and the hired help alike find themselves in grave danger.

The Changeling (1979)
Colour, 107 minutes.
Director: Peter Medak. Producers: Joel B. Michaels, Garth Drabinsky. Screenplay: William Gray, Diana Maddox. Photography: John Coquillon. Production Designer: Trevor Williams. Editors: Lou Lombardo, Lilla Pederson. Music: Rick Wilkins. Special Effects: Gene Grigg.
Cast: George C. Scott (John Russell),

Trish Van Devere (Claire Norman), Melvyn Douglas (Senator Carmichael), John Colicos (Captain DeWitt), Barry Morse (Parapsychologist), Jean Marsh (Joanna Russell).

A bereaved husband and father takes up residence in a cavernous old house, only to find that an angry ghost already holds the lease.

The Child (1994)
a.k.a. Relative Fear
Colour, 94 minutes.
Director: George Mihalka. Producers: Tom Berry, Stefan Wodoslawsky. Screenplay: Kurt Wimmer. Photography: Rodney Gibbons. Production Design: Patricia Christie. Editor: Ion Webster. Music: Marty Simon. Special Makeup Effects: Adrien Morot. Special Effects: Ryal Cosgrove/Cineffects.
Cast: Darlanne Fluegel (Linda), Martin Neufeld (Peter), James Brolin (Atwater), Denise Crosby (Connie), M. Emmet Walsh (Earl), Matthew Dupuis (Adam).
A mix-up in the maternity ward leads to terror ten years later when a psychotic child shows his true colours.

City in Panic (1987)
Colour, 85 minutes.
Director: Robert Bouvier. Producers: Robert Bouvier, Andreas Blackwell. Screenplay: Andreas Blackwell, Peter Wilson. Photography: Mark McKay. Art Director: Ray Lorenz. Editor: Wayne Ryan. Music: Dave W. Shaw. Special Effects Makeup: Gary Boisvert. Special Effects: Gerald Lukaniuk.
Cast: Dave Adamson (Dave Miller), Leann Nestegard (Elizabeth Price), Ed Chester (Barry McKee), Peter Roberts (Alex Ramsey), Gary Bryant (Dr. Farthing).
A serial killer targets homosexuals in Toronto, and it's up to a hard-boiled, free-thinking radio host to make the steam baths safe for men again.

The Clown at Midnight (1998)
Colour, 92 minutes.
Director: Jean Pellerin. Producers: Gary Howsam, Giles Paquin. Screenplay: Kenneth J. Hall. Photography: Barry Gravelle. Art Director: Rejean Labrie. Editor: Robert Lower. Music: Glenn Buhr. Special Effects Supervisor: Kenneth J. Hall. Special Makeup Effects: Doug Morrow. Special Effects: Rory Cutler.
Cast: James Duval (George), Sarah Lassez (Kate), Tatyana Ali (Monica), Margot Kidder (Miss Gibby), Christopher Plummer (Caruthers),

Melissa Galianos (Walnut).
A killer clown stalks an old theatre currently being renovated by high school students.

The Clown Murders (1975)
Clour, 94 minutes.
Director/Screenplay: Martyn Burke. Producer: Christopher Dalton. Photography: Dennis Miller. Editors: Alan Collins, Ronald Sanders. Music: John Mills Cockell.
Cast: Stephen Young (Charlie), Susan Keller (Alison), Lawrence Dane (Phillip), John Candy (Ollie), Gary Reineke (Rosie), Al Waxman (Police Officer).
A group of friends kidnap another man's wife as a joke, but when they hole up at an abandoned farmhouse they are hunted down and killed by a maniac.

The Club (1993)
Colour, 93 minutes.
Director: Brenton Spencer. Producer: Ilana Frank. Screenplay: Robert C. Cooper. Photography: Curtis Petersen. Art Director: Ian Brock. Editors: Nick Rotundo, Michael McMahon. Music: Paul Zaza, Peter Breiner. Special Effects: Brock Jolliffe. Prosthetic Effects: Francois Dagenais.
Cast: Joel Wyner (John), Andrea Roth (Amy), Zack Ward (Kyle), Rino Romano (Evan), Kim Coates (Mr. Carver), Kelli Taylor (Laura).
A medieval-themed prom night proves to be a devilish ruse to send suicidal teens to hell. Or something like that.

The Corpse Eaters (1974)
Colour, 57 minutes.
Directors: Donald R. Passmore, Klaus Vetter. Producer/Screenplay/Ghoul Make-up: Lawrence Zazelenchuk. Photography: Klaus Vetter. Editor: Michelle Jones.
Cast: Michael Hopkins, Edmond LeBreton, Terry Leonard, Michael Krizanc, Helina Carson.
Zombies rise from their graves and munch on a group of Sudbury-area loogans.

Creature of Comfort (1968)
Colour. 118 minutes (?).
Director: Graham Driscoll. Producer: Donald Adams. Screenplay: Robert Stuart [Laird Stuart].
Cast: Donald Pleasance (Shopkeeper).
A living duvet, repeatedly sold by a complicit shopkeeper, eats its more objectionable coverees.

Cries in the Night (1982)
a.k.a. Funeral Home
Colour, 92 minutes.
Director/Producer: William Fruet. Screenplay: Ida Nelson. Photography: Mark Irwin. Production Designer: Roy Forge Smith. Editor: Ralph Brunjes. Music: Jerry Fielding. Makeup: Shonough Jabour. Special Effects: Dennis Pike.
Cast: Kay Hawtry (Grandma), Lesleh Donaldson (Heather), Barry Morse (Mr. Davis), Dean Garbett (Rick) Stephen Miller (Billy Hibbs), Harvey Atkin (Harry).
A young girl working at her grandmother's hotel is curious about why the residents are disappearing. Could granny's super-strength and violent mood swings have anything to do with it?

Curtains (1983)
Colour, 89 minutes.
Director: Jonathan Stryker [Richard Ciupka]. Producer: Peter R. Simpson. Screenplay: Robert Guza Jr. Photography: Robert Paynter, Fred Guthé. Production Designer: Roy Forge Smith. Editor: Michael MacLaverty. Music: Paul Zaza. Director of Special Effects: Colin Chilvers. Prosthetics: Greg Cannom.
Cast: John Vernon (Jonathan Stryker), Samantha Eggar (Samantha Sherwood), Linda Thorson (Brooke Parsons), Lynne Griffin (Patti), Lesleh Donaldson (Christie), Anne Ditchburn (Laurian), Maury Chaykin (Monty).
A group of actresses attend a mass audition at director Jonathan Stryker's country house, but a maniac kills them off one by one.

The Dark (1993)
Colour, 88 minutes.
Director: Craig Pryce. Producers: Robert Bergman, Craig Pryce. Screenplay: Robert Cooper. Photography: Michael Storey. Art Director: Nicholas White. Editor: Michael Todd. Music: Guy Zerafa, Alun Davies. Score: Paul Zaza. Creature Design: Ron Stefaniuk. Prosthetics: Colin Penman.
Cast: Stephen McHattie (Hunter), Cynthia Belliveau (Tracy), Jaimz Woolvert (Ed), Brion James (Buckner), Neve Campbell (Jesse).
A giant shaggy rat creature lives under a cemetery, munching on corpses and any live humans it can get its paws on. A scientist, several cops, and an obsessed FBI man are all on its trail.

Dead Stop (1995)
Colour, 91 minutes.
Director/Screenplay: Nick Rotundo.
Producer: Paco Alvarez. Photography:
Edgar Egger. Production Design: Gabi
Milius. Editor: Nick Rotundo. Music:
Mychael Danna. Special Effects: Brock
Jolliffe.
Cast: Robert McFaul (Jay Looker), Chris
Chinchilla (Kyle Garrett), Tina Mosner
(Carol Mannings), Gina Brunton
(Michelle Devrise), Walter Lane (Dr.
Moebius).
*An organ-harvesting operation causes havoc
in a small town.*

Deadly Eyes (1982)
a.k.a. The Rats
Colour, 87 minutes.
Director: Robert Clouse. Producers:
Jeffrey Schechtman, Paul Kahnert.
Screenplay: Charles Eglee. Photography:
René Verzier. Art Director: Ninkey
Dalton. Editor: Ron Wisman. Music:
Anthony Guefen. Special Makeup Effects
and Animal Prosthetics by Makeup
Effects Labs. Special Effects: Malivoire
Productions Inc.
Cast: Sam Groom (Paul Harris), Sara
Botsford (Kelly Leonard), Scatman
Crothers (George Foskins), Lisa Langlois
(Trudy), Lesleh Donaldson (Martha),
Cec Linder (Dr. Louis Spenser).
*Steroid-enhanced rats terrorize a city, and
it is up to a teacher and his health-official
girlfriend to save the day.*

Death Ship (1980)
Colour, 91 minutes.
Director: Alvin Rakoff. Producers: Derek
Gibson, Harold Greenberg. Screenplay:
John Robins, based on a story by Jack
Hill and David P. Lewis. Director of
Photography: René Verzier. Production
Designer: Chris Burke. Editor: Mike
Campbell. Music: Ihor Slaney. Special
Effects: Mike Albrechtson, Peter Hughes.
Cast: George Kennedy (Captain
Ashland), Richard Crenna (Trevor
Marshall), Nick Mancuso (Nick), Sally
Ann Howes (Margaret Marshall), Kate
Reid (Sylvia), Victoria Burgoyne (Lori),
Saul Rubinek (Jackie).
*A possessed old rust-bucket of a ship tor-
ments and kills the group of shipwreck
survivors it had earlier pointlessly saved.*

Death Weekend (1976)
a.k.a. The House by the Lake
Colour, 89 minutes.
Director/Screenplay: William Fruet.
Producer: Ivan Reitman. Photography:
Robert Saad. Art Director: Roy Forge

Smith. Editors: Jean Lafleur, Debbie
Karjala. Special Effects: Tony Parmalee.
Makeup: Maureen Sweeney.
Cast: Brenda Vaccaro (Diane), Don
Stroud (Lep), Chuck Shamata (Larry),
Richard Ayres (Runt), Kyle Edwards
(Frankie), Dan Granberry (Stanley).
*A woman is taken up to a lakeside man-
sion by a rich dentist, but they are attacked
by a group of crazed, sadistic louts.*

Decoys (2004)
Colour, 93 minutes.
Director: Matthew Hastings. Producer:
Franco Battista. Screenplay: Tom Berry,
Matthew Hastings. Photography: Daniel
Villeneuve. Production Designer: Csaba
András Kertész Editor: Isabelle Levesque.
Music: Daryl Bennett, Jim Guttridge.
Special Makeup Effects: George Tucci.
Cast: Corey Sevier (Luke Callahan),
Stefanie von Pfetten (Lilly), Kim Poirier
(Constance), Nicole Eggert (Detective
Watts), Richard Burgi (Detective Kirk),
Meghan Ory (Alex).
*A college student discovers that two beau-
tiful campus blondes are aliens who first
seduce and then freeze their victims.*

Deranged (1974)
Colour, 82 minutes.
Directors: Jeff Gillen, Alan Ormsby.
Producer: Tom Karr. Screenplay: Alan
Ormsby. Photography: Jack McGowan.
Art Director: Albert Fisher. Editor
[uncredited]: Bob Clark. Music: Carl
Zittrer. Makeup and Special Effects: Alan
Ormsby, Tom Savini, Jerome Bergson.
Cast: Roberts Blossom (Ezra Cobb),
Marion Waldman (Maureen Selby),
Cosette Lee (Ma Cobb), Micki Moore
(Mary), Pat Orr (Sally), Leslie Carlson
(Narrator).
*The story of Ezra Cobb, a sub-moronic
farmer who kills women to please the pre-
served corpse of his mother.*

Le Diable est parmi nous (1972)
a.k.a. Satan's Sabbath, The Possession of
Virginia
Colour, 91 minutes
Director: Jean Beaudin. Producers: John
Dunning, Yrene Nold. Screenplay: John
Dunning, André Link. Photography: René
Vérzier, Denis Gingras. Editors: Jaques Jean,
Jean Lafleur. Music: Francois Cousineau.
Cast: Louise Marleau, Daniel Pilon,
Danielle Ouimet (Virginie), Rose-Rey
Duzil (The Grandmother), Henri Norbert.
*A sleepy reporter is drawn into the machi-
nations of a devil cult looking for a few
good sacrificial victims.*

Dracula: Pages From A Virgin's Diary
(2001)
B/W with tinted sequences, 74 minutes.
Director/Screenplay: Guy Maddin.
Producer: Vonnie Von Helmolt.
Photography: Paul Suderman.
Production Designer: Deanne Rohde.
Editors: Guy Maddin, deco dawson.
Special Effects: Ken Hart Swain. Special
Makeup Effects: Doug Morrow.
Cast: Zhang Wei-Qiang (Dracula), Tara
Birtwhistle (Lucy), David Moroni (Van
Helsing), CindyMarie Small (Mina),
Johnny Wright (Harker).
*A twinkle-toes vampire arrives in England
from his ancestral home in Transylvania
and proceeds to drain the blood of the
living until old Van Helsing and his friends
manage to still his evil heart and happy
feet forever.*

Evil Judgment (1984)
Colour, 93 minutes.
Director: Claudio Castravelli. Producers:
Claudio Castravelli, George Amsellem.
Screenplay: Victor Montesano, Claudio
Castravelli. Photography: Mario
Romanini, Roger Racine. Editors: Susan
Shanks, Gerald Vansier. Music: Corkey
Laing. Special Effects Makeup: Michelle
Burke, Catherine Cossault.
Cast: Pamela Collyer (Janet), Jack
Langedyck (Dino), William Massey
(Ron/Robertson), Nanette Workman
(April), Ronald Nincherl (Armstrong),
Suzanne DeLaurentiis (Liz).
*A murderous ex-judge targets prostitutes
along with women he thinks might be pros-
titutes.*

Flick (1970)
a.k.a. Dr. Frankenstein on Campus
Colour, 81 minutes.
Director: Gilbert W. Taylor. Producer:
William Marshall. Screenplay: David
Cobb, William Marshall, Gilbert W.
Taylor. Photography: Chris Slagter.
Editor: Eric Wrate. Music: Paul Hoffert,
Skip Prokop. Makeup: Ken Brooke.
Cast: Robin Ward (Viktor Frankenstein),
Kathleen Sawyer (Susan Harris), Austin
Wells (Cantwell), Sean Sullivan
(Professor Preston), Ty Haller (Tony
Bayles), Tony Moffat-Lynch (David).
*Young doctor Frankenstein uses mind con-
trol and murder to revenge himself on those
who would see him thrown out of school.*

The Fly (1986)
Colour, 96 minutes.
Director: David Cronenberg. Producer:
Stuart Cornfeld. Screenplay: Charles
Edward Pogue, David Cronenberg.

Photography: Mark Irwin. Production Design: Carol Spier. Editor: Ronald Sanders. Music: Howard Shore. The Fly Created and Designed by Chris Walas Inc. Cast: Jeff Goldblum (Seth Brundle), Geena Davis (Veronica Quaife), John Getz (Stathis Borans), Joy Boushel (Tawney), Les Carlson (Dr. Cheevers), David Cronenberg (gynecologist).
A scientist discovers the secret to teleportation, but an accident with a fly puts a crimp in both his research and his romance.

Food of the Gods II (1989)
a.k.a. Gnaw: Food of the Gods II
Colour, 86 minutes.
Director: Damian Lee. Producers: Damian Lee, David Mitchell. Screenplay: Richard Bennett, E. Kim Brewster. Photography: Curtis Petersen. Production Designer: Reuben Freed. Editor: David Mitchell. Music: Steve Parsons, Dennis Haines. Creature Designs by David B. Miller. Visual Effects by Ted Rae.
Cast: Paul Coufos (Neil Hamilton), Lisa Schrage (Alex Reed), Michael Copeman (Lt. Weizel), Colin Fox (Edmund Dellhurst), Frank Pellegrino (Joshua), Jackie Burroughs (Dr. Treger).
Giant rats, inadvertently created by scientists and released by animal rights activists, munch on college students on a campus which looks suspiciously like that of York University.

Freakshow (1988)

Full Circle (1977)
a.k.a. The Haunting of Julia
Colour, 97 minutes.
Director: Richard Loncraine. Producers: Peter Fetterman, Alfred Pariser. Screenplay: Dave Humphries, Harry Bromley Davenport. Photography: Peter Hannan. Editor: Ron Wisman. Music: Colin Towns.
Cast: Mia Farrow (Julia), Keir Dullea (Magnus), Tom Conti (Mark), Jill Bennett (Lily), Robin Gammell (Mr. Swift).
A guilt-ridden woman who has lost her daughter to a household accident finds herself haunted by the ghost of another little girl.

The Gate (1986)
Colour, 85 minutes.
Director: Tibor Takacs. Producer: John Kemeny. Screenplay: Michael Nankin. Photography: Thomas Vamos. Production Designer: William Beeton. Editor: Rit Wallis. Music: Michael Hoenig, J. Peter Robinson. Special Visual Effects: Randall William Cook. Special

Makeup Effects: Craig Reardon.
Cast: Stephen Dorff (Glen), Louis Tripp (Terry), Christa Denton (Al), Deborah Grover (Mom), Scot Denton (Dad), Ingrid Veninger (Paula).
Two heavy-metal loving kids discover the portal to hell in their suburban Toronto back yard. Imps, demons and the zombified corpse of a workman pour out and wreak terrifying havoc.

The Gate II (1989)
Colour, 93 minutes.
Director: Tibor Takacs. Producer: Andras Hamori. Screenplay: Michael Nankin. Photography: Bryan England. Production Designer: William Beeton. Editor: Ronald Sanders. Music: George Blondheim. Special Effects: Frank Carere. Special Makeup Effects: Craig Reardon. Special Visual Effects: Randall William Cook.
Cast: Louis Tripp (Terry), Simon Reynolds (Moe), James Villemaire (John), Pamela Segall (Liz), Neil Munro (Art).
In an effort to help out his alcoholic father, one of the kids from the first film manages once again to re-open the portal to hell, and once again this proves a very bad idea.

Ghostkeeper (1981)
Colour, 87 minutes.
Director: James Makichuk. Producers: Harold J. Cole. Screenplay: Douglas McLeod, James Makichuk. Photography: John Holbrook. Art Director: Barry Anderson. Editor: Stan Cole. Music: Paul Zaza. Special Effects: Mel Merrills. Makeup: Kirstie McLellan.
Cast: Riva Spier (Jenny), Murray Ord (Marty), Sherinne Fadden (Chrissy), Georie Collins (Ghostkeeper), John MacMillan (Wendigo).
A skidoo-riding trio of vacationers finding themselves trapped in an old mountain resort, are forced to deal with a creepy old caretaker lady and the hulking monster she keeps in a closet.

Ginger Snaps (2000)
Colour, 108 minutes.
Director: John Fawcett. Producers: Steve Hoban, Karen Lee Hall. Screenplay: Karen Walton. Photography: Thom Best. Production Designer: Todd Cherniawsky. Editor: Brett Sullivan. Music: Michael Shields. Special Make-up and Creature Effects by Paul Jones. Special Effects: Brock Jolliffe.
Cast: Emily Perkins (Brigitte), Katherine Isabelle (Ginger), Kris Lemche (Sam), Mimi Rogers (Pamela Fitzgerald), Jesse Moss (Jason).

A teenage girl is bitten by a werewolf, and bloody havoc in her suburban neighborhood is the result.

Ginger Snaps 2: Unleashed (2004)
a.k.a. Ginger Snaps: The Sequel
Colour, 95 minutes.
Director: Brett Sullivan. Producers: Steve Hoban, Paula Devonshire, Grant Harvey. Screenplay: Megan Martin. Photography: Gavin Smith, Henry Less. Production Designer: Todd Cherniawsky. Editor: Michele Conroy. Music: Kurt Swinghammer. Special Makeup and Creature Effects: Howard Berger, KNB.
Cast: Emily Perkins (Brigitte), Katherine Isabelle (Ginger), Tatiana Maslany (Ghost), Eric Johnson (Tyler), Janet Kidder (Alice), Brendan Fletcher (Jeremy).
Brigitte, the dead Ginger's sister, is thrown into a drug rehab centre where the lycanthropic shenanigans begin anew.

Graveyard Alive: A Zombie Nurse in Love (2003)
B/W, 80 minutes.
Director/Screenplay: Elza Kephart. Producers: Patricia Gomez, Elza Kephart, Andrea Stark. Photography: John Ashmore. Art Direction: Sarah Hagen, Chantal Houtteman, Caroline Meyer. Editor: Stéphane Oliver. Music: Martin Pelland. Special Effects: Marc Thibault.
Cast: Anne Day-Jones (Patsy Powers), Karl Gerhardt (Dr. Dox), Samantha Slan (Goodie Tueshuze), Monik Vincent (Head Nurse), Rollande Laroche (Kapotsky).
A homely nurse is bitten by a zombie woodcutter, which complicates her budding romance with a handsome doctor as well as her relationship with the rest of the hospital staff.

Graveyard Shift (1987)
a.k.a. Central Park Drifter
Colour, 89 minutes.
Director/Screenplay: Gerard Ciccoritti. Producers Michael Bockner, Robert Bergman, Gerard Ciccoritti. Photography: Robert Bergman. Production Designer: Lester Berman. Editors: Robert Bergman, Norman Smith. Music: Nicholas Pike. Special Makeup Effects: Timothy Mogg.
Cast: Silvio Olivero (Stephen Tsepes), Helen Papas (Michelle), Cliff Stoker (Eric Hayden), Dorin Ferber (Gilda), Dan Rose (Robert Kopple).
A suave vampire finds that working the night shift as a cab driver is a good way to find victims.

Happy Birthday To Me (1980)
Colour, 110 minutes.
Director: J. Lee Thompson. Producers:
John Dunning, André Link. Screenplay:
John Saxton, Peter Jobin, Timothy Bond.
Photography: Miklos Lente. Production
Designer: Earl Preston. Editor: Debra
Karen. Music: Bo Harwood, Lance
Rubin. Special Effects: King Hernandez,
Bill Doane, Warren Keillor, Ron
Otteson. Special Makeup Effects: The
Burman Studios.
Cast: Melissa Sue Anderson (Virginia),
Glenn Ford (Dr. Faraday), Lawrence
Dane (Hal Wainwright), Sharon Acker
(Estelle), Frances Hyland (Mrs.
Patterson), Tracy Bregman (Ann), Louis
Del Grande (Surgeon).
*A series of bizarre murders decimate the
population of an exclusive academ. Could
troubled young Virginia be the culprit?*

Happy Hell Night (1992)
a.k.a. Frat Fright
Colour, 87 minutes.
[as Happy Hell Night] Director: Brian
Owens. Producer: Pavlina Proevska.
Screenplay: Brian Owens, Ron Peterson,
Michael Fitzpatrick. Photography: Sol
Negrin. Music: Nenad Bach. Special
Makeup Effects: Gabe Bartalos, Joel
Harlow, Stanislaw Zaric.
[as Frat Fright]
Director/Screenplay/Editor: David
Mitchell. Producers: Curtis Petersen,
Damien Lee. Photography: Curtis
Petersen. Additional Photography: David
Pelletier. Music: Mark Sanders.
Cast: Laura Carney (Liz), Nick Gregory
(Eric), Franke Hughes (Sonny), Ted
Clark (Ned Bara), Darren McGavin
(Henry Collins), Charles Cragin
(Malius).
*A killer priest slices his way through a
frat party.*

Hello Mary Lou: Prom Night II (1987)
a.k.a. The Haunting of Hamilton High
Colour, 96 minutes.
Director: Bruce Pittman. Producer: Peter
Simpson. Screenplay: Ron Oliver.
Photography: John Herzog. Additional
Photography: Brenton Spencer.
Production Designer: Sandy Kybartas.
Editor: Nick Rotundo. Music: Paul Zaza.
Special Makeup Effects: Nancy Howe.
Special Mechanical Effects: Jim Doyle,
Theatrical Engines.
Cast: Michael Ironside (Bill Nordham),
Wendy Lyon (Vicki Carpenter), Justin
Louis (Craig Nordham), Lisa Schrage
(Mary Lou Maloney), Richard Manette
(Father Cooper).

*A prom queen is accidentally incinerated,
and years later her spirit returns to seek
revenge.*

Humongous (1981)
Colour, 94 MINUTES
Director: Paul Lynch. Producer: Anthony
Kramreither. Screenplay: William Gray.
Photography: Brian R. R. Hebb. Art
Directors: Carol Spier, Barbara Dunphy.
Editor: Nick Rotundo. Music: John Mills
Cockell. Special Effects: Martin
Malivoire. Special Effects Apparatus:
Gordon Smith and the Gore Boys.
Humongous Make-Up: Brenda Kirk.
Humongous Head Created By Maureen
Sweeney Donati.
Cast: Janet Julian (Sandy), David Wallace
(Eric), Janet Baldwin (Carla), John
Wildman (Nick), Joy Boushel (Donna),
Layne Coleman (Bert), Garry Robbins
(Ida's Son).
*A group of youngsters wash up on Dog
Island, where a shaggy half-human crea-
ture stalks and kills them one by one*

The Incubus (1981)
Colour, 92 minutes.
Director: John Hough. Producers: Marc
Boyman, John M. Eckert. Screenplay:
George Franklin [Sandor Stern].
Photography: Bert Dunk. Production
Design: Ted Watkins. Editor: George
Appleby. Music: Stanley Myers. Special
Makeup Effects: Maureen Sweeney.
Special Effects: Colin Chilvers, Martin
Malivoire.
Cast: John Cassavetes (Sam Cordell),
John Ireland (Hank Walden), Kerrie
Keane (Laura Kincaid), Helen Hughes
(Agatha Galen), Erin Flannery (Jenny
Cordell).
*A demon rapist cuts a swath of terror
through a small California village, and the
local coroner begins to suspect that someone
in town knows more than they are telling.*

Island of the Dead (2000)
Colour, 91 minutes.
Director: Tim Southam. Producers:
Christine Kavanagh, Luciano Lisi.
Screenplay: Peter Koper, Tim Southam.
Photography: Daniel Jobin. Production
Designer: Mario Hervieux. Editor: Heidi
Haines. Music: Gaétan Gravel, Serge
Laforest. Special Effects: Ryal Cosgrove.
Special Makeup Effects: Texa FX Group.
Cast: Malcolm McDowell 9Rupert
King), Talisa Soto (Melissa O'Keefe),
Bruce Ramsay (Tony Matos), Mos Def
(Robbie J.), Kent McQuaid (James
Neely).
Killer flies attack a real estate developer, a

cop and several convicts when they visit a
New York City burial island.

The Jitters (1989)
Colour, 79 minutes.
Director/Producer: John Fasano.
Screenplay: Jeff McKay, Sonoko Kondo.
Photography: Paul Mitchnick. Art
Director: Wojtek Kozlinski. Editors: Ray
Van Doorn, John Fasano. Music: Dann
Link, Tom Borton. Special Makeup
Effects: Richard Alonzo. Special Creature
created by Steve Wang. Special Effects:
Michael Cavanough, Al Cotter.
Cast: Sal Viviano (Michael Derrick),
Marilyn Tokuda (Alice Lee), James Hong
(Tony Yang Sr.), Doug Silberstein
(Leech), Frank Dietz (Rat).
*A Chinese storekeeper is murdered and
returns as a "hopping vampire" to take on
the vicious, blazer-wearing gang terrorizing
Toronto's Chinatown.*

Junior (1984)
Colour, 82 minutes.
Director: Jim Hanley. Producer: Don
Carmody. Screenplay: John Maxwell,
Don Carmody. Photography: Maurice
De Ernsted. Art Director: Paola
Rudolph. Editor: Jacques Jean. Music:
Ken Roberts, Allen Gerber. Special
Effects: Neil N. Trifunovich. Special
Effects Makeup: Donald James Mowat.
Cast: Suzanne DeLaurentis (K.C.), Linda
Singer (Jo), Jeremy Ratchford (Junior),
Michael McKeever (Bud), Ken Roberts
(Sheriff), Cotton Mather (Luke).
*Two ex-prostitutes try to start a new life in
a small town, but fail to reckon on the
local group of louts and their slobbering,
chainsaw-wielding, mother-obsessed resi-
dent psychopath, Junior.*

The Keeper (1976)
Colour, 88 minutes.
Director/Screenplay: T.Y. Drake.
Producer: Donald Wilson. Photography:
Doug McKay. Art Director: Keith
Pepper. Editors: Sally Paterson, George
Johnson. Music: Erich Hoyt. Special
Effects: Al Razutis.
Cast: Christopher Lee (The Keeper), Tell
Schreiber (Dick Driver), Sally Gray (Mae
B. Jones), Ross Vezarian (Inspector
Clarke), Ian Tracey (The Kid), Bing
Jenson (Danny).
*An asylum keeper attempts to become the
richest man in all the world by stealing the
family fortunes of his charges.*

The Kiss (1988)
Colour, 98 minutes.
Director: Pen Densham. Producers: Pen

Densham, John Watson. Screenplay: Stephen Volk, Tom Ropelewski. Photography: Francois Protat. Production Designer: Roy Forge Smith. Editor: Stan Cole. Music: J. Peter Robinson. Makeup and Creature Effects: Chris Walas Inc. Special Effects Supervisor: Louis Craig.
Cast: Joanna Pacula (Felice), Meredith Salenger (Amy), Mimi Kuzyk (Brenda), Nicholas Kilburtus (Jack), Jan Rubes (Tobin), Peter Dvorsky (Father Joe).
A succubus who travels in the guise of a harmless black-sheep aunt arrives to stay with her unsuspecting family.

Lady of the Lake (1999)
Colour, 80 minutes.
Director/Screenplay/Editor: Maurice Devereaux. Producers: Maurice Devereaux, Martin Gauthier. Photography: Richard Labelle, Denis Nöel Mostert. Production Designer: Jean-Philippe Hèbert. Music: Martin Gauthier. Lady of the Lake Demon Effects: Adrien Morot.
Cast: Eirik Rutherford (David Lowry), Tennyson Loeh (Viviane), Emidio Michetti (Anthony Vinchenzo), Chris Piggins (Richard the Knight), Marty Daniels (Jake Lowry).
A present-day fellow battles demons and travels through time to save his medieval lady-love from a horrific curse.

The Little Girl Who Lives Down The Lane (1976)
Colour, 92 minutes.
Director: Nicholas Gessner. Producer: Zev Braun. Screenplay: Laird Koenig. Photography: René Verzier. Art Director: Robert Prévost. Editor: Yves Langlois. Music: Christian Gaubert. Special Effects: Christophe Harbonvie.
Cast: Jodie Foster (Rynn), Martin Sheen (Frank Hallet), Alexis Smith (Mrs. Hallet), Mort Shuman (Migliori), Scott Jacoby (Mario).
A young girl living a life of mystery in a small town, apparently on her own, is plagued by a child molester, his mother, and other assorted nosy townspeople.

The Mangler 2 (2001)
Colour, 96 minutes.
Director/Screenplay: Michael Hamilton-Wright. Producer: Glen Tedham. Photography: Norbert Kaluza. Production Design: Matthew Budgeon. Editor: Anthony A. Lewis. Music: Ferocious La Fonque. Makeup Design: Ingrid Bauer.
Cast: Chelse Swain (Jo Newton), Lance Henriksen (Headmaster Bradeen),

Philipe Bergeron (Chef Lecours), Dexter Bell (Will Walsh), Daniella Evangelista (Emily Stone).
A private school's computerized security system goes haywire, killing students and faculty alike.

The Mark of Cain (1985)
a.k.a. Identity Crisis
Colour, 83 minutes.
Director: Bruce Pittman. Producer: Tony Kramreither. Screenplay: John Sheppard, Peter Colley, Bruce Pittman. Photography: John Herzog. Art Director: Rob Bartman. Editor: Margaret Van Eerdewijk. Music: Bruce Ley. Makeup: Nancy Howe.
Cast: Robin Ward (Sean O'Neil/Michael O'Neil), Wendy Crewson (Dale O'Neil), Antony Parr (Dr. Clifford), August Schellenberg (Otto), Deborah Grover (Molly).
Which twin is the crazed psycho? That's the question uppermost in the mind of the woman visiting their ancestral home.

The Mask (1961)
a.k.a. The Eyes of Hell, Face of Fire, The Spooky Movie Show
B/W, 85 minutes.
Director/Producer: Julian Roffman. Screenplay: Sandy Haber, Frank Taubes, Franklin Delessert. Hallucination Sequences Devised and Written by Slavko Vorkapich. Photography: Herbert S. Alpert. Art Director: David S. Ballou. Editors: Stephen Timor, Robert Schultz. Music: Louis Applebaum. Special Photographic Effects: Linwood G. Dunn, James B. Gordon, Film Effects of Hollywood. Special Effects: Herman Townsley.
Cast: Paul Stevens (Dr. Allen Barnes), Claudette Nevins (Pamela Albright), Bill Walker (Police Lieutenant Martin), Anne Collings (Jill Goodrich), Martin Lavut (Michael Radin), Leo Leyden (Dr. Soames).
A haunted Aztec mask causes addictive hallucinations and murderous rage in all who dare to don it.

Massacre Up North (2001)
Colour, 99 minutes.
Director/Producer/Screenplay: Paul Stoichevski. Photography: Geoff Bland. Editor: James Weisbrod. Special Makeup Effects: Iantha Goldberg, Ty Batterham, Andrew Parker. Special Effects: Gerald Lukane, Art Effects Theatrical Ltd.
Cast: Paul Stoichevski (Leslie Rejck), Lorn Eisen (Patrick), Labe Kagan (Detective Fred Pagluca), Kieren Hart (Deputy O'Malley), Allison Leigha

Taylor (Joclyn).
Young Leslie is disfigured in a terrible camping accident. Maniacally resentful of "normals" by the time he reaches adulthood, he becomes a homicidal maniac who can only be stopped by a hail of police bullets.

Matinee (1989)
Colour, 93 minutes.
Director/Screenplay: Richard Martin. Producers: Kim Steer, Cal Shumacher. Photography: Cyrus Block. Production Designer: Kim Steer. Editors: Bruce Lange, Debra Rurak. Music: Graeme Coleman. Special Effects: Paller Special Effects, Robert Comer. Prosthetics: Danny Nowak.
Cast: Ron White (Al Jason), Gillian Barber (Marlyn), Jeff Schultz (Lawrence), Beatrice Boepple (Sherri), Timothy Webber (Geoff Oslam), William B. Davis (Heath Harris).
A small town's horror film festival is plagued by a series of murders.

Micro-Nice (2002)
a.k.a. Disciples of Darkness
Colour, 37 minutes.
Director: Myles Langlois. Producers/Screenplay: Myles Langlois, Drue Langlois. Photography: Caelum Vatnsdal. Art Director: Drue Langlois. Editors: Myles Langlois, Drue Langlois, Carla Mundweiler.
Cast: Danny Stevens (Theobald Bogarde), Carla Mundweiler (Petrolia), Sharon Johnson (Medusa), Sarah Johnson (Salvail Keller), Joanne Rodriguez (Vienna Headache), Krista Gowenlock (Chinabark), Jenny O' (Kipp Jerli).
A coven of witches attempts to evilize an innocent young woman, but this proves much more difficult than usual, due to such obstacles as a recalcitrant gorgon, a murderous zombie and an angry barber.

My Bloody Valentine (1982)
Colour, 91 minutes.
Director: George Mihalka. Producers: André Link, John Dunning, Stephen Miller. Screenplay: John Beaird. Photography: Rodney Gibbons. Art Director: Penny Hadfield. Editor: Jean Lafleur. Music: Paul Zaza. Special Makeup Effects: Tom Burman, Ken Diaz, Tom Hoerber.
Cast: Paul Kelman (TJ), Lori Hallier (Sarah), Neil Affleck (Axel), Don Francks (Chief Newby), Keith Knight (Hollis), Alf Humphreys (Howard), Cynthia Dale (Patty), Helen Udy (Sylvia).
A Cape Breton mining town is the scene of deadly revenge when a pick-axe wielding killer stalks the streets and mine shafts.

A Name For Evil (1970)
Colour, 78 minutes.
Director/Screenplay: Bernard Girard.
Producer: Reed Sherman. Photography:
Reginald Morris. Art Director: Cameron
Porteous. Editor: Maurice White. Music:
Dominic Frontiere.
Cast: Robert Culp (John Blake),
Samantha Eggar (Joanna Blake), Sheila
Sullivan (Luanna Baxter), Mike Lane
(Fats), Sue Hathaway (Mary), Clarence
"Big" Miller (Jimmy).
*A disaffected architect relocates to his
grandfather's ruined lakeside mansion,
bringing his reluctant wife along, but the
ghost of the old paterfamilias causes deadly
discord between the couple.*

The Neighbor (1993)
Colour, 93 minutes.
Director: Rodney Gibbons. Producer:
Tom Berry. Screenplay: Kurt Wimmer.
Photography: Ludek Bogner. Production
Designer: Claude Paré. Editor: Robert
Newton. Music: Milan Kymlicka. Special
Effects: Ryal Cosgrove.
Cast: Rod Steiger (Dr. Myron Hatcher),
Linda Kozlowski (Mary), Ron Lea
(John), Bruce Boa (Bishop), Sean
McCann (Lieutenant Crow), Benjamin
Shirinian (Young Myron).
*A young couple are alarmed at the mani-
acal interest their new neighbour takes in
the woman's pregnancy.*

Night of the Demons 3 (1996)
Colour, 85 minutes.
Director: Jimmy Kaufman. Producer:
Claudio Castravelli. Screenplay: Kevin S.
Tenney. Photography: Walter Bal.
Production Designer: David Blanchard.
Editors: Daniel Duncan, Kevin S.
Tenney. Music: Raymond C. Fabi.
Special Effects Makeup: SOTA Effects.
Cast: Amelia Kinkade (Angela), Kris
Holdenreid (Vince), Gregory Calpakis
(Nick), Patricia Rodriguez (Abbie),
Vlasta Vrana (Dewhurst).
*A murderous demon named Angela terror-
izes and kills anyone who comes near the
dilapidated mansion she inhabits.*

The Night Walk (1972)
a.k.a. Deathdream, The Night Andy
Came Home, Dead of Night
Colour, 88 minutes.
Director: Bob Clark. Producers: Bob
Clark, John Trent, Peter James.
Screenplay: Alan Ormsby. Photography:
Jack McGowan. Art Director: Forest
Carpenter. Editor: Ron Sinclair. Music:
Carl Zittrer. Makeup: Alan Ormsby, Tom
Savini. Special Effects: Tom Savini.

Cast: Richard Backus (Andy Brooks),
Lynn Carlin (Christine Brooks), John
Marley (Charles Brooks), Henderson
Forsythe (Dr. Phillip Allman), Anya
Ormsby (Cathy Brooks).
*A young man killed in Vietnam returns to
his family nevertheless, but, observing that
he now wears sunglasses all the time and
likes to drink blood, they soon suspect he's
not quite the same lad they sent off to war.*

Of Unknown Origin (1983)
Colour, 89 minutes.
Director: George P. Cosmatos. Producer:
Claude Héroux. Screenplay: Brian
Taggert. Photography: René Verzier.
Production Designer: Anne Pritchard.
Editor: Roberto Silvi. Music: Ken
Wannberg. Special Effects: Jacques
Godbout, Louis Craig. Special Makeup
Effects: Stéphan Dupuis.
Cast: Peter Weller (Bart Hughes),
Jennifer Dale (Lorrie Wells), Lawrence
Dane (Eliot Riverton), Kenneth Welsh
(James Hall), Louis Del Grande (Clete),
Maurey Chaykin (Dan Errol), Shannon
Tweed (Meg Hughes).
*A man finds his self-renovated brownstone
invaded by a large, increasingly belligerent rat.*

Phobia (1980)
Colour, 91 minutes.
Director: John Huston. Producer: Zale
Magder. Screenplay: Lew Lehman,
Jimmy Sangster, Peter Bellwood.
Photography: Reginald Morris. Art
Director; David Jaquest. Editor: Stan
Cole. Music: André Gagnon. Special
Effects: Martin Malivoire.
Cast: Paul Michael Glaser (Dr. Peter
Ross), Susan Hogan (Jenny St. Clair),
John Colicos (Inspector Barnes), David
Bolt (Henry Owen), Patricia Collins (Dr.
Alice Toland).
*The patients of a psychologist specializing
in phobia begin dying in manners
reflecting their respective fears. It becomes
clear that the psychologist might just have a
few emotional problems of his own.*

Pin… (1988)
a.k.a. Pin: A Plastic Nightmare
Colour, 102 minutes.
Director/Screenplay: Sandor Stern.
Producer: René Malo. Photography: Guy
Dufaux. Art Director: Francois Séguin.
Editor: Patrick Dodd. Music: Peter
Manning Robinson. Pin Design and
Construction: Atelier P&P.
Cast: David Hewlett (Leon), Cyndy
Preston (Ursula), Terry O'Quinn (Dr.
Linden), Bronwen Mantel (Mrs.
Linden), John Ferguson (Stan Fraker),

Helene Udy (Marcia Bateman).
*An anatomically correct dummy named
Pin insinuates himself into the lives of a
neurotic family in small-town Quebec. The
teenage boy becomes his best friend in the
world, willing to help Pin do anything to
anybody.*

The Pit (1981)
a.k.a. Teddy
Colour, 96 minutes.
Director: Lew Lehman. Producer: Bennet
Fode. Screenplay: Ian A. Stuart.
Photography: Fred Guthé. Art Director:
Peter E. Stone. Editor: Rik Morden.
Music: Victor Davies. Special Effects
Costuming: Dahl Delu, Yvonne
Bromovitz Delu, Tracey Reid.
Cast: Sammy Snyders (Jamie), Jeannie
Elias (Sandra), Laura Hollingsworth
(Marg Livingstone), Sonja Smits (Mrs.
Lynde), Richard Arden (Mr. Benjamin),
Laura Press (Mrs. Benjamin).
*A maladjusted child with a talking teddy
bear discovers a pit full of proto-human
creatures, into which he pushes townspeople
who have annoyed him. He eventually gets
his comeuppance.*

The Playgirl Killer (1966)
a.k.a. Decoy For Terror
Colour, 85 minutes.
Director/Screenplay: Erick Santamaria.
Producer: Maxwell A. Sendel.
Photography: Roger Moride. Editor:
Jacques Gagné. Music: Georges Savaria.
Special Effects: Omega Productions,
Batchelor.
Cast: William Kerwin (Bill), Jean
Christopher (Arlene), Andrée
Champagne (Nicki), Mary Lou Collins
(Betty), Neil Sedaka (Bob).
*A maniacal artist kills his models in an
attempt to recreate the vision which tor-
ments his every waking moment.*

Possession—Until Death Do You Part
(1987)
Colour, 92 minutes.
Directors: Lloyd A. Simandl, Michael
Mazo. Producers: Lloyd A. Simandl,
John A. Curtis. Screenplay: Lyne J.
Grantham. Photography: Nathaniel
Massey. Editors: Bert Bush, Michael
Mazo. Music: Tom Lavin, Rick Kilburn.
Special Effects: Jeff Butterworth.
Cast: John Robert Johnston (Frankie),
Melissa Martin (Madeline), Cat Williams
(Amy), Leanne Jaheny (Janie), Samra
Wolfin (Barbara).
*A psycho momma's boy rampages through
the woods of British Columbia, killing
indiscriminately and without reason.*

Prom Night (1980)
Colour, 95 minutes.
Director: Paul Lynch. Producer: Peter
Simpson. Screenplay: William Gray,
Robert Guza Jr. [uncredited: John
Hunter]. Director of Photography:
Robert New. Art Director: Reuben Freed.
Editor: Brian Ravok. Music: Carl Zittrer,
Paul Zaza. Special Effects: Al Cotter.
Prosthetics: Warren Keillor.
Cast: Leslie Nielsen (Principal
Hammond), Jamie Lee Curtis (Kim),
Casey Stevens (Nick), Eddie Benton
(Wendy), Michael Tough (Alex), Robert
Silverman (Sykes).
*Four pre-teens cause the accidental death of
a younger girl, and six years later, on prom
night, someone is seeking bloody revenge.*

**Prom Night II—see Hello Mary Lou:
Prom Night II**

Prom Night III: The Last Kiss (1990)
Colour, 93 minutes.
Directors: Ron Oliver, Peter Simpson.
Producers: Ray Sager, Peter Simpson.
Screenplay: Ron Oliver. Photography:
Rhett Morita. Production designer:
Reuben Freed. Editor: Nick Rotundo.
Music: Paul Zaza. Special makeup effects:
Nancy Howe. Special effects: The Light
and Motion Corporation.
Cast: Tim Conlon (Alex), Cyndy Preston
(Sarah), David Stratton (Shane),
Courtney Taylor (Mary Lou), Roger
Dunn (Mr. Weatherall).
*A remedial high school student falls in with
the re- resurrected prom queen Mary Lou,
who renews her spree of revenge-seeking.*

Prom Night IV: Deliver Us From Evil
(1991)
Colour, 93 minutes
Director: Clay Borris. Producer: Ray
Sager. Screenplay: Richard Beattie.
Photography: Ludek Bogner. Production
Design: Ian Brock. Editor: Stan Cole.
Music: Paul Zaza. Makeup: Nancy
Howe. Special Effects: Brock Jolliffe.
Cast: Nikki de Boer (Meagan), Alden
Kane (Mark), Joy Tanner (Laura), Alle
Ghadban (Jeff), James Carver (Father
Jonas).
*A deadly priest murders some sinful high
school students and then goes into a coma
for thirty years. Upon awakening, he stalks
a new group of iniquitous teens.*

Psychic (1992)
Colour, 92 minutes.
Director: George Mihalka. Producer:
Tom Berry. Screenplay: Miguel Tejada-
Flores, Paul Koval. Photography: Ludek

Bogner. Production Designer: Perri
Gorrara. Editor: Paul Ziller. Music:
Milan Kymlicka. Special Effects: Brock
Jolliffe, Ted Ross, Special Effects
Prosthetics: Performance Solutions.
Cast: Zach Galligan (Patrick), Catherine
Mary Stewart (Laurel), Michael Nouri
(Steering), Albert Schultz (Nick), Ken
James (Markewitz), Clark Johnson
(Spencer).
*A psychic college student sees visions of
murder, but the police, ever skeptical of
supernatural phenomena, assume him to be
the killer.*

Psycho Girls (1985)
Colour, 92 minutes.
Director: Gerard Ciccoritti. Producer:
Michael Bockner. Screenplay: Gerard
Ciccoritti, Michael Bockner.
Photography/Editor: Robert Bergman.
Art Director: Craig Richards. Music: Joel
Rosenbaum. Special Makeup Effects:
Timothy Mogg.
Cast: John Haslett Cuff (Dan), Darlene
Mignacco (Mrs. Dan), Rose Graham
(Vicky), Agi Gallus (Sarah), Silvio
Olivero (Oates).
*A group of asylum escapees kidnap, ter-
rorize and torture a dinner party
comprised entirely of smug Toronto yuppies.*

The Pyx (1973)
a.k.a. The Hooker Cult Murders
Colour, 111 minutes
Director: Harvey Hart. Producer: Julian
Roffman. Screenplay: Robert Schlitt.
Photography: René Verzier. Production
Design: Earl Preston. Editor: Ron
Wisman. Music: Harry Freedman.
Makeup: Julia Grundy.
Cast: Karen Black (Elizabeth Lucy),
Christopher Plummer (Det. Sgt. Jim
Henderson), Donald Pilon (Det. Sgt.
Pierre Paquette), Jean-Louis Roux
(Keerson), Yvette Brind'Amour (Meg).
*A high-class call girl is found at the base of
a Montreal apartment building, and the
detective assigned to the case slowly dis-
covers the diabolical circumstances behind
her death.*

Rabid (1977)
Colour, 91 minutes.
Director/Screenplay: David Cronenberg.
Producer: John Dunning. Photography:
René Verzier. Art Director: Claude
Marchand. Editor: Jean Lafleur. Special
Makeup Design: Joe Blasco Makeup
Association. Special Makeup Artist: Byrd
Holland.
Cast: Marilyn Chambers (Rose), Frank
Moore (Hart Read), Joe Silver (Murray

Cypher), Howard Ryshpan (Dr. Dan
Keloid), Patricia Gage (Dr. Roxanne
Keloid).
*Experimental surgery on a motorcycle-crash
victim (Chambers) results in a vampiric
plague unleashed on the citizens of
Montreal. Using a penile spike which
emerges from her armpit, Chambers sucks
blood and spreads her disease until she is
finally killed and tossed into the garbage.*

Reaper (1998)
Colour, 94 minutes.
Director: John Bradshaw. Producer:
Stefan Wodoslawsky. Screenplay: Vincent
Monton, Matt Dorff. Photography:
Bruce Chun. Art Director: David
Gaucher. Editor: Isabelle Levesque.
Music: Normand Corbeil. Special Effects
Makeup: Djina Caron, Marie-Josée
Lopez.
Cast: Chris Sarandon (Luke Sinclair),
Catherine Mary Stewart (Sonya
Lehrman), Vlasta Vrana (Norris), Joanna
Noyes (Wilma), Rob Pinnock (Deputy
Hopps).
*One of those direct-to-video programmers
notable only for their plodding lack of inci-
dent and narrative drive. Stewart plays a
cop on the trail of a serial killer who may
or may not be the writer (Sarandon) whose
serial-killer novels are identical in every
detail to the actual crimes.*

Red Blooded American Girl (1990)
Colour, 89 minutes.
Director: David Blyth. Producer:
Nicholas Stiliadis. Screenplay: Allan
Moyle. Photography: Ludek Bogner.
Production Designer: Ian Brock. Editor:
Nick Rotundo. Music: Jim Manzie.
Special Effects: Brock Jolliffe.
Cast: Andrew Stevens (Owen Augustus
Urban III), Heather Thomas (Paula
Bukowsky), Christopher Plummer (Dr.
Alcore), Kim Coates (Dennis), Lydie
Denier (Rebecca Murrin).
*Modern-day vampires are created through
a power-hungry mad doctor's weird science,
and only an eccentric researcher can help
put a stop to them.*

The Reincarnate (1971)
a.k.a. The Dark Side, Le Sacrifice d'une
Vierge
Colour, 95 minutes.
Director: Donald Haldane.
Producer/Screenplay: Seeleg Lester.
Photography: Norman C. Allin. Art
Director: Harry Maxfield. Editor: George
Appleby. Music: Milan Kymlicka.
Cast: Jack Creley (Everet Julian), Jay
Reynolds (David Payne), Trudy Young

(Ruthie), Terry Tweed (Ann), Hugh Webster (Berryman), Anthony Kramreither (Van Brock).

A many-times reincarnated lawyer searches for a body in which to live out his next life. He approaches a passionate sculptor about the position, and in the meantime arranges the virgin sacrifice necessary for the transmogrification to take place.

Ripper: Letter From Hell (2001)
Colour, 114 minutes.
Director: John Eyres. Producers: Evan Taylor, John Curtis. Screenplay: Pat Bermel. Photography: Thomas M. Harting. Production Designer: Mark Harris. Editor: Amanda I. Kirpaul. Music: Peter Allen. Special Effects: Bill Mills. Prosthetics: Christ Stanley.
Cast: A.J. Cook (Molly Keller), Bruce Payne (Marshall Kane), Jurgen Prochnow (Detective Kelso), Ryan Northcott (Jason Korda), Kelly Brook (Marisa Tavares).
A Jack the Ripper-inspired killer stalks and kills the students of a university course on serial killers.

Rituals (1978)
Colour, 99 minutes.
Director: Peter Carter. Producer: Lawrence Dane. Screenplay: Ian Sutherland. Photography: René Verzier. Art Director: Karen Bromley. Editor: George Appleby. Music: Hagood Hardy. Makeup Effects: Carl Fullerton. Special Effects: Doug Wardle.
Cast: Hal Holbrook (Harry), Lawrence Dane (Mitzi), Robin Gammell (Martin), Ken James (Abel), Gary Reineke (D.J.), Jack Creley (Jesse).
A quintet of vacationing doctors are stalked by a misshapen woodsman, who happens to hate medicos, in the forest near Sault Ste. Marie.

Rock 'n' Roll Nightmare (1987)
a.k.a. The Edge of Hell
Colour, 83 minutes
Director: John Fasano.
Producer/Screenplay: Jon Mikl Thor.
Photography: Mark Mackay. Art Director: Wolfgang Siebert. Editor: Robert Williams. Music: Thor and Tritonz. Special Makeup Effects: Arnold Gargiulo and Fascination Film Effects.
Cast: Jon Mikl Thor (John Triton), Jillian Perri (Lou Anne), Frank Dietz (Roger Eburt), Dave Lane (Max), Rusty Hamilton (Seductress).
A heavy-metal bodybuilder and his entourage move into a deserted farmhouse to make their next record. Unfortunately the building is haunted by a variety of

foam-rubber sock puppets in the service of Satan. The bodybuilder, however, has a few tricks up his leather sleeves.

Savage Island
Colour, 92 minutes.
Director / Editor: Jeffery Scott Lando. Producers: Michelle Czernin von Chudenitz, Renee Giesse, Steven Man. Screenplay: Kevin Mosley. Photography: Geoff Rogers. Production Designer: Robin Ferrier. Music: Chris Nickel. Special Makeup Effects: Gene McCormick.
Cast: Winston Rekert (Eliah Savage), Don S. Davis (Keith Young), Steven Man (Steven Harris), Kristina Copeland (Julia Young Harris), Brendon Beiser (Peter Young).
An island-dwelling family doesn't cotton to the arrival of some rowdy outlanders.

Samhain (2003)
Director/Screenplay: Christian Viel. Producers: Christian Viel, Dawne Everett. Photography: Dan Goyens. Art Director: Kevin Grant. Editors: J Deschamps, Christian Viel. Special Effects Makeup: Adrien Morot.
Cast: Richard Grieco (Mark), Bobbie Phillips (Karen), Ginger Lynn Allen (Pandora), Jenna Jameson (Jenny), Neil Napier (Jim), Mark Borchardt (Andrew).
A group of youngsters go to Ireland, where they are attacked and eaten by a cannibal family.

Seizure (1973)
Colour, 94 minutes.
Director: Oliver Stone. Producers: Garrard L. Glenn, Jeffrey D. Kapelman. Screenplay: Edward Mann, Oliver Stone. Photography: Roger Racine. Art Director: Najwa Stone. Editors: Nobuko Oganesoff, Oliver Stone. Music: Lee Gagnon. Makeup/Special Effects: Thomas Brumberger.
Cast: Jonathan Frid (Edmund), Martine Beswick (The Queen), Joe Sirola (Charlie), Christina Pickles (Nicole), Mary Waronov (Mikki), Hervé Villechaize (The Spider).
A writer of horror fiction is terrorized by his own creations over a long weekend at his rural Quebec home.

Sexcula (1973)
Colour, 86 minutes.
Director: John Holbrook [credited as Bob Hollowich]. Producer: Clarence Newfeld [credited as Clarence Frog]. Screenplay: David F. Hurry.

Photography: John Goode [credited as Boris Von Bonnie]. Editing/Music: John Holbrook, Keith Woods.
Cast: Debbie Collins (Sexcula), Jamie Orlando (Fellatingstein), John Alexander (Frank), Tim Lowerie (Orgie), Bud Coal (Gorilla/Logger).
A very low-budget ($85,000.00) sex/horror/comedy filmed in Vancouver, but apparently never released. Too bad—any movie with a character named "Fellatingstein" deserves at least a couple of screenings.

Shivers (1975)
a.k.a. The Parasite Murders, They Came From Within, Orgy of the Blood Parasites, Starliner,
Colour, 87 minutes.
Director/Screenplay: David Cronenberg. Producers: Ivan Reitman, John Dunning, André Link. Photography: Robert Saad. Editor: Patrick Dodd. Special Makeup and Creatures created by: Joe Blasco.
Cast: Paul Hampton (Roger St. Luc), Joe Silver (Rollo Linsky), Lynn Lowrey (Forsythe), Allan Migicovsky (Nicholas Tudor), Susan Petrie (Janine Tudor), Barbara Steele (Betts).
A mad doctor has created parasites which travel from victim to victim by sexual intercourse and render their hosts mad. The creatures quickly spread through an apartment complex located on a Montreal island, despite the best efforts of the resident doctor and his sexy nurse.

Shock Chamber (1985)
Colour, 94 minutes.
Director/Screenplay/Editor: Steve DiMarco. Producer: Sharon Haxton. Photography: N. "Kuri" Kurita. Music: Peter Dick. Special Effects Makeup: Randi Daudlin.
Cast: Doug Stone (The Peddler/Cameron/Stan), Bill Zagot (Nick), Jackie Samuda (Linda), Russell Ferrier (Ron), Karen Cannata (Blanche), Andy Adoch (Oral).
A trilogy of shot-on-video stories related by an old lady to a reporter during a funeral.

Skulduggery (1983)
Colour, 95 minutes.
Director/Screenplay: Ota Richter. Producers: Peter Wittman, Ota Richter. Photography: Robert New. Art Director: Jill Scott. Editor: Ian McBride. Music: Eugen Illen.
Cast: Thom Haverstock (Adam), Wendy Crewson (Barbara/Donigen), David Main (Chuck), Clark Johnson (Dave), Geordie Johnson (Jake), Kate Lynch (Janet).
A role-playing game spells trouble for a group of fantasy-minded young adults.

Someone is Watching (*1998*)
Colour, 93 minutes.
Director: Douglas Jackson. Producers: Pierre David, Elisabeth Ann-Gimber, Geoffrey S. Patenaude. Screenplay: Charles Klausmeyer, Mark Kinsey Stephenson. Photography: Bruno Philip. Art Directors: Joseanne Brunelle, Tristan Tondin. Editor: Robert E. Newton. Music: Richard Bowers. Special Effects: Ryal Cosgrove.
Cast: Stephanie Powers (Michelle Dupré), Mickey Toft (Cory Dupré), Barry Flatman (Charles Jensen), Margot Kidder (Sally Beckert), Martin Neufeld (Bobby (B.J.) Culley), Stewart Bick (Joe Carvelli).
The former Mrs. Hart is a single mom in a duplex being watched by the pathetic lunatic next door. When they finally meet…it's murder!

Spasms (1983)
a.k.a. Death Bite
Director: William Fruet. Producers: John G. Pozhke, Maurice Smith. Screenplay: Don Enright. Photography: Mark Irwin. Art Director: Gavin Mitchell. Editor: Ralph Brunjes. Music: Eric N. Robertson. Serpent's Theme by Tangerine Dream. Makeup Illusions by Dick Smith, Carl Fullerton and Stéphan Dupuis. Monster Designed and Produced by Raymond A. Mendez.
Cast: Peter Fonda (Dr. Thomas Brazilian), Oliver reed (Jason Kincaid), Kerrie Keane (Suzanne Kincaid), Al Waxman (Crowley), Miguel Fernandes (Mendez), George Bloomfield (Reverend Thanner).
A rich industrialist is plagued by his psychic connection to a legendary devil snake. He unwisely imports it back to North America where it breaks loose and causes deadly havoc.

Terror Train (*1980*)
a.k.a. Train to Terror
Colour, 97 minutes.
Director: Roger Spottiswoode. Producer: Harold Greenberg. Screenplay: T.Y. Drake. Photography: John Alcott. Production Designer: Glenn Bydwell. Editor: Anne Henderson. Music: John Mills Cockell. Special Effects Make-Up: Alan Friedman.
Cast: Jamie Lee Curtis (Alana), Ben Johnson (Charlie), Hart Bochner (Doc), Sandee Currie (Mitchy), Derek McKinnon (Kenny Hampson), David Copperfield (Magician), Joy Boushel (Pet), DD Winters (Merry).
A trainload of college students is decimated by the vengeful nerd on whom they'd played a cruel joke years before. The combined

efforts of train conductor Johnson and good-girl scream queen Curtis are required to pitch the demented dweeb out the door and into the snow.

Things (1989)
Colour, 84 minutes.
Director: Andrew Jordan.
Producers/Screenplay: Andrew Jordan, Barry J. Gillis. Photography: Dan Riggs. Art Director: Sandra Fullerton. Editor: Nancy Ellison. Music: Stryk-9, Familiar Strangers, Jack Procher. Special Effects: Glenn Orr.
Cast: Barry J. Gillis (Dan Drake), Amber Lynn (Reporter), Doug Bunston (Doug Drake), Bruce Roach (Fred Horton), Patricia Sadler (Susan Drake), Jan W. Pachul (Dr. Lucas).
Some people go to a house and drink beer, and there's some monsters and gore. Something about a mad doctor doing experiments. Porn star Amber Lynn, pretending to be a reporter, keeps tabs on the action from in front of a television set.

Tomcat (1993)
Colour, 95 minutes.
Director/Screenplay: Paul Donovan. Producers: Robert Vince, William Vince. Photography: Peter Wunstorf. Production Design: Lynne Stopkewich. Editor: David Ostry. Music: Graeme Coleman. Special Effects: Garry Paller. Special Makeup Effects: Tibor Farkas.
Cast: Richard Grieco (Tom), Natalie Radford (Imogen), Maryam D'Abo (Jacki), Serge Houde (Dr. Pace), Sean Orr (Dale).
A scientist experimenting with kitty-cat hormones turns her boyfriend into a murderous cat-man.

The Uncanny (1977)
Colour, 88 minutes.
Director: Denis Héroux. Producers: Claude Héroux, René Dupont. Screenplay: Michael Parry. Photography: Harry Waxman. Production Design: Wolf Kroeger, Harry Pottle. Editors: Michel Guay, Keith Palmer, Peter Weatherley. Music: Wilfred Josephs. Special Effects: Michael Albrechtsen. Makeup: Brigitte McCaughry, Tom Smith.
Cast: Peter Cushing (Wilbur Gray), Ray Milland (Frank Richards), Donald Pleasance (Valentine De'ath), Samantha Eggar (Edina Hamilton), John Vernon (Pomeroy).
An author tries to convince his publisher of the central premise of his new book—that cats are intelligent creatures who are the actual masters of the earth. He tells a trio of stories to illustrate this.

The Understudy: Graveyard Shift II (1988)
Colour, 88 minutes.
Director/Screenplay: Gerard Ciccoritti. Producers: Stephen R. Flacks, Arnold H. Bruck. Director of Photography: Barry Stone. Production Designer: Gerard Ciccoritti. Editor: Neil Grieve. Music: Philip Stern. Special Makeup Effects: Adrianne Sicova, Andrea Sicova.
Cast: Wendy Gazelle (Camilla/Patti), Mark Soper (Matthew), Silvero Olivero (Baisez), Ilse Von Glatz (Ash), Timothy Kelleher (Duke/Lenny), Lesley Kelly (Martina).
A seductive vampire causes trouble on the set of a low-budget vampire movie after he is cast in the lead role.

The Untold (2003)
a.k.a. Sasquatch
Colour, 85 minutes.
Director: Jonas Quastel. Producers: Rob Clark, Craig Denton. Screenplay: Jonas Quastel, Chris Lanning. Photography: Shaun Lawless. Production Designer: Piotr Polak. Editor: Gabriel Wrye. Music: Larry Seymour, Tal Bergman. Creature Effects: Jason Palmer. Special Effects Supervisor: Rory Cutler.
Cast: Lance Henrikson (Harlan Knowles), Andrea Roth (Marla Lawson), Russell Ferrier (Clayton Tyne), Erica Parker (Tara), Phil Granger (Winston Burg), Jeremy Radick (Plazz), Taras Kostyuk (Bigfoot).
A rich industrialist searches for his daughter in the mountains of the west coast, and discovers that a certain shaggy anthromorph may have had a hand in her disappearance.

Videodrome (1982)
Colour, 87 minutes.
Director/Screenplay: David Cronenberg. Producer: Claude Héroux. Photography: Mark Irwin. Production Design: Carol Spier. Editor: Ronald Sanders. Music: Howard Shore. Special Makeup Design and Creation: Rick Baker.
Cast: James Woods (Max Renn), Sonja Smits (Bianca O'Blivion), Deborah Harry (Nicki Brand), Peter Dvorsky (Harlan), Les Carlson (Barry Convex), Jack Creley (Brian O'Blivion).
The owner of a marginal cable television station discovers a mysterious channel that causes hallucinations and death in its viewers—starting with him.

The Vindicator (1986)
a.k.a. Frankenstein '88
Colour, 92 minutes
Director: Jean-Claude Lord. Producers:

Don Carmody, John Dunning. Screenplay: Edith Rey, David Preston. Photography: René Verzier. Production Designer: Douglas Higgins. Editor: Debra Karen. Music: Paul Zaza. Special Effects: George Easchbamer, Bill Orr. Frankenstein designed and created by Stan Winston Studios.
Cast: Teri Austen (Lauren Lehman), Richard Cox (Alex Whyte), Pam Grier (Hunter), Maury Chaykin (Bert), David McIlwraith (Carl Lehman/Frankenstein).
A scientist is nearly incinerated in an accidentally-on-purpose lab explosion, but is transformed into a monstrous half-human robot who then goes looking for revenge.

Visiting Hours (1981)
Colour, 105 minutes.
Director: Jean-Claude Lord. Producer: Claude Heroux. Screenplay: Brian Taggart. Photography: René Verzier. Art Director: Michel Proulx. Editors: Jean-Claude Lord, Lise Thoulin. Music: Jonathan Goldsmith. Special Effects: Gary Zeller. Special Makeup Effects: Stephan Dupuis.
Cast: Lee Grant (Deborah Ballin), Michael Ironside (Colt Hawker), William Shatner (Gary Baylor), Linda Purl (Sheila Munroe), Michael J. Reynolds (Porter Halstrom).
A psychotic misogynist stalks a women's libber through the strangely deserted halls and boiler rooms of a hospital.

The Vulture (1966)
a.k.a. Manutara
Colour, 91 minutes.
Director/Producer/Screenplay: Lawrence Huntington. Photography: Stephen Dade. Art Director: Duncan Sutherland. Editor: John S. Smith. Music: Eric Spear.
Cast: Robert Hutton (Eric Lutens), Akim Tamiroff (Professor Koniglich), Broderick Crawford (Brian Stroud), Diane Clare (Trudy Lutens).
A nuclear scientist and his wife ponder the mystery of the half-man, half vulture creature who seems bent on murdering her entire family.

Whispers (1989)
Colour, 93 minutes.
Director: Douglas Jackson. Producers: Don Carmody, John Dunning. Screenplay: Anita Doohan. Photography: Peter Benison. Production Designer: Charles Dunlop. Editor: Jacques Jean. Music: Fred Mollin. Special Effects Supervisor: Jacques Godbout. Dead Twin Design: Joe Blasco. [Additional Makeup Effects: Ed French.]

Cast: Victoria Tennant (Hilary), Jean Leclerc (Bruno), Chris Sarandon (Tony), Peter MacNeill (Frank), Linda Sorenson (Kayla), Jackie Burroughs (Mrs. Yancy).
A woman is stalked by a set of cockroach-maddened twins.

The Wisher (2002)
a.k.a. Spliced
Colour, 86 minutes.
Director: Gavin Wilding. Producer: Mark Reid. Screenplay: Ellen Cook. Photography: Mark Dobrescu. Production Designer: Kathy McCoy. Editor: Dean Evans. Music: Chris Ainscough. Special Makeup Effects: Lee Stearns. Special Effects: Eric Vrba, Ryan Bobart. Special Visual Effects: Jack Tunnicliffe.
Cast: Liane Balaban (Mary), Ron Silver (Morgan), Drew Lachey (Brad), Siri Baruc (Debbie), Jared Van Snellenberg (Shane).
A horror-loving teen is terrorized by an evil character from a hit movie called The Wisher.

Witchboard: The Possession (1995)
Colour, 93 minutes.
Director: Peter Svatek. Producer: Robin Spry. Screenplay: Kevin S. Tenney, Jon Erzine. Photography: Barry Gravelle. Production Designer: Richard Tassé. Editor: Denis Papillon. Music: Richard Grégoire. Special Effects Director: Jean Lafleur. Creature and Prosthetic Special Effects: Olivier Xavier. Mechanical Effects: Jacques Godbout. Digital Effects: Buzz Image Group.
Cast: David Nerman (Brian), Locky Lambert (Julie), Cedric Smith (Francis), Donna Sarrasin (Lisa), Danette Mackay (Dora).
An unemployed broker falls for the charms of an evil Ouija board. Diabolic possession and murder are the results.

Yeti, the Giant of the 20th Century (1977)
a.k.a. Yeti
Colour, approximately 95 minutes.
Director: Frank Kramer [Gianfranco Parolini]. Producers: Nicolo Pomilia, Wolfranco Coccia, Gianfranco Parolini, Mario DiNardo.Screenplay: Mario DiNardo, Gianfranco Parolini, Marcello Coscia. Photography: Sandro Mancori. Art Director: Claudio DeSantis. Editor: Manlio Camastro. Music: Sante Maria Romitelli. Special Effects: Ermanno Biamonte.
Cast: Phoenix Grant [Antonella Interlenghi] (Jane), Mimmo Crau (Yeti),

Jim Sullivan (Herbie), Tony Kendall [Luciano Stella] (Cliff Chandler), John Stacy (Professor Wasserman), Eddie Faye (Hunnicutt).
A giant revived Yeti goes on the rampage in modern-day Toronto.

Zombie Nightmare (1986)
Colour, 83 minutes.
Director: Jack Bravman. Producer:Pierre Grisé. Screenplay: David Wellington. Photography: Roger Racine. Art Director: David Blanchard. Editor: David Franko. Music: Jon Mikl Thor. Special Effects: Andy Clemens, Tony Bua, Jean Marc Cyr.
Cast: Adam West (Churchman), Jon Mikl Thor (Tony Washington), Tia Carrere (Amy), Marushka (Molly Mokembo), Frank Dietz (Frank Sorrell), Linda Singer (Maggie).
A heavy-metal bodybuilder is reincarnated as a zombie to take revenge on the punks who killed him.

Photo Credits

Cover image and photos on pages 3, 123, 125, 201 and 203 courtesy of the Canadian Film Reference Library and René Malo.

Photos on pages 10, 13, 15, 25, 41, 43, 59, 61, 63, 65, 67, 69, 71, 73, 75, 94, 97, 99, 101, 103, 105, 107, 109, 119, 120, 127, 129, 131, 133, 141, 143, 145, 147, 151, 153, 159, 161, 163, 165, 168, 173, 175, 185, 189, 191, 193, 205, 207, 209, 211 and 219 courtesy of the Canadian Film Reference Library.

Photos on pages 17, 135, 137 and 139 courtesy of the *Winnipeg Free Press*.

Photos on pages 19, 23, 57 and 81, and all colour poster images courtesy of the David DeCoteau Collection.

Photos on pages 20, 27, 29, 31, 33, 35, 37 and 39 courtesy of Peter Roffman.

Photos on pages 45, 47, 49, 51 and 53 courtesy of Jack F. Murphy.

Photos on pages 54, 89, 91 and 83 courtesy of the Canadian Film Reference Library and William Alexander/Critical Mass.

Poster image on page 111 courtesy of T.Y. Drake.

Photos on pages 115 and 117 courtesy of the Canadian Film Reference Library and TVA International.

Poster image on page 167 courtesy of Hysteria Lives.

Photos on pages 177 and 213 courtesy of Ed French.

Photos on pages 195, 197 and 199 courtesy of Jon Mikl-Thor.

Photo on page 220 courtesy of Guy Maddin.

Photo on page 225 courtesy of Theorius Champton.

Photo on page 227 courtesy of Rapid Heart Pictures.

Index

Acomba, David, 84, 103
Act of the Heart, 55
Adams, Brooke, 172
Adams, Donald, 57
Adams, Julie, 143, 199
Adams, Lawrence, 58
Adams, Lynne, 206
Agincourt Productions, 60
Alcocer, Santos, 82
Alcott, John, 131, 135
Aldrich, Robert, 43
Alfred Hitchcock Presents, 67
Alien, 187, 218
Aliens, 156, 184, 187
Alien 3, 200
All in the Family, 142
All the King's Men, 46, 48
Allarcom, 188
Allen, Barry, 72, 143, 144
Allen, Nancy, 138
Allen, Tom, 140
Allen, Woody, 183
Alliance Atlantis, 230
Allin, Norman, 65
Almond, Paul, 55
Alonzo, Richard, 199-200
Alpert, Harry, 36
Alpert, Herb, 36, 41
Altered States, 159
American Gothic, 46
American International Pictures, 30, 47, 56, 74, 76, 89
American Nightmare, 16, 165-66, 176, 213
American Psycho 2, 45
American Werewolf in London, An, 152, 159, 162
Amicus, 43, 45, 56, 172
Amityville Curse, The, 15, 205, 206
Amityville: Dollhouse, 206
Amityville Horror, The, 15, 125, 150, 170, 202
Amityville 1990: It's About Time, 204
Anderson, Melissa Sue, 145-46
Anderson, Michael, 128
Andy Williams Show, The, 108
Angry Red Planet, The, 13
Animal House, 59, 77
Another 48 Hrs., 200
Anspach, Susan, 187
Appice, Carmine, 199
Applebaum, Louis, 38, 40
Arcand, Denis, 84
Argento, Dario, 208
Arkoff, Samuel Z., 74, 76, 78
Arlen, Richard, 154
Around the World in Eighty Days, 128
Astral-Bellevue Pathé, 70, 72-75, 83, 115
Atkinson, Dennis, 81

Atlantic City, 122, 152
Attack of the Brain Demons, The, 78
Attack of the Flesh-Eating Tree, The, 223
Attack of the Killer Squirrel, The, 223
Attack of the Killer Tomatoes, 223
Atwill, Lionel, 25
Audrey Rose, 125
Aurum Film Encyclopedia of Horror, 117, 131, 136, 152, 184, 191
Avco Embassy, 129, 142
Avenging Angelo, 106
Aykroyd, Dan, 170

Back to Bataan, 156
Back to God's Country, 23
Backus, Richard, 85, 86
Bad Moon, 221
Badham, John, 188
Badlands, 112
Baker County, U.S.A., 142
Baker, Henry, 82
Baker, Rick, 162
Balaban, Liane, 227
Bambi Meets Godzilla, 109
Band, Albert, 36
Barker, Clive, 29
Barney, Matthew, 224
Barry, George, 57
Barry, John, 128
Barrymore, John, 26
Bartel, Paul, 178
Battle Beyond the Stars, 156
Bava, Mario, 43, 99
Bay, Frances, 170
Bay of Love and Sorrows, The, 224
Baye, Nathalie, 213
Baywatch, 213
Beachcombers, The, 216
Beaird, John, 148
Beast From 20,000 Fathoms, The, 26
Beaudin, Jean, 44, 65
Beattie, Richard, 211
Bedlam, 26
Behind the Green Door, 112
Believe, 218, 219
Believers, The, 170
Bellamy, Ralph, 25
Bells, 128, 164
Bergeron, Philippe, 226
Bergman, Ingmar, 41
Bergman, Robert, 179-80, 182
Bernstein, Leonard, 72
Berry, Tom, 206, 212-213
Beswick, Martine, 82
Better Off Dead, 213
Big Meat Eater, 62, 109
Big Trouble in Little China, 200
Bigfoot, 226

Billy the Kid vs. Dracula, 78
Bing Crosby Productions (BCP), 56
Black, Karen, 68, 69, 177-78
Black Cat, The, 25, 48
Black Christmas, 61, 88, 90-92, 105, 119, 146, 148, 152, 213
Black Roses, 192, 198-200
Black Sunday, 99
Blackout, 117
Blacula, 46, 193
Blade, 231
Blade Runner, 215
Blair, Linda, 158
Blair Witch Project, The, 228
Bland, Geoff, 222
Blasco, Joe, 100, 112, 159
Bleeders, 215, 218, 228
Blob, The (1958), 13, 164
Blood and Donuts, 216-217, 229
Blood and Guts, 137, 138
Blood Feast, 43, 50
Blood Games, 154
Blood Relations, 203, 204, 206, 207, 218
Blood Relatives, 45, 128
Blood Sisters, 192
Blood Symbol, 211
Bloody Birthday, 204
Bloody Brood, The, 33, 34
Bloomfield, George, 158
Blossom, Roberts, 88, 89
Bluebeard, 156
Blue Man, The, 177-78, 203
Blue Monkey, 186-87, 205, 214
Blue Murder, 189, 217
Blue Velvet, 170, 190
Bluhdorn, Charles, 150
Blumer, Ronald, 116
Boam, Jeffrey, 171, 174
Bochner, Hart, 27, 131
Bochner, Lloyd, 27, 131
Bockner, Martin, 181
Bockner, Michael, 180-182
Body Parts, 214
Bond, Timothy, 57, 89, 90, 146
Boot, Das, 225
Borris, Clay, 211
Borrower, The, 138
Borsos, Phillip, 154, 204
Botsford, Sara, 128, 164
Boushel, Joy, 141, 142, 185
Boyman, Marc, 150, 151
Bradley, Paul, 166
Brady Bunch, The, 138
Brain, The, 64, 201, 204-206
Brainiac, The, 43
Bram Stoker's Legend of the Mummy, 27
Brandis, Jock, 57, 160
Brault, Michel, 112
Bravman, Jack, 192-94
Breakfast Club, The, 217

Bregman, Tracy, 145
Breznahan, Tom, 205
Brind'Amour, Yvette, 68
Brisson, Ed, 200
Broadway Melody of 1938, 36
Bromley, Karen, 91, 115, 116
Bronson, Charles, 144
Brood, The, 98, 110, 122-125, 137, 162, 173
Brooks, Albert, 170
Brooks, Mel, 156, 185
Brooksfilms, 185
Brotherhood III: Young Demons, The, 16
Browning, Tod, 25, 225
Bruck, Arnold, 182-83
Brumberger, Tom, 82
Bryant, Peter, 165
Bua, Tony, 194-95, 199
Buck Rogers in the 23rd Century, 123
Buell, John, 68
Bugsy Malone, 223
Burgoyne, Victoria, 129
Burke, Martyn, 106
Burman, Tom, 146, 148, 149
Burnt Offerings, 125
Burroughs, Jackie, 172, 218
Busgang, Howard, 178
Burton, Richard, 156, 174
Buza, George, 205
Bydwell, Glenn, 135

Cagney and Lacey, 158
Caine Mutiny, The, 156
Calhoun, Rory, 86
Calling the Shots, 216
Cameron, James, 156, 184, 186, 225
Campbell, Neve, 125, 126, 170, 215
Campbell, Nicholas, 172
Canadian Broadcasting Corporation, 30, 31, 65, 67, 89, 95-97, 111, 115, 158, 184, 202
Canadian Co-operation Project, 53, 166
Canadian Film and Television Production Association, 77
Canadian Film Centre, 216
Canadian Film Development Corporation (Telefilm Canada), 17, 44, 52, 53, 55, 56, 60, 65, 66, 70, 72, 73, 83, 97-99, 101, 102, 107, 108, 111, 113, 188
Canadian Film Reference Library, 64
Canadian Film Weekly, 32, 40-42
Candy, John, 106
Cannes Film Festival, 73-75, 133
Cannibal Girls, 71-78, 80, 99, 100, 143, 148, 230
Cannom, Greg, 151

Cannon Films, 181-82
Canuck-O-Vision, 14, 110, 129, 207
Canuxploitation! (website), 231
Cape Fear, 144
Capital Cost Allowance, 73
Car, The, 86, 129
Carlin, Lynne, 85, 86
Carlson, Les, 88, 89, 91, 161, 162, 172
Carmody, Don, 110, 112, 130, 131, 135, 136, 176
Carnival of Souls, 43
Carpenter, The, 195-96, 206, 213
Carpenter, John, 90, 92, 136, 150, 157, 158, 170, 172, 174, 191, 200
Carradine, John, 45, 78, 205
Carradine, Robert, 117
Carrere, Frank, 192
Carrere, Tia, 193-94
Carrie, 138, 189
Carry On, Sergeant, 11
Castravelli, Claudio, 176
Carter, Peter, 106, 113, 115, 116
Casa de los Sombras, La, 46
Cassandra Crossing, The, 135, 136
Cassavetes, John, 86, 150, 151, 181
Castle, William, 26, 27, 37, 46, 76
Castle of the Living Dead, 45
Castravelli, Claudio, 57
Cat People (1942), 26
Cat People (1982), 87
Cathy's Curse, 44, 116, 117
Cellar Dweller, 46
Chabrol, Claude, 45, 128
Chamberlain, Richard, 128, 129
Chambers, Marilyn, 112
Chambre blanche, La, 55
Champagne, Andrée, 50, 52
Champlin, Charles, 127
Chan, Jackie, 198
Chaney, Lon, 217
Changeling, The, 47, 122, 125-127, 137
Chase, Chevy, 170
Chaykin, Maurey, 186
Cheever, John, 62
Chester Angus Ramsgood, 108
Child, The, 213
Children of the Corn, 174, 186
Children Shouldn't Play With Dead Things, 84, 87, 92
Christina's House, 227
Christine, 174, 213
Chuvalo, George, 185, 207
Ciccoritti, Gerard, 55, 65, 179-184
Cinema Canada, 68, 92, 102, 103, 105, 106, 116, 157
Cinemuerte (film festival), 231
Cinépix, 44, 56, 62, 65, 66, 77, 97, 99-101, 104, 111, 112, 119, 144, 186, 204
Cinevision, 70
Circle of Two, 122
Citizen Kane, 26, 119
City in Panic, 16, 176, 198
City on Fire, 129, 130

Ciupka, Richard, 151, 152
Clare, Diana, 48
Clark, Bob, 23, 45, 61, 84-86, 88, 90-92
Clark, Rob, 226
Clement, Andy, 194-95
Clive, Colin, 25
Clouse, Robert, 164
Clown at Midnight, The, 217
Clown Murders, The, 106, 217
Club, The, 187, 214, 215
Coal, Bud, 107
Coates, Kim, 206, 210, 214
Cocteau, Jean, 41
Cohen, Barney, 178
Cohen, Larry, 191
Cole, Janis, 216
Colicos, John, 126
Colley, Peter, 176
Collins, Alan, 98
Coquillion, John, 47, 49, 126
Collins, Debbie, 107
Color Me Blood Red, 50
Color of Money, The, 170
Columbia Pictures, 146, 151
Columbus of Sex, The, 70
Conners, Stompin' Tom, 88
Conti, Tom, 119
Cook, A.J., 225
Cook, Randall William, 191-92
Cool Sound from Hell, A, 31
Cooper, Robert, 214
Copperfield, David, 132
Coppola, Francis, 170, 188
co-productions, 44, 116, 117-119, 129, 213
Corman, Roger, 15, 30, 42, 56, 60, 98, 99, 124, 156, 195, 204
Corpse Eaters, The, 78-81, 83, 84, 100, 195
Corupe, Paul, 231
Cosmatos, George P., 135, 174, 175
Countess Dracula, 143
Crabtree, Arthur, 29
Crackers, 122
Craft, The, 170
Craven, Wes, 108, 170, 171, 228
Crawford, Broderick, 48
Crazies, The, 100
Creature from the Black Lagoon, 143, 199
Creature of Comfort, 56, 57, 78, 103
Creepshow, 156
Creley, Jack, 64, 65, 114, 146, 161
Cremaster, 224
Crenna, Richard, 129, 131
Cries in the Night, 143, 145
Crimes of the Future, 95, 96, 100
Criswell, 40
Critters, 191
Critters 3, 170
Cronenberg, Cassandra, 96
Cronenberg, David, 12, 14-17, 29, 30, 36, 44, 46, 56-58, 64, 65, 81, 84, 88, 92, 95-102, 105, 110-13, 122-25, 137, 138, 148,

150, 154, 161-64, 169, 171-74, 184-86, 202, 204, 205, 214, 216, 217, 219, 225, 230
Cronenberg on Cronenberg, 96, 124, 173
Cronyn, Hume, 27
Crothers, Scatman, 164
Cruising, 171
Cry of the Banshee, 47
Cube, 201, 221
Cujo, 174
Culp, Robert, 61, 108
Curnick, David, 108-110
Currie, Gordon, 216
Curse of the Crimson Altar, 47, 58
Curse of the Fly, 28, 29
Curse of the Voodoo, 31
Curtains, 122, 137, 151, 152
Curtis, Jamie Lee, 131, 132, 138-140, 143, 211
Cusack, John, 213
Cushing, Peter, 118
Cypher, 225

d'Abo, Maryam, 213
Dade, Stephen, 48
Dagenais, Francois, 214
DAL, 56
Dale, Holly, 216
Dalen, Zale, 107, 109
Dane, Lawrence, 106, 113-115, 145
Dangerous Age, A, 31, 32
Dante, Joe, 99, 156
Dark, The, 170, 215, 218
Dark Intruder, 67
Dark Shadows, 46, 47, 82
Darkman, 229
Darkness Falls, 200
David, Pierre, 137, 162, 174, 202-203, 212
Davis, Bette, 91
Davis, Geena, 184, 185
Davison, Jon, 99
Dawn of the Dead (1979), 80
Dawn of the Dead (2004), 231
Day of the Animals, 156
Day of the Nightmare, 46
Dead Meat, 216
Dead of Night, 118
Dead of Winter, 203, 204
Dead Ringers, 137, 214
Dead Zone, The, 163, 171-174
Deadly Eyes, 128, 129, 155, 164, 175
Deadly Harvest, 146
Death Bed: The Bed that Eats, 57
Death Ship, 122, 129-131, 133, 156
Death Valley, 215
Death Weekend, 44, 77, 103-106, 142
De Carlo, Yvonne, 42, 46
Degrassi Junior High, 206
Dekker, Fred, 138
De Laurentiis, Dino, 171, 173-74
Del Grande, Louis, 145, 185

Deliverance, 113, 115, 116, 142, 276
Demme, Jonathan, 99
Demon Seed, 123
De Niro, Robert, 159
Densham, Pen, 203
Dentist, The, 137
Denton, Christa, 191-92
Denton, Clive, 105, 106
De Palma, Brian, 91, 139
Deranged, 87-89, 100
Deschanel, Caleb, 156
Desgagnés, Eric, 231
Devereaux, Maurice, 211-212
Devil Bear, The, 24
Devil Dog: Hound from Hell, 27
Devil Doll, The (1936), 225
Devil Doll, The (1964), 31
Devil's Advocate, 170
Devil's Daughter, 47
Devil's Rain, The, 45, 146
Diable dedans, Le, 231
Diable est parmi nous, Le, 44, 65-67, 69
Diary of a Sinner, 204
Dickens, Charles, 25
Die! Die! My Darling, 45
Dietz, Frank, 194-95, 198-200
Director's Guild of Canada, The, 164
Disappearance, The, 126
Dmytryk, Edward, 155, 156
D.O.A., 91
Dr. Blood's Coffin, 31, 48
Dr. Jekyll and Mr. Hyde, 26
Dr. Terror's House of Horrors, 45, 56
Doctor X, 25
Donahue, Troy, 82
Donaldson, Lesleh, 143-146, 165
Donen, Stanley, 171
Donner, Richard, 69
Don't Be Afraid of the Dark, 123
Don't Look Now, 45, 67
Dorff, Stephen, 190-92
Douglas, Melvyn, 63, 127
Doyle, Jim, 189, 190
Dracula (1931), 25
Dracula (1992), 170
Dracula: Dead and Loving It, 156
Dracula: Pages from a Virgin's Diary, 225
Drabinsky, Garth, 125-127
Drake, T.Y., 107-110, 133-137, 200
Dream House, 154
Driscoll, Graham, 56, 57
Drylanders, The, 63, 103
Dufaux, Guy, 201
Duguay, Christian, 177
Duke, Robin, 187
Dullea, Kier, 91, 119
Dunning, John, 43, 44, 56, 62, 65, 66, 77, 97, 99, 111, 112, 144, 147, 150, 176, 177
Dunwich Horror, The, 27
Dupuis, Roy, 218
Dupuis, Stéphan, 146, 159, 215

Dutton, Syd, 191
Dvorsky, Peter, 203

Earth Vs. the Spider (2001), 170
Earthquake, 26
Eastwood, Clint, 215
Ebert, Roger, 116, 149
Edison, Thomas, 22
Edwards, Blake, 27
Edwards, Natalie, 69, 92
Eggar, Samantha, 61, 62, 118, 123, 124
Elvira, 42
Embattled Shadows (book), 24
Emergency Ward 10, 202
Empire Records, 210
Enter the Dragon, 164
Entity, The, 31
Euro Trip, 76
Evangeline, 23
Evil Dead, The, 208
Evil Judgment, 57, 176
Evil Spawn, 217
Evils of the Night, 78
Exorcist, The, 68, 84, 116, 125, 159
Experiment in Terror, 27
Explosion, 55
Exterminator, The, 198
Eyres, John, 225

Face at the Window, The, 26
Faces, 86
Faculty, The, 189
Falk, Peter, 33
Famous Players, 44
Fangoria (magazine), 83, 140, 147, 163, 172, 196, 205, 211, 214
Fantasia Film Festival, 231
Farrow, Mia, 119
Fasano, John, 82, 192-200, 206, 228
Fast Company, 122, 205
Fast Kill, The, 57
Fatal Attraction, 212
Fawcett, John, 222
FDR – Hyde Park, 32
Ferrigno, Carla, 199
Ferrigno, Lou, 199
Field of Dreams, 179
Fields, Verna, 174
Fiend, 57
Fiend Without a Face, 29
Film Effects, 73, 74
Findlay, Roberta, 192, 197
Firestarter, 174
Flacks, Stephen, 182-83
Flaherty, Joe, 187
Flesh Eaters, The, 43
Flick (a.k.a. **Dr. Frankenstein on Campus**), 58-61, 123, 172, 176
Fluegel, Darlanne, 213
Fly, The (1958), 15, 28, 29
Fly, The (1986), 14-16, 141, 162, 169, 184-85, 187, 190, 203, 219
Fode, Bennett, 204
Fog, The, 138
Fonda, Peter, 116, 158

Food of the Gods, 146,155
Food of the Gods II, 204
Footsteps in the Snow, 51
Ford, Glenn, 26, 45, 46, 144-146
Ford, Harrison, 204
Forsythe, Henderson, 86
Fortune and Men's Eyes, 67
48 Hrs., 171
Foster, Jodie, 117
Foster, Ralph, 32, 68
Fothergill, Robert, 108
Foxy Lady, 70, 71, 73
Francks, Don, 149
Franco, David, 196
Franco, Jesus, 43
Franju, Georges, 33
Frank, Ilana, 189-90
Frankenheimer, John, 188
Frankenstein (1910), 22
Frankenstein (1931), 24
Frankenstein and Me, 218
Freaked, 170
Freddy vs. Jason, 15, 215
Freed, Reuben, 187
Freer, James, 22
French, Ed, 177-78
Freund, Karl, 25
Frid, Jonathan, 46, 47, 82
Friday the 13th, 15, 92, 140, 148-150
Friday the 13th part 2, 148
Friday the 13th part 4, 178
Friday the 13th (TV series), 57
Friedkin, William, 68, 69, 171
Frogs, 47, 117
From the Drain, 96
Frontiere, Dominic, 62
Fruet, William, 16, 44, 57, 103-105, 115, 121, 142-144, 148, 158-161, 178-79, 186-87
Fruitman, Orval, 137
Fujiwara, Chris, 28
Fulford, Robert, 17, 100, 102
Full Circle, 99, 119, 126, 129
Fullerton, Carl, 159
Funhouse, The, 191
Furie, Sidney, 30-32, 45, 48, 67, 125

Gaga Communications, 200
Galaxy of Terror, 156
Gale, David, 205
Galligan, Zach, 210
Gammell, Robin, 113-115
Gargiulo, Arnold, 197
Gate, The, 169, 190-92, 198
Gate II, The, 192
Gazzara, Ben, 218
Gein, Ed, 87, 88, 143
Gélinas, Gratien, 66
Genie awards, 127
Gentleman Jekyll and Driver Hyde, 28
Gessner, Nicholas, 117
Getting Your Money's Worth, 32
Getz, John, 185
Ghost Ship, The (1943), 26
Ghost Ship (2002), 131

Ghostbusters, 77, 170, 191
Ghostkeeper, 107, 122, 153, 154
Gibbons, Rodney, 147, 149, 205
Gift, The, 170
Gillen, Jeff, 87-89
Gillis, Barry J., 208
Gilmour, Clyde, 41
Ginger Snaps, 16, 23, 171, 216, 221-222, 224, 228, 229
Ginger Snaps II: Unleashed, 228-229
Girard, Bernard, 61
Girdler, William, 24, 156
Glaser, Paul Michael, 127, 128
Glen Warren Productions, 60
Glickenhaus, James, 198, 199
Globe and Mail, The, 60, 101, 102
Gloria, 151
Gluck, Lew, 159
Godfather, The, 86
Godzilla, 13, 30
Goin' Down the Road, 53, 91, 103, 105, 115, 148, 166, 211, 230
Goldberg, Daniel, 70-76, 100, 180
Goldbloom, Jeff, 184
Golden Harvest, 164
Goldsmith, George, 186
Gone With the Wind, 230
Good Earth, The, 36
Good Son, The, 212
Goode, John, 107
Goosebumps, 218
Gordon, Bert I., 155
Gordon, James, 37, 38
Gordon, Richard, 31
Gordon, Stuart, 170
Gore, Tipper, 198, 199
Gorilla At Large, 42
Gorky Park, 203
Gorshin, Frank, 195
Gossett Jr., Lou, 27
Graham, Superstar Billy, 193-95
Grant, Lee, 156, 157
Graver, Gary, 70
Graveyard Alive: A Zombie Nurse in Love, 231
Graveyard Shift, 65, 182-83
Gray, Sally, 108
Gray, William, 126, 137, 141
Great Shadow, The, 23
Green, Martin, 50, 51
Greenberg, Harold, 70, 75, 83, 104, 115, 131
Grefé, William, 51
Gremlins, 210
Grey Fox, The, 122
Grier, Pam, 186
Grierson, John, 27, 28, 32, 33, 42, 100
Griffen, Lynne, 152
Grizzly, 24
Grodnik, Daniel, 133
Groom, Sam, 164
Guess Who, The, 207
Guns of Navarone, The, 144
Guthé, Manfred, 72, 152
Guza, Robert, 137, 151

Haber, Sandy, 34, 35, 41
Haim, Corey, 15, 204, 214
Haldane, Don, 30, 31, 62, 63, 103
Hall, Kenneth J., 217
Haller, Daniel, 27
Halloween, 15, 56, 90, 92, 133, 135, 136, 140, 144, 152, 157, 189
Halloween H2O, 226
Halloween: Resurrection, 15
Hamilton-Wright, Michael, 226
Hammer Films, 43, 48, 56, 107, 109, 110, 128, 151, 172, 215, 225
Hamori, Andras, 192
Hand, The, 83
Hand of Night, 48
Hand that Rocks the Cradle, The, 212
Handling, Piers, 105
Hangin' In, 175
Hanka, 36
Hanks, Tom, 176
Hanley, Jim, 176
Happy Birthday To Me, 27, 44, 57, 128, 144-148, 225
Happy Hell Night (a.k.a. **Frat Fright**), 210
Happy Hooker Goes to Washington, The, 178
Hard Part Begins, The, 137
Hard Rock Zombies, 191
Harkness, John, 157, 212
Harmon, Robert, 171
Harrington, Curtis, 27
Harry, Debbie, 161
Harry and the Hendersons, 226
Hart, Harvey, 30, 31, 62, 67-70
Harvey, Grant, 229
Harvey, Laurence, 46
Hauer, Rutger, 218
Haunting, The, 42, 48
Hauser, Wings, 206
Hayward, Louis "Deke", 74, 75
He Is My Brother, 156
Hebb, Brian R. R., 141
Heely-Ray, Ken, 131
Heely-Ray Sound System, 131
Hegyi, Steve, 224
Heinlein, Robert A., 45
Hello Mary Lou: Prom Night II, 188-90
Hemingway, Ernest, 161
Henriksen, Lance, 225
Herbert, James, 165
Héroux, Claude, 162, 174
Herzog, John, 189
Hess, Jon, 204
Hewlitt, David, 201
Hide and Go Shriek, 135
High-Ballin', 116
Highpoint, 116
Hilarious House of Frightenstein, The, 224
Hill, Debra, 171, 172
Hill, Jack, 129, 130
Hill, Walter, 150, 171
Hills Have Eyes, The, 141, 228
Hitchcock, Alfred, 26, 146
Hindle, Art, 123

Hoffert, Paul, 60
Hoffman, 130
Hoffman, Dustin, 159
Hofsess, John, 70
Holbrook, Hal, 113-116
Holbrook, John, 106, 107, 154
Holland, Byrd, 112
Hollywood North (book), 60
Hollywood Reporter, The, 152
Homeric Productions, 48
Hong, James, 200
Hookers on Davie, 216
Hooper, Tobe, 157, 158, 226
Horner, James, 211
Horrors of the Black Museum, 29
Hough, John, 46, 151
Houghton, Buck, 177
House of Dark Shadows, 47
House of Seven Corpses, The, 46
House of the Dead, 215
Housekeeper, The, 213
Houseman, John, 128
Howard, Sandy, 129, 131, 133, 135, 141, 146, 186
Howe, Nancy, 189
Howes, Sally Ann, 129
Howling, The, 159
Howling Nightmare, 224
Hud, 63
Humongous, 64, 122, 126, 141, 142, 143, 185, 189, 214
Hunger, The, 182
Hunt, Ed, 204
Hunter, Russell, 126
Huntington, Lawrence, 47, 49
Hussey, Olivia, 91
Hustler, The, 33
Huston, John, 110, 126-128, 155
Huston, Walter, 128
Hutton, Robert, 48, 49
Hyams, Peter, 147
Hysteria, 128
Hysteria Lives (website), 142

I Bury the Living, 36
I Drink Your Blood, 56
I Love a Man in Uniform, 195, 206
I, Madman, 192
I Saw What You Did, 46
Iliad Productions, 48
Ilsa, Tigress of Siberia, 44, 77
Impulse, 27
In the Mouth of Madness, 170
Incubus (1966), 45
Incubus, The (1981), 46, 150, 151, 202, 205
Indiana Jones and the Last Crusade, 172
Innerspace, 172
Initiation, L', 44
Interview (magazine), 76
Intruder Within, The, 116
Invaders from Mars, 13
Invasion of the Body Snatchers, The (1956), 13
Invasion of the Body Snatchers (1978), 45

Invisible Invaders, 48
Ireland, John, 45, 46, 150, 151
Ironside, Michael, 144, 156, 157, 204
Irwin, Mark, 123, 138, 143, 159, 185-86, 198, 204
Island of the Dead, 224
Isle of the Dead, 26, 224
It Lives Again, 86
It's Alive, 84, 86
Italian Machine, The, 111

Jackson, Douglas, 213
Jackson, Peter, 123
Jacoby, Scott, 117
Jacqueline Susann's Once is Not Enough, 104
James, Brion, 215
James, Ken, 113-115
Jansens, Maris, 204
Jarvis, May, 72
Jason X, 15
Jaws, 24, 84, 128, 135, 156, 174, 175
J.B. and the Playboys, 51, 52
Jewison, Norman, 216
JFK, 106
Jitters, The, 200
Jobin, Peter, 146
Johnson, Ben, 131, 132, 135
Johnston, Bob, 69
Jordan, Andrew, 209
Jory, Victor, 27
Judy Marsh Modelling Agency, 58, 59
Julian Roffman: Man of Action (essay), 33
Junior, 176

Kael, Pauline, 152
Kahnert, Paul, 164
Kamen, Michael, 173, 174
Kane, Carol, 103
Kantor, Robert, 115
Kapelman, Jeffrey, 82
Karloff, Boris, 22, 25, 26, 218
Karr, Tom, 87-89
Kaufman, Jimmy, 216
Kaufman, Phillip, 45
Keane, Kerrie, 151
Keeper, The, 107-110, 133
Keitel, Harvey, 89
Keller, Susan, 106
Kelman, Paul, 199
Kennedy, George, 129-131
Kephart, Elza, 231
Kerner, Ben, 63
Kerwin, Bill, 50
Kerwin, Harry, 50
Khaner, Julie, 158
Kidder, Margot, 90, 91, 125, 170, 213, 217
Killer Bs, 188
Killer Party, 161, 178-79, 214
Killer Shrews, 164
King Kong, 25
King of Kensington, 158
King, Stephen, 116, 156, 171,

173, 174, 226, 231
Kingdom of the Spiders, 45
Kingfish, 72
Kingston Trio, The, 108
Kinski, Klaus, 152
Kiss, The, 203
Kleinburg Studios, 14, 32, 33, 38, 48, 64, 104, 116, 184
KNB Effects Group Inc., 228
Knelman, Martin, 60, 100
Kolchak: The Night Stalker, 27
Konchalovsky, Andrei, 171
Koontz, Dean R., 15, 44, 204
Kozlowski, Linda, 213
Kramer vs. Kramer, 122
Kramreither, Anthony, 64, 65, 165, 176
Kruschen, Jack, 46
Kubrick, Stanley, 135, 153
Kuersten, Erich, 29
Kwaidan, 43
Kybartas, Sandy, 189
Kymlicka, Milan, 213

LaBute, Neil, 156
Lady of the Lake, 211
Lafleur, Jean, 44
Lake, Veronica, 51
Lamont, Jack, 47
Lamontagne, Maurice, 52
Lancaster, Burt, 62, 174
Landis, John, 152, 171
Langlois Brothers, 223
Langlois, Lisa, 128, 164
Lantos, Robert, 44, 182
Last Chase, The, 106
Last Picture Show, The, 135
Lawless Land, The, 204
Lawnmower Man 2, The, 226
Lea, Ron, 213
Lear, Norman, 142
Lee, Christopher, 69, 107, 109, 204
Lee, Damian, 204
Legacy, The, 125
Legend of Hell House, The, 151
Lehman, Lew, 155, 164
Lemche, Kris, 171, 222
Leonard Maltin's Movie and Video Guide, 131
Lesage, Jean, 52
Lester, Seeleg, 63, 64
Letting Go, 63
Levy, Eugene, 71, 72
Lewis, David, 129
Lewis, Herschel Gordon, 43, 50, 56, 188
Lewton, Val, 26, 224
Lighthouse, 58-60
Lightshow Communications, 179-82
Limelight Productions, 60
Linder, Cec, 164
Lindley, John, 178-79
Link, André, 43, 44, 56, 62, 65, 66, 75, 77, 97, 99, 111-12, 144, 147-48, 177
Lion's Gate Films, 44

Little Girl who Lived Down the Lane, The, 44, 99, 117-18
Little House on the Prairie, 146
Logan's Run, 128
Loiselle, André, 231
Lom, Herbert, 172-73
Lombardo, Lou, 126
Loncraine, Richard, 119
Long Day's Journey Into Night, The, 195, 206
Lord, Jean-Claude, 44, 157, 186
Lord of the Rings, The, 42, 109, 191
Loren, Sophia, 174
Lorimar Productions, 171
Los Angeles *Times*, 127, 190
Lost Boys, The, 172, 191
Louis, Justin, 189
Love Story, 86
Loving and Laughing, 97
Lowerie, Tim, 107
Lowrey, Lynn, 100
Lucky Pierre, 43
Lugosi, Bela, 25, 48, 49
Lynch, David, 30
Lynch, Paul, 137-142, 164, 165
Lynn, Amber, 208
Lyons, Wendy, 189
Lytle, Andrew, 61

Mabe, Ricky, 218
Mackay, Mark, 198
Mad Butcher, The, 46
Maddin, Guy, 31, 224-225
Maddox, Diana, 126
Magnificent Ambersons, The, 26
Makichuk, James, 154
Malick, Terence, 112
Malle, Louis, 152
Malo, René, 202-203
Mamet, David, 156
Mancuso, Nick, 129, 130
Mangler 2, The, 225-226
Maniac, 128
Manitou, The, 123
Manners, David, 25, 26
Manoir du Diable, Le, 22
Mantis in Lace, 58
maple-syrup porn, 56, 62, 204
Margheriti, Antonio, 43
Marins, Jose Mojica, 43
Mark of Cain, The, 58, 176, 188, 189
Marleau, Louise, 66
Marley, John, 85, 86
Marriage Trap, The, 23
Mars Needs Women, 13
Marshall, Bill, 60
Martin, Andrea, 71, 72, 91
Martin, John, 199
Martin, Richard, 204
Martin, Terry, 139
Martz, Neil, 159
Maryk, Michael, 159
*M*A*S*H*, 45
Mask, The, 34-42, 63, 64, 91, 110
Massacre Up North, 222-223
Massey, Raymond, 26, 45

Massey Report, 53
Matalon, Eddy, 117
Matinee, 16, 204
Matrix, The, 170, 229
Maximum Overdrive, 156
McCowan, George, 47
McDowell, Malcolm, 224
McGavin, Darren, 210
McGrath, Doug, 91, 92
McHattie, Stephen, 215
McKay, Doug, 109
McKay, Jeff, 200
McKee, Lucky, 231
McLuhan, Marshall, 65
McNaughton, John, 138
McRae, Henry, 23
McTiernan, John, 170
Meatballs, 77
Meatballs III, 176
Medak, Peter, 126, 127
Medjuck, Joe, 76, 102
Méliès, Georges, 22
Mendez, Ray, 159, 160
Meredith, Burgess, 195
Meridian Productions, 32, 56, 68
Metro-Goldwyn-Mayer, 179
Miami Golem, 46
Michaels, Joel B., 126
Michaels, Lorne, 98, 123
Micro-Nice, 223-224
Mihalka, George, 16, 44, 142, 147-150, 177, 210, 212-213
Mikels, Ted V., 84
Milland, Ray, 47, 117, 118
Millenium, 225
Miller, Clarence "Big", 62, 72
Miller, Stephen, 147
Milligan, Andy, 56
Mr. Patman, 122
Mr. Smith Goes to Washington, 36
Mr. Vampire, 200
Mitchnick, Paul, 199
Monahan, Brent, 160
Monster Club, The, 119
Monthly Film Bulletin, 42, 49, 151
Moore, Demi, 170
Moore, Roy, 89, 90
Moosehead Beer, 149, 150
Moran, Jim, 38-41
Morello, Tony, 211
Morita, Rhett, 207
Morot, Adrien, 212, 215, 218
Morris, Peter, 24
Morris, Reginald, 62, 91, 129
Morse, L.A., 196
Most Dangerous Game, The, 26
Moyle, Allan, 210
Mummy, The, 25
Mummy's Rampage, The, 78
Munsters, The, 46
Murder By Decree, 45
Murder My Sweet, 156
Murdoch, Cindy, 224

Murphy, Jack, 147
My Big Fat Greek Wedding, 143
My Bloody Valentine, 16, 44, 53, 144, 147-150, 157, 177, 205, 210, 213, 229
My Bodyguard, 87
My Little Eye, 171
Myers, Mike, 26
Mystery of Edwin Drood, The, 25
Mystery of the Million Dollar Hockey Puck, The, 216
Mystery of the Wax Museum, The, 25
Mystery Science Theatre 3000, 196

Name for Evil, A, 61, 62, 72, 106, 107, 108
Nankin, Michael, 192
Narizzano, Silvio, 45
Naschy, Paul, 56
Natali, Vincente, 221, 225
National Archives of Canada, 81
National Film Board of Canada, The, 11, 12, 21, 27, 28, 30, 32, 34, 37, 38, 53, 62, 63, 75, 148, 174
National Lampoon, 147
Necromancy, 155
Negin, Louis, 111
Neiderman, Andrew, 202
Neighbor, The, 170, 213
Nelson, Ida, 143
Nerman, David, 216
Nevins, Claudette, 38, 41
New Line Cinema, 42
New, Robert, 138, 140, 175
New Waterford Girl, 210, 227
New World Pictures, 98, 124
Newfeld, Clarence, 107
Newland, Marv, 109
Newman, Paul, 170
Newton, John, 159
Nicholson, Jack, 153
Nielsen, Leslie, 18, 67, 139, 156, 193, 211
Nightbreed, 29, 30, 200
Night Life, 84
Nightmare, 128
Nightmare on Elm Street, A, 15, 42, 176, 188, 189
Night of Bloody Horror, 56
Night of the Creeps, 138
Night of the Demons III, 16, 215, 216
Night of the Living Dead, 55, 62, 81, 111
Night Shadows, 206
Night Walk, The, 23, 84-87, 90, 92
Night Walker, The, 27
1984, 128
99 44/100% Dead, 188
Niven, David, 174
Nixon, Richard, 69
Nocturna, 46
Nomads, 170
Norstar Releasing, 153, 188, 189, 214
Nothing But Trouble, 170

O'Bannon, Dan, 218
Oblong Box, The, 47, 49
Oboler, Arch, 41
O'Brien, Edmund, 91
October Crisis, 63, 64, 112
Of Unknown Origin, 136, 156, 174-75, 216
Ohashi, René, 171
Old Dark House, The, 26
Old School, 76
Oliver, Ron, 188-90, 207-208
Oliviero, Silvio, 183
Omen, The, 84, 116, 125
Omen IV, The, 15
One Magic Christmas, 204
One Plus One, 41
Onibaba, 43
Ontario Securities Commission, 127
Ontkean, Michael, 155
O'Quinn, Terry, 201
Orca, 128
Ord, Murray, 153
Ordres, Les, 112
Orlando, Jamie, 107
Ormé, Stuart, 45
Ormsby, Alan, 84, 85, 87-89
Ormsby, Anya, 85
Ottawa *Citizen*, 125
Outer Limits, The, 63

P4W: Prison For Women, 216
Pacific Heights, 212
Pack, The, 164
Pacula, Joanna, 203
Paperboy, The, 170
Paramount Pictures, 48, 148, 149, 150, 173
Paranoiac, 127
Pariser, Alfred, 99, 119
Parker III, Chauncey G., 174
Parks, Michael, 108
"Parnell, Julian", 65
Party of Five, 170
Passmore, Donald, 80
Passport to Sdhame, 130
Pastore, Vincent, 199
Pat Garrett and Billy the Kid, 47
Paul, Alexandra, 213
Payne, Bruce, 225
Paynter, Robert, 152
Peachment, Chris, 151
Peckinpah, Sam, 47, 103, 126, 135
Peggy Sue Got Married, 188
Penn, Arthur, 204
Penthouse Pictures, 61
Perenchio, Jerry, 142
Peterson, Dean, 48, 49
Phantom of the Opera, The, 27
Phobia, 110, 126-128, 155
Phoenix Pictures, 204
Pickford, Mary, 26
Pickles, Christina, 82
Pick-Up Summer, 141, 147
Piemonte, Pee Wee, 193-94
Pike, Dennis, 124
Pike, Karen, 138

Pilon, Daniel, 66
Pin, 150, 151, 169, 201-03, 205, 206
Pinsent, Gordon, 46, 115
Piranha, 99
Piranha II: The Spawning, 156
Pit, The, 152, 154, 155, 164, 215
Pit and the Pendulum, The (1990), 170
Pitt, Ingrid, 143
Pittman, Bruce, 58, 176, 188, 190
Pizza to Go, 147
Plague of the Zombies, 48
Planes, Trains and Automobiles, 106
Platoon, 214
Play Dead, 46
Playgirl Killer, 50-52
Pleasance, Donald, 56, 57, 103, 118, 119
Pleasantville, 179
Pleasure Palace, 204
Plumb, Eve, 138
Plummer, Christopher, 68, 109, 210, 217
Pogue, Charles Edward, 15, 185
Point of No Return, 204
Polanski, Roman, 62, 69
Pollack, Sidney, 171
Polley, Sarah, 187
Poltergeist, 191
Poltergeist (TV series), 170
Porky's, 131
Powell, Michael, 183
Power, The, 46
Powers, Stephanie, 213
Predator, 227
Premier Operating, 72
Presner, Bob, 147
Pressberger, Emeric, 183
Preston, Cyndy, 201, 205, 206
Price, Vincent, 109, 224
Prochnow, Jurgen, 225
Producer's Releasing Corporation, 49
Prokop, Skip, 60
Prom Night, 16, 122, 126, 136-141, 143, 151, 152, 156, 175, 182, 187, 219, 228
Prom Night III: The Last Kiss, 201, 206-208
Prom Night IV: Deliver Us from Evil, 210-211
Prophecy, 146
Protector, The, 198
Proudest Girl in the World, The, 32
Pryce, Craig, 215
Psychiatrist, The, 108
Psychic, 210
Psycho, 87, 128, 143, 144, 203
Psycho Girls, 180-182
Pug-Dog Crisis, The, 224
Pump Up the Volume, 210
Puppet Masters, The, 45
Purl, Linda, 157
Pyx, The, 31, 67-69, 72, 117, 177

Q, 191

Quadrant Films, 84, 87, 90
Quastel, Jonas, 226
Quiet Revolution, 52
Quigley, Linnea, 143
Quiller Memorandum, The, 128
Quota Quickies, 24

Rabid, 64, 77, 100, 110-112, 122,
  123, 154, 173, 185, 203, 210
Racine, Roger, 82, 176, 194
Ragozzino, Ed, 29
Railsback, Steve, 187
Raimi, Sam, 170, 196, 208, 229
Rakoff, Alvin, 130
Rambo, 136
Ratopolis, 174, 175
Raw Meat, 114
Razutis, Al, 109
Re-Animator, 205
Reardon, Craig, 191-92
Red Blooded American Girl,
  209-210
Red Shoes, The, 183
Reed, Carol, 63
Reed, Oliver, 123, 158, 160, 186
Reeltime, 197
Reeves, Keanu, 170
Reeves, Michael, 45, 58
Reflections of Fear, 188
Regan, Laura, 171
Reid, Kate, 129, 130
Reincarnate, The, 31, 63-65, 70,
  103, 177, 178, 203, 213
Reineke, Gary, 106, 113-115
Reiner, Rob, 174
Reitman, Ivan, 70-77, 99, 100,
  104, 110, 170, 180, 191
Rekert, Winston, 177-78
Relic Hunter, 193
Return of the Fly, 28
Return of the Living Dead, 143
Reynolds, Burt, 218
Reynolds, Jay, 64
Reynolds, Michael J., 157
Rice, Anne, 182
Richards, David Adams, 224
Richler, Mordecai, 74
Richter, Ota, 175
Riding the Bullet, 231
Riel, 158
Riley, Doug, 73
Riou-Garand, Suzanne, 100
Rip-Off, 103
Rituals, 106, 113-116, 129, 159
Return of the Living Dead, 218
Return to Sleepaway Camp, 199
Ripper: Letter from Hell, 225
Road Trip, 76
Robbins, Gary, 141, 142
Robert Lawrence Productions, 48
Roberts, Eric, 221
Robertson, John S., 26
Robins, John, 129
Robocop, 175
Robson, Mark, 26, 42, 224
Rock 'n' Roll High School, 82
Rock 'n' Roll Nightmare, 192,
  196-98

Roddenberry, Gene, 108
Rodley, Chris, 95, 124, 171, 173
Rodriguez, Robert, 189
Roeg, Nicolas, 45
Roffman, Julian, 31-38, 40, 42, 56,
  60, 63, 64, 68-70, 95, 110, 231
Roffman, Peter, 41
Rogers, Mimi, 222
Rollin, Jean, 56
Rolling Stone, 102
Romano, Rino, 214
Romeo and Juliet, 91
Romero, George, 55, 63, 81, 100,
  156
Rona Jaffe's Mazes and Monsters,
  176
Rosemary's Baby, 47, 62, 63, 65, 125
Rosenblum, Ralph, 183
Ross, John, 48, 49
Ross, Sinclair, 63
Roswell: The Aliens Attack, 154
Roth, Andrea, 214
Roth, Eli, 87, 92
Roth, Phillip, 63
Rotundo, Nick, 190
Rowdyman, The, 46, 115
Royal Ontario Museum, 38
Rubes, Jan, 203-206, 218
Rubinek, Saul, 129, 130
Runaway Train, 171
Russell, Ray, 150, 151
Ryshpan, Arden, 141

Saad, Robert, 72, 99
Saddest Music in the World, The,
  31, 225
Sager, Ray, 188
St. Elsewhere, 82
Sakai, Sonoko, 200
Salomé – Where She Danced, 46
Saltzman, Harry, 70
Samhain, 228
Samuel Goldwyn Company, The,
  188
Samuels, Maxine, 67, 68
Sanders, Ronald, 123, 185
Sandler, Bob, 71, 76
Sangster, Jimmy, 127
Santamaria, Erick, 51
Santo, 43
Sasquatch (1977), 29, 226
Sasquatch (2002), 226-227
Satan's Cheerleaders, 46
Satan's Mistress, 78
Satan's Paradise, 23
Satan's School for Girls, 27
Saturday Night (magazine), 17,
  100, 112
Saturday Night Live, 98, 123
Saturn 3, 171
Saving Jessica Lynch, 200
Savini, Tom, 80, 87, 89
Saxon, John, 91
Saxton, John, 146
Scanner Cop, 16
Scanners, 16, 137, 146, 162, 163,
  173, 185
Scanners II, 177

Scanners III, 177
Scarborough Bluffs, 64, 139, 160
Scary Pictures, 71, 72
Schickel, Richard, 127
Schouten, Dick, 90
Schrader, Paul, 87
Schreiber, Live, 108
Schreiber, Tell, 108
Schuster, Frank, 32
Schwartz, "Skin", 37, 38
Schwarzenegger, Arnold, 186, 227
Scorsese, Martin, 82
Scott, George C., 125, 126
Scream, 108, 170
Scream and Scream Again, 47
Screamers, 177
S.C.T.V., 61, 71
Sear, Walter, 192, 197
Search and Destroy, 142
Seaway, 47
Secret Window, 231
Secrets of Chinatown, 24
Secter, David, 95
Sedaka, Neil, 50-52
Seeing Things, 145
Seizure, 47, 82, 83, 176
Self Defence, 23
Sendel, Maxwell A., 51
Sennett, Mack, 70
Sensurround, 131
Sentinel, The, 125
Serendipity Point Films, 44
Serpent and the Rainbow, The, 179
Seventh Victim, The, 26
Sexcula, 106, 107, 154
Shamata, Chuck, 104
Shane, Bob, 108
Shapiro, Leonard, 197
Shapiro Entertainment, 197-98
Shapiro-Glickenhaus
  Entertainment, 198
Shatner, William, 45, 146, 157,
  193
Shaver, Helen, 170
Shaye, Robert, 41, 42, 64
She Cried Murder, 90
Shebib, Don, 84, 91, 103
Sheen, Martin, 117, 172
Sheppard, John, 176, 188
Sherman, Bobby, 156
Sherman, Harvey, 90
Shining, The, 135, 153, 164
Shipman, Ernest, 23, 69
Shipman, Nell, 23
Shivers, 17, 77, 96-102, 105, 107,
  111, 112, 173, 174, 185
Shonteff, Lindsay, 31
Shore, Howard, 60, 173, 174,
  185
Shuftan, Eugene, 33
Shusett, Ron, 218
Silence of the Lambs, 159
Silent Partner, The, 126
Silent Scream, 46
Silla, Felix, 123
Silver, Joe, 100
Silver, Ron, 227
Silver Streak, 133

Silverman, Robert, 138
Simcom, 137, 151-153
Simpson, Peter, 137, 138, 140,
  151, 152, 188-90, 203, 207,
  210, 214
Single White Female, 212
Siskel, Gene, 116, 149
Sisters, 91
Sitges International Festival of
  Fantastic and Horror Cinema,
  105, 225
Sixteen Candles, 199
Skerritt, Tom, 172
Skip Tracer, 107, 109
Skullduggery, 138, 175
Slap Shot, 155
laher$, 211-212
Slaughter, Tod, 26
Slaughterhouse Rock, 192
Sleepaway Camp, 177
Slime People, The, 48
Smith, Dick, 158, 159
Smith, Gordon, 179, 214-215
Smits, Sonja, 154, 161
Snake Woman, The, 31, 48
Snider, Norman, 98
Snyders, Sammy, 154, 155
Soames, Richard, 135, 136
Society, 163
Sole, Alfred, 138
Sole, John, 97
Solnicki, Victor, 137, 162
Someone Is Watching, 213
Something About Love, 206
Sopranos, The, 199
Sorcerers, The, 58
Sorrell, Cindy, 198
Southam, Tim, 224
Spacek, Sissy, 112
Spasms, 57, 159-161
Speed, 170
Spencer, Brenton, 187, 189, 214
Spencer, Michael, 53, 60, 66, 73,
  95, 97, 99, 111
Spider, 123, 225
Spielberg, Steven, 108
Spier, Carol, 123, 185
Spier, Riva, 153, 154
Spottiswoode, Raymond, 34, 35,
  135
Spottiswoode, Roger, 135
Stalked, 213
Stallone, Sylvester, 106
Star Wars (film series), 109
Starship Invasions, 204
Starsky and Hutch, 128
Stay Tuned, 147
Steele, Barbara, 99, 100, 143
Steiger, Rod, 213
Stein, David, 205
Stepfather, The, 179, 201, 211
Stereo, 95, 96, 100
Stern, Sandor, 125, 150, 151,
  202-203
Sternberg, Josef von, 25
Stevens, Andrew, 210
Stevens, Paul, 38, 41
Sting of Death, 51

Stoichevski, Paul, 222
Stoker, Bram, 225
Stone, Oliver, 82, 83, 106, 194, 214
Storaro, Vittorio, 152
Strange Brew, 214
Straub, Peter, 119
Straw Dogs, 47, 103, 104, 276
Stroheim, Erich von, 25
Stroud, Don, 104, 105
Stuart, Laird, 56
Stunt Man, The, 62
Subotsky, Milton, 119
Sugar Cookies, 82
Sullivan, Brett, 229
Sullivan, Sean, 58, 172
Sundown, 46
Sur le Seuil, 231
Suspiria, 84, 188
Sutherland, Donald, 45, 46, 56, 67
Sutherland, Ian, 115
Svatek, Peter, 216, 218
Swain, Chelse, 226
Swanson, Greg, 132
Sweeney, Maureen, 142
Swimmer, The, 62
Swofford, Ken, 199

Taggart, Brian, 156, 157, 174
Takacs, Tibor, 190, 192
Take One, 76, 102, 103, 105, 231
Tamiroff, Akim, 48, 49
Tanya's Island, 138
Tarantino, Quentin, 181
Tarantula, 28
Taste of Blood, A, 50
Taubes, Frank, 34, 35, 41
tax shelter era, 24, 121, 122, 129, 134, 138, 144, 147, 149, 166, 174, 203, 211
Taxi Driver, 117, 141, 159
Taylor, Bill, 191
Taylor, Gilbert W., 60
Taylor, Nat, 32-34, 37, 38, 40, 60, 63, 64
Taylor-Roffman Productions, 33, 35, 41
Taylor, Yvonne, 33
Tedham, Glen, 226
Tenement, 192
Tenney, Kevin S., 216
Terezakis, Bill, 215
Terminator, The, 156, 186
Terror Night, 46
Terror Train, 15, 27, 122, 131-36, 141, 152, 157, 178
Terror Trap, The (website), 143
Tessier, Eric, 231
Texas Chainsaw Massacre, The, 84, 87, 88, 157, 276
Then came Bronson, 108
They, 171
Thing, The, 150, 191
Things, 208-209, 223
13 Ghosts, 26
13 Platoon, 32
Thomas, Heather, 210
Thompson, J. Lee, 144, 146

Thomson, David, 27
Thor, Jon-Mikl, 194, 196-98, 200
Three's Company, 153
Thresher at Work, The, 22
Threshold, 86
Tigon, 43
'Till Death Do Us Part, 146
Time (magazine), 127
Time Out (magazine), 102, 151
Tinnell, Robert, 218
Titanic, 156
Tokuda, Marilyn, 200
Tombstone, 200
Toronto *Citizen*, 69
Toronto International Film Festival, 137
Toronto *Telegram*, 41
Torture Garden, 48
Touch of Evil, 48
Townsley, Herman, 37
Tracey, Ian, 109
Transcendental Hopheads, 223
Transfer, 96
Travolta, John, 139
Traynor, Chuck, 112
Tremors 2: Aftershock, 170
Trick or Treat, 191
Tripp, Louis, 190-92
Trog, 48
Trucks, 156
Trudeau, Pierre, 52, 55, 64, 96
Trudeau (mini-series), 184
Tushingham, Rita, 213
Twentieth-Century Fox, 184
Twilight Zone, The, 45
Twilight Zone: The Movie, 170
Twin Peaks, 155
Twin Peaks: Fire Walk With Me, 30, 170
Twins of Evil, 151
2000 Maniacs, 50
2001: A Space Odyssey, 91

Udy, Hélène, 149, 201-203
Ulmer, Edgar, 25
Uman, Joel, 57
Uncanny, The, 47, 117-119, 123, 129
Under the Volcano, 128
Understudy, The: Graveyard Shift II, 183-84
Unforgiven, 215
Universal Pictures, 25, 131, 163, 172, 202
Unlawful Entry, 212
Up Uranus!, 57
Uptown Theatre, 65, 190, 230
Urban Legend, 15

Vaccaro, Brenda, 104, 105
Valerie, 56
Valley of the Dolls, 26
Vampire Bat, The, 25
Vampire Hookers, The, 78
Van Devere, Trish, 125, 126
Variety, 49, 57, 60, 76, 102, 127, 136, 190
Vaughn, Robert, 204

Vernon, John, 118, 128, 152, 187
Verzier, René, 69, 112, 117, 130, 157, 165, 175
Vetter, Klaus, 80
Vice Squad, 206
Victory, 128
Video Trash and Treasures, 196
Videodrome, 65, 88, 154, 158, 161-164, 171-173, 203-205
Viel, Christian, 228
Viens, Mon Amour, 44
Viking, The, 11
Village Voice, The, 140
Villechaize, Hervé, 82
Vindicator, The, 44, 176, 186
Virus (1980), 27
Virus (1998), 45
Vision IV, 90
Visiting Hours, 45, 144, 146, 156-57, 186, 212
Viviano, Sal, 199-200
Vogel, Matt, 177-78
Von Sydow, Max, 206
Vorkapich, Slavko, 36, 37
Vrana, Vlasta, 144, 178, 203, 216
Vulture, The, 47-50, 100

Walas, Chris, 185, 203
Waldman, Marian, 88, 91
Walken, Christopher, 58, 89, 172-73
Walsh, Gwynyth, 187
Walton, Karen, 222
Wang, Steve, 200
Warner Bros., 37, 38, 41, 63, 91, 131, 165, 178, 179
Warner, Jack, 70
Watanabe, Gedde, 199
Watcher, The, 170
Watchers, 15, 16, 204
Watchers 3, 206
Watchtower, The, 16
Ward, Robin, 58, 176
Waxman, Al, 158, 159
Waxworks II: Lost in Time, 46
Wayne, Johnny, 32
Wayne's World, 193
Webster, Ben, 48
Wedding in White, 103, 105
Welcome to Arrow Beach, 46
Welk, Lawrence, 100
Well, The, 63
Weller, Peter, 174-75
Welles, Orson, 48, 155
Wellington, David, 195-97, 206, 213
Werewolf, The, 22
West, Adam, 193-96
Whale, James, 26
Whatever Happened to Baby Jane?, 42
When A Stranger Calls, 90, 103
Whispers, 44, 177
Whitlock, Albert, 191
Why Shoot the Teacher?, 45
Wicker Man, The, 69, 84
Wickman, Caryl, 135
Wightman, Dana, 205

Wild Bunch, The, 126
Williams, Dick, 37
Williams, Mark, 187, 205
Williams, Trevor, 126
Wilson, Donald. 108-110
Wimmer, Kurt, 212-213
Wincott, Jeff, 139
Wind, The, 206
Winnipeg Film Group, The, 224
Winnipeg Manifesto, 84
Winter Kept Us Warm, 95
Winters, Shelley, 109
Wise, Robert, 42
Wise Blood, 128
Wisher, The, 227-228
Wishmaster, 15
Witchboard: The Possession, 16, 215-216, 218
Witchcraft, 48
Witchfinder General, The, 47
Witness, 204
Wizard of Gore, The, 188
Wizard of Oz, The, 230
Wodoslawsky, Stefan, 212-213
Wojeck, 152
Wood, Ed, 40, 131
Wood, Robin, 86, 102
Woods, Donald, 26
Woods, James, 161, 162, 163
Woods, The, 231
Woolvett, Jaimz, 215
Woronov, Mary, 82
Wray, Fay, 25
Wrong Turn, 141
Wuerich, Hugo, 37
Wyner, Joel, 214

X-Men, 215
Xtro, 15

Yacower, Maurice, 102
Yeux Sans Visage, Les, 33
Yeti – Giant of the 20th Century, 119
You Only Live Twice, 56, 118
Young, Jack, 124
Young Lions, The, 156
Yuzna, Brian, 163

Zaza, Paul, 14, 149, 211
Zazelenchuk, Lawrence, 77, 78, 80, 81
Zeffirelli, Franco, 91
Znaimer, Moses, 98
Zombie Nightmare, 192-98, 206

Acknowledgements

MORE THAN A FEW PEOPLE HELPED IN MORE THAN A FEW ways with the writing of this book. David DeCoteau has been an incredible and thoroughly invaluable help in this book: helping me track down movies, artwork and people, and providing much inspiration to me as well as a dandy foreword to the book. Dave Barber at the Cinematheque has been helpful in many, many ways, and letting me curate a small Canadian horror festival at his theatre was certainly not the least of them. Chris Boyce and the rest of the folks in the DNTO office gave me the first forum for a piece on Canadian horror movies. It was a radio piece, but at the end of it I thought to myself "Hey…this might be a book…" Paul Corupe was also extremely helpful in providing information and material, and he runs a heck of a website too. Check page 235 for the address of his site.

Many books and magazines were consulted in the research of this project, but it seems fitting to cite two of them in particular, *Cinema Canada* and *Fangoria*, for their unwitting assistance. They are the chocolate and peanut butter which came together and provided much of the material herein. Michael Gingold of *Fangoria* was helpful in a number of ways as well.

Thanks go to Arbeiter Ring, my lovely publishers: specifically John Samson, Todd Scarth, Esyllt Jones and Carolynn Smallwood. The kind people at the Canadian Film Library were helpful with research and photographs. Randall King from the *Winnipeg Free Press* provided kind assistance, as did Tim Murphy. Helpful in numerous Toronto-related ways were Evan Kroeker, Pattie Chalmers, Alex Anderson and Kathleen Olmstead. Grateful thanks go to my parents, who have always been supportive and who bought the computer upon which this book was written, and gave more direct help at times as well.

And then there were the people involved in making the movies themselves who took the time to answer my questions. Karen Bromley, Don Carmody, Gerard Ciccoritti, William Fruet, Robert Fulford and Vlasta Vrana all met with me in person to talk about their work and recollections. Peter and Bonnie Roffman welcomed me into their home and told me a great deal about Peter's father Julian Roffman, his life and his films. Dennis Atkinson, Frank Dietz, Sally Drake, T.Y. Drake, John Fasano, Ed French, Gary Graver, Manfred Guthé, Maris Jansons, Paul Lynch, George Mihalka, Ron Oliver, Bruce Pittman, Garry Robbins, John Ross, Peter Simpson, Laird Stuart and Hélene Udy all spent time telling me their stories or otherwise helping out over the phone or by email. The generosity and enthusiasm of all these people is gratefully acknowledged.

Anyone who's ever made or worked on a Canadian horror movie is deserving of some thanks here, and some respect too. Obviously this book would not exist without you and your labours. It's not easy to make a movie, and though this book is not uncritical (and sometimes, perhaps, a little harsh), know that I'm always much happier that you made your movies than if you had not. So if I run your work through the wringer, please don't take it the wrong way. You're all champs in the end to me, and this book is dedicated to you and your efforts.

Lastly (but firstly in my heart), there is Alicia Smith, my wife. It's no picnic to sit through countless hours of Canadian horror movies if you're not naturally predisposed to do so. Since there are no medals to reward such a feat, she'll have to settle for my thanks, my admiration and my love.